W0016925

WOMEN'S STUDIES QUARTERLY

VOLUME 40   NUMBERS 1 & 2   SPRING/SUMMER 2012

An educational project of the Feminist Press at the City University of New York and the
Center for the Study of Women and Society at The Graduate Center, City University of New York

EDITORS
Amy Herzog, Queens College and The Graduate Center, City University of New York
Joe Rollins, Queens College and The Graduate Center, City University of New York

GUEST EDITORS
Patricia Clough, Queens College and The Graduate Center, City University of New York
Jasbir Puar, Rutgers University

ART EDITOR
Margot Bouman

FICTION/NONFICTION/PROSE EDITOR
Jocelyn Lieu

POETRY EDITOR
Kathleen Ossip

EDITORIAL ASSISTANTS
Meredith Benjamin
Elena Cohen

EDITORS EMERITAE
Victoria Pitts-Taylor 2008–2011 ▪ Talia Schaffer 2008–2011
▪ Cindi Katz 2004–2008 ▪ Nancy K. Miller 2004–2008 ▪
Diane Hope 2000–2004 ▪ Janet Zandy 1995–2000
▪ Nancy Porter 1982–1992 ▪ Florence Howe 1972–1982; 1993–1994

The Feminist Press at the City University of New York
EXECUTIVE DIRECTOR
Gloria Jacobs

EDITORIAL DIRECTOR
Amy Scholder

MANAGING EDITOR
Jeanann Pannasch

ART DIRECTOR
Drew Stevens

MARKETING & SALES MANAGER
Cary Webb

WSQ: Women's Studies Quarterly, a peer-reviewed, theme-based journal, is published in the summer and winter by the Feminist Press at the City University of New York, The Graduate Center, 365 Fifth Avenue, Suite 5406, New York, NY 10016.

COVER ART
Laura Splan, Detail of Surface Tension series, 2011. Graphite and soap residue on Clayboard, 18 x 24 x 2 in.

WEBSITE
feministpress.org/wsq

EDITORIAL CORRESPONDENCE
WSQ: Women's Studies Quarterly, The Feminist Press at the City University of New York, The Graduate Center, 365 Fifth Avenue, Suite 5406, New York, NY 10016; wsqeditorial@gmail.com.

PRINT SUBSCRIPTIONS
Subscribers in the United States: Individuals—$40 for 1 year; $90 for 3 years. Students—$28 for 1 year. (Student subscribers must provide a photocopy of current student identification.) Institutions—$75 for 1 year; $180 for 3 years. Subscribers outside the United States: Add $25 per year for delivery; add $50 per year for expedited delivery. To subscribe or change an address, contact WSQ Customer Service, The Feminist Press at the City University of New York, The Graduate Center, 365 Fifth Avenue, Suite 5406, New York, NY 10016; 212-817-7915; info@feministpress.org.

FORTHCOMING ISSUES
Enchantment, Ann Burlein, Hofstra University, and Jackie Orr, Syracuse University
Fashion, Eugenia Paulicelli, Queens College and The Graduate Center, City University of New York, and Elizabeth Wissinger, The Graduate Center, City University of New York

RIGHTS & PERMISSIONS
Fred Courtright, The Permissions Company, 570-839-7477; permdude@eclipse.net.

SUBMISSION INFORMATION
For the most up-to-date guidelines, calls for papers, and information concerning forthcoming issues, write to *WSQ: Women's Studies Quarterly* at the Feminist Press at the City University of New York, wsqeditorial@gmail.com or visit feministpress.org/wsq.

ADVERTISING
For information on display-ad sizes, rates, exchanges, and schedules, please write to *WSQ* Marketing, the Feminist Press at the City University of New York, The Graduate Center, 365 Fifth Avenue, Suite 5406, New York, NY 10016; 212-817-7915; marketing@feministpress.org.

ELECTRONIC ACCESS AND SUBSCRIPTIONS
Access to electronic databases containing backlist issues of *WSQ* may be purchased through JSTOR at www.jstor.org. Access to electronic databases containing current issues of *WSQ* may be purchased through Project Muse at muse.jhu.edu, muse@muse.jhu.edu; and ProQuest at www.il.proquest.com, info@il.proquest.com. Individual electronic subscriptions for *WSQ* may also be purchased through Project MUSE.

ISSN: 0732-1562   ISBN: 978-155861-792-6 $25.00

Contents

Marina Zurkow, *Heraldic Crests for Invasive Species: North American Gray Squirrel*, 2011. Letterpress print on Somerset paper, 18 x 16 in. Edition of 10. Drawing assistant Ellen Anne Burtner. Courtesy of bitforms gallery.

Editors' Note

Our machines are disturbingly lively, and we ourselves frighteningly inert.

Donna Haraway, "A Manifesto for Cyborgs"

97% of our DNA looks like gibberish.

Page Hill Starzinger, "A Karstic"

The parasite . . . does not even have to speak; it resonates. It makes noise, like the gnawing rats. It produces toxins, inflammations, fever. . . . It intervenes in the networks, interrupting messages and parasiting the transmissions.

Michel Serres, The Parasite

Prescient nearly thirty years ago, Haraway's observation retains its foreboding accuracy. And yet, as the genetic material of that single thought encounters and infects the quotes to follow, other cellular structures appear; the epigraph is recombinant. Transmission; vaccination; replication; infection; reproduction; immunity; vulnerability; permeability; meme, median, mode; words; ideas; code: these are just some of the ironies, pleasures, and paradoxes of our inquiry here in the *Viral* issue of *WSQ.*

The discovery of vaccines that could prompt the body to resist viral infection happened almost a century before viruses were discovered; their effect—immune responses that could prevent disease—long preceded discovery of a cause. Viruses themselves were first identified by a botanist studying disease in tobacco crops, an attempt to stop unseen forces wreaking havoc in the agricultural economy. Biological viruses are parasitic, infectious agents dependent on the bodies of the hosts in which they replicate. They maintain a highly paradoxical relationship to the entities and systems that provide for their very existence, yet which they mimic,

***WSQ: Women's Studies Quarterly* 40: 1 & 2 (Spring/Summer 2012)** © 2012 by Amy Herzog and Joe Rollins. All rights reserved.

incorporate, mutate, and potentially destroy. Viruses share a tremendous capacity for adaptation, and for disruption—unruly, noisy forces that can divert systemic flows. Rather than viewing viruses as alien others, infiltrating systems from the outside, we might consider the virus's ability to bring to light aspects of discord inherent in the networks in which they thrive. In this sense, echoing work on the role of viruses as formative agents in evolutionary biology, the virus functions as an element of difference that is constitutive of the larger system. "The difference is part of the thing itself," Michel Serres writes of the parasite-system complex, "and perhaps even produces the thing. . . . In the beginning was the noise."[1]

The relationship between the virus and the viral builds upon the slippages each term connotes between material effects and latent codes. Virality denotes the speed with which information moves across cyberspace at the same time that it invokes our fears of contagion, worries about the loss of information, and threats to health, borders, identities, economies, and politics. Like viruses, viral processes are vexingly unpredictable, simultaneously capable of radical intervention and regressive cooptation. Moreover, as guest editors Patricia Clough and Jasbir Puar observe in their introduction, viral denotes processes that require us to interrogate anew our assumptions about the actual and the virtual. In so doing, scholars are called upon to rethink how we understand biopolitics, security, race, sexuality, gender, technologies of communication, forms of embodiment, and aesthetics, particularly in the institutional settings of the market, the family, religion, health, the military, education, media, and the state.

The articles assembled in this volume come from a range of interdisciplinary academic spaces and many of the authors are themselves artists. Read as a group, they simultaneously trace and analyze an intellectual arc that spans the asymptotic realms of the imaginary to the actualized and from there to the unmeasurable—overlapping categories to say the least. At the risk of reductionist summarizing, several prominent themes thread across the scholarly works included here, in particular those of race, disease, and politics. The juxtaposition of approaches is remarkable for the jarring similarities they force us to recognize regarding questions of agency and control in diverse systems. What are the possibilities and limitations for radical political action within networks of informatics (Blas, Franklin)? How does the infrastructure of online social activism intersect with colonial legacies and contemporary global politics (Nyong'o)? How is mobility (of viruses, bodies, and capital) regulated in transnational contexts, and how are issues of security, disability, and vulnerability mobilized defensively (White, Chen)? How are categories of race produced, labored, and transmogrified within accelerating technological networks (Balance, Rai)? Can crowds, swarms, or alien codes evade the icy hard limits of the systems that seek to generate and contain them (Rogers, Glasberg)? What role can art play in engaging with viral processes, and what sorts of ethical cominglings might parasitic encounters set into motion (Chung, Lukes, Fisher, Berrigan)?

We are privileged and excited to note that our Classic Revisited for this issue is Donna Haraway's "A Manifesto for Cyborgs." In the age of the viral, the insightful brilliance of the "Manifesto" takes on new urgency and relevance as it simultaneously reminds us of how far we have evolved, and how much more evolving we might do. Haraway's contribution to this volume refashions her insights from the "Manifesto" and reminds us to attend as well another moment of prescience from elsewhere in her oeuvre: we are gestating in the womb of a pregnant monster. In this section we are also pleased that Fouché, Orr, and Schneider have shared with us their contemplations on the Manifesto as their collective efforts put on display the productivity and intellectual satisfaction to be found in Haraway's viral thought.

One of our goals as editors is to enhance the artistic presence in each issue and to integrate the artwork with the scholarship as fully as possible. With *Viral*, this objective is achieved with particular clarity. Not only is there exceptional artistry on display in the scholarly works, the poetry, prose, and images selected here resonate particularly well with the theme of the Issue. Visual works by Laura Splan, Ranjit Kandalgaonker, and Marina Zurkow push our understanding of the viral in unexpected directions. We are especially pleased to introduce a new section to the journal, curated by Margot Bouman, who joins us as art editor with this issue. The commissioned project for *Viral* was created by Melanie Crean, who parasitizes actual redacted PowerPoint slides created by the U.S. military related to their operations in Iraq. *Hypnotizing Chickens* highlights the contradictory role these slides play, serving at once to confound the press with deliberately byzantine graphics, and to construct and rationalize policies internally. The use of PowerPoint technology across corporate, military, and academic fields raises stark questions about the ways in which information is being distilled, coded, and disseminated in our contemporary technosphere. A version of this project will be posted online, in the hopes that it might engender broader, viral debate. Similarly, David Oscar Harvey's "Red, Red, Red," should inspire readers to explore for themselves the visual pleasures of the film from which this printed work arose. Book reviews by

Hantel, Mills, and Goldberg offer readers a sampling of scholarly works that expand the reaches of the viral into even wider scholarly domains.

Johanna Blakley, deputy director of the Lear Center at the University of Southern California's Annenberg School, bring us the Alerts and Provocations in this issue. Blakely's recent work on gender, social media, fashion, and copyright, has gone viral as her TEDTalks circulate across the Internet and she, herself, circles the globe speaking about the center's work. In this issue, she draws from her research on media, culture, and politics to examine rapidly changing economies of taste and knowledge production in a viral world. She argues that traditional demographic categories are being replaced by "transnational taste communities," mobile interest-based clusters that coalesce within, and are amplified by, social media networks. The conversations within these networks tend to be dominated by female voices, presenting a fascinating opportunity for rethinking questions of audience, identity, agency, and gender. The word-cloud portraits that accompany Blakely's text obscure her subjects' demographic markers as they simultaneously make manifest their tastes and interests, rendering new physiognomies from latent metadata.

Patricia Clough and Jasbir Puar have assembled in this volume a series of works that invite us to think deeply about the viral, and we are grateful for all their diligent efforts and incisive work as guest editors. As ever, we are indebted to our associates Meredith Benjamin and Elena Cohen, and all the talented people at the Feminist Press who do the hard work of bringing each issue to print: Jeanann Pannasch, Drew Stevens, and Gloria Jacobs. We owe special thanks to Jocelyn Lieu for her efforts as prose editor for the past few years and wish her well as she moves on to other scholarly endeavors. Finally, we are delighted to welcome Nicole Cooley as she takes over in that role.

Amy Herzog
Associate Professor of Media Studies
Queens College
PhD Program in Theater
The Graduate Center
City University of New York

Joe Rollins
Associate Professor and Executive
Officer of Political Science
Queens College and
The Graduate Center
City University of New York

Notes

1. Michel Serres, *The Parasite*, trans. Lawrence R. Schehr (Minneapolis: University of Minnesota Press, 2007), 13.

Introduction

Patricia Clough and Jasbir Puar

Wall Street; Madison, Wisconsin; Spain; Egypt; Greece; and London—
the sites continue to proliferate—offer examples of what has been tagged
a viral politics protesting a viral capitalism. Although this is a recent and
spectacular instance of the viral, there are the repeating and more ordinary
ones. Fear-raising reports of the threat of biological terrorism that at any
moment might go viral are released with some regularity; in Fall 2011, the
New York Times Magazine led with a story about the 2001 anthrax attacks
that announced, "We are still not ready." Nor does a week go by without
some study claiming to document the loss of our ability to think logically
because of our susceptibility, if not addiction, to digital media, the form
of which is more affective than its content. One only has to turn to books
like David Weinberger's *Too Big To Know* (2012) to read how the web's
structure is destroying the institutions of knowledge production as we have
known them. If social protests, the structure of digital media, and threats
of terrorist attacks on the health and welfare of nations can all be described
in viral terms, this special issue of *WSQ* would propose that the viral has
itself *gone viral*. The "viral" has come to describe a form of communication
and transmission in and across various and varying domains: the biological, the cultural, the financial, the political, the linguistic, the technical, and
the computational.

But what is contagious about the social protests of today, or infectious
about threats of biological terrorism, or addictive about the form of digital media is not so much about the transfer of messages or ideologies, or
the production of a singular solidarity or a clearly defined collectivity, but

rather the process of transformation. The viral is transformative; it has an open-ended relation to form itself. In this sense, the viral takes on characteristics, albeit selectively, which usually are attributed to the virus. At play is the virus's ability to change itself as it replicates and disseminates, or what Alexander Galloway and Eugene Thacker refer to as the virus's capacity for "replication and cryptography" (2007). In its replications, the virus does not remain the same, nor does that which it confronts and transits through. Viral replication swerves from the performative "repetition with a difference"; it is replication without reproduction, without fidelity, without durability. It is this generative differentiation that is repeated. It is the repetition that *is* the difference, the difference that *counts* and that is expressed numerically in code as "a continual replication of numerical difference." The virus, it might be said, seeks out code as its medium. It is through code that the virus performs its mutation in and across species, as well as all technical platforms or domains.

While the viral may differ from the virus in that the former seems only to signal exuberant capacities of rapid replication and distribution without the capacity for mutation accorded the latter, nonetheless, the difference between the viral and the virus is not one of opposition, a point explored by Zack Blas in this issue. Rather, the characteristics of the virus, we would argue, serve as a threshold, an horizon against and alongside which virality takes its action. There is the becoming of the virus in the viral. Or to put it another way, the viral seeks to be an infecting form, to have the virus's capacity for mutation, its sensitivity to the timing of repetition, the rhythm of the speeds of repetition, and the resonances of its numerical vibrations. As such, the viral has invited economic, political, social, and cultural investment in new processes of quantification that would allow code to be applied to what Luciana Parisi has described as "the full densely packed zones of information that are the intensive surrounds of zero and one," or the seemingly infinite series of numbers between zero and one. These processes of quantification enable a "numerical variability, which remains computationally open." (2009, 363).

Providing code with a computational openness may only further erase differences between the viral and the virus; quantification that is computationally open allows "active and passive parasitic forces" to inform measure, so that measure can measure where "stability is mobile, directed by vectors of attraction and repulsion" (2009, 364). Here, however, measure only modulates or affects what already is mobile; it affects a self-affecting or self-infecting numerical variability. With the viral, measure and all its relata—values, norms, if not reality, truth, and objectivity—become a matter of modulation, not relative but affected and affecting. In relationship to the viral, measure becomes speculative in its aim; it activates, if it does not preempt, futurity and potentiality in probing for the not-yet-calculated, the excess incalculability in calculation. Measure is no longer representational or if representational, representation functions as modulation.

In its effect on subjectivity, memory, desire, and history, virality suggests a move away from identity; it is a move away from those sorts of representational forms or strategies that privilege interiority, depth, and integrity. Virality proposes its own strategy of creativity in its being attracted to or aligned with what Gilles Deleuze called the "virtual." As Heather Lukes suggests in this issue, the viral binds representation to virtuality. As such, the viral returns measure to the aesthetic in that aesthetic measure is a singular, or what we have called a "subjective," measure, one, that like the virus, changes its metric or perspective with each measure or modulation, allowing measure to probe again and again for the incalculable excess of calculation. Thus the subjective perspective of aesthetic measure does not refer specifically to the human subject. With the viral, aesthetic measure goes beyond human perception, consciousness, and cognition, drawn to a futurity or potentiality that today is an object of political, cultural, economic, and technical contention.[1] If the virus can invoke anxieties about trespassing borders, the containment of contagion, or failure thereof, the viral can instigate a panic around measure or measuring that takes us beyond human perception, consciousness, and cognition to the incalculable or the yet-to-be-calculated. Yet both the virus and the viral also signal a positivity in the conviviality of the numerical and the virtual, the calculable and the aesthetic, the bodily and the technological, the inorganic and organic, the living and the nonliving. The viral brings a porosity of boundaries, with the ease of crossing them, or the requisite to cross them with the expectation of transformation. Indeed it is not surprising that in biotechnological circles, for one, it is suggested that metaphors for describing our relationship with infectious agents be more ecologically informed, taking into account the microbes on our skin, in our guts, and in our mucous membranes, how these are more often protective rather than destructive. They are part of us as well as of the biosphere. Recent reports indicate that very old viruses, some called Mimi, once reproduced without a host and were even the condition of possibility for the development of the genome.

This shift in seeing the virus and the viral as life giving as well as central to communication and transmission might suggest that the viral is becoming what Deleuze (1988) referred to as "diagrammatic," thus, informing strategies of practice across governing, economic, and social formations. Writing about the viral as diagrammatic, Jussi Parikka has proposed that virality is a specific mode of action that is crossing institutions, contexts, and scales and is "inherently connected to the complex, non-linear order of a network society" (2007). This network is not a stable structure, but can be seen as an active principle for assembling actors: not only the action of human actors but the action of various and varying entities. As such, the viral presents itself as "a key tactic in commercial, security and technological contexts" and is therefore useful for questioning "the complex ontology of contemporary capitalist culture" (2007). In this formulation, the viral easily is connected to what has been called "the affective turn," "the new materialisms," "posthuman and interspecies studies," "speculative realism," and "object-oriented ontologies."[2]

Each of these strands of thought has a purchase on imagination in the present moment, when the human is being displaced as the central concern in critical theoretical engagements with perception, cognition, bodily feeling, or affect. In each of these strands of thought, there is a rebooting of ontology in order to give weight to the *a*human, the *a*norganic, and the *a*subjective as ground of being and knowing. That is to say, there is a move beyond deconstruction to what necessarily is a speculative philosophy, a philosophical speculation on what is beyond human perception, cognition, and consciousness.[3] There is also the return to aesthetics. There is an elevation of aesthetics to first philosophy such that aesthetics comes to inform measure when measure has become speculative, or a mode of modulating futurity or potentiality. All this is giving shape to the viral as diagram, as the viral invites a rethinking of measure and method in the arts, the humanities, the sciences, and the social sciences, as well as practices of governance and economy.

The essays to follow not only arise out of the abstract contexts, offered above, of the becoming virus of the viral and the becoming viral of transmission and communication; they also offer specific meditations on virality. They bring us news of the viral from the various domains already infected and infecting cultures, local and global, while providing spaces in which to judge the present-day effects of virality—multiple, complex, if not contradictory—and to strategize about political, economic, and aesthetic responses. As already indicated, Zach Blas, in his essay, goes beyond any opposition of the virus and the viral, allowing him to consider what positive strategies for progressive, even revolutionary, politics virality might model, complicating the reduction of the viral to a mere effect of globalization, digital control, or vectors of illness. Instead he points especially to those ways of understanding the viral that allow for speculation on the virus's affective states or its perceptions. What does it feel like to become viral? What kinds of "abilities, capacities, and debilities" are involved (Puar 2009)? Is the virus dead, alive, undead? Does the virus emote? Here, Blas, taking a lead from Ian Bogost's "alien phenomenology," (forthcoming 2012) promotes the viral an opportunity for an *a*human poetics in the context of a nonhuman unknown becoming human speculation on what Eugene Thacker calls a "world-without-us" (2010). Blas suggests that the viral's political potential is best estimated in these terms.

In his essay, Seb Franklin also raises questions about the political, but unlike Blas he is more skeptical of those practices linked to the viral that have been touted as progressive. Interrogating the practices of hacking and networking, Franklin is disappointed in their potential for progressive politics because politics has depended on the novel types of social interaction these practices afford; therefore these practices cannot make claim to being able to transform the technical structure of computation. Rather, they depend on who is hacking or networking. Franklin is no more impressed with the contagious aspects of the virus, as if anything viral is automatically resistant to or deconstructive of given power relations. Instead Franklin finds potential for progressive politics in the excess of the virus, in the in-between-ness or the yet-to-be-calculated of viral excess. Thus behind Franklin's evaluations is his concern about the reduction that calculation is judged to affect or the appropriation of the excess of the viral as a matter of biopolitical control. Franklin also argues that since it is this drive for appropriation that motivates the development of mathematical technologies of measure, it is these technologies that become objects of political, cultural, and economic contention, for which aesthetic measure must give expression and be a critical intervention.

Kenneth Rogers's essay also draws a connection between the viral and a mathematical technology that makes "crowdsourcing" possible. Rogers gives a genealogy of the crowd, beginning in the nineteenth century, when fear of the crowd's expression of a need for equality led to a view of it as irrational, a threat to civic life, while in the economic sphere of the market the crowd was considered rational or an expression of individuals together pursuing individual gain through rational choice. Taking this genealogy as a backdrop, Rogers goes on to address the 2008 death of a Wal-Mart temp worker who was asphyxiated in the crush of bodies entering the store on Black Friday. Tracing the indirect racism of the descriptions of the crowd of mostly African American shoppers as barbaric, uncivil, and irrational, Rogers notes that at the time of this event, the crowd already was being rethought as an economic resource as well; in a transformation of crowd psychology, a market logic increasingly was being ascribed to various non-market behaviors. Through making use of a mathematical technology that would be the basis for modern derivatives and hedge funds, it became possible to collapse the difference between the irrationality of the crowd and the rationality of individual self-interest through bundling risks for investment. Crowdsourcing, then, is a matter of drawing users' participation into some scheme about services or social networking that appeals to both self-interest and communal belonging. Once there is a critical mass of users, Rogers explains, the value of the online crowd can be monetized. Here too the mathematical technology also serves politics offering an image of possibility. In contrast to the top-down design of crowdsourcing, Rogers suggests the "open source crowd" as an image of the crowd's removing itself from exploitation.

In her essay, Melissa Autumn White turns our attention to biology, one of the preeminent discourses of the viral. White also returns us to racialized populations that play a part in Rogers's discussion of Black Friday as well. However, White focuses primarily on populations of migrants or guest workers. Taking Canada as her example and starting with the recent H1N1 flu scare; its failure to become an epidemic; and the subsequent excuse offered by the World Heath Organization that epidemics, like viruses, are unpredictable, White shows how the uneven distribution of capacities for health across populations has become a way the state shores up its increasingly porous borders. While capital and commodities move swiftly, if not easily, across national boundaries and financial markets, labor moves differently. In controlling immigration even while inviting guest workers, states reproduce a geopolitical stratification of vulnerabilities as they ensnare vitality in relations of power. For example, in linking immigration to the fear of the H1N1 epidemic, the Mexican migrant worker became what White describes as "a vector of disease," an "informational node," or a "potential transmitter of viral code." Mexican guest workers invited to do agricultural work in Canada became a resource of another kind, a population that could be declared a health threat to the nation and thus denied rights of residency, even the right to have rights. They became a political resource for strengthening national boundaries. So the vulnerable populations described as irrational consumers in Rogers's essay are vulnerable as workers in White's essay, while vulnerability in both cases racializes the population.

In her essay, Caitlin Berrigan continues to engage the viral in the context of biological discourse, the biology of plants, blood, and disease. Focusing on hepatitis C, a disease that had not yet invited a legible interest group, Berrigan raises interest through performance art. She does so by rendering palpable or cultivating more intensively a sense of reciprocity between plant and human. The performance described by Berrigan makes use of hepatitis C–carrying blood, thought harmful to humans, in order to nourish dandelion plants, a weed thought of as "bad" for lawns, but having curative potential for hepatitis C. Berrigan's interspecies performance shows complicated antagonisms, codependencies, and evolution in our relationship to pathogens. Here is a commingling and becoming that is at ease with the virus and suggests a ceasefire in fighting disease with Big Pharma drugs. By investigating evolution as a matter of alliances rather than evolution as a matter of filiation, Berrigan demonstrates that viruses show the way to lateral genetic transfers among unrelated organisms that may be health giving. They even suggest an image of life that does not privilege the bounded organism. Unfortunately, as Berrigan reports, the installation of her "weed" performance was deemed a threat to health and was not allowed to stand, a reminder of the way the potential of the virus circulates in a global capitalist economy where health is all but inseparable from a financialized, militarized security.

It is in the context of a financialized, militarized security that, in her/his essay, Mel Chen takes up the mask against the current fixation on the veil. For Chen, masking functions to evoke projections of otherness, especially terrorist otherness, and at the same time to manage environmental insecurity through biological protection. Thus Chen's treatment of the viral works in that space of crossing between the virus as biological and the viral as political or communicative. As such, the mask, for Chen, is to be understood as a prosthetic, as a biopolitical strategy that modulates debility and capacity. As bodily prosthesis, the mask speaks through the individual to the debility of a nation, to protect it from its vulnerabilities while simultaneously disavowing them. The mask points to the nation's displacement of its vulnerabilities, projecting them elsewhere, rather than owning them. Further, the mask as prosthesis moves racialized populations beyond the visual registering of otherness in the nation's self-representation; in reconfiguring bodily matter as prosthetic, the mask also points to the "new" materialisms of *a*human assemblages and their potentiality for reconfiguring boundaries and security.

The chances for such a reconfiguration as a function of the fast circulation of calls for freedom and the establishment of sexual rights as human rights is, however, doubtful, as Tavia Nyong'o sees it. Offering a reading of a gone-viral tweet appeal to support defeating the Ugandan antigay measure becoming law, Nyong'o, in his essay, points to the difficulty of getting beyond the short-circuiting of such appeals into giving new life "to old clichés about African alterity, violence, and dependency." Drawing on Jodi Dean's work on rapid connectivity through virtual proximity, Nyong'o shows how "Africa" easily fits the process of short-circuiting. Not only has the African, nearly-starved-to-death child become iconic of global poverty and illegitimate governance, but more recently the engagement with Africa by queers in nations such as the United States, decrying those who would punish those practicing "African homophobia," has shown the difficulty of disconnecting human rights and humanitarian appeals from the effects of their circulating in capital-invested information technology. It is not so much that the form of circulation simply is overcoming the content of the messages circulated; rather, Nyong'o argues that the content is short-circuited, not only foreclosing a deeper critique of the "fantasy of participation," but also often reducing politics to single issues. The short-circuiting of content also makes it easy for messages to be taken over by what Nyong'o sees as a perverse discourse. Focusing on how the fast circulation of messages, like those of Twitter and Facebook, are dissolving symbolic identities into imaginary ones, Nyong'o suggests that the "neoliberal pervert" has displaced the postcolonial subject. That is to say, both those messages critiquing so-called African homophobia and those resistant to those critiques are not guided by a prohibitive law or authority; the perversion is not that of homosexuality. It is that the messages and their various viral permutations all wind up soliciting enjoyment and disavowal.

While Christine Balance also is critical of social media, especially for the way it makes use of uncompensated affective labor, she nonetheless registers some of the positive uses of DIY online production. In her essay, Balance takes up the surveys and reports that indicate that Asian Americans are dominating DIY online production. Focusing on the inclination of Asian Americans to use new media to create, notably, vlogs, webisodes, musical covers, and parodies, Balance suggests that Asian Americans, while doing affective labor for free, are also performing their identities in novel ways they have not been able to perform otherwise. The online productions, with predecessors in forms thought to be narcissistic and self-indulgent, allow, in Balance's view, Asian Americans to sift out their identities both from the catchall term "Asian American" and from other stereotypes, including that of the model minority. It is an affective labor that transforms alienation into expression of various emotions: anger, rage, heartache.

Not all uses of the epistolary and diaristic forms have gone online, nor, as Balance suggests, are they all deserving of the labels "narcissistic" and "self-indulgent." After all, there has been a wealth of critical revisioning of these forms in much scholarship of identity politics, especially feminist scholarship. In her essay, Anna Fisher draws on artists Chris Kraus and Sophie Calle to demonstrate how the work of younger feminist artists remake the feminist project enabling it to assimilate "irony and equivocality for its tactical gain." Fisher shows how both artists use epistolary and diaristic practices to challenge heterosexual romance's complicity in women's abjection: Kraus by chronicling her romantic obsession with a famous author, Dick Hebdige, and Calle by providing analysis of breakup emails. Fisher argues that the artists' works are parasiting in that they do not flee from charges hurled at women, such as "hyperfemininity and over-dependence." Rather, they hold on to them more tightly. Here parasiting is a matter of overidentification, where one pretends to take the system at its word and play it so closely that ultimately it cannot bear the intensity. As Fisher concludes, Kraus and Calle swell in critical import as each feeds on her male host, "who is suddenly dwarfed by its parasite."

Heather Lukes also turns to aesthetic production, to examine anxieties about speed, consumption, contagion, mass culture, and artistic politics during the 1930s—the time period during which she claims the virus moves from scientific visual capture to "metaphorical menace." Tracing the tropes of infection and virality in Nathanael West's last novel, *The Day of the Locust* (1939), Lukes dissects the social malaise haunting Southern

California's landscape, typically analyzed in this novel through an over-determined binary of the intentionality of the author and the (Frankfurt School–inflected) complicity of that author/artist as a mere puppet within the culture industry. An infectious mass culture threatens to mechanize all aesthetic performance. Like Rodgers, Lukes is interested in theories of crowd contagion, what she calls "the virus of mob affect," as a trans-human feeling. Reading against the grain of typical interpretations of West, she articulates a relation between viral affect and the psychoanalytic "symptom," rethought here as viral effect.

As a cultural artifact that delves with enthusiasm into themes of virality and also has had an interesting path of viral replication, *The Thing* is explored by Elena Glasberg as a fictional production that is continually revived from the edge of extinction. Glasberg's timely "re-review" of John Carpenter's 1981 sci-fi classic *The Thing* follows on the heels of a 2011 (largely failed) "prequel" and also is situated amid memes of a pulp fiction short story, an early film called *The Thing from Another World*, fanzines, video games, and documentaries. In all these versions the pivotal narrative moment is when the Thing and the human become indistinguishable. Noting that Carpenter relocates the story of the Thing to Antarctica to use the ice as an "environmental hard limit" that contains the Thing, Glasberg argues that virality actually thrives through and because of the hard limits, redefining the notion of a limit itself as that which allows for replication. The ice is thus the ideal setting for thinking about the posthuman, where the human seems not to be natural, or native. In reexamining the Thing and its prolific recounting across multiple media, Glasberg demonstrates the imbrication of the story and the means of its telling as a form of viral imitation. The Thing lives on.

Focusing on Alfred Hitchcock's *The Birds*, Una Chung, like Glasberg, looks at the perceived horror of the viral and suggests that the viral diagram offers the possibility of practices that would allow us to "cross over horror." Taking up the rhythm of attack and rest of the birds, the massed onslaught of speed and force and unabated intensity, Chung links crossing over horror with practices in the art of power befitting an aesthetic measure that is computationally open. With these practices, Chung proposes that we not be drawn back into, or become overwhelmed by, depressing descriptions of these times. Or that we not follow critics of *The Birds* like Žižek, who proposes, on the one hand, that horror must be accepted as central to human existence and, on the other, that horror is the psychotic core of the machine, its becoming speed unattached to representation, memory, or history. For Chung, crossing over horror is the displacement of the opposition of human and machine in a practiced or practical recognition that "human impotence no longer [need make] us mad." Chung ends by pointing to the practice of Apichatpong Weerasethakul, maker of films and multimedia installations, which as Chung sees it, refuses to put a "chalk line around a human form" and instead engages the quality of light that encourages time travel, reincarnation, through flashes of dreams that one can shift through at one's own pace and thereby remember, forget, desire, and make history anew.

In tune with Chung, Amit Rai in his essay takes up race and experiments with its affirmative possibilities. Rai suggests that in the viral diagram race would be better engaged in terms of ecologies of sensation or affect rather than seen as a matter of nominalization, a naming that works at the molar level to capture the molecular movement of race, or what Rai calls "race racing." Instead of an antiracist politics driven by the reactive representational strategies of naming, race racing is the intensive processes of becoming that entail the multiplicity of race so that it is no longer familiar to itself. As such, "race racing" points to the embodied duration of race that makes possible its variation across populations. Rai argues further that this multiplication of race racing is coemergent with technoassemblages that make possible experimentation in new bodily habituations and the feedback loops from experimentation. Rai opens with a diagnosis that by the end of the essay becomes a provocation: "Antiracism must become something else, experimenting with duration, sensation, resonance, and affect."

We close our introduction with a return to the feminist classic for this special issue, Donna Haraway's 1985 "Manifesto for Cyborgs," without which a feminist method for critically engaging technoscientific visions would have been greatly impoverished; nor would the many proposals for life-giving practices of epistemology or ontology have been envisioned. And in her response to the well-deserved praise and gratitude offered her in this issue by Jackie Orr, Joseph Schneider, and Rayvon Fouché, Haraway just starts up again, casting her wisdom, her humor, and her aesthetic over the future, once again hoping to orient potentiality by encouraging projects that are political, ethical, and daringly imaginative. If with her early scholarship, she already would teach us about "creatures simultaneously animal and machine, who populate worlds ambiguously natural and crafted," (1991, 149) over the years, her work simply would make clearer how urgent is the task of refusing any forms of knowing and being that privilege human perception, consciousness, and cognition by a too easy dismissal of other lives, organic and nonorganic. From the start, Haraway has been calling for a criticism of technoscience that is subtle, a criticism that recognizes what we are faced with and takes account of it with what she described in the "Manifesto" as a double-vision or perspective. As she put it:

> From one perspective, a cyborg world is about the final imposition of a grid of control on the planet, about the final abstraction embodied in a Star Wars apocalypse waged in the name of defense, about the final appropriation of women's bodies in a masculinist orgy of war. . . . From another perspective, a cyborg world might be about lived social and bodily realities in which people are not afraid of their joint kinship with animals and machines, not afraid of permanently partial identities and contradictory standpoints. The political struggle is to see from both perspectives at once because each reveals both dominations and possibilities unimaginable from the other vantage point. Single vision produces worse illusions than double vision or many-headed monsters. Cyborg unities are monstrous and illegitimate; in our present political circumstances, we could hardly hope for more potent myths for resistance and recoupling (1991, 154).

While the viral may raise new challenges to double vision and require us to worry about those violated bodies, besides women's, Haraway's proposal for criticism still is a sound one. It is one that has been undertaken by all the authors writing for this special issue, those who authored the essays highlighted above and those who authored reviews, including Mara Mills, Max Hantel, and Greg Goldberg. And there is the mesmerizing art of Ranjit Kandalgaonker and Marina Zurkow, and the poems by Amy Evans, Deborah Fried-Rubin, Kate Greenstreet, Page Hill Starzinger, Anna Rabinowitz, Danielle Pafunda, Leah Umansky, and David Oscar Harvey. With all of them we say, "Here's to the future."

Patricia Ticineto Clough is professor of sociology and women's studies at the Graduate Center and Queens College of the City University of New York. She is author of *Autoaffection: Unconscious Thought in the Age of Teletechnology* (University of Minnesota Press, 2000); *Feminist Thought: Desire, Power and Academic Discourse* (Wiley, 1994), and *The End(s) of Ethnography: From Realism to Social Criticism* (Sage, 1992). She is editor of *The Affective Turn: Theorizing the Social*, (Duke University Press, 2007) and co-editor, with Craig Willse, of *Beyond Biopolitics: Essays on the Governance of Life and Death* (Duke University Press, 2011). She is currently working on Ecstatic Corona: Philosophy and Family Violence, an ethnographic, historically researched, experimental writing project about where she grew up in Queens, New York.

Jasbir Puar is a professor of women's and gender studies at Rutger's University. She is the author of *Terrorist Assemblages: Homonationalism in Queer Times* (Duke University Press, 2007), which won the 2007 Cultural Studies Book Award from the Association for Asian American Studies. Her articles have appeared in *Gender, Place, and Culture*; *Social Text*; *Radical History Review*; *Antipode: A Radical Journal of Geography*; and *Signs: Journal of Women in Culture and Society*. She is currently working on a new book project focused on queer disability studies and theories of affect and assemblage.

Notes

1. For a more developed discussion of aesthetics, measure, and new media, see Clough, forthcoming.
2. Important texts include Clough 2007; Livingston and Puar 2011; Bryant, Srnicek, and Harman 2011; Coole and Frost 2011.
3. It is not surprising that it is with considerable interest, if not concern, that the recent turn to speculative realism is being monitored. Not only does it question what has been labeled "correlationism," that is, the presumed impossibility of a world without human knowing or without a primordial rapport between human and world; it instead supports a speculative grasp of "a world-without-us," which Thacker describes as "a nebulous zone that is at once impersonal and horrific," that is beyond "the world-in-itself' that is finally always for us (2010, 5-6).

Works Cited

Bogost, Ian. Forthcoming 2012. *Alien Phenomenology*. Minneapolis: University of Minnesota Press.

Bryant, Levi R., Nick Srnicek, and Graham Harman, eds. 2011. *The Speculative Turn*. Melbourne: re.press.

Clough, Patricia. 2007. *The Affective Turn*. Durham: Duke University Press.

———. Forthcoming. "In the Aporia of Ontology and Epistemology: Toward a Politics of Measure." *Scholar and Feminist Online*.

Coole, Diane, and Samantha Frost, eds. 2010. *New Materialisms*. Durham: Duke University Press.

Deleuze, Gilles. 1988. *Foucault*. Minneapolis: University of Minnesota Press.

Galloway, Alexander, and Eugene Thacker. 2007. *The Exploit, A Theory of Networks*. Minneapolis: University of Minnesota Press.

Haraway, Donna J. 1985. "A Manifesto for Cyborgs: Science, Technology, and Feminism in the 1980s." *Socialist Review* 80:65–107.

———. 1991. *Simians, Cyborgs, and Women.* New York: Routledge.

Livingston, Julie, and Jasbir Puar. 2011. "Interspecies." *Social Text 106, 29.1: 3-14.*

Parikka, Jussi. 2007. "Contagion and Repetition: On the Viral Logic of Network Culture." *Ephemera* 7(2):287–308.

Parisi, Luciana. 2009. "Symbiotic Architecture: Prehending Digitality." *Theory Culture and Society* 26:347–79.

Puar, Jasbir. 2009. "Prognosis Time: Notes Towards a Geopolitics of Affect, Debility, and Capacity." *Women and Performance: A Journal of Feminist Theory,* 19:2,161-172.

Thacker, Eugene. 2010. *In the Dust of This Planet.* Washington: Zero Books.

Weinberger, David. 2012. *Too Big to Know: Rethinking Knowledge Now That the Facts Aren't the Facts, Experts Are Everywhere, and the Smartest Person in the Room Is the Room.* New York: Basic Books.

PART I. **ARTICLES**

Laura Splan, *Doilies (Herpes)*, 2004. Freestanding, computerized, machine-emboidered lace mounted on velvet, 8 in. diameter.

571

Kate Greenstreet

Poor, or whatever comes first.

restore / resist
answer / count
what I'd give

He's afraid
the baby will be born like him, but the baby is fine.
On the legend, must the blue be the sea? It's a story about this.

Fill in the blank: People are always _____ .

Missing. One way or another.

Kate Greenstreet is the author of *The Last 4 Things* and *case sensitive*, both from Ahsahta Press, and five chapbooks. Her work can be found in *Chicago Review*, *Colorado Review*, *Fence*, *Guernica*, *Boston Review*, and other journals. Ahsahta will publish her third book, *Young Tambling*, in 2013.

 WSQ: Women's Studies Quarterly 40: 1 & 2 (Spring/Summer 2012)

Virus, Viral

Zach Blas

In a recent article titled "After Life: *De Anima* and Unhuman Politics," Eugene Thacker writes, "If our global context of climate change, disasters, pandemics, or complex networks tells us anything, it is that political thought today demands a concept of life adequate to its anonymous, unhuman dimensions, an unhuman politics, for unhuman life" (2009, 40). Thacker's use of the unhuman, rather than the inhuman or nonhuman, alludes to the strange worlds and weird lives that reveal themselves by turning toward the emergent, unexpected, and challenging interactions, engagements, and limits between the human and nonhuman.

Thacker's call for an unhuman politics arises in a swarm of viral hype. Everything has seemingly gone viral: Alongside repeated panics of virus outbreaks, there are also fears of vaccine shortages—but there are plenty of Anti-Viral Kleenex; the rise of PC computer viruses are fought with antivirus security software; and just as Michael Hardt and Antonio Negri have described the new world order's institutional structure as being "like a software program that carries a virus along with it, so that it is continually modulating and corrupting the institutional forms around it," there is now viral marketing, viral advertising, and viral media to aid, support, and propagate this structure (Hardt and Negri 2000, 197–98). Concurrently, the emergence of theories like viral ecology, viral philosophy, viral capitalism, viral politics, viral affect, and viral aesthetics to diagnose our culture today suggests that the virus perhaps is the major trope of the postmodern condition (Bardini 2006). The virus|viral looms as an exemplar for considering Thacker's unhuman politics, as the nonhuman virus comes to bear multifariously upon the human, in part, through the human nam-

WSQ: Women's Studies Quarterly **40: 1 & 2 (Spring/Summer 2012)** © 2012 by Zach Blas.

ing or classification of what is permitted to be considered viral. What a virus is and does cannot only be extracted into the qualifier viral just as the qualities of the viral cannot be reduced to the virus. To think the virus and the viral is to engage in their continuous states of flux, transformation, and movements toward and between as well as diversions away from one another, attending to the fact that there is some kind of recognition or identification process that binds or links the virus and viral together for the human. The virus is difficult to conceptualize not only because it can exist in so many material substrates and is constantly changing but also because the virus has historically produced different generations of itself that operate in greater or lesser degrees of complexity, in both biological and computational forms. Thus, a dizzying array of viralities have emerged and continue to rapidly proliferate; the viral has indeed gone viral.

The viral emphasizes a break, or rupture, between fiction and reality that is hazy, fluid, unstable. Imitations of the virus, commonly labeled "viral," are more like creative openings into fictions or poetics of the virus. These framings of the virus are unhuman, and unhuman politics is a framing for the examination of the overlappings, differences, and irreducibilities—*mediations*—of the virus and the viral.

What are our viral politics today? While Alexander Galloway and Eugene Thacker have written that "viruses and diseases are obviously not to be looked at as models for progressive political action," our contemporary moment forces us to look there (Galloway and Thacker 2007, 96). Galloway and Thacker hint that the virus, as a product of globalization and conquest as well as computer security and digital control, is a dead end for radical politics. Yet political art collectives like the Electronic Disturbance Theater and Queer Technologies use the virus as an anticapitalist tactic. If these groups create a notion of the virus|viral that does not simply coincide with capitalism, are there other possibilities for a radical viral politics?

In this essay, I will explore the potentials of a viral, or unhuman, politics. I will commence by considering two axes of the virus|viral relation. The first is from the virus to the viral based on action, or replication and cryptography: this is the most common usage of the viral today, what Galloway and Thacker call the "becoming-number" of the virus. The second is from the virus to the viral based on affect: in this speculative section, the work of Jakob von Uexküll and Ian Bogost will be used to generate a conception of the viral through an "alien phenomenology" of the virus's perceptual world, or Umwelt. Finally, I will discuss queer theorist Tim Dean's recent study on gay male barebacking. Dean describes barebacking as "an arena of invention that involves experiments in how to *do* things with viruses" (2009, 47). Deploying Foucault's concept of "ascesis," defined as the creative work one performs to transform and develop a way of life, I will argue that barebacking is a form of viral ascesis, that is, a creative styling of viruses. I will suggest that viral ascesis, while attempting to engage both virus|viral axes, is one instantiation of a possible viral politics.

Virus|Viral 1: Action

Representations of the virus|viral today typically hinge on rapid spreadability and mutation. In fact, wherever one looks, the virus has gained the most attention through its abilities to replicate and disseminate. From SARS and H1N1 to the latest computer virus or meme, the virus is commonly perceived as that which quickly generates copies of itself and infectiously breaks through barriers or quarantines.

In line with this perspective of the virus, Alexander Galloway and Eugene Thacker, two theorists who have written extensively on viruses, state that the virus is "life exploiting life," that is, viruses take advantage of their host entities to generate more copies of themselves (2007, 83). The virus succeeds in producing its copies through a process Galloway and Thacker refer to as "never-being-the-same" (87). Maintaining within itself the ability to continuously mutate its code with each reproduction, the virus propagates itself. Defining the virus based on action, they write:

> Replication and cryptography are thus the two activities that define the virus. What counts is not that the host is a "bacterium," "an animal," or a "human." What counts is the code—the number of the animal, or better, the numerology of the animal. . . . The viral perspective is "cryptographic" because it replicates this difference, this paradoxical status of never-being-the-same. . . . What astounds us is that the viral perspective presents the animal being and creaturely life in an *illegible* and *incalculable* manner, a matter of chthonic calculations and occult replications. (87)

Galloway and Thacker conclude by claiming that this becoming-number of the virus *is* its identity.

This conception of the virus, as that which is solely concerned with replication and mutation, is representative of what has become known as viral today. It seems that everything has "gone viral" based on this dominant understanding of the virus as a becoming-number. Particularly, in social media, the viral is representative of the virus-as-replication. For something to go viral in social media platforms all that is required is that things spread within a system or network. For example, a viral marketing campaign will use a preexisting social network to circulate advertisements for its products, but the viral in this campaign is not the self-replicating, mutating contagion of the virus that Galloway and Thacker discuss; it is only half their formulation. Contagion in this viral sense is not even self-replicating or mutating. Viral marketing requires *users* in a network to circulate advertisements, and the advertisements will typically remain unchanged, having only been copied and circulated by other agents, usually humans. This is the standard occurrence in viral media as well: a video going viral on YouTube simply means that it has received a large number of views in a short period of time and has spread to other sites.

While social media stresses the replication and spreadability of the virus and ignores its mutating never-being-the-sameness, current theorizations of capitalism focus on *both* the replication and mutation of the virus. Media theorist Jussi Parikka takes Hardt and Negri's assertion that capitalism is like a virus further in his writings on viral capitalism. He notes that capitalism is now viral in that it is capable of continuous modulation and heterogenesis (Parikka 2007, 96). "The commodity," he writes, "works as a virus—and the virus part of the commodity circuit" (97). Viral capitalism replicates itself through a mutating act of never-being-the-sameness, that is, it continuously modulates and reproduces to maintain a global infection. Viral capitalism is another gesture toward theorizing our phase of control capitalism, which has many other labels—ludic capitalism, Empire, protocological control, Deleuzian capitalism, and digital and liquid capitalism, all underscoring unstable, rapid fluxes of unhuman flows that induce a general commodification of life itself. Viral capitalism highlights the "infectious" nature of this multiplicitous, morphing control process.

In this axis of the virus|viral relation, that mysterious, allusive thing called a virus, evolving over time in biological matter and silicon, existing in ever complexifying, generational forms, somewhere between life and death, instigating excessive panic, hype, and thrill, is reduced to its properties of action. It is easy enough to argue that today's viral hype is a fictional relation to—or break from—the virus, creating a poetics or distortion of its movement and action. Perhaps this particular viral is rightly dominant because its focus on speedy replication and mutation is at the heart of contemporary capital, neoliberalism, and globalization, and even though there are uses of this viral form that proffer and fight for an anticapitalism, can the viral go *elsewhere*? To another viral that might drastically depart from replication, mutation, speed, and capitalism?

Virus|Viral 2: Affect

While there certainly appears to be a becoming-number of the virus based on its replicating and cryptographic existence, is a configuration of the viral based on this numeric paradigm a reduction not only of what could count as viral but also of the virus itself? Viruses not only change through replication, they also change their embodied contexts, in that all viruses require a host and can be spread from one host to another. Galloway and Thacker state that the material substrate of the virus—its materiality paired with its host—is not as necessary in understanding the virus's existence as is its mathematical identity, but given that a virus cannot survive unless residing within a host, it seems that the host is crucial, in that there would be no "number" without the host. To understand the virus as becoming-number leaves unanswered questions of a virus's affects, sensations, and desires. Are there not multiplicitous potentialities for the virus to become? Perhaps the code is what counts if the virus is to be understood as primarily a mathematical abstraction, but what of the perceptions of the virus, its affects, embodiments, and host organisms? Could their be another viral that emerges from these qualities?

The prospects of constructing a viral based on these criteria of the virus have an air of inaccessibility. What is the affect of the virus and how could it ever be corralled into a viral if it is irreducible to the human? How does one gain access to such affective knowledge of another thing? What this impasse makes clear is that all virals are ethical, aesthetic, and political treatments of the virus; they are configurations that gesture toward the overall inaccessibility of fully knowing a virus. This section will present the possibilities of another viral, not popular or in use, through a speculative practice on the impossible question of affect and phenomenology.

Jakob von Uexküll gives us the first conceptual tool needed, the Umwelt, or the perceptual world of an animal or creature. Uexküll, a biologist of the early to mid-twentieth century who popularized biosemiotics, developed the concept of the Umwelt to think about the radically diverse sensory worlds that different creatures exist within; he refers to these worlds as bubbles or islands of senses, arguing that each animal can never leave or escape its self-world, or Umwelt. Crucial to Uexküll's phenomenological thought is the premise that things do not have an autonomous existence from the creatures that perceive them: "No one, who has the least experience of the Umwelten of animals will ever harbour the idea that objects have an autonomous existence that makes them independent of the subjects" (von Uexküll 2001, 108). While Uexküll's speculative Umwelten provide a potential framework for developing a notion of the viral from the virus's affects or perceptions, his argument against autonomy requires a second theoretical tool, media theorist Ian Bogost's alien phenomenology, which helps break from this position.

Alien phenomenology is part of a new philosophical movement called "speculative realism," primarily rooted in the continental tradition, that argues for an ability to *speculatively* gain access to that which exists beyond or outside the correlation of being and world. Within the strand of object-oriented ontology or philosophy, Ian Bogost is developing a "pragmatic," or "applied," speculative realism, which he calls "alien phenomenology" (Bogost, n.d.). For Bogost, the "true alien" is right in front of us, not hidden in the farthest reaches of another galaxy but in everything everywhere, from our kitchenware to the sidewalk cement to the electronics in our cell phones. He asks about the microcomputer: "But what do they experience? What is their proper phenomenology? In short, what is it like to be a thing? If we wish to understand a microcomputer . . . on its own terms, what approaches might be of service? . . . When we ask what it means to be something, we pose a question that exceeds our own grasp of the being of the world. These unknown unknowns characterize things about an object that may or may not be obvious, clear, or even knowable" (Bogost, n.d.). While Bogost claims, similarly to Uexküll, that all things infinitely recede from human grasp, he surprisingly argues that it is the philosopher's duty to speculate on these unknown unknowns. He writes that speculation is poetic and creative, a "phenomenology that explodes like shrapnel" away from the terrain of the human.

Fascinatingly, Bogost refers to this practice of speculation in terms of disturbance: "A speculum is a mirror, but not in the modern sense of the term as a device that reflects back the world as it really is, unimpeded and undistorted. . . . The speculum of speculation is . . . a funhouse mirror made of hammered metal, whose distortions show us a perversion of a unit's sensibilities" (Bogost, n.d.). Alien phenomenology operates as a break or distortion, from the nonhuman unknown to human speculation, creatively paving the way for an unhuman poetics. When Bogost asks, "What is it like to be a thing?" can this be expounded upon to ask, "What is it like to be a virus?" More precisely, can the idea of alien phenomenology be used to speculate upon the virus's Umwelt and, as a result, conceive a new viral? This viral would surely bring about a different viral, or unhuman, politics.

This other viral—a minor viral?—would have to take into account questions like How does the virus sense? Is the virus dead, alive, undead? Does the virus emote? How does desire play into the virus's drive toward multiplicity? How does it feel to replicate and spread in a particular substrate, such as silicon, animals, or plants? How does the virus affect and how is it affected in different symbiotic encounters? If viruses assemble spontaneously within cells, what is the poetic dimension to such a choreography? If these affective dimensions of the virus are ambivalent toward capitalism or sexuality, how does one speculate on such relations?

Barebacking and Viral Ascesis

Tim Dean's book *Unlimited Intimacy: Reflections on the Subculture of Barebacking* charts practices of gay male unprotected anal intercourse. While Dean is interested in keeping a continuity between general unprotected sex and barebacking, he is careful to point out that barebacking subculture is based on a community of gay men who have formed around the specific erotic practice of deliberately seeking unprotected anal sex. Dean suggests that barebackers not only play with the risks of HIV infection but also form an ethics of alterity through their openness to sex with strangers. Barebacking, Dean writes, is about creativity and experimentation.

While some might consider barebackers' desire for HIV infection as the desire to die like previous generations of gay men from HIV/AIDS, barebackers approach the virus as a gift that contributes to generating their social organization. Barebackers do many creative things with viruses: they name them, metaphorically describe their operations, and imaginatively engage and relate with them. While Dean insists in his book that barebacking is a practice against identity politics, the creative work barebackers do to HIV forms specific identities of the virus. Interestingly, while barebacking may be against an identity politics on the scale of the human, it crafts an identity politics on the scale of the virus. Foucault's concept of ascesis, as the creative work done on oneself, aids in explaining the production of barebacking subculture. Barebackers engage in an ascesis with the virus, and I will suggest that this viral ascesis heightens the identificatory work done on the virus. These new imaginings and constructions of the virus are accomplished through attempting an engagement with both axes of the virus|viral relation. Barebacking, through inventions with viral ascesis, is an experiment in unhuman politics.

In his own discussion of ascesis, Foucault insists time and again that "to be 'gay' . . . [is] to try to define and develop a way of life" (1997a, 138). He writes that "we have to create a gay life. To become. . . . We have to create culture . . . [and the] innovations those practices imply. . . . It's the real creation of new possibilities of pleasure" (1997b, 163–65). Foucault, like Dean, privileges a doing that is a continuous, modulating, nonteleological openness and transformation. This mode of living evades dominant identity formations in favor of multiplicities of relationships, actions, behaviors. Foucault defines such a way of living as ascesis: "It's the work that one performs on oneself in order to transform oneself. . . . Yet it's up to us to advance into a homosexual ascesis that would make us work on ourselves and invent—I do not say discover—a manner of being that is still improbable" (1997a, 137). Ascesis is an invention of living, a creative forming of life; it is living like art, an "art of living" (1997c, 146). In turn, viral ascesis is creative, inventive experimenting with viruses; it also highlights a paradox within barebacking subculture: while the work done on the self may transform the human into acts, relations, behaviors rather than identity, the work done on the virus transforms the radically nonhuman otherness of the virus in a humanly conceptualized identity through acts of poetic anthropomorphization.

Dean claims that these actions deliver barebackers to an unlimited intimacy. He writes, "The virus itself permits unlimited intimacy, in the sense that it traces the persistence of multiple prior bodily contacts in the present moment . . . [through its] immortality" (2009, 88). Of course, the virus is not immortal, nor is it traceable in such a manner. Dean continues: "Through HIV it is possible to imagine establishing an intimate corporeal relation with somebody one has never met, or, indeed, could never meet— somebody historically, geographically, or socially distant from oneself. What would it mean for a young gay man today to be able to trace his virus back to, say, Michel Foucault?" (88–89). The use of the word "imagine" is crucial, as again, this tracing of a corporeal relation through the virus itself is impossible; it can only be imagined. Dean's unlimited intimacy is unlimited by the creative work of viral ascesis. This unlimited intimacy requires a virus|viral relation, a fabricated, imagined identity of the virus, to reach such unlimitedness. Let's turn to three specific examples of viral ascesis in barebacking subculture.

Bug Chasers

Dean defines bug chasers as "men who want the human immunodeficiency virus inside their bodies" (2009, 48). In barebacking subculture, men do not seek to be infected by HIV but rather chase a bug. The move from viral infection to bug chasing is significant, as the term "bug" not only transforms the virus but it also affects the men who bareback. Dean notes that "bug chasing" can be a euphemism for HIV as well as a keeping up with the latest trends and fetishes (48). Dean also suggests that bug chasing aligns with a history of gay men being referred to as animals for performing or desiring specific sexual acts; wolves and pigs are his examples.

Bug chasing is an invention of viral ascesis that stylizes the virus. Barebackers chase a bug, not bugs and, therefore, not the multiplicitous never-being-the-sameness of the virus. A bug is extractable and exchangeable, not necessarily a parasite, and can be traded between individuals without dying. A bug is also typically visible to the naked human eye, while a virus is not. Bug chasing brings the otherness of the virus closer to the human by making it more familiar to human perceptual registers.

Seed

Dean quotes the blogger Geek Slut on "seed," or semen: "'Seed is a gift, it's love, it's acceptance. Taking a man's cum—in your ass, down your throat, rubbed into your skin, whatever—even if you don't know his name, is *closeness*'" (Dean 2009, 54). "Seed," a term for semen, suggests a number of creative capacities that the substance is able to enact or execute for barebackers. "Breeding culture" is a term commonly used to refer to the subculture, and while this again stresses the generative aspects of seed, it also complicates any understanding because of the potential for semen to be a carrier of HIV (84–89). Semen, even when carrying an infectious agent that can and does kill, is still thought to affirmatively produce love, intimacy, and closeness when exchanged. Indeed, Dean notes that "seroconversion can feel like becoming pregnant" (88).

Seed emphasizes the possible virus in semen as a gift, as that which breeds the subculture of barebacking: seed not only as the material substance of semen but also as inventions through viral ascesis. Dean tells us that "gift giving represents a basis for social organization rather than merely a sign of individual desire. . . . To give [seed] is thus not to lose but to gain" (76). To gain from seed follows the logic that seed typically grows into something more than itself, such as with fruit or tree seeds. Notably, the virus does not operate under this rubric. It replicates but remains no more or less than it was before; it does not generate an excess to its materiality, just more of it. Viral ascesis turns potentially HIV-infected semen in an affirmative social generator.

Cruising

In the introduction to *Unlimited Intimacy*, Dean writes that promiscuity is on "the route to something new. Promiscuity, in other words, concerns more than new sex partners: it also concerns new ideas and new ways of doing things. . . . [It is] a synonym for creativity. Sexual adventurousness gives birth to other forms of adventurousness—political, cultural, intellectual" (2009, 5). Dean returns to this new kind of expansive creativity in his final chapter, titled "Cruising as a Way of Life." Dean contends that cruising is an ethics of openness and alterity, an ethics of the stranger. He writes that an ethics of cruising is concerned with "how one treats the other . . . [and] how one treats his or her own otherness" (177). What kind of way of life is created when the barebacker and the virus are ethically thought and brought together? How do they treat one another?

In barebacking subculture, the intimate connectedness of the human and the virus is the stuff of the unhuman. Yet while Dean's ethics of openness is an unhuman ethics, it lacks a radical openness to the alterity of the virus. Even though the barebackers' viral ascesis veers far afield from the popular terrain of the viral as rapid spreadability and also enters into a powerful and passionate affective relation with the virus, these creative acts hyperbolize the virus in an anthropomorphic styling that restricts the otherness of the virus. As such, the viral remains a mediation of the virus that favors the human. Following this, can viral ascesis—or any virus|viral relation for that matter—ever stay open to the nonhumanness of the virus? How else can one ethically cruise for the alterity of the virus?

Coda

The virus|viral relations presented reveal that a mediation, or distortion, always exists between the virus and the viral, and while the viral typically has a political leaning or inclination, the virus itself is politically ambiguous. All virals are captures, identifications, speculations; and yet the virus always escapes. Thus, the determination of what is viral generates political, poetic, and ethical schemas. These are the stakes of the unhuman: how the virus is framed to the human, through the viral, has social effects. Yet, as Eugene Thacker's call for an unhuman politics mandates, there must be a conception of the virus|viral relation that is "adequate to its anonymous, unhuman dimensions" (Thacker 2009, 40). What might such an adequacy entail? Pursuing such questions is the next step in understanding viral politics today.

Zach Blas is an artist-theorist working at the intersections of networked media, queerness, and the political. He is a PhD student in literature, information science and information studies, visual studies, and women's studies at Duke University and creator of the art group Queer Technologies.

Works Cited

Bardini, Thierry. 2006. "Hypervirus: A Clinical Report." *CTheory*. http://www.ctheory.net/articles.aspx?id=504.

Bogost, Ian. Forthcoming. "Alien Phenomenology, Or What It's Like To Be A Thing." University of Minnesota Press.

Dean, Tim. 2009. *Unlimited Intimacy: Reflections on the Subculture of Barebacking*. Chicago: University of Chicago Press.

Foucault, Michel. 1997a. "Friendship as a Way of Life." In *Ethics: Subjectivity and Truth*. New York: New Press.

———. 1997b. "Sex, Power, and the Politics of Identity." In *Ethics: Subjectivity and Truth*. New York: New Press.

———. 1997c. "Sexual Choice, Sexual Act." In *Ethics: Subjectivity and Truth*. New York: New Press.

Galloway, Alexander R., and Eugene Thacker. 2007. *The Exploit: A Theory of Networks*. Minneapolis: University of Minnesota Press.

Hardt, Michael, and Antonio Negri. 2000. *Empire*. Cambridge, MA: Harvard University Press.

Parikka, Jussi. 2007. *Digital Contagions: A Media Archaeology of Computer Viruses*. New York: Peter Lang.

Thacker, Eugene. 2009. "After Life: *De Anima* and Unhuman Politics." *Radical Philosophy* 155.

Uexküll, Jakob von. 2001. "An Introduction to Umwelt." *Semiotica* 134(1/4).

Queer Africa and the Fantasy of Virtual Participation

Tavia Nyong'o

"This Law Could Lead to Genocide"

As I write this, I get a tweet. BradNYC wants me to know that "this Ugandan anti-gay law could easily lead to genocide."[1] I click the provided link, which takes me to the website for CNN and the headline "Ugandan Anti-gay Measure Will Be Law Soon, Lawmaker Says" (McKenzie 2010). Alarming to be sure, as is the video clip one can play immediately below, featuring the article's author, CNN's Nairobi-based correspondent David McKenzie, interviewing the editor of a Ugandan tabloid that has published the names, photos, and addresses of "Uganda's top 100 gays" and called for them to be hanged. After being redirected to a short advertisement urging me to invest in Korea's free economic zones, I watch a clip of McKenzie interviewing Giles Muhame, introduced as the "youthful editor" of the tabloid *Rolling Stone* (confusion with the venerable rock magazine of the same name is in all likelihood intentional). In a striking exchange, Muhame calmly parries McKenzie's increasingly exasperated attempts to get him to deny the worst of what he is accused of. Yes, Muhame affirms, he *did* intend to gain quick publicity for his new venture through outing gays. Yes, he *does* believe that homosexuality is immoral, criminal, and a sickness more dangerous to the Ugandan body politic than terrorism. And yes, he hopes that his publicity stunt *will* lead to the arrest and the hanging of gays. Indeed, as Muhame calmly adopts the posture of African alterity, and McKenzie performs his astonishment on behalf of those whom he names as his "Western viewers," the confrontation devolves into a curious short-circuit. There seems to be no characterization of his position that McKenzie can get Muhame to disagree with except, notably, the claim that the *Rolling Stone* story has led to extralegal "mob" violence against individuals. That, Muhame hotly denies, is a flat-out lie.

My analysis of the protean subject of discursive incommensurability draws upon African postcolonial theory while sidestepping the temptation to resurrect an innocent African subject. Instead I look to theorists of neoliberalism as a global political project, and communicative capitalism as its dominant mode of discursive production. This perspective frames my approach to the exchange between Muhame and McKenzie and to similar scenes in contemporary media that are staging anxieties over an "African homophobia" cast as at once atavistic, protean, and portentously necropolitical (Mbembe 2003). *Rolling Stone*'s campaign against gays certainly seems to fit under the rubric of a death-driven politics (particularly given that, shortly after it occurred, a prominent Ugandan gay activist was brutally murdered in his home) (Rice 2011).[2] This may tempt us to accept @BradNYC's characterization of proposed legislation in Uganda's parliament—the so-called Bahati bill, which would extend severe penalties, including death, to offenses ranging from "promoting" homosexuality to the seduction of the innocent—as protogenocidal. Especially within a media context that often frames contemporary sub-Saharan Africa as a charnel house of horror, we may see the antigay campaign in Uganda as joining the long list of what postcolonial African theorist Achille Mbembe terms the "new and unique forms of social existence in which vast populations are subjected to conditions of life conferring upon them the status of the living dead"(2003, 40). Indubitably, queer activism, rights, and existence in sub-Saharan Africa, as elsewhere, can be a matter of life or death (see, for instance, Kato 2010). But, insofar as Mbembe's essay is a call to expand and render more complex our accounts of contemporary sovereignty, we might want to use the concept of necropolitics to question, rather than ratify, the stereotyped horror that the CNN television and webcast affirms. In particular, we require an analysis of necropolitics that accounts for its presence within communicative capitalism, rather than one that extends stereotypes of a violent Africa. Is the necropolitical an atavistic force of alterity, outside communicative reason and action, requiring intervention, pacification, and control? Or is it a figure or fantasy elicited from within the short circuit of discursive confrontation? This essay shall argue the latter.

Necropolitics can be used to pivot between two lines of critical thought that differently evoke viral metaphors. The first is that line of thought that identifies the tropology of infectiousness and contagion with racial blackness, exposing the associations between blackness and communicable diseases such as HIV/AIDS, associations that insinuate that blackness is a racialized form of the death drive itself (I am drawing in particular on the work of Browning 1998). The paradox of this death-bound African figure—a paradox distilled in the humanitarian West's preferred image of Africa as an emaciated and starving child—is that it is also a figure of life. Africa breeds forms of life that are given over to death. Discourses of Africa as the wellspring of enthusiastic, orgiastic violence link the excitability of primitive vitality to the unpredictable but catastrophic expenditure of waste or disposable life. (My thinking on vitalism and race-thinking has been shaped by the work of Jones 2010.) The contagiousness of African culture—from the pulsating rhythm of the drums to the frenzy of African worship—is held to both transfix and horrify the onlooker. Such racialized reason—and the various technologies of segregation, apartheid, and quarantine that colonial and neocolonial regimes have developed as a consequence—is rarely brought up in the contemporary debate around the efficacy of remote activism organized under the rubric of human rights. When it is, it is from the perspective of a postcolonial *ressentiment*, as when the homophobic Anglican archbishop of Nigeria, Peter Akinola, denounces church tolerance of homosexuality as a form of "spiritual slavery" (qtd. in Rubenstein 2010). Such mobilizations of the history of slavery and colonialism by and for a contemporary clerical and state patriarchy are only further enabled by an unwillingness on the left to confront the complicity of the humanitarian and human rights impulse in the reproduction of hegemony over the global South. Such an awareness could complement the equally urgent need to develop alternative "usable pasts" for African same-sex sexuality (such a deconstructive approach to the myth of a singularly straight African past is mounted in Epprecht 2008).

This will not be the place to mount a full critique or defense of human rights, nor to adequately limn the nuanced distinctions between "human rights" and "humanitarian intervention" as they operate in the field of international law (Douzinas 2007). Instead, I want to focus on one particular tactic that emerges out of the rich tradition of human rights and humanitarian work and rethink its function in the era of what Dean (2009) calls "communicative capitalism". Dean is among the theorists insisting most forcefully that we cannot disconnect the democratic and humanist messages disseminated across networks from the hierarchical and anti-humanist infrastructure of capital-intensive information technology that carries them. Neither, of course, can we simply collapse the message into the information. It is rather the analytical short circuit produced by these two layers of analysis—which cannot be resolved but must be preserved theoretically and politically—that protects against premature foreclosures utopian and dystopian (Shirky 2008; Lanier 2010).

As the notion of spreading a tiny "meme" of information about Uganda over SMS and web via Twitter suggests, action alerts are increasingly "going viral." The tradition of the letter-writing campaign (which dates back to the origins of the modern human rights organizations but indeed possesses roots in abolitionist humanitarian campaigns of the nineteenth century) has taken a new concrete shape as it has shifted onto new electronic communications platforms. Already there have been several waves of techno-euphoria around the liberating prospects of Facebook and Twitter for social movements, particularly in the Middle East, and a countering techno-realism pointing to the highly increased surveillance capacities these technologies endow repressive state apparatus (Morozov 2011; Mejias 2010). In terms of the kind of Internet-based progressive activism pioneered by domestic U.S. organizations like MoveOn.org and its internationalist counterpart, Avaaz.org, the enthusiastic embrace of the cascading potential of millions of tiny actions to add up to a wave of significant political force has been met with skepticism in some quarters.

In order to address such skepticism, certain questions seem appropriate. Among them: what exactly is the relationship, in contemporary Uganda, between popular homophobia, extralegal violence, and the law? How does the language of humanitarian intervention ("genocide") clarify or cloud the issue, when it comes to the human rights of LGBT Ugandans? What is the nature of the journalist Muhame's influence, if any, relative to any of these domains? What was his relationship to the "lawmaker" and "anti-gay measure" of the article to which this interview was attached? And beyond such questions regarding Muhame are questions about the interview itself. How does this moral showdown between "the West" and Africa over human rights give voice to the struggles of queer Ugandans? What needed background information—for instance about the conflicts over Uganda's abstinence and monogamy-based programs to fight HIV/ AIDS—is omitted from a decontextualized discussion of the Bahati bill? To what degree does such media consolidate the discursive construction of homophobia, in the sovereign eyes of the donor community, as the latest locus of bad governance in sub-Saharan Africa? Does such a confrontation not cast, as Neville Hoad puts it, "African nationalism as a site of displaced resistance to a perceived encroachment on neocolonial nationalism by the forces of globalization" (2007, 77)? And doesn't McKenzie a bit hastily claim gay rights as a "Western value" when, as Gary Younge has shrewdly noted, one might much more logically cast gay rights among the *critiques* of Western civilization (Younge 2010; see also Abelove 2005, 70–88; 2010, 341)?

It is far too easily presumed—especially in the wake of Tunisia and Egypt—that web 2.0, along with the proliferation of print, radio, and television media in the neoliberal, deregulated African communications sector, is positively affecting long-standing struggles for democracy, human dignity, and human rights in Africa (Nyong'o 1987). We leap too quickly to the assumption that information and communications technologies are extending "peer-to-peer" contact with other people across the globe, deepening our ability to intervene positively in their lives. The scale and rapidity of response to subjects in distress seem beyond reproach, and, lest reproach nonetheless be offered, those organizations that disseminate action alerts will quickly assert that real activists on the ground demand them.[3] Such pragmatic responses foreclose a more extended critique of activist praxis and narrow the field of legitimate discussion to single-issue politics. This has particularly short-sighted consequences for the analysis of homophobia, insofar as it is often presented, as in the CNN interview, as an inexplicable excess of violence gratuitously added to the misery already meted out on Africans by the cruelty of fate. It promotes the view that African homophobic violence circulates in a "general economy" of waste and expenditure of life that defies the "political economy" of impoverishment and need within which Africans in the neoliberal global order are typically consigned (Bataille 1988). Integrating an analysis of "African homophobia" as an effect of the short circuit within communicative capitalism avoids this trap of exoticizing evil.

The need for such a nonpragmatic analysis of the effects of single-issue exposés of "African homophobia" was literally on display at bookstores and magazine racks in September 2010, when the U.S. national LGBT magazine the *Advocate* ran a (thorough and well-researched) article on the influence of American evangelicals on antigay campaigns in Uganda and elsewhere under the inflammatory cover headline "Get Out of Africa." Who exactly is in Africa here, and what position are they in to get out? The headline is

FIG. 1: Cover of *The Advocate*, September 2010. Courtesy of The Advocate/Here Media Inc. © 2010 Here Publishing Inc. All rights reserved.

much more than an obvious play on the classic 1937 colonial romance, Karen Blixen's *Out of Africa*. It stages the fantasy of a pink and purple Africa in need of rescue from a globally ambitious Christian evangelicalism that, while originating in the United States, is seen as finding particularly fertile conditions where "fervor is so welcome that it threatens to sweep the entire continent." While the author of the more nuanced article within is not responsible for the way his research is presented and publicized, it is precisely the visual and semiotic logic of distillation for ease of circulation that is at issue (Sharlet 2010). As Mary-Jane Rubenstein (2010) notes, exposés of U.S. evangelical missionizing in postcolonial African nations like Uganda neglect to take the long view of Christianity's presence in Africa. "Taken alone," she argues, "they leave us with the impression that everything ultimately comes from Western Europe and North America. If we assert that the bishops of the South are fighting someone else's battle— that they are defending a gospel that came from the North against a new sexual ethic that's also coming from the North, by means of a Northern-style homophobia enforced with Northern cash—then it begins to look as though nothing is really African, or Asian, or South American at all." This perplexing dissolution of the African subject is reflected in the ambiguous addressee of that directive "Get out of Africa." Is it a warning to the potential gay Western tourist to a homophobic African country? Advice to imperiled African queers? Or even an imperative to interfering U.S. Christian evangelicals? This ambiguity doesn't need to cohere into a stable or singular interpellation, insofar as its primary objective seems to be the broadcast of ambient affects of worry, alarm, and imperative.

Rubinstein goes on to tease out the complex triangulation of Christianity, tradition, and globalization that is being performed in the Anglican communion (where battles over the ordination of gay clergy have raged most fiercely), as a corrective to such one-sided views of Africa as overly susceptible to pernicious "fervor." But such attempts to increase the circulation of expert knowledge can also spur an enlightened self-deception of the variety "We know very well, but anyway, something must be done," or "Everyone's heard that critique before, but what are we are going to do in the meantime?" What spurs such disavowals? Why does global connectivity not seem to stoke a greater appreciation of the complexity of situations? (Ironically, the founder of both MoveOn.org and Avaaz.org has written a new book exposing precisely this phenomenon, which he attributes to the increasingly self-selective way information and opinion circulates on the Internet (see Pariser 2011). Does communicative capitalism elevate the transmission of affect over the accomplishment of political objectives, reducing politics to what Dean calls a fantasy of participation?

I assume here both that fantasies are necessary props to the stable functioning of reality and that the disrupting of those fantasies is potentially political insofar as it can make that reality run a little less smoothly, forcing it to account for itself in terms it officially proscribes. The method of immanent critique I have adopted for this essay entails my traversing this fantasy of participation, in part by participating in the networks I discuss and critique. I hesitate, however, to present myself as an objective researcher into those networks, insofar as the materiality of the phenomena I wish to investigate requires a greater reflexivity. Here, I am persuaded by Žižek's claim that "materialism is not the direct assertion of my inclusion in objective reality (such an assertion presupposes that my position of enunciation is that of an external observer who can grasp the whole of reality): rather, it resides in the reflexive twist by means of which I myself am included in the picture constituted by me—it is this reflexive short circuit, this necessary redoubling of myself as standing both outside and inside my picture, that bears witness to my 'material existence.'" (2006, 17)

Correlatively, the short circuit is object, method, and symptom of my effort to make sense of the declining symbolic efficiency of action alerts and other forms of remote "democratic" and "human rights" participation, and the accompanying increase in certainty that, after all, they must be doing *something*. It is the felt sense of urgency, which viral political messaging depends upon, that requires further analysis, insofar as it produces a subject of global participation, seemingly proximate to, and caring about, and assisting, queer Africans in dire need.

"We Have Just Days Left"

Let me enter into this discussion of the fantasy of participation through another story from Uganda. Or, rather, from Facebook. In August of 2010, a friend posts a link to his "wall," which shows up in my "newsfeed," to a website called Avaaz.org. He has just signed a petition to President Yoweri Museveni of Uganda, asking him to shelve the Bahati bill, and he urges his friends to do so as well. David Bahati, member of Parliament from Ndorwa West, had first introduced the bill in October of 2009. Investigative journalist Jeff Sharlet (author of the *Advocate* cover story) revealed Bahati's connections to a U.S. fundamentalist organization known as the Family, which strove to disentangle itself from Bahati's bill once its links to him became public. Because I had been following this story, I was immediately attracted to and alarmed by my friend's urgent action alert. I thought the bill *had* been shelved months earlier, in May 2010, in part because of such international protests as I was now being urged to involve myself in. Worrying that a new development had occurred, I rushed to the website. There I read:

> Gay Ugandans may be sentenced to death if legislation being debated right now passes.
>
> High level international condemnation has just pushed the President to send the bill for review, but Ugandan allies say only a worldwide outcry could tip Parliamentarians away from discrimination, alarming them with global isolation.
>
> We have just days left—sign the petition to oppose Uganda's anti-gay law below and send it on to friends and family and it will be delivered to Uganda's politicians, donors and embassies around the world. (http://www.avaaz.org/en/uganda_rights_5/?vl)[4]

Here we are given no information about Uganda, not even where in the world it might be, only that its government is contemplating putting gays to death. The call seeks to compensate for this absolute minimum of knowledge provided with a sort of maximum of participation urged, envisioning a "worldwide outcry," expressed through petition signatures, as the only way to tip the balance in favor of clemency for Ugandan queers. Although the language of this call was highly indexical—these events are happening "now," there are only "days" are left to act—no calendar date is listed. To my concerned friend, who received the link from another friend, there was no reason to doubt the sincerity or urgency of the alert. Believing I knew better, I poked around the site further and eventually reached another page that brought the story up to date. A list of Avaaz achievements included this claim:

> In an unprecedented show of public opposition to the proposed law that would sentence gay Ugandans to death, Avaaz worked with church leaders and human rights activists to deliver a 450,000-strong petition to the Speaker of Uganda's parliament. . . .
>
> Parliament had been expected to debate the bill in February 2010 [but] in the face of local and global pressure, formal discussion still hasn't begun. Some say the bill may be left to die in committee, potentially a quiet but extraordinary victory for human rights. Avaaz continues to work closely with allies to monitor the bill—and stands ready to take action once more if it regains momentum. (http://www.avaaz.org/en/highlights—human-rights.php)

What explains the simultaneity of these messages on the web platform of a single activist site?[5] I don't wish to single out a well-meaning, multi-issue activist organization for undue criticism, simply for failing to keep a webpage updated. The dynamic of the story is undoubtedly complex: the Bahati bill has wound an unpredictable way through Uganda's legislative procedure, periodically appearing to be on the verge of adoption before being semipermanently "shelved" in May 2011 (although its author vows to reintroduce a new version after elections due in February 2012) ("Uganda's Anti-gay Bill 'Shelved'" 2011). Without unfair criticism, I do want to point out how the Internet is shaping the communicative strategy of humanitarian and human rights activism.[6] Technology theorist Jaron Lanier (2010) calls these design "lock-ins," structures that become self-sustaining because of mass adoption and the consequent nigh impossibility of conversion to more optimal systems. Because of one such arbitrary structure of the web, for instance, the call to action and the follow-up reports are on different webpages (in this case not even hyperlinked to each other). The sharing mechanism of web 2.0 sites like Facebook and Twitter further isolate individual pages from the sites they originate from, and add their own independent commenting and archiving that can perpetuate the life of the page even if it is updated or removed on the original server.

The rhythmic urgency and delay produced by the series of action alerts and updates on the Avaaz website can thus not exactly be mapped directly onto the chronology of the Bahati bill's progression through Uganda's parliament. Because of the peculiar temporality of alerting an indefinite number of people via the Internet, Avaaz activists deliberately composed their alert to be chronologically ambiguous. Rhetorically, the call combines temporal urgency with no specific time frame.[7] A webpage, instantly accessible globally at low cost, is best left ambiguous, all the better to capture the marginal utility of the least committed, least informed browser who can be convinced to click a button and send an email. The homepage of Avaaz.org at any given point in time is a bewildering array of flash points from that day's or week's media, drawn from all corners of the globe. Encountering it, one is confronted with the prospect of the Sisyphean task of involving oneself comprehensively, and with a peculiar kind of indifference, to all issues equally. But the site appears to work best as a kind of clearinghouse, where issues work more like nodal entry points, with no attempt to discourage involvement with an exhaustive presentation (or integrated analysis) of world crisis. As Ulises Mejia (2010) notes, such "nodocentrism" has performative effects on the activism it ostensibly facilitates, shaping and structuring what can be known and done even as it greatly magnifies and accelerates the means by which such knowledge and action can occur. In converting activism into a kind of informatics—the crucial objective is the count of signatures and the rapidity with which they can be gained and deployed—a specific kind of discourse is mobilized and, with it, another short circuit. This raises questions regarding our easy convictions about the causative role of sheer numbers in swaying decision makers, cast in the role of masters being confronted with a demand to exchange reasons (a role I will return to and query in my conclusion).

The deliberate reduction of information in order to ease the threshold of participation can actually have the effect, I argue, of disorienting the subject in the process of mobilizing her or him to action. I mean here to go beyond the quite familiar critique that information on the Internet is unreliable to note how unreliability and affective intensity can enter into a negative feedback loop, such that the less reliable information we can glean, the more we attach ourselves to intensities that seem plausible insofar as they conform to imaginary structures. This is what Žižek calls the decline in symbolic efficiency. Jodi Dean comments on the idea in the following passage:

> Žižek's notion of a decline in symbolic efficiency . . . highlights our perpetual uncertainty, our sense that we never really know whether what we say registers with the other as what we mean as well as our sense that we are never quite sure what "everybody knows." . . . Imaginary identities sustained by the promise and provision of enjoyment replace symbolic identities. . . . Imaginary identities are incapable of establishing a firm place to stand, a position from which one can make sense of one's world. . . . The flip side of the multiplicity of imaginary identities, then, is the reduction and congealing of identity into massive sites or strange attractors of affective investment (2009, 63–67).

The subject of the urgent action alert, we could hypothesize, is increasingly imaginary, rather than symbolic. That is, she or he is mobilized by a presymbolic image of threat or lure, one that proliferates independent of secure symbolically efficient knowledge. Uganda becomes a strange attractor of imaginary identities gathered around a "world outcry," and Ugandan queers are framed within an updated version of what Anne McClintock calls "panoptical time," or "the image of global history consumed—at a glance—in a single spectacle from a point of privileged invisibility"(1995, 37). In this current case, Ugandan LGBT folk are depicted through the metaphor of the closet, globally and transhistorically construed and, through that metaphor, placed at a prior point in a historical development that the West has already progressed through (see, for example, Gettleman 2010). As McClintock's stresses, this is above all an optical effect that produces a fantasy of the other as somehow occupying a different order of time. Outcry is organized around what *might* happen or may already be happening in Uganda, that is, around temporal uncertainty, and we are urged to invest affect to the extent that we remain uncertain. How could it possibly hurt, after all, to quickly express our indignation to President Yoweri Museveni for presiding over plans to execute gays? It's less important that we truly understand the situation and believe in the efficacy of this action than it is to believe that *someone* believes in it. We are thus yoked to our activism through a relation of interpassivity.

The decline of symbolic efficiency presents a challenge to more empirical approaches to the study of human rights in Africa. The shock of the "Kill the Gays" bill as a strange attractor of global affect could indeed be parlayed into a more sustained, deeply historical knowledge of the situation in Uganda. Such a sustained ethnographic, historical, and political engagement would place the recent events in the context of prior controversies, going back to the 1990s, over Uganda's ABC (Abstinence, Be Faithful, Condoms) HIV/AIDS education strategy. Uganda's approach was seen as an outlier in the global mainstream, and its efficacy became the subject of sharp ideological dispute as evangelical groups, among others, championed Uganda's "just say no" approach (Hoad 2010). The sexual regulation of the citizenry had thus been established as the basis of a displaced struggle over sovereignty well before the Bahati bill had been introduced and provides the necessary context for understanding how global action against it is perceived in Uganda. Once the bill drew international censure, from the administration of President Barack Obama and other foreign governments and agencies, it was drawn into the complex diplomatic and political calculus of a regime balancing a variety of concerns. The legal and moral proscriptions against homosexuality were hardly primary among those concerns, given that Uganda's penal code—derived from the British colonial era—already punishes homosexuality. Rather than a question of the symbolic order of the law, as most activism assumed it to be, homosexuality became a strange attractor for imaginary identities aggressively competing within the communicative terrain of neoliberalism, such as the evangelical scourge of the gay seducer, and the humanitarian angel swooping in to rescue the endangered and helpless African queer. While such imaginary identities do have real-world effects, their allure often encourages implausible leaps, such as the miscategorization of a human rights violation as an imminent humanitarian catastrophe, which the free-floating circulation of the term "genocide" encouraged.

The patient, retrospective, and time-consuming work of piecing together the full picture of a situation is precisely what a politics organized around rapid mobilization militates against, particularly when it is a single issue. Interminable analysis is disparaged in situations where a decision is needed. It is certainly the case that activists must act with less than total information. And furthermore, activism is a performative agency designed to *change* a situation, not merely to adequately understand it. But this does not answer the question of how the decision actually operates under conditions of declining symbolic efficiency. How do we know, in other words, that the outcry has worked, even if we agree to participate in it? What chain of causation, exactly, links our participation in the plight of queer Africa to the eventual decision (or nondecision) to shelve the Bahati bill?

Who is the master to whom we are addressing our demands, and does a figure like Giles Muhame speak his discourse?

Participation as a Neoliberal Fantasy

Something tells me to check out the Facebook page of *Rolling Stone* and its editors. That thing, I think, is my memory that what originally got me active on Facebook was the realization that all my extended cousins, aunts, and uncles in Kenya and its diaspora were using it. Instantly I am cruising the pages of Giles Muhame and his colleague Cliff Abenaitwe, recent journalism graduates of Makerere University, once a jewel of African higher education that has been decimated, as George Caffentzis has recently written, by World Bank structural adjustment policies designed to strip-mine free public higher education and foster in its place a system of paying students and entrepreneurial-minded faculties competing for tuitions. The entrepreneurial, opportunistic, and cynical affective tonality of the *Rolling Stone* editors is thus not a symptom of African alterity, but of their subjectivation within the uneven but singular landscape of neoliberalism (on cynicism as the affective tonality of the neoliberal multitude, see Virno 2003).

Students exiting the neoliberal African university, Caffentzis writes are "a displaced, unemployed, increasingly proletarianised, and potentially revolutionary class of 'knowledge workers'" (2010, 35). They are also part of the Facebook generation, if profiles of Muhame and Abenaitwe are any indication. Those profiles are indeed incongruous. Abenaitwe, while calling for the death of gays, also describes himself as "a down to earth, caring, loving, friendly person." Giles Muhame spells out his name in an acrostic: *G* is for "generous," *I* is for "intelligent," *L* is for "lovin," and so on. Most intriguingly, for a man interviewed on CNN as agreeing with the view that homosexuality is an abomination, Muhame lists himself as "interested in" both women and men. Another short circuit. Is this person near from me, or far? Are we speaking the same language, using the same platform, meshing through the same computer code, or not? In its very imagined proximity and invitation to link, like, comment, and connect, Facebook enacts the dissolution of symbolic efficiency into an eddy of imaginary identities that lack "a position from which one can make sense of one's world." In the place of such stable positions, we confront waves and oscillations of affect that buffet us into opportunistic alignments. It is not necessarily a contradiction, I am arguing, for Muhame to present himself as a "lovin'" person interested in both men and women on Facebook and a dutiful protopatriarch calling for the death of gays on CNN. Such cynicism is the emotional tonality of the multitude under conditions of the decline of symbolic efficiency.

At one level, reading Dean alongside recent controversies over homosexuality in East Africa might be taken for the familiar tactic of showing how representations of the other actually reveal more about us than about them. Africa becomes a kind of projection screen upon which the decline of participatory democracy, the rise of evangelicalism, and so on, in the United States, can be mapped. But the power of a symptomatic analysis of democracy as a neoliberal fantasy, I argue, goes beyond this tactic. Rather than just reflecting Western identity back upon itself, what the short circuits of communicative capitalism do, under Dean's analysis, is expose the lack and the split in that Western identity, revealing how liberal democracy is not at all identical to itself. This, I think, is a much more arresting theoretical tactic. Rather than fruitlessly rehearsing the argument of whether it is just or right to "export" our values or democracy, Dean asks whether such values and democracy are powerful self-deceptions, things we cannot give because they are things we do not have.

Dean insists that it is ruinous to take democracy (and I would add, human rights) as the horizon of left politics, arguing that democracy under neoliberalism has become increasingly separated from the political and sutured to the economic. That is to say, democratic participation is being rendered increasingly isomorphic with consumer choice, both because participation is becoming more passive and, conversely, because consumerism is becoming more active and widely available. The productions of nationally or globally conscious individuals increasingly flow through the same channels—Skype, Facebook, AT&T, Blogger.com—that any other lifestyle, interest, purchase, or interpersonal relation takes. A gay activist in Berlin can post an irate comment on the Facebook page of a homophobic journalist half a world away. Indeed, many of the pictures of "Uganda's top gays" were scraped from social networking sites like Facebook. All this furious, contestatory activity, while registering to us as political action, is registering to Facebook, and so forth, as "user-generated content." To switch to a Deleuzean metaphor, such activist contributions are inscribed upon the same recording surface of capital as that of all other forms of postmodern production. They become subject to the logic of accumulation through dispossession.

This logic increasingly subtends all activism—or simply activity—that invests in the hope that a neoliberal order contains the resources within itself to erect a world of greater freedom. But before we can even begin that project, the moment of accumulation has occurred. Recall the almost comically literal example of neoliberal globalization in the ad before the CNN interview. Whoever CNN thinks I am, clearly it is someone whose interest in international affairs might extend to investing in "free economic zones" in Korea. Even before I have watched the video, in other words, my "eyeballs" have been "monetized," in industry jargon. Even before I have been invited to share in the CNN reporter's gaping astonishment at the barbaric African other, my participation has already been short-circuited, its value accrued, and, at one economic level, it doesn't matter whether what I see is misleading or not, the entire picture or not. Information, advertisement, and affect are all brought together in what Dean calls "a knot of hope and despair (2009, 75–94).

This is why it's relevant to tell the story through the Twitter feed and the CNN website. The ideology inheres to the mode of participation, in this case including the affective labor of @BradNYC in posting the link, and mine to feel impelled to click it. As Dean puts it, "Rhetorics of access, participation, and democracy work ideologically to secure the technological infrastructure of neoliberalism" (2009, 23). In extending this argument to a transnational perspective, it is important to keep in mind the structural unevenness of this infrastructure, *pace* Thomas Friedman and his paeans to a "flat" world of global competition. One symptom of the unevenness of these global effects is the complex way that the biopolitical and necropolitical affect each other in a way that works against a single horizon of human rights strategy.

In their insistence on a binarism between an able and ethical world community and a disabled and corrupt African sovereignty, human rights interventions reveal their biopolitical basis, that is, their hope to intervene at the level of life. This form of power is attached to the Foucauldian dynamic of governmentality, which describes the modes of increased surveillance, pastoral care, and subjectifying intervention that the European state increasingly deployed in the nineteenth and twentieth centuries. This account is contrasted in the work of Mbembe by a necropolitics, in which the state intervenes less to preserve life than to manifest its power over death. With his concept of necropolitics, Mbembe points out the specificity of postcolonial struggles over the terms of an African sovereignty characterized by a relatively weak state power, in biopolitical sectors like health care, education, sanitation, and civil engineering, in contrast to a relatively stronger sovereignty in areas like the military, paramilitary, police, and communications sectors. Hence the relative indifference of the necropolitical to life, which is simply "permitted" to live, in contrast to death, which is carefully organized, industrialized, and deployed, whether in war, genocide, or starvation.

When Giles Muhame hotly denies inciting violence in his interview with CNN, we see the dynamics of bio/necropolitics at work. His denial seems to reflect less a humanitarian reflex in the face of the consequences of his rhetoric than it does his negotiation for position within an authoritarian state that reserves for itself the deployment of the power to make death. By participating in a populist, public demand for gays to be identified and hanged, he can appeal to the necropolitical state in terms that flatter its sovereignty, even if it outrages the international community. But such a call tips into sedition if it leads to unauthorized extralegal pogroms, so he must couch his protests against the neoliberal immiseration and normlessness of Uganda in the very language of patriarchy and gerontocracy that dominates people of his generation, making gays and lesbians scapegoats for globalization. *Rolling Stone*'s homophobic aggression against the strange attractor of homosexuality cannot be read as simply lining up with the patriarchal order of an authoritarian (and nondemocratic) regime. It is, rather, symptomatic of the new inchoate subjects formed by neoliberal globalization, which the canny trademark infringement of the name of their enterprise should telegraph.

Given the disqualification and derogation of the university by neoliberalism, producing the roving and opportunistic "knowledge worker," where should the traditionally constituted university discourse intervene? The structural imbalances of neoliberalism militate against its dream of better knowledge supplied by native informants. Indeed, the university discourse establishes a social bond based on its own particular fantasy, which is of a public sphere founded in the exchange of reasons. What evidence do we have that communicative capitalism is constructing such a sphere? Activism displaces theoretical reflection in favor of closer knowledge of what is really happening on the ground. But no one is placed in a position of cognitive privilege with regard to what is really happening on the ground. Africans themselves lack fluency in the dozens of requisite languages and colonial histories, or the ability to navigate the continent's many borders with the ease of high flying international experts, researchers and do-gooders. A Kenyan colleague sighs as he relates being asked for his expert commentary on the situation elsewhere in queer Africa, and clicking on Wikipedia (Macharia 2010). The gay international, especially in its media projects, seems to long for the return of anthropology's native informant (Massad 2007). But what if we now only encounter the digitally native informant? What if everywhere we turn Africans are plugged into the same circuits of power, knowledge, and enjoyment, albeit from a position of radical inequality? How then is the stable binarism of us rescuing them possibly to be maintained?

From Postcolonial Hybrid to Neoliberal Pervert

If it is foolhardy to enter into the naive attempt to know the African subject completely, transparently and, as it were, peer to peer, then it might be past time to revisit a famous, nigh, fabulous, figure—the postcolonial hybrid—and ask whether such a figure is sufficient to the task of mounting a political challenge to the present neoliberal order. Homi Bhabha developed a theory of postcolonial hybridity in *The Location of Culture* that is based upon what he identifies as a "time-lag" and "temporal break in representation" (Bhabha 1994, 274). It is through such time lag, he suggests, that "new and hybrid agencies and articulations" emerge (275). In colonial and postcolonial contexts, such a hybrid agency might be seen in the unexpected fluency of the colonized or formerly colonized in the terms of the colonial order. But what happens in the neoliberal present when the compression of time and space voids the possibility of lag? The postcolonial hybrid occupied a future competence that the colonial order officially recognized, but temporally delayed (we have all encountered the astonishment of the Western visitor, impressed that the Ugandan speaks English *so well*). But now we see the uncanny specter of the supposedly atavistic African with the Facebook profile, spelling out his own name as a kooky acrostic like any daydreaming ninth grader from Omaha. Or my own experience of flying to Nairobi to meet with young Kenyan queers, only to encounter a room full of computers and cell phones, with one group of boys huddled around a terminal displaying the Germany-based website GayRomeo. When time lag is displaced by the short circuit, it is no longer clear that any position enjoys a perspective from which to perceive the other as lagging. Panoptic time is perturbed, which does not mean that it disappears as an effect, just that the dislocation of colonial privilege within the symbolic order produces more aggressive imaginary efforts to resurrect it.

The reduction of agencies and articulations to a single plane of antagonistic identities, conducted over an infrastructure of uneven and militarized neoliberal capitalism, does not produce the liberatory or subversive postcolonial hybrid. Rather, it gives way to a new figure I call the neoliberal pervert, invoking not the moralistic language of sexual perversion, but the analytic deployment of the pervert's discourse as one of several possible instantiations of the social bond (Feher-Gurewich 2003). The fantasy of global participation in queer Africa is a manifestation of the pervert's discourse, not because homosexuality is a perversion, but because the opposition to homosexuality, in navigating the current political field, increasingly has shifted from the master's discourse—prohibitive and lawlike—to the pervert's discourse, soliciting enjoyment and disavowal.

For Dean, the classic neoliberal pervert was George W. Bush. Although anti-Bush protesters assumed that Bush, as U.S. president, spoke the master's discourse, Dean perceptively notes how Bush's reliance on both jingoistic nationalism and fervent evangelical belief repeatedly allowed him to cast himself as an agent of a higher power or mission, rather than a father issuing denials. He was, of course, famously, the "decider," but the decision he took was not self-authorized, she argues, but the mechanism through which he could evade the hysterical protester's demand that he supply reasons and exchange in rational, democratic deliberation. Dean comments, "Insofar as he is merely the executor [Bush] doesn't speak for himself or participate in the exchange of reasons. The reasons, or knowledge, already underpin his decision and are subject to his servicing of them. . . . The pervert doesn't recognize himself in the address of the hysteric because he is merely an instrument" (2009, 85–6). The neoliberal pervert may resemble the master insofar as neither participates in the exchange of reasons (and thus neither responds well to the university discourse founded on such an exchange). They differ in that the master can be opposed by exposing the source of his hidden enjoyment, since his authority rests on a certain shrouding of his authority. The pervert, by contrast, exhibits his enjoyment, and insofar as his is merely an instrument of knowledge, it is not susceptible to the traditional tactics taken against a prohibitive patriarchal "no" (for instance, the traditional tactic of exposing the patriarch's hypocrisy, or demanding he submit his decision making to rational deliberation).

The distinction might be made clear by contrasting the positions of a traditional patriarchal figure like Ugandan president Museveni and a neo-liberal pervert like Martin Ssempa, one of the most prominent Ugandan campaigners against condoms, sex outside marriage, and homosexuality and a key supporter of the Bahati bill. With some qualification, we could describe the abstinence/monogamy approach to HIV education (at least, this seems to describe the way that approach is fantasized by a pro-abstinence documentary like *Miss HIV* of 2008) as partaking of the master's discourse. Just don't have sex, or have sex only with one's single heterosexual marital partner, and don't demand reasons (which are obvious: father knows best, and HIV will kill you). As a promulgator of this message, Museveni seems to function as a traditional master. We see footage of him speaking in *Miss HIV*, but are granted interview access only to his wife, first lady Janet Museveni. In this way, Mr. Museveni is distanced from the exchange of reasons, and even Mrs. Museveni speaks primarily of further delegating "the truth" about HIV/AIDS to the church, which already has the role of truth telling in society. So far, a master's discourse appears to be in operation. But when the function of truth telling is delivered over to the church, in the figure of pastor Martin Ssempa of the Makerere Community Church, an important shift occurs.

Appearing in the documentary, Ssempa is a warm, fun-loving person who, far from appearing anxious to deliver the truth, wants to draw his hearers into a relaxed and confident enjoyment of the superiority of Christian chastity. He laughingly mocks the hysterical antagonism of pro-sex HIV/AIDS educators, who are portrayed in the film as furthering an ideology that began in the promiscuous culture of Western gay men. And he underscores the youthful, fun-loving, and hip basis of his ministry, as Bob Marley plays over footage of him dancing with college students at a "Keep Ya Underwear On" campus party. Where, Ssempa demands, is there a commandment that says, "Thou shalt not have fun?" No reference is made in the film, as Neville Hoad (2010) notes, to Ssempa's involvement in a condom-burning episode on that same campus in 2004. And the film was released before a notorious speech Ssempa gave in 2010, in which he attacked homosexuals in the most virulent of terms and displayed downloaded gay male pornography to a horrified audience. The apparent contrast between the warm/friendly and angry/frothing Pastor Ssempa notwithstanding, I want to argue that both stances show how his discourse is taken up within a perverse social bond, rather than being the discourse of the patriarch/master.

With 3.5 million views on YouTube and climbing, Ssempa's explicit rant against anal sex, fisting, and coprophagy has become a viral hit, inspiring parodies and responses but, as of yet, no lucrative record deal. Universally known as the "Eat da Poo Poo" video, Ssempa's speech spread so rapidly because of the cartoonish explicitness with which it claimed to represent gay male sex. His vivid images and hand gestures, and frequent recourse to pornographic computer images, seemed to exemplify the stereotypical sexually repressed homophobe, obsessed with the object of his anathema. But such a reading would mistake him as a traditional master, invested in hiding the obscene source of his enjoyment, rather than a pervert, obeying a higher power and positioned in relation to the obscenity of his enjoyment through a logic of disavowal.

This distinction becomes apparent when one considers the attempts to satirize Ssempa by taking the speech, cutting and looping the most incendiary phrases, and adding effects like beats, autotune, and funny graphics. Such satires, at least ostensibly, deflate the incendiary charge of Ssempa's speech by turning it back on its source. But does this miss the mark? Dean argues that the pervert "is acting in the service of a cause, principle, and design of nature that is incommensurate with his will. . . . This hysterical process produces, but does not depend on, the authority of the master. The pervert doesn't recognize himself in the address of the hysteric because he is merely an instrument" (2009, 86). This is why, strictly speaking, parody fails to reveal Ssempa's personal obsessions. They are rather caught up in the same contagious circuit of enjoyment, within which Ssempa and his audience can consolidate a horrific, obscene image of coprophagic homosexuals. The implied critique of looping and mocking Ssempa's infantile phrase "They eat the poo poo" misses the mark insofar as he carries around his up-to-date Apple laptop to show graphic pictures of homosexuality not to titillate or because he is titillated, but in order to be the instrument of a higher power, and to deploy coprophagy as a strange attractor for imaginary and aggressive identities. Satirizing his speech as an example of extreme, ignorant, or atavistic "African homophobia" merely replays the short circuit, rather than contesting it.

And however easy the enjoyment to be derived from laughing at the frothing, deluded evangelical, under conditions of declining symbolic efficiency, such mockery is truly politically ambiguous: the first place I encountered a hip parody of Ssempa's speech was on the Facebook page of *Rolling Stone* itself.

Tavia Nyong'o is associate professor of performance studies at New York University, where he researches and teaches black diasporic culture and aesthetics, feminist and queer theory, and popular music studies.

Notes

1. Personal Twitter IDs have been changed.
2. The Ugandan gay activist David Kato, whose name, photo, and address were published in *Rolling Stone*, was murdered on January 26, 2011. International condemnation followed the murder, along with calls for a full investigation.
3. When giving this essay as a talk, I often met this objection, as if it would be a clear refutation of all the concerns I was raising, that nevertheless *real* Africans, in *real* conditions of emergency, had authorized and urged international petition campaigns. This reflects the individualizing logic both of neoliberal governmentality and, more specifically, of the "prisoner of conscience" as prototypical benefactor of international petition campaigning. Methodological individualism, however, produces both blindness and insight. It is never simply the case that a specific African voice, or voices, can authenticate an international campaign, particularly when such campaigns are calibrated to hear certain voices or discourses and not attend to others. Gayatri Spivak's (1988) germinal critique of the discursive privileges of rescuing brown others is a needed antidote to such easy convictions that the subaltern speaks through the international human rights community.
4. I first read these words in August 2010. As of August 18, 2011, as I complete final edits on this article, this page is still active and is the third result when "avaaz uganda petition" is searched on Google. The top result for this search is a new page titled "Uganda's anti-gay bill stopped," now (August 18, 2011) up elsewhere on the Avaaz.org website, at https://secure.avaaz.org/en/uganda_stop_homophobia_petition/. Curiously, even though the campaign is declared a success, the petition is still actively accepting signatures. Adelaide from Switzerland just signed it, one hour prior to this writing. And the original page, which is not linked to the updated page, has yet to be taken down.
5. As pointed out in note 4, subsequently Avaaz.org has added a third page, bringing the story up to May 13, 2011. Crediting the petition and calls with the ultimate shelving of the Bahati bill, this page noted, "Together, we've won a major fight for equality and justice. Over 1.6 million of us signed the petition opposing the anti-gay bill, tens of thousands of us called our heads of state, and we helped make the attack on gay rights in Uganda a major international news story—and it worked" (https://secure.avaaz.org/en/uganda_stop_homophobia_petition/).

6. Again, I conflate humanitarianism and human rights in this essay not because I fail to register their distinctive regimes within international law, but rather because activist websites like Avaaz.org conflate them in urging petitionary action. On any given day, its front page urges its readers to take action in broadly ranging causes, from the famine in Somalia, to the genocide in Sudan, to the disappeared in Syria and the arrest of an anticorruption activist in India.

7. Here we see one way viral activism is diverging from traditional rights campaigning. Such lack of temporal specificity would be highly unlikely in a traditional mailer or phone call. In order to commit resources to a paper-and-postal campaign, any activist organization would have had to place its actions in a clearer chronology. Its call would go out to an established mailing or call list of committed, possibly dues-paying members. Even collecting signatures door to door or on the street from random individuals would require an investment of resources that would give focus to the campaign and embed it in time and space. But leveraging the long tail of Internet activism promotes new logics of interpellation, in which such chronological and strategic specificity declines in significance.

Works Cited

Abelove, Henry. 2005. *Deep Gossip*. Minneapolis: University of Minnesota Press.
———. 2010. "A Moderately Gay History." *Criticism* 52(2):339–41.
Bataille, Georges. 1988. *The Accursed Share: An Essay on General Economy*. New York: Zone Books.
Bhabha, Homi. 1994. *The Location of Culture*. New York: Routledge.
Browning, Barbara. 1998. *Infectious Rhythm: Metaphors of Contagion and the Spread of African Culture*. New York: Routledge.
Caffentzis, George. 2010. "The World Bank and the Double Crisis of African Universities." *EduFactory Web Journal*, No. 0 (January):27–41.
Dean, Jodi. 2009. *Democracy and Other Neoliberal Fantasies: Communicative Capitalism and Left Politics*. Durham: Duke University Press.
Douzinas, Costas. 2007. *Human Rights and Empire: The Political Philosophy of Cosmopolitanism*. London: Routledge.
Epprecht, Marc. 2008. *Heterosexual Africa?: The History of an Idea from the Age of Exploration to the Age of AIDS*. New African Histories. Athens: Ohio University Press.
Feher-Gurewich, Judith. 2003. "A Lacanian Approach to the Logic of Perversion." In *The Cambridge Companion to Lacan*, ed. Jean-Michel Rabaté. Cambridge, UK: Cambridge University Press.

Gettleman, Jeffrey. 2010. "Gay in Uganda, and Feeling Hunted." *New York Times*, January 4. http://www.nytimes.com/2010/01/04/world/africa/04gay.html

Hoad, Neville. 2007. *African Intimacies: Race, Homosexuality, and Globalization*. Minneapolis: University of Minnesota Press.

———. 2010. "Miss HIV and Us: Beauty Queens Against the HIV/AIDS Pandemic." *CR: The New Centennial Review* 10(1):9–28.

Jones, Donna. 2010. *The Racial Discourses of Life Philosophy: Négritude, Vitalism, and Modernity*. New York: Columbia University Press.

Kato, David. 2010. "A Matter of Life and Death: The Struggle for Ugandan Gay Rights." Lecture at the University of Cambridge, England, February 24. http://www.polis.cam.ac.uk/cghr/events_2010_catouganda.html

Lanier, Jaron. 2010. *You Are Not a Gadget: A Manifesto*. New York: Knopf.

Macharia, Keguro. 2010. "Knife-Edge: A Fiction on Africanity." *Gukira* (blog), June 8. http://gukira.wordpress.com/2010/06/08/knife-edge-a-fiction-on-africanity/

Massad, Joseph. 2007. *Desiring Arabs*. Chicago: University of Chicago Press.

Mbembe, Achille. 2003. "Necropolitics." *Public Culture* 15(1):11–40.

McClintock, Anne. 1995. *Imperial Leather: Race, Gender, and Sexuality in the Colonial Contest*. New York: Routledge.

McKenzie, David. 2010. "Ugandan Anti-gay Measure Will be Law Soon, Lawmaker Says." CNN.com. http://edition.cnn.com/2010/WORLD/africa/10/27/uganda.antigay.bill/index.html

Mejias, Ulises A. 2010. "The Limits of Networks as Models for Organizing the Social." *New Media and Society* 12(4):603–17.

Morozov, Evgeny. 2011. *The Net Delusion: The Dark Side of Internet Freedom*. New York: PublicAffairs.

Nyong'o, Peter Anyang', ed. 1987. *Popular Struggles for Democracy in Africa*. London: Zed Books.

Pariser, Eli. 2011. *The Filter Bubble: What the Internet Is Hiding from You*. New York: Penguin.

Rice, Xan. 2011. "Ugandan Gay Rights Activist David Kato Found Murdered." *Guardian*, January 27. http://www.guardian.co.uk/world/2011/jan/27/ugandan-gay-rights-activist-murdered

Rubenstein, Mary-Jane. 2010. "Notes from the Tangled Anglican Web." *Killing the Buddha*, April 1. http://killingthebuddha.com/mag/dogma/tangled-anglican-web/

Sharlet, Jeff. 2010. "Dangerous Liaisons." *Advocate*, August. http://www.advocate.com/printArticle.aspx?id=131500

Shirky, Clay. 2008. *Here Comes Everybody: The Power of Organizing Without Organizations*. New York: Penguin Press.

Spivak, Gayatri. 1988. "Can the Subaltern Speak?" In *Marxism and the Interpretation of Culture,* ed. Cary Nelson and Lawrence Grossberg. Chicago: University of Illinois Press.

"Uganda's Anti-gay Bill 'Shelved.'" BBC, "Africa," May 13. http://www.bbc.co.uk/news/world-africa-13392723

Virno, Paolo. 2003. *A Grammar of the Multitude.* Los Angeles: Semiotext(e).

Younge, Gary. 2010. "Gay Equality Can't Yet Be Claimed a Western Value, But It Is a Human Right." *Guardian,* June 7. http://www.guardian.co.uk/commentisfree/2010/jun/07/racism-islamophobia-homophobia-far-right

Žižek, Slavoj. 2006. *The Parallax View.* Cambridge, MA: MIT Press.

Race Racing: Four Theses on Race and Intensity

Amit S. Rai

In what follows I attempt to wrest the concept of race away from reactive dialectics and give it its full positivity. I desire, in other words, to make an affirmation of becoming in the processes of race racing. By "race racing" I don't mean a faster conception of race, but it does involve diagramming speeds as intensive rates and gradients internal to assemblages of technology and perception. For example, the shrinking average shot duration of an average Hollywood blockbusters creates a feedback with forms of attention and anticipation constituting the perceptual mode of power in dominant cinema (Massumi 2005, 2010). In what sense, through what vectors of force could such a perceptual mode of power become a question of race in its mode of becoming, that is, race racing? Thus, what I mean by "race racing" is moving toward a "common notion" of race (a notion of race that is common to at least two multiplicities), one that unfolds the feedbacked processes of racialization as intensive variation, continuous, qualitative duration, and vectors of embodied habituation immanent to historically specific media assemblages. On the "face" of it, race would most obviously be seen as a mode (and modification) of the attribute of extensity (space): the epidermal schema is a variable organization of the space, distribution, arrangement, and color of the body (Deleuze and Guattari 1987, 144–48). But in what sense can we say that race racing, its being in becoming, is an intensive process?

What I think is clear is that the politics of antiracism must move beyond reactive dialectics and representational strategies that have by and large determined the forms of antiracist interventions. Antiracism must become something else, experimenting with duration, sensation, reso-

 WSQ: Women's Studies Quarterly **40**: 1 & 2 (Spring/Summer 2012) © 2012 by Amit S. Rai.

nance, and affect. This experimentation would summon Deleuze's famous gloss on Henri Bergson's two multiplicities as an inspiration. Deleuze insisted that for Bergson duration was "susceptible to measurement only by varying its metrical principle at each stage of the division," taking the problem into the "sphere of two kinds of multiplicity": quantitative and qualitative (Deleuze 1991, 40; Ansell-Pearson 2001, 16–17).

In his fine, Deleuzian-inspired study of the philosopher of intuition, Keith Ansell-Pearson shows that the significance of Bergson's attempt to think about duration in a new way is that it puts into question the ontological confines of esprit by not returning to the "assimilating act of consciousness" the alterity of novelty. Thinking about the radical alterity of duration allows thought to pragmatically conceptualize the material conditions of becoming, to pose the question, in other words, of why and how it is that we dwell among badly analyzed composites and are "badly analyzed composites ourselves" (Deleuze 1991, 10; Ansell-Pearson 2001, 28).

Which brings me to my first thesis: practices of race racing affirm the capacity of embodied, qualitative duration to give race its immanent intensive variability across and within populations. What are the virtual and actual relations between sensation and race? This question must come to terms with the "time of life" itself, which is not a universally given quanta, obviously.

In light of this question, we would want to move beyond resistant acts of naming (queer, freak, nigger, etc.) as "indispensable" to politics. For instance, Arun Saldanha argues for the importance of naming as a strategy in radical politics. Writing of the Goa "freaks" involved in trance cultures, he writes, "In naming themselves freaks, white youths immediately called attention to their desire for the escape from normality and from the past" (Saldanha 2007, 54). In his work Saldanha rigorously poses the question of the relation between (raced) naming and intensity, but in what sense is naming anything other than a capture of bodily sensation? Let me be more precise: molecular revolutions have no language or signification because they are not of the order of consciousness, and they have, therefore, no "true" name. They are of an ecological order of embodied composites whose processes of sensation pass a critical threshold of difference-in-repetition and thus effect a counteractualization toward the virtual. Thus race racing is a method of counteractualizing sensation toward a plane of immanence, toward relations that are exterior to their terms (Deleuze and Boyman 2001, 37). This approach to racial processes has received the most considered attention in certain forms of feminist and queer praxis, yet because duration remains a marginal consideration in theorizations of identity, the conception of the politics of race tends toward the molar and the spatial (the White Man or even the reterritorialized Freak), even as contemporary theory celebrates the molecular. This happens, for instance, in some forms of queer identity politics where the molecular destabilization of identity through new viral or contagious organizations of sense and sensation becomes a pre-given mold through which the norm is queered, capital is made homonormative, or even the Israeli occupation is recuperated for queer tourism (Puar 2010, 2007).

But virality involves/evolves into representation in an adventure that is always also purely virtual. Why is it then that we continue to find in contemporary forms of antiracism an overreliance on representational strategies that turn out to be by and large interventions in consciousness? I think this focus on antiracist nomination has broad implications for how we conceptualize and practice the "and" in the "race and intensity" of this essay's title. A decisive posing of the problem comes about when we think of the method of antiracism. Can antiracism escape the ressentiment of reactive dialectics? Perhaps this is the problem with all politics that root themselves in the "anti-"—they remain defensive in character. But the ontological and political processes of race racing do not stop at the "White Man Himself" (a phrase used in Deleuze and Guattari's description of European racism), which is simply to say that sensation moves beyond categories in consciousness and language (Deleuze and Guattari 1987, 178). In other words, isn't there (1) something deeply Eurocentric about contemporary antiracism (especially in its nominalist avatar) and (2) something fundamentally representational about the "anti-"? This also brings to the fore the curious status of the universal in antiracist practice: what is it that gives a certain universality to the antiracist name? Isn't it in fact the White Man Himself?

But Deleuze's virtual philosophy gives us another method to think about intensive, concrete universals, and they are of a different nature from that of the universal name. Manuel DeLanda helps us grasp Deleuze's very different concept of universality. First, universality is tied to the generative processes of multiplicities, those processes that render them mechanism independent. While essences are abstract and general entities, "multiplicities are concrete universals." That is, multiplicities are actualized sets of attractors (realized as tendencies in physical processes) linked together by bifurcations (realized as abrupt transitions in the tendencies of physical processes). Gradually a more or less effective (i.e., weaponized) diagram emerges: "Unlike the generality of essences, and the resemblance with which this generality endows instantiations of an essence, the universality of a multiplicity is typically divergent: the different realizations of a multiplicity bear no resemblance whatsoever to it and there is in principle no end to the set of potential divergent forms it may adopt." In other words, if one is to consistently think of race racing as an intensive process, the multiplicity of race lacks any resemblance to itself; race racing multiplicities give form to processes, not to this or that final product (a race, a name . . .). Indeed, the end results of processes realizing the same multiplicity may be highly dissimilar from one another, like the spherical soap bubble and the cubic salt crystal, or like jazz music and the narrative novel, "which not only do not resemble one another, but bear no similarity to the topological point guiding their production." The multiplicity of race racing is of an obscure yet distinct nature quite different from the clear and distinct identity of rationalistic essences. More, and again unlike essences, which as abstract general entities coexist side by side sharply distinguished from one another, race racing as a concrete universal must be thought of as meshed together with other multiplicities into a continuum. "This further blurs the identity of multiplicities, creating zones of indiscernibility where they blend into each other, forming a continuous immanent space" (DeLanda 2002, 21). The continuous immanent space of race racing is an ecology of sensation.

To my mind a much sharper distinction must be made between race as reactive dialectics and intensive processes of becoming. It is the latter that leads directly to a consideration of the complex ontology of sensation; the former leads circuitously (that is, arbitrarily) to identity and representation. And this for four main reasons: First, becomings are not inversions of discourse (or if they are, they are that only secondarily): they are qualitative, virtual multiplicities that change in kind by dividing themselves immanently (see above). Second, to assemble and give direction to a set of becomings is basically to quantify and spatialize what are qualitatively distinct durations (thus the difference of a becoming is a "real" distinction insofar as it is invested with a definite but variable duration, scale, tempo, pattern, intensity, resonance, etc.). In other words, assemblages of becoming are forms of intensity-capture that qualitatively modify the becomings themselves. Third, and again, the ambivalent focus on the overthrow of the White Man threatens to turn into an elaborate recentering of Europe; there are large parts of Asia and Africa, not to mention the East End of London, where biopolitical projects both in terms of becomings and captures have little if anything to do with overthrowing the White Man (the traditionally defensive position of antiracism). But why is that? It's not because white racism is not a palpable reality in these areas—the history of colonial anthropology, white supremacy, eugenics, craniometry, and Nazism is a lived and felt reality. Why then would I say that overthrowing the White Man is not the target of these forms of racial becomings? It is because white supremacy has become biopolitical in these domains and, in the process, has qualitatively changed by dividing itself through new and yet genealogically continuous and topologically plastic strategies, mutated sensations, emergent habituations with different rates of attention, technoperceptual assemblages, algocratic governmentalities—new capacities, part-subjects, and populations (Aneesh 2001). Consider, in this regard, the list of themes from the forthcoming "European Conference on Artificial Life" (in tribute to the late Francisco Varela):

> Synthesizing artificial cells, simulating large-scale biological networks, storing and making intelligent use of an exponentially growing amount of data (e.g., microarrays), exploiting biological substrates for computation and control, and deploying bio-inspired engineering are all cutting-edge topics today. "Life itself": ECAL 2011 will leverage the remarkable development of biological modeling and extend the topics of Artificial Life to the fundamental properties of living organisms: their multiscale pattern-forming morphodynamics, their autopoiesis, robustness, capacity to self-repair, cognitive capacities, and co-adaptation at all levels, including ecological ones. (Life August 2011)

These becomings are no longer simply reactive and defensive, they can be affirmative and creative; indeed, they become reactive when they are separated from what they can do. (Deleuze 2006; Rai 2010). In other words, and finally, the first becomings are not racial: the first becomings are viral mutations in ecologies of sensation, when a set of intensive processes crosses a critical threshold and self-differentiates. My first thesis therefore has a scholium: race racing, the being of racial becoming, is a modification in technoperceptual composites through an experimental practice of duration, attention, sense, sensation, and time scale. We need today to seize every opportunity to experiment with the "and" in "race and intensity" by finding for it new conjunctions in sense and sensation—race racing to the nth degree.

Let us consider a more overtly political example. In 1994 there were around 3 million Indians waiting to get a telephone line, and some had already waited for over ten years. Because of entrenched bureaucratic control of telecommunications, telephony was an elite technology. By 2011, the entire media ecology had been transvaluated and mutated. Following the liberalization of the Indian economy in the early 1990s, the entire telecom industry was marked for rapid reform in 1994, and a process of privatization was initiated. Sixteen years later pro-governmental discourse narrates that event as a milestone for postcolonial India:

> The telecommunication services have improved significantly since independence with the sector witnessing a series of reform measures that included, announcement of National Telecom Policy in 1994 that defined certain important objectives, including availability of telephone on demand, provision of world class services at reasonable prices, ensuring India's emergence as major manufacturing / export base of telecom equipment and universal availability of basic telecom services to all villages. Telecom Regulatory Authority of India (TRAI), the independent regulator was established in 1997 and New Telecom Policy was announced in 1999, which further laid stress on providing an enabling framework for the development of this sector and to facilitate India's vision of becoming an IT superpower and develop a world class telecom infrastructure in the country. (Government of India 2010, 177–78)

The aspirations of the Indian nation are writ large in this inventive narration of the transition from what might be termed post-colonial development to the aspirational world-class superpower. Indian neoliberalism (its history doesn't quite fit the label, given the socialist and Gandhian commitments of the constitution) has developed antinomies, or pockets of tension, through rapid economic growth: growing internal disparities; ongoing communal tensions; emergent sexualities and gender roles; and a reorganization of work in a move toward flexible, precarious, globalized services. Despite the general tendency of transnational capital toward monopoly, corruption, and elite hegemony, today there are over 1 billion mobile handsets in India, and the national market continues to be the most competitive mobile service market in the world. In the broader study from which I have abstracted this example, I ask: What has happened to the assemblage of populations and telephony in the twenty years from 1991 to 2011? What are the implications of mobile telephony becoming the third-largest attractor of foreign direct investment (after services and computer hardware and software)? How has mobile telephony become one of the fastest-growing contributors to India's gross domestic product? What kinds of innovations in the informal economy are facilitating and in turn catalyzed by this rapid proliferation of mobile media? How has the elite telephone become the mundane mobile, and with what effects at the level of population, habit, movement, affect, security, sensation, and perception?

I believe that this example pushes us to diagram race as sets of intensive variations in ecologies of sensation distributed unevenly and with uneven effects across populations through processes that form assemblages of perception and media. Thus, one of the most important aspects of thinking about race "and" intensity, it seems to me, is the relation of race to the machinic phylum. An intensive ontology of becoming is a diagram of coevolutionary processes, whose variability stabilizes around definite but always temporally bound basins of attraction, and whose asymptotic oscillations are always open to shock or stochastic resonance (DeLanda 2002; Varela, Thompson, and Rosch 1991).

Thesis 3, then: These coevolutionary processes suggest that all becomings are ecological in that they mobilize important available resources to refunction correlated flows of energy, information, biomass, sensation, and technology. A corollary of coevolution in media-machinic assemblages of bodies and technologies is that there will always also be emergent properties, capacities, and affordances as an effect of this refunctioning of correlated processes. Technoscience and queer feminists such as Donna Harraway, Anne Balsamo, Luciana Parisi, Tiziana Terranova, Patricia Clough, and Jasbir Puar have shown that contemporary war machine-bodies have emerged as infomatic technologies for mapping and policing exceptionalized battle spaces in Iraq, Afghanistan, Abu Ghraib, Guantánamo Bay, Gaza, and so on.

Today, all racial becoming, all race racing is to a greater or lesser extent cyborgian (but no racial becoming was ever not also technologically feedbacked). The emergence of the cyborg marks the shift from discipline to control, as mobile, digital always connected networks allow for continuous and flexible modulation in real time, "like a *self-deforming* cast that will continuously change from one moment to the other, or like a sieve whose mesh will transmute from point to point" (Deleuze 1995, 179). The coevolution immanent in technoperceptual assemblages in societies of control, in biopolitical projects of gene splicing and neuromarketing, suggests that a new ecology of sense and sensation in the mode of the digital bodies forth a cyborg race.

But we would miss the crucial dimension of the virtual if we were to reduce the cyborg merely to the synchronized, controlled instrument of military technologies. This is not only because the newly machinic soldier is not the same assemblage as was the white supremacist, but rather because her cyborg capacities emerge from a mutating technoperceptual multiplicity; this virtual-actual circuit makes of her both a race apart and yet continuously meshed within other ecologies of sensation. Thus, the problem of cyborg-becoming needs to be diagrammed as an ontology of the complex, rather than in terms of a representational, and ultimately epistemological, analysis (Ansell-Pearson 2002). The type of analysis that leads to the negative critiques of militarized white supremacy is piously drawn from the ressentiment of the subaltern. But feminist technoscience has already broached the ontological question of the cyborg-soldier: what are her emergent capacities, her newly machined ecology of sensations, her forms of perceptual habituation, her styles of comportment; and what new analytical tools are at hand for diagramming, and so experimenting with, her embodied composites, her media assemblages (video games as/ in military training)?

The question of habituation beings me to my final thesis: race racing involves/evolves habituation (thesis 4). A critique of habit is foregrounded in practices of race racing. For instance, consider this set of fragmentary observations on the quotidian functioning of a mobile phone from a twenty-year-old Mumbaite:

> If I'm travelling—daily travelling—like from place A to place B, whether I'm going to hurry or not has to do with whether I'm using my phone or not. So if I'm going somewhere and I'm in touch with someone who's already there I'll tend to hurry up a bit or speed up my trip. Or it might work the other way as well where if I'm going for some work and someone's already there having taken care of it—I would know on the phone and probably relax. So the phone has a bearing on how urgent I consider a trip. If I'm going to meet someone somewhere, I'll call to check if they've left so that I don't have to wait. Or if I reach early I'll call someone up and talk to them while I'm waiting. If I'm outside and I'm alone for a while and I have nothing else to do then I'll call someone up or I'll start fiddling with my phone. When I don't know what to do with my

hands I take my phone out and start to use it. Also if I'm walking across the room and another person is sitting somewhere on the other side and I'm going towards them—because I'm a somewhat awkward, shy person—most of the time if I'm walking and I think someone's watching, I'll take out my phone and fiddle with it. It changes the way I walk—in these situations—I can't say how, but I use it as a . . . um . . . decoy. If I want to avoid someone I'd pick up my phone and start talking or pretend. I'd say, "excuse me". I use this for awkward moments. Out of all my numbers maybe four or five I communicate with on a regular basis. And obviously I use the cell—it's different from a landline . . . more personal. (Inteview conducted by Ajinkya Shenava, March 20, 2010, Mumbai.)

It is in fact a range of affective dispositions that gives virtual tendencies to the human-mobile assemblage. In the broader study from which I have drawn this interview excerpt, I ask, What happens between this woman's body, her halting gestures, public space, and the mobile phone? The mobile becomes an affective trigger, a fashion statement, a decoy, an early warning device, an excuse, and sometimes a phone; and it even allows for a different bodily comportment in space (Venkatesh et al. 2010). Without overreading this response, it seems safe to say that there is a gendered dimension to this mutation in embodiment: for a city whose public spaces are still populated by no more than 28 percent women at any given time, the mobile seems to have become for some (and more and more) women a way of renegotiating male-dominated spaces (Phadke 2011).

The processes of habituation involve relations that are constantly moving outside their terms, in patterned but unpredictable processes correlated across an open nonspatial virtual multiplicity, or a noncoinciding resonant unity. We aspire to a diagrammatics commensurate with the obscure yet distinct nature of habits embodied in autonomic processes, reflexes, aesthetic styles, neural pathways, memory, precognitive associations, and so on. All of which implies, first, that as method the diagramming of an ontology of race moves toward its ecology of sensation, its immanent virtual multiplicity. Race racing, its rhythmic character in its entirety, expresses and hence modifies sensation itself. Second, that while race is a particular organization of sensation, its ecology is always already before and ahead of it (its past and future are both differently potential). This confusion in clearly demarcating the relation between race and sensation leads quite often to a reactive critique of habituation: bad racist habits are all we get in much of contemporary antiracist discourse. But habituation is a process that in its repetitions is productive of difference (Deleuze 2004, 30, 148), a process that is both quantitative (e.g., hyper-Taylorized, post-Fordist factory production breaks bodily movement down into measurable milliseconds) and intensive (a new mutant capacity of movement and perception, habit's clinamen, emerges swerving from strategies of value accumulation, by "varying its metrical principle at each stage of the division") (Deleuze and Boundas 2004).

But that is because racial habits are actualizations of a virtual multiplicity, an ecology of sensation, an ecology that is modified by these habits themselves. And it is here, then, where we would locate an <u>ethics</u> of race racing: the being of becoming of race is in an ethics, not of nomination, but of (de-/re-/non-)habituation. An ethics of race racing would begin by offering a better diagram of emergent affects and functional correlations in the composition of at least two multiplicities leading to new experimental practices of racial becoming.

To summarize these four theses on race and intensity:

1. Embodied duration gives race its immanent intensive variability across and within populations. A racialized body is both a modification of the attribute of extensity and a mode of a historically specific but virtually plastic ecology of sensation (Deleuze 1992, 76–79). We give the name "race racing" to this process of embodied duration.

Scholium: race racing, the being of racial becoming, modifies technoperceptual composites through experimental practices of duration, attention, sense, sensation, and time scale. Race is a mode of matter's (life's, nature's, the world's, substance's) attribute of extensity. But race racing is a modification of sensation; race racing is expressed in this or that mode in the sense that race racing is a modification of the affectivity of sensation itself (Deleuze 1992, 110–11).

2. The essential power of race, that is, its specific capacity to affect and be affected, is of the nature of an embodied style of composing differential forces into a noncoinciding resonant unity: an aesthetico-ontological style. This composition of forces is both human and technological at once. The history of race is inseparable from the historical tendencies immanent in the machinic phylum; this is why the concept of technoperceptual media assemblages roots itself in diagrams of ecologies of sensation. The power of race is a gradient that goes from sensation or affectivity to identity or representation, following Spinoza's insight that the more power a

thing has the more it can be affected in a great number of ways (intensive dimensions of qualitative change) (Deleuze 1992, 102). The expressive forms of race affirm the absolute quality of sensation (80).

3. Coevolutionary processes of becomings mobilize important available resources in a given ecology to refunction correlated flows of energy, information, biomass, sensation, and technology. Media-machinic assemblages of bodies and technologies have specific emergent properties because of a continuous, but unstable, refunctioning of correlated processes. The coevolution immanent in technoperceptual assemblages in societies of control, in biopolitical projects of gene splicing and neuromarketing, suggests that a new ecology of sense and sensation in the mode of the digital bodies forth a cyborg race.

4. Race racing involves/evolves into habituation. By developing ethological diagrams of habit, which proceed through common notions of technoperceptual assemblages, collective practices of experimentation in and with habituated sensations will mutate race.

What, finally, is the epistemological status of these four theses? If what I have argued is a sensible shift in the politics and theorization of race toward the common notion of race racing as a diagram of speeds and slownesses, intensive rates and gradients internal to manifold assemblages of technology and perception, then these theses should perform an experimentation on race itself. This experimentation would continuously mutate, never resembling itself, changing the metric of its own measure through a resonance that moves beyond its terms.

Amit S. Rai is senior lecturer in new media and communication in the School of Business and Management at Queen Mary, University of London. His study of new media in India, *Untimely Bollywood: Globalization and India's New Media Assemblage*, was published by Duke University Press in 2009. His blog on the history of media assemblages and the politics of perception can be found at http://mediaecologiesresonate.wordpress.com.

Works Cited

Aneesh, A. 2001. Virtual Migrations: Indian Programmers in the US-based Information Industry (PhD dissertation, Rutgers, New Brunswick).

Ansell-Pearson, Keith. 2001. Philosophy and the Adventure of the Virtual: Bergson and the Time of Life. London: Routledge.

DeLanda, Manuel. 2002. Intensive Science and Virtual Philosophy. London: Continuum.

Deleuze, Gilles. 1991. Empiricism and Subjectivity: An Essay on Hume's Theory of Human Nature. New York: Columbia University Press.

———. 1992. Expressionism in Philosophy: Spinoza. New York: Zone Books.

———. 1995. "Postscript on Control Societies." In Negotiations. New York: Columbia University Press.

———. 2004. Difference and Repetition. London: Continuum.

———. 2006. Nietzsche and Philosophy. New York: Columbia University Press.

Deleuze, Gilles, and Constantin V. Boundas. 2004. The Logic of Sense. London: Continuum.

Deleuze, Gilles, and Anne Boyman. 2001. Pure Immanence: Essays on a Life. New York: Zone Books.

Deleuze, Gilles, and Félix Guattari. 1987. A Thousand Plateaus: Capitalism and Schizophrenia. London: Athlone.

Government of India. 2010. India 2010: A Reference, annual. New Delhi: Publications Division, Ministry of Information and Broadcasting, Government of India.

European Conference on Artificial Life. Alife-announce: Announcement for Alife listserv, November 30, 2010. http://lists.idyll.org/listinfo/alife-announce

Massumi, Brian. 2005. "Fear (the Spectrum Said)." In Against Preemptive War. Special issue, Positions: East Asia Cultures Critique13(1):31–48.

———. 2010. "Perception Attack: Brief on War Time." Theory and Event 13(3) http://muse.jhu.edu/journals/theory_and_events/v013/13.3.massumi.htmi

Phadke, Shilpa. 2011. "Middle-Class Women, Hetero-sexuality, and the New Spaces of Consumption in Mumbai." Department of Sociology, University of Mumbai, India.

Puar, Jasbir. 2010. "Israel's Gay Propaganda War." Guardian. November, 2010.

———. 2007. Terrorist Assemblages: Homonationalism in Queer Times. Durham: Duke University Press.

Saldanha, Arun. 2007. Psychedelic White: Goa Trance and the Viscosity of Race. Minneapolis: University of Minnesota Press.

Varela, Francisco J., Evan Thompson, and Eleanor Rosch. 1991. The Embodied Mind: Cognitive Science and Human Experience. Cambridge, MA: MIT Press.

Venkatesh, Alladi, Annamma Joy, John F. Sherry Jr., and Jonathan Deschenes. 2010. "The Aesthetics of Luxury Fashion, Body and Identify Formation." Journal of Consumer Psychology 20(4):459–70.

Masked States and the "Screen" Between Security and Disability

Mel Y. Chen

I open with a typical poster from a hospital emergency room that advises on contingent measures taken to prevent the spread of H1N1, showing calm, gently smiling eyes behind a biological mask secured around a blue surgical cap (fig. 1). The poster reassures us—acknowledging that the sight of a mask *could* be frightening—that masks, benevolently, not threateningly ("you may see others . . . it does not mean that someone has the swine flu"), protect everyone.

Such evocation of all possible parties does not at first seem a standard security apparatus, but in fact its language mimics the all-embracing appeal

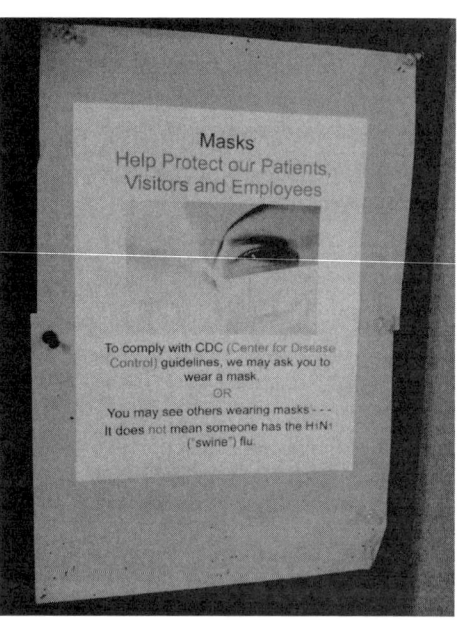

FIG. 1: Poster in hospital emergency room, North Adams, Massachusetts, 2011: "Masks Help Protect Our Patients, Visitors and Employees." Photo by the author.

of "for your protection" slogans found today in many security genres, from extraordinary extensions of airport search techniques to digital passcode access. This mask, when worn in health or medical contexts, is urged as necessary protection from the transmission of disease, while other masks are coded as threat—for instance, facial coverings that occlude individual features potentially thwart facial-recognition surveillance software. Masks can, in these versions, render the face unmappable to security operations of the vulnerable state.

In light of heightened contagion scares in the contemporary United States, we might consider the medicalized mask as a newer prosthetic disability form in light of the concurrence of modern public health conventions, the increasing potential for rapid transnational communicability of disease, and the significant incidence of breathable pollution for the common citizenry. But before drawing such a conclusion, we might ask: what counts, and doesn't count, as a mask; and what is, and isn't, disability? Mask forms and figurations are multiple and complex and deserve a closer look; the value of "disability" is similarly mobile, attachable variously to human bodies, notions, and abstract entities.

From a broad viewpoint, facial masks certainly symbolize more than illness or its possibility. They also suggest (and have historically been used to symbolize) the "horror" of disfigurement, the use of ritual, the protection of self and other. Indeed, much work has been done in drama studies and anthropology on the theatrical and ritual effects of masks. In today's political environment, how does the role of masks in obscuring the face work within a national public? And, observing that masks can incite complex emotions from various perspectives, how does the visage itself enable, disable, or compound affect?

For the purposes of this experimental essay, "the mask" is considered quite openly. Visiting an array of mask citations (public announcements, journalistic photos, artistic re-creations, television series), I discuss questions of security and sensitivity before turning to a consideration of Levinasian facial ethics as well as Deleuze and Guattari's articulation of masks. I propose that masks could be understood as roving, material instances of a *screen*, one that bars access to the visage while functioning as a device of projection for others. In specific sites, such a screen functions epistemologically to translate for or against the face, where the face is understood as a prioritized site of human engagement.

To clarify, this essay intends to undo any singularly assured "mask" visual trope by running among diverse exemplars (with all their anthropological, horroristic, and ethnic trappings) to map their sensible geographies, and to ask what their often polarized and racialized valences might tell about the investments of nationalistic self-imagining. Ultimately, my hope is that the masks appear less as concrete objects per se than as screens with affective resonance. Thinking through Deleuze and Guattari and others, such screens are what I will claim most stably undergird projects of securitized, nondisabled whiteness. I discuss how this screen today might bear ever greater affective intensities, since it occupies a primary symbolic position within overlapping discourses of security.

Security

Commonly mouthed within the post-9/11 U.S. climate is the notion that heightened security efforts, including the recently extended USA PATRIOT Act, are instituted for the "protection" of U.S. citizens. This occurs against a global terrain in which today's empires are finding that effective protection is hard to come by; that is, military and strategic "security" are unstable. Contrary to a prevalence of accounts that speak to the ever growing military counterparts of an ever present war on the part of the United States and, to a lesser degree, European and UN nations (and also to an associated, also perpetually growing prison-industrial complex), I wish to attend to what I see as a quiet construction of weakness—not weakness as attenuated masculinity, but weakness in disability terms—a kind of threatened *immunity* wherein the "body" of the nation is vulnerable to attack. On the part of these Western states, this weakness is the requisite underside of frenzied war-making. Given that economic and military security have in many ways merged as critical interests of state formations, it is telling that U.S. economic sovereignty is being interpreted as increasingly fragile (indexed by such events as the historic Standard and Poor's credit downgrade of August 2011) in the same period in which surveillance of "terrorism" grows to unprecedented levels.

We can then ask: When immunity is historically premised on a collective body such as the state, then when that state is felt to be either incomplete or impaired, what are the prostheses mustered to protect against threat? If we were to map the biopolitical links between individual and national body, what are the confluences between ways that people and nations protect against visible and invisible threats? In this section,

I consider masks as emblematic of new kinds of prostheticized integrities that supplement the human body in its defense against threats (where a prosthesis is defined as an "artificial" limb to replace a missing or impaired part of the body). I argue that masks also quietly emerge in the symbolic economies of national "defense," wherein mask symbolization is deployed to project a nation's own broken state onto certain racialized others.

Masks both symbolize and effect security; by both representing and doing, they are performative technologies of a sort. As such, they bespeak action and transformation. Yet at the same time, they cover, conceal, and hide, and in so doing simultaneously perform a very different sort of vulnerability. They suggest the robbing of sentience as a cost of that security, and thus a radically different model of personhood. This is precisely why the ideological fear felt by certain Americans intensively focuses on Islamic facial and head coverings, in that these garments' implication of apparently self-cancelling personhood seems to perform the threat of Arab collectivity to Western democracy—one that is, like socialism, felt to be violent to U.S. self- (individualistic) representation and distinction.

Among the most potent (and hence most threatening) forms of "masks" for contemporary U.S. politics is the burqa, along with other Muslim facial coverings. The image of the burqa has been made potent not simply, of course, because it is just any old facial covering. It is connected to a racialized construction of Islam, and to a perverse femininity. But I also believe that its appearance as a symbol of international strife at this moment makes sense in terms of the embodied, gendered imagination of security. Rather than focus on the "veil" as an ordinary garment, or even as an instrument of pseudofeminist democratic expansionism, both of which have been extensively discussed (see, e.g., Yegenoglu 1998; Scott 2010; Mahmood 2004; Ahmed 2011), I consider here its curious entanglement in discourses of security.[1]

The cover of the June 2011 issue of the *Atlantic*, while it might first appear to rehearse a particular combination of "women's rights" as a justification for the spread of Western political-economic systems, is a case in point (fig. 2). What doubles as the cover image and the background to stark white text is the image of a woman's face in a niqab (Muslim headwear that covers most of the face), her eyes staring back at the viewer in the "direct gaze" style so often used in photojournalistic documentations of the "Third World" (see, e.g., Szorenyi 2004; Lutz and Collins 1993). In the cover story's title, "Is This the Face of Arab Democracy?" the words

"Arab Democracy" appear in particularly large, bold capital letters. The letters deploy alarmist red on black, the inverse color scheme of that used
for the "True Crime" banner at upper left, which announces coverage of a
Los Angeles murder story (one that turns out to concern white-on-white
crime). Words referring to threat are made explicit: the subtitle is "Why
the New Middle East Is More Hopeful—and More Hazardous." Within
the cover story, by Jeffrey Goldberg, the templative notion that "Muslim
women are oppressed," employed with seeming abandon by politicians in
the United States and Europe and sometimes forming part of an explicit
strategy to legitimate war, is generally presumed to be valid (Goldberg
2011).[2]

The cover's wider insinuation is not so much that a "hazard" to feminist civic values exists in the form of covered women under an unrecogniz-
able patriarchal structure; it is rather that the covering is itself a threat to
democracy, a threat that inevitably leads to terrorism. The title blurb reads,
"As dictatorships crumble across the Middle East, what happens if Arab
democracy means the rise of radical Islamism?" *Muslimah Media Watch*, a
feminist Muslim blog, identifies this exploitative cover, humorously titling
the blog entry "Arab Women: They're in Niqabs, Gettin' in Ur Democracy" (2011).

How do masks produce such judgment, if we could say that they did?
It has been argued that, for one thing, they create distance. In a recent article on the aesthetic mediation of torture, including covering the face or

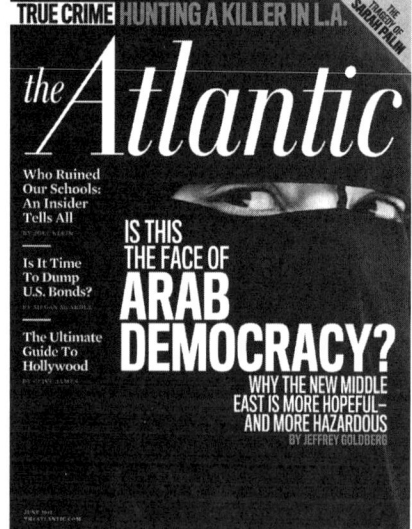

FIG. 2: Cover of the *Atlantic*,
June 2011. Reprinted with
permission.

head of victims, Marita Sturken (2011) describes distancing devices that support the "modes of innocence and comfort culture." These devices, she argues, are necessary for the U.S. public to disavow the torture of innocent people, even as that torture is openly acknowledged. Central to her argument is the depersonalizing hooded figure, arms outstretched, in Abu Ghraib who achieved a kind of iconic status as martyrlike (evoking Christ). She credits that iconicity with creating a certain distance for the American "comfort culture" that becomes more accustomed to torture. Anne McClintock (2009) further reminds us of an underlying reason we see such coverings: masks are used as a sensory deprivation torture technique at Abu Ghraib and Guantánamo Bay. She notes, "There is a terrible tension here of the bright visibility of the scene and the unseeable darkness of the prisoner's torment, the invisible obscene of their suffering" (65).

Does this image participate straightforwardly in Sturken's culture of comfort (even if for self-reassurance)? Despite her sense that "in the image's iconic status, it does not matter who he is" (2011, 429), the hooded figure, in my reading, must be racialized and thereby achieves affective ambiguity. Sturken passes too quickly over the protest poster variation of this image, created by Forkscrew Graphics, that she describes as putting the Statue of Liberty into a Ku Klux Klan hood. Presumably, this poster makes use of the fact that the Klan hood can be easily viewed in the United States as worn by the *perpetrator* of violence rather than by its victim. This iconic perpetrator of violence, the Ku Klux Klan, diverts violence to history even as it calls forth the association of a timeless symbol, the Statue of Liberty, with modern-day racism. A faceless symbol of the police state, for example, hooded riot police, does not enjoy the same symbolic consensus. Instead, Sturken prefers a somewhat deescalating reading of the figure as Christ-like.

In its nonwhiteness, it is difficult to see the hooded figure evoking only Christian martyrdom—even, as W. J. T. Mitchell (2005) argues, it was "as if the MPs at Abu Ghraib sensed that their mission was to realize America's Crusade against infidels, its Holy War against the Unholy Terrorists, with the staging of an Arab man as a Christ-like sacrifice" (304). In my calculation, the assumed-to-be person of color under the mask stands for something else: literally, a veiled threat upon whom violence must be obligatorily—necessarily—unleashed.[3] The icon in itself does not guarantee distance; some icons are proximating, enlivening, affectively valenced.

Sensitivity

Ed Cohen's (2009) recent work traces the history of immunity as an initially political/legal notion that was taken up into biomedical discourses.[4] What is most interesting to me here is the translatability of this political notion into biopolitical understandings of self and world. On the basis of belonging to a worldly community predetermined by civic codes of face and faciality ascribed to Western possibilities of subjectivity, individual immunity gives way to a certain vulnerability. Yet, as Priscilla Wald notes in her theorization of "imagined immunities," epidemiological narratives resolutely align themselves in terms of national boundaries (2008, 65). We might consider a tension between political immunity and resolute sovereignty, on the one hand, and a felt vulnerability that codes as a state of emergency in Western regimes inchoately aware of their brokenness, on the other. Ultimately, concerns of health and political sovereignty come together and blend, seemingly irretrievably, in the heightened figure of the mask.

When discussing masks, then, it is fitting to discuss their involvements with disability discourses. Wearing a mask as an evident prosthetic "outs" a person who otherwise passes as nondisabled. It visibly marks as invisibly "damaged" (or at least, vulnerable) a body that might otherwise seem healthy. While some prosthetics "enable" or "restore ability" while remaining cosmetically indiscernible, others are evident, as is the cane or wheelchair; conventionally these draw attention to the disability. The chemically sensitive person's mask falls into this latter category.[5]

While multiple chemical sensitivity (MCS) has often been regarded as peripheral or even external to conventional understandings of disability, Anna Mollow and others with MCS argue that it is appropriate to discuss this condition, like other disabilities, precisely in terms of access, despite the fact that "our requests seem to fall far outside the realm of what's 'reasonable'" (2011, 194). Although Mollow's excellent piece in a recent issue of *WSQ* does not mention—perhaps does not imagine it possible?—the mask, it is one rather practical way to approach, and protect oneself from, at least some of the threatening everyday chemicals in our environment. It is indeed a prosthetic in the sense that it is an extension of a chemically sensitive person's breathing apparatus, comparable in at least some ways to the prosthetic limb's operating as an extension of a partially amputated extremity.

In "The Other Arms Race," David Serlin (2006, 49–67) writes a history of prosthetics particularly in relation to World War II male amputees. He points out that there exists a bifurcation of types of disability that have consequences for gender: "disability induced by modern technology or warfare," on the one hand, subject to even higher valorization and secured masculinity because of service to nation or to industrial capitalism, and, on the other hand, "hereditary disability," which subjects a disabled person to suggestions of effeminizing (or feminine) weakness (54).

Prosthetic masks, too, have gendered valences. Feminist artist Allison Smith, in her 2009 project *Needle Work*, painstakingly re-created cloth gas masks used in World Wars I and II. Their fragility, she has reported, was literally and figuratively palpable (fig. 3). Arguably, we can think of such masks as the first environmental prosthetics made en masse, linking them genealogically to the contemporary prosthetic practices of people with MCS in ways that mirror Serlin's history connecting the timing of

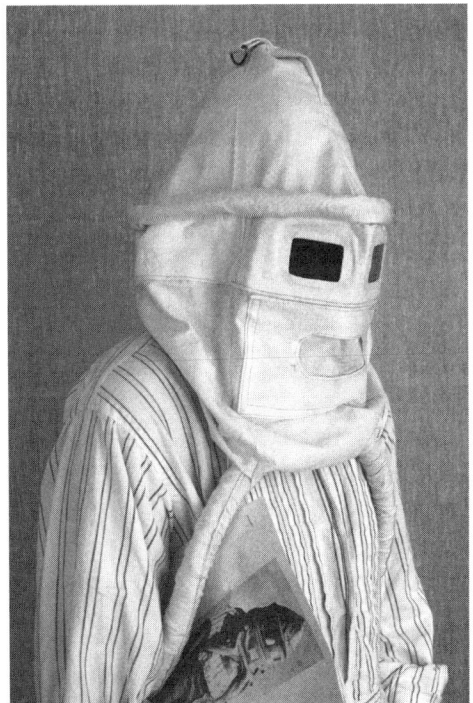

FIG. 3: Allison Smith, *Needle Work*, 2010. Re-creation of cloth gas masks. Photo courtesy Allison Smith.

expanded prosthetic limb manufactures with disabilities due to World War II.

Smith points to these masks' "handmade quality, which seems to suggest simultaneously a level of loving care as well as functional inadequacy. . . . I have begun to see these objects as remnants of an as-yet unwritten history of needlework" (Smith 2009). In so doing, Smith restores the gendered making by women of the early cloth gas masks for provision to European and American males on the war front. Smith's work further demonstrates that across this historical reach back in time, certain things remain: the fragility, the faltering promise of the gas mask and its haunting transnationality as a symbol of a war against people—of whatever location—deemed criminals or war opponents.

In current culture, images of masks proliferate; they have become symbolic fodder for all sorts of imaginative posthumanisms. For example, consider a regular event in 2011 at Café Guru, a cosmopolitanized Indian-

FIG. 4: Poster for Cafe Guru, Contagious Behaviour event, Leeds, England, 2011. Photo by the author.

style restaurant and event venue in Leeds, England. Café Guru hosts an invite-only dance/entertainment evening called "Contagious Behaviour." fig. 4). The launch poster presents a young, apparently white female, with decorous swirls emerging from her head that look sometimes like oily hair, suggesting a punk aesthetic, sometimes like background decoration. She wears a chemical filter mask, with plastic cartridges, rubber noseguard, and fiber gaskets, of the general type used by painters and others who work with fumes. One end of the mask appears to be attached to a lit fuse. The typeface, with the raised lettering of a punch-style roll labeler, nostalgically evokes former eras, possibly the simpler techne of 1980s science fiction. That the wearer of the mask is a white female modulates the affective threat of the mask, fetishizing and aestheticizing it.

Interestingly, photo shoots from the events posted on the Internet show not young white women with chemical masks, as in the poster, but women wearing a different kind of facial covering: many women are wearing ensembles of fake veils (revealing the eyes) *and* bindis, both of which presumably have been provided to guests of the parties. Such coincident images draw on existing links between discourses of health, security, safety, religion, and sexuality.

David Mitchell and Sharon Snyder (1997) point out the tendency among posthumanist theorists to consider virtual technologies as prostheses; according to the authors, N. Katherine Hayles "forgoes a discussion of disabled people's more obvious status as 'cyborgs' in order to privilege the chosen prosthetic identification of computer hackers and video junkies" (8). In a site in which media are materially altering the felt world of its denizens, it is important to condition or delimit (as Hayles herself recognizes) the locatedness of the posthuman figure and its chosen prosthetic identifications, while the spread of media icons like the racialized woman in the burqa or niqab needs to be triangulated with race and disability both.

Genuine chemical (vapor) mask iconographies of the sort on the Contagious Behaviour poster, unlike that of the aestheticized and essentially ineffective surgical mask Julianne Moore wears as a woman suffering from MCS in the 1995 film *Safe*, necessarily build upon sites in which they were made en masse: military histories of wartime protection—in particular, the gas masks deployed as early as World War I to protect against poison and irritant gases. Yet MCS, building as it does upon a popularization of sick building syndrome, seems to bespeak neither war nor the physically disabling work of industrial capitalism, but rather the service-related office

jobs of late capitalism. [6] It resolutely folds into imagined primary employ-
ments of middle-class white women. For all these reasons, it is not surprising that the iconic persona of MCS remains a white woman, a fact noted
by Mollow.[7]

The iconic persona of multiple chemical sensitivity—someone like
Moore's economically privileged character in *Safe*—is also precisely *not*
a man or woman of color, as much as the bodies who occupy present-day
service economies have changed. The wearing of masks by white women
or men, I argue, cannot quite arouse the kind of heightened, transnationalizing security sentiment that a woman of color (or a man of color, for
that matter) in a mask might. For instance, an article titled "Fashionable
MCS Terrorist Goes for a Bike Ride" (2008) in *The Canary Report*, an
online publication about multiple chemical sensitivity, shows a photo by a
masked male bicyclist with MCS of his reflection in a bus, with a quote in
which he humorously contemplates the possibility that he might be perceived as a terrorist, but only with benevolence: "I can only imagine what
the people inside the bus were thinking, probably something like 'Well, it's
nice to see the terrorists are making an effort to be a little more fashionable now.'" One senses that the bicyclist's whiteness is what makes merely
humorous the possibility that this masked person with MCS could be perceived as a terrorist. His clear recognition of a likeness between masks, or
his feeling that both are screens of a sort, does not lead to a meditation
on the possible structural relationships—polarizations as well as resonances—between one person's sensory protection and another's sensory
deprivation.

Indeed, discussions of masks in accounts by white women with MCS
seem largely to have to do with their own chemical insecurity in an otherwise racially (though not always economically) secure world. There is no
acknowledgment that one's wearing a mask could arouse terror, or even a
reading of hostility, in others. From the other side, there is no equivalent
righteous pronouncement that such women need reveal their faces in an
open society. For such use of masks is easily read as "functional necessity,"
except when it is not—in the case of burqas. The juxtaposition of MCS
masks and Muslim veils and the qualitatively different affects attaching to
them suggest a different, yet curiously analogous, pairing of the kind that
Lennard Davis offers in his consideration of the Venus de Milo as a register
of the visual-psychic economies of ability discourses. For Davis, the Venus
de Milo, with her missing limbs, facial disfigurements, "scars," and missing

toes, is a specter of disability whose threat requires that the disability must be covered over and replaced with a corrective idealization of perfection; Davis notes that art historians have regularly overlooked Venus's missing and scarred parts. But Medusa is a "poignant double . . . the disabled woman to Venus's perfect body," playing a different part in scopic regimes of ability and disability. Davis writes, "In this moment, the normal person suddenly feels self-conscious, rigid, unable to look but equally drawn to look. The visual field becomes problematic, dangerous, treacherous. The disability becomes a power derived from its otherness, its monstrosity, in the eyes of the 'normal' person" (1995, 132). The pairing in this essay is not obviously of one disabled person against another. Yet there is a way in which disability can itself double upon another form that may or may not be disabled. We can imagine in the preceding discussion of MCS masks and Muslim veils that one person's disability prosthetic, read as protective device, can be "overlooked"—or, to be more realistic, redeemingly accommodated, at the cost of demonizing (or, indeed, disabling?) another's—in the eyes of a Western "normal"—yawning and horrible "missingness."

Returning to the promotional image for Contagious Behavior, Cafe Guru's poster graphic runs roughshod over the division between chemical and biological, since a biological mask that would more directly link to notions of contagion either generally covers the entire face, in the extreme version, or is a simpler piece of synthetic cloth, rigid or slack, secured by an elastic band and with no valve. It is therefore quite unlike the hospital mask that opened this essay. I read the Cafe Guru mask's contemporary conflation of biological and chemical toxic agents less as a sign of popular ignorance or a recognition of the fact that both biological and chemical agents can constitute threats, than as an overdetermination of tropes of immunity and the attraction of the mask's ranging affective touch in a context of global political flux.

Screen

I have argued that masks are contested sites of security and disability. The term "masks" also, I contend, is a complicated one within debates about ethics and affect. For what *happens* to the face when it is masked? In his *Totality and Infinity*, philosopher Emmanuel Levinas writes of the ethical first importance of the face, in particular the primacy of the face-to-face encounter (1969, 194–219). The face itself, to Levinas, is phenomenologically distinct and, indeed, is likened to a *force*, the capacity to affect; it affects even before being judged. The naked face presents a vulnerable other, demanding compassion in the ethical encounter. But taking this phenomenological abstraction to its limit, what becomes of the ethical encounter when—in the case of a mask—an altered face, a covered face, or a non-face, presents itself?

Here, Deleuze and Guattari's *A Thousand Plateaus* presents a compelling, if problematic, discussion of face and faciality in the context of Westernized culture. In their account, what counts as "face" is but a production of an "abstract machine of faciality," a machine that facializes many more things than heads: "The face is produced only when the head ceases to be a part of the body, when it ceases to be coded by the body, when it ceases to have a multidimensional, polyvocal corporeal code—when the body, head included, has been decoded and has to be *overcoded* by something we shall call the Face. . . . What accomplishes this is the screen with holes, the white wall/black hole, the abstract machine producing faciality" (Deleuze and Guattari 1987, 170).

For Deleuze and Guattari, then, not only is "face" a particular kind of material-discursive production, rather than a biological self-evident given, but also integral to this production is the surrounding screen: it is a determinative, calculative, generative "white" screen against which a "black" face emerges as a distinct hole. They write, "The face is not a universal. It is not even that of the white man; it is White Man himself, with his broad white cheeks and the black hole of his eyes. The face is Christ. The face is the typical European, what Ezra Pound called the average sensual man." (196). They further explain that the production of such a Christ-like "face" creates the possibility for racist judgment against faces that do not resemble this idealized face. In her description of the hooded figure in Abu Ghraib as "martyric," Sturken (2011) claims it is because of iconicity that it doesn't matter (or matters less?) who is inside the hood. The concealment of a (racialized) face presumably permits the iconic image to float even more. But what kind of identity matters against what kind of nonidentity?

For Deleuze and Guattari, when a "mask" appears, it is merely the accouterment of the primitive. They breezily claim that for the primitive, face (and facial expression) symbolically means nothing and hence doesn't, or didn't, exist ("The mask assures the head's belonging to the body, its becoming-animal, as was the case in primitive societies" [181]).

Against their confident historicization of "the primitive," I wish to affirm the material presence of the mask in contemporary society, a mask that continues to signal primitivity for believers in the Western political ideology's creation of the modern moment in a way that neatly aligns with Deleuze and Guattari's temporalization of the mask.

I see the mask in contemporary transnationalized security frameworks as a screen in itself, a screen of projection, and as a negative screen for what lies beyond it. It offers no vulnerability to a Levinasian ethics of encounter; it seems to insult that nakedness and, as such, stands as a figure of violence toward the idea of encounter itself. To others, the mask (as burqa) is a screen on Muslim women, seeming to cancel them in the eyes of Christian Westerners seeking to find Deleuze and Guattari's White Man there instead; in other cases, a mask (as biological: antiviral, antivapor, or antiparticulate) for protection seems to threaten its viewer rather than simply affirm the possibility of the viewer's own threat to the sensitivity of the person wearing it. The mask wearer has broken the civic pact necessary for communitas: you must offer the vulnerability of your face, because this is part of your contract.

The burqa has been seen as causing a rupture in that civic pact and has been the contested site of legal restriction in European nations such as France. An op-ed piece in the United Kingdom's *Catholic Herald* in April 2011 was titled "Wearing the Burqa in Our Streets Is a Hostile Act: The French Are Right to Ban It." The author goes on to say, "To be a society at all, we have to be able to see each other. That's the beginning of any communication between individuals" (Oddie 2011). The author quotes another commentator: "Common citizenship involves trust, and trust cannot exist where one cannot see people's faces in public. Obviously there can be necessary functional reasons for concealment—surgical masks, beekeeper's helmets, extremes of cold—but concealment in normal circumstances in an open society amounts to a hostile act." Still another quoted person points to the security threat of "the woman with a bulging shopping bag and a hidden face who is sitting opposite us in the Tube." This writer identifies such functions as protection of the body undergoing surgery, protection of the beekeeper's face from stings, and protection from the elements, but the quieter condition he imposes is one of exception. In normal circumstances, masks should not be worn.

What the opinions in the *Catholic Herald* do not acknowledge is that "normal circumstances" are subject to interpretation, and the author has unwittingly absorbed the perspective that the United Kingdom is, to use Agamben (1998)'s words, in its own state of exception. "Normal circumstances" were the aesthetic goal, if not the true condition, of the postspill Gulf shores, and they are precisely why, for a time, the Latino disaster workers cleaning the spill in Louisiana were threatened by BP with losing their jobs if they dared to wear protection like masks and gloves, for fear the public would be aroused to "mass hysteria" (read: feminized weakness, psychological disability) upon seeing them (Kennedy 2010).[8]

We might therefore say that the mask-screen can operate negatively, precisely when what is at stake is the loss of *face* as the necessary translating mechanism for what is inside. In the case of the burqa, Islam—the United States' "unfathomable obscurity"—displaces idealized American affiliation amid a growing nationalist securitization via a communalism of the body, a biopolitical demand by which a body must become eminently accessible to others. The mask-screen in Western scopic regimes scrambles the affectivities of risk with its subjects and objects, resulting in violent social and physical acts of "protection."

Such politics of the screen, I suggest, is precisely what produces interesting *affective* coincidences that are not otherwise attainable between masks of torture, figures of terrorism like the "concealing burqa," and biological or chemical protection. All of these—what we might call specular productions which are subject to judgments from an interested perspective of "global security"—betray confusions between subject and object, threat and victim. Such specular productions are closely tied to contemporary geopolitical conditions and environmental knowledge productions.

In this light, the mask participates in security assemblages that have effects within and without, much like the Sikh turban that Jasbir Puar (2010) considers. Puar argues against a purely specular model of terrorist visualities and for "information bodies" subject to racial and sexual biopolitics, into which certain bodies fall. It is crucial, as well, to examine the curious links between various figures of war/security and disability, as little as they might first have to do with one another. Robert McRuer (2010, 163–178) helpfully theorizes, tweaking Puar's generative formulation, "disability nationalism in crip times," urging a transnational perspective on disability, sexuality, and politics from directions of disability, postcolonial, and queer studies. Indeed, I wonder what happens to essentially white feminine representations of disability as they might become staged against certain bodies of color that, despite being similarly prostheticized, would fall too easily in line with Puar's terrorist corporealities.

I conclude by considering questions of facial legibility and deception, visibility and security, with a somewhat unlikely case: the TV persona of Dexter, a serial killer who articulates his own concealing actions, as well as his psychological complexity/disability. In the pilot episode of the Showtime television series *Dexter* (2006), the titular character steers his boat through the waterways of Miami after he has murdered a man. Dexter introduces himself: "I don't know what it is that made me the way I am, but whatever it was left a hollow place inside. People fake a lot of human interactions, but I feel like I fake them all, and I fake them very well." He works as a blood-splatter forensics analyst for the Miami police (selecting his victims by identifying presumed habitual killers from police cases), part of the very team who seeks to capture this skilled killer. In later episodes Dexter repeatedly invokes the descriptor of "mask" to describe his social conundrum, having the need to perform a self that in his view does not exist, to conjure apparent emotion and connection where it cannot be felt. Indeed, even his sexuality must be conjured, and the girlfriend he acquires is but a cover for his persona of normalcy; to us there is no evidence of his attraction to her.

This mask is occasionally literalized. In the first episode's nod to the bondage value of plastic wrap in BDSM sex play, Dexter pulls the wrap tight around his face, distorting his facial features and frightening his victim; he later wears a splatter shield while dismembering another live victim. Yet while Dexter stalks his prey, he relies not on disguise, but on simply evading detection. In the course of this day job, he does not wear a literal mask (at one point, his unprotected face is splattered with blood spurting from a body), though one could say that because of Dexter's double life, his "mask" (of "normalcy," of human emotion) is dissolved into his proper face, or is integral to his character. The hidden double construction has been capitalized upon in a recent marketing joke: you can purchase a "Michael C. Hall Limited Edition" of Kiehl's Rare Earth Deep Pore Cleansing Masque, with proceeds benefitting environmental causes. What kind of temporary concealment, and ultimate salutary revealing, is on offer here?

The invocation of a mask in a crime show is not novel; concealment and detection were built into the early definition of criminality and have been thematized in endless crime, adventure, and horror movies—to name a few, *Texas Chainsaw Massacre* (dir. Marcus Nispel, 1974), *Point Break* (dir. Kathryn Bigelow, 1991), *Set It Off* (dir. F. Gary Gray, 1996).[9] Yet the figure of the mask as an appurtenance is increasingly operationalized in modern-day criminal surveillance and detection techniques, making Dexter's citation both predictable and curiously insular in a time of expanded, transnational geographies of crime. Furthermore, Dexter's mask serves two purposes for him: meticulous affectation of nondisability and concealment of crime. *Dexter* illuminates the complex status of masks as they appear and disappear in contemporary U.S. culture—and how those facial coverings have consequences for current debates about states of security, affect, health, race, and gender.

While he may at first seem to be an interior fantasy and the newest instantiation of domestic crime tropes, Dexter—white, male, gainfully employed—suggests a shadow version of the threats to security and health that the United States feels itself surrounded by; his vigilante version of eye-for-an-eye "justice" mimics the extralegality of U.S. operations domestically and abroad. What is more, Dexter can choose to use the mask to literalize his own duplicity, but in the show the masks remain an infrequent device. The nonhuman/inanimate appurtenances of prosthetic masks have become part of the immune system itself, but made invisible on "proper" national self-representations; this is why we see a superficially "normal" and nondisabled body but one that is described as masklike, such as in the case of Dexter. Thinking of Dexter's mask economies as a register of the complexities of regime vulnerability/immunity, it is interesting to note that the earliest documented sense of the word "vulnerable," a meaning now declared obsolete by the *Oxford English Dictionary*, was in fact one of potential aggression, not fragility: "having the power to wound." Definitions resembling the contemporary meaning of "susceptibility to *being* wounded, injured, or attacked" appeared immediately thereafter, possibly in response to the passivizing "-able" suffix. The chronology of meanings of "vulnerable"—spanning the English seventeenth century—suggests a psychic economy imbued with the fortuitous exchange of rival roles.

Levinas, confronting the possibilities and difficulties of the presentation of the self, writes, "To seek truth I have already established a relationship with a face which can guarantee itself, whose epiphany itself is somehow a word of honor. . . . Every language as an exchange of verbal signs refers already to this primordial word of honor" (1969, 202). Dexter exploits what Levinas calls the "primordial word of honor," and this thwarted facial authenticity has a pedagogical value for Americans. In the early episodes, the rare choice of mild masking, in which the character's face can still be identified or detected, serves its own allegorical function: (white) Americans can self-mask, but even if they regard themselves as duplicitous, as other than presentation, there is no need to consider themselves burdened by a permanent prosthesis. In fact, vulnerabilities must be projected, externalized, rather than owned; they cannot and should not occur on the white U.S. body, only elsewhere. This is another way of expressing that states of fragility can only be lightly acknowledged to the point of an ever growing war and an ever increasing surveillance mechanism. But disability—read as necessary prosthesis on the body—is to be considered beyond the ken, or visual register, of the self-representing domain of the United States. If the state is fragile, it is not yet disabled.

Acknowledgments

I would like to thank Julia Bryan-Wilson and Dana Luciano for fruitful discussion about masks; Julia was a generous and productive critic of my drafts. Special thanks to an anonymous reviewer, only some of whose excellent comments I was able to address in this version. Any errors remain mine alone.

Mel Y. Chen is assistant professor of gender and women's studies at the University of California–Berkeley, with research interests in critical race, disability, and queer theory; environmental and animal studies; and language. Mel's forthcoming book (Duke University Press, 2012), *Animacies: Biopolitics, Racial Mattering, and Queer Affect*, explores questions of racialization, queering, disability, and affective economies in animate and inanimate "life."

Notes

1. Diverse feminist work exists on the veil. One strand focuses on Western colonialist legacies residing in political ideologies' deployment of discourses of racial and sexual difference in relation to the veil historically and contemporarily. Another strand takes up questions of the veil from a necessarily more complex Muslim feminist perspective.
2. For a critical response to the popular conception that Iraqi women have been "liberated" in some way by the U.S. occupation, see Sadig Al-Ali and Pratt 2009.

3. Jasbir Puar, however, refuses this economy, associating the iconic hooded figure with both the Ku Klux Klan and the veil/burqa (Puar 2007, 102).

4. Interestingly, the metaphor of immunity seems to travel within its own theorization: Roberto Esposito (2008) describes the political concept of immunitas as a "poisoned affect of gratitude" in the interest of belonging to a community that paradoxically reduces the individual's immunity.

5. Tobin Siebers's book *Disability Theory* (2008) has an extensive discussion of passing in relation to disability. Building on a discourse that identifies some prosthetics as normalizing, and others as disabling in the eyes of others, he identifies the strategic use of prosthetics (or prosthetic gestures) as what he calls the disability "masquerade." While Siebers's analysis works well for the strategic deployment of exaggerated movements (like limping) and the use of prosthetic devices like canes, it seems to falter when it comes to one prosthesis, the mask. This is mentioned in Chen 2011. I should note that Siebers's not identifying the actual mask as part of disability accouterments is not surprising, for his schema somewhat neatly follows popular disability studies renderings of disability, in which chemical sensitivity is not typically included.

6. For a history of sick building syndrome in the United States and its gendered and classed racialization as white, female, and middle class, due to a combination of activist visibility, illness representation, and structural racism, see Murphy 2006.

7. There is much more to the classed, gendered racialization of MCS. In addition to the work of Murphy, for a study of environment, environmental justice, and body materialities, see Alaimo 2010. Chapter 5 in particular theorizes the construction of MCS in relation to class and race.

8. Kerry Kennedy of the Robert F. Kennedy Center for Justice and Human Rights (www.rfkcenter.org) reports that workers were discouraged from using respirators. From interviews with workers, Kennedy (2010) found that "workers were not only denied protective equipment but, after arriving for work wearing respirators, were threatened with the loss of their jobs if they chose to wear these 'unnecessary' devices which only serve to 'spread hysteria.'"

9. For one feminist consideration of horror films, see Clover 1992.

Works Cited

"Arab Women: They're in Niqabs, Gettin' in Ur Democracy." 2011. *Muslimah Media Watch* (blog). http://muslimahmediawatch.org/2011/05/arab-women-theyre-in-niqabs-gettin-in-ur-democracy/.

Agamben, Giorgio. 1998. *Homo Sacer: Sovereign Power and Bare Life*. Stanford: Stanford University Press.

Ahmed, Leila. 2011. *A Quiet Revolution: The Veil's Resurgence, from the Middle East to America*. New Haven: Yale University Press.

Alaimo, Stacy. 2010. *Bodily Natures: Science, Environment, and the Material Self*. Bloomington: Indiana University Press.

Chen, Mel. 2011. "Toxic Animacies, Inanimate Affections," *GLQ: A Journal of Lesbian and Gay Studies* 17(2–3):265–86.

Cohen, Ed. 2009. *A Body Worth Defending: Immunity, Biopolitics, and the Apotheosis of the Modern Body*. Durham: Duke University Press.

Clover, Carol. 1992. *Men, Women, and Chain Saws: Gender in the Modern Horror Film*. Princeton: Princeton University Press.

Davis, Lennard. 1995. *Enforcing Normalcy: Disability, Deafness, and the Body*. New York: Verso.

Deleuze, Gilles, and Félix Guattari. 1987. *A Thousand Plateaus: Capitalism and Schizophrenia*. Minneapolis: University of Minnesota Press.

Esposito, Roberto. 2008. *Bios: Biopolitics and Philosophy*. Minneapolis: University of Minnesota Press.

"Fashionable MCS Terrorist Goes for a Bike Ride." 2008. *The Canary Report*, September 29. http://www.thecanaryreport.org/2008/09/29/the-fashionable-mcs-terrorist/

Goldberg, Jeffrey. 2011. "Danger: Falling Tyrants," *Atlantic Monthly* 307(5): 46–55.

Kennedy, Kerry. 2010. "Gulf Needs Concrete Actions That Respect Residents' Rights." *HuffPost Green*, June 11. http://www.huffingtonpost.com/kerry-kennedy/gulf-needs-concrete-actions_b_609827.html

Levinas, Emmanuel. 1969. *Totality and Infinity: An Essay on Exteriority*. Pittsburgh: Duquesne University Press.

Lutz, Catherine, and Jane Collins. 1993. *Reading "National Geographic."* Chicago: University of Chicago Press.

Mahmood, Saba. 2004. *The Politics of Piety: The Islamic Revival and the Feminist Subject*. Princeton: Princeton University Press.

McClintock, Anne. 2009. "Paranoid Empire: Specters from Guantánamo and Abu Ghraib." *Small Axe* 13(1):50–74.

McRuer, Robert. 2010. "Disability Nationalism in Crip Times." *Journal of Literary and Cultural Disability Studies* 4(2):163–178.

Mitchell, David T., and Sharon L. Snyder. 1997. *The Body and Physical Difference: Discourses of Disability*. Ann Arbor: University of Michigan Press.

Mitchell, W. J. T. 2005. "The Unspeakable and the Unimaginable: Word and Image in a Time of Terror." *English Literary History* 72(2):291–308.

Mollow, Anna. 2011. "No Safe Place," *WSQ: Women's Studies Quarterly* 39(1–2):188–199.

Murphy, Michelle. 2006. *Sick Building Syndrome and the Problem of Uncertainty: Environmental Politics, Technoscience, and Women Workers.* Durham: Duke University Press.

Oddie, William. 2011. "Wearing the Burqa in Our Streets Is a Hostile Act: The French Are Right to Ban It." *Catholic Herald,* April 20.

Puar, Jasbir K. 2007. *Terrorist Assemblages: Homonationalism in Queer Times.* Durham: Duke University Press.

Sadig Al-Ali, Nadje, and Nicola Christine Pratt. 2009. *What Kind of Liberation? Women and the Occupation of Iraq.* Berkeley: University of California Press.

Scott, Joan Wallach. 2010. *The Politics of the Veil.* Princeton: Princeton University Press.

Serlin, David. 2006. "The Other Arms Race." In *The Disability Studies Reader,* ed. Lennard Davis. New York: Routledge.

Siebers, Tobin. 2008. *Disability Theory.* Ann Arbor: University of Michigan Press.

Smith, Allison. 2009. *Needle Work.* St. Louis: Kemper Art Museum.

Sturken, Marita. 2011. "Comfort, Irony, and Trivialization: The Mediation of Torture." *International Journal of Cultural Studies* 14(4):423–40.

Szorenyi, Anna. 2004. "The Face of Suffering in Afghanistan: Identity, Authenticity, and Technology in the Search for the Representative Refugee." *Australian Feminist Law Journal* 21(1):1–22.

Wald, Priscilla. 2008. *Contagious: Cultures, Carriers, and the Outbreak Narrative.* Durham: Duke University Press.

Yegenoglu, Meyda. 1998. *Colonial Fantasies: Towards a Feminist Reading of Orientalism.* Cambridge, UK: Cambridge University Press.

The Life Cycle of a Common Weed:
Viral Imaginings in Plant-Human Encounters

Caitlin Berrigan

It was like a scene from *Repo Man* (1984) in which all the products are brandless and packaged with the same blue-on-white text, indicating exactly what they are and nothing else: milk, beer, corn flakes. The hardware and garden supply in my farm community sold forty-pound bags labeled "DRIED BLOOD" in generic red-on-white. The huge bags were piled by the door, as if to remind you to grab one on your way out among other sundries like chewing gum, flashlights and pocket screwdrivers. I marveled to think that more than my own body weight in dried blood slouched by the cash registers, and what was it for anyway? My mother, an amateur botanist, explained that blood is a fertilizer high in nitrogen and can be dried and sold as a by-product of industrial slaughterhouses. Though blood is not new to agricultural systems. Lush gardens sprouted with the blood of slain beasts appear in the Talmud and in twelfth-century Persian poetry (Stanley 1993; Bynum 2007; Khayyám 1901). The blood of mortal wounds from protagonists of ancient Greek tales gave rise to hyacinths, violets, and crocuses, as well as mythological plants, such as the *prometheion* and the *moly* (Conticelli 2001). I am enamored of blood as a substance and as a symbol of vitality. But as I am a lifelong carrier of the hepatitis C virus, my own blood carries with it the sinister potential of seeding another person with disease. I was intrigued that my own blood— hazardous to humans—could nonetheless be useful to plants.

This nugget of horticultural information lay dormant until the concept for an artwork germinated years later: *Life Cycle of a Common Weed*. The idea is to stage an encounter between plants and humans involving the exchange of nutrients. Blood from a human body nourishes dande-

WSQ: Women's Studies Quarterly 40: 1 & 2 (Spring/Summer 2012) © 2012 by Caitlin Berrigan.

lions with nitrogen. In turn, the root and leaves of the dandelion provide nutritious and medicinal sustenance to the human. The artwork exists as a performance, visual documents, an event, and a perpetual cultivation. In the narrative that follows, I describe the emergence of *Life Cycle of a Common Weed* from a web of embodied knowledges, multispecies encounters, cultural symbols and practices, dialogues, and lateral transfers. I infect the philosophical abstractions of the artist's statement genre with a situated autoethnography that joins the artwork to nodes of questions and contexts, but by no means circumscribes its entire network of connectivity.

A growing fatigue with the militancy used to address human-viral encounters led me to develop a series of artworks, including *Viral Confections, Tea Party to Befriend a Virus*, and *The Knit Virus* (2006–2008). The sculptures are activated in public settings to invite nondidactic discussion about chronic illness, hepatitis C, art, and medicine. The arrangement facilitates free-form, public conversation about matters typically confined to private medical settings. The artworks engage what anthropologist Heather Paxson (2008) calls a "post-Pasteurian microbiopolitics." Paxson extends Foucault's (1976) concept of "biopolitics," to describe the "potentialities of collaborative human and microbial culture practices" (Paxson 2008, 17) among artisanal cheese makers who cultivate the triumph of tasty and edible bacteria over pathogenic ones. Beyond cheese, Paxson's microbiopolitics imply the structuring of interspecies transactions. They are at once intimately *micropolitical* in the sense of Deleuze and Guattari's (1987) detailed, supple movements of power and subversion that complement the rigid centralization of *macropolitics* (208–231); and *microbiological* in scale, extending out into the molar realm of populations through globalized trade and travel, where the (micro)biopolitical becomes a geopolitical concern of sovereign powers (see generally Braun 2007). In resistance to this sovereign language, I am interested in delineating a micropolitical space to air the complicated antagonisms, codependencies, and evolutions in our relationships to pathogens. The friend-or-foe model hardly suffices for human interrelations; how could it suffice for human-microbial relations? Fear-inducing and xenophobic language used to describe disease frightens people away from learning how to safely and intentionally coexist with microbes. In these artworks, I seek not to normalize viral encounters but to amplify them such that microbial "actors" (see generally Latour 2005) must be recognized as part of what being-in-the-world is about.

Life Cycle of a Common Weed emerged from my prior work about coexistence with microbes. It also germinated from my routine of self-care and my body's inability to respond to biomedical pharmaceuticals. Raised by working-class, back-to-the-land, white hippies, I was taught at a young age to forage for herbal remedies in the Redwood Forest as well as at the grocery store—operated by a lesbian commune. Among the therapeutic plants to treat hepatitis C is the common dandelion, *Taraxacum officinale.*

Despite its place in pharmacopoeias of many centuries, the dandelion is listed among weeds by the U.S. federal government (USDA 2009). A PubMed search for "Taraxacum officinale" produces as many studies on the therapeutic effects of dandelions for humans as it does the efficacy of various herbicides on them. A prolific weed that contaminates lawns in one context, the dandelion is a rarified medicinal commodity in another. The dialectic of the dandelion matches the dialectic of blood, which may be a contaminant in one context and a rich source of nutrition in another. My artwork involves feeding virally contaminated blood to dandelions as a cultivation of reciprocity. The disputed merits of the materials foreground how relating to bodies and diseases are just as complex, codependent, and antagonistic—layered with tenderness and brutality.

The common dandelion, *Taraxacum officinale*, populates sidewalks, industrial wastelands, fields, and the manicured lawn. Each part of the dandelion is edible. The long, brittle taproot and leaves contain the richest nutrients and can be processed for tea and herbal remedies. Dandelion is a safe and popular medicinal plant that promotes the flow of bile and reduces inflammation in the liver and gallbladder. It is higher in beta-carotene than carrots, has more iron and calcium than spinach, and contains many B vitamins, as well as vitamins C, E, P, and D and biotin, inositol, potassium, phosphorus, magnesium, zinc, and insulin. Dandelion root is a helpful remedy for hepatitis C, all kinds of liver conditions, kidney disease, diabetes, hypoglycemia, and stress. (Brill and Dean 1994; Balch and Balch 2000)

Native to Europe and Asia, the dandelion is widely recognized as a medicinal plant, first noted in tenth-century Persian medical manuals (Carr et al. 1998, 141). European colonists intentionally introduced dandelions into the United States circa the seventeenth century to stave off scurvy and malnutrition at the end of the winter (Gade 1991; Mack and Erneberg 2002; Mack 2003). Dandelions propagate easily in human-modified landscapes, swiftly proliferating in the disturbed soil of lawns and empty urban lots. It is noninvasive, as it does not prohibit the growth of other plants. Today, over half a million pounds of herbicides are purchased in the United States (Kiely et al, 2004, 20), most of them applied to dandelions and other unwanted plants, in the country's largest irrigated crop: the lawn (Milesi et al. 2005). Dandelions are among the key targets of chemical industry advertising campaigns, such as in ads that tell consumers, "Don't eat 'em defeat 'em" (Robbins and Sharp 2003, 431).

Contagion/Cultivation

Hepatitis C is a blood-borne virus that, according to the World Health Organization (1997), accounts for chronic liver illness in 3 percent of the world's population (over 200 million people if calculating with 2011 figures). Among the top ten causes of death in Americans aged twenty-four to seventy-four (St. John and Sandt 2005), hepatitis C kills at least fifteen thousand people a year in the United States (Manos et al. 2008). There is no vaccine. It is the most common, chronic, blood-borne viral infection in the United States (St. John and Sandt 2005) but is not widely understood by the public. With a confusing and bland name, hepatitis C affects motley demographics: people with a history of injection drug use, health and emergency workers, veterans, incarcerated persons, blood transfusion recipients, and kidney dialysis patients prior to 1992. No other forms of social identity or class are dominant among these groups that might otherwise band them together. What Rabinow (1996) names "biosociality"—a collective identity grounded in a shared, technoscientific biological experience—has not appeared for hepatitis C; there is no biosocial patient advocacy proportionate to the magnitude of the epidemic. Hepatitis C is distributed and heterogeneous; it is, for example, racially complicated, as white men represent the quantitative majority of those infected, while the greatest prevalence is among African American men (Fleckenstein 2004).

Nor does hepatitis C have what cultural historian Priscilla Wald (2008) calls an "outbreak narrative," like the "emerging infections" that sent frissons around the globe at the end of the twentieth and beginning of the twenty-first centuries, foretelling apocalypse accomplished by microbial agents. Xenophobic narratives surrounded the emergence of HIV, SARS, Ebola, West Nile, bird flu, and H1N1 swine flu (Wald 2008). Hepatitis C, on the other hand, has had a slow and insidious emergence over twenty years, with research correspondingly sluggish. Like the dandelion, hepatitis C is relatively inconspicuous, yet it is all around you once you look. It is this ubiquitous, weedy quality of the hepatitis C virus that I wished to instrumentalize in my artwork. Lacking an outbreak narrative, hepatitis C could perhaps serve as a model for being-with microbes once their outbreak narratives have cooled into complacency. Often reinforcing social stigmas, xenophobia, and moralized behavior, the outbreak narrative favors rhetoric of battle, fear, and heroic drug innovation. Yet questions of contagion, proximity, communication, and communicability remain underexamined. Wald reminds us that "the interactions that make us sick also constitute us as a community" and diseases dramatize "the most basic of human narratives: the necessity and danger of human contact" (2008, 2). What outlives the outbreak narrative are these questions of commingling and becoming in ongoing social-viral encounters—questions I sought to interrogate with art.

Life Cycle of a Common Weed (*LCCW*) is thus a gesture of reciprocity in which I cultivate dandelions and fertilize them with my own blood. Blood containing human pathogens remains a good fertilizer for plants. I can give to the dandelions what would be a danger to any human, emphasizing the fertility of contaminated blood and the nourishment of weeds in a reciprocal plant-human exchange of sustenance. The standard Western treatment for hepatitis C has changed little in the past ten years. It remains expensive and is only about 50 percent effective. *LCCW* is a microbiopolitical tactic to circumnavigate Western medicinal orthodoxy and corporate interests (Paxson 2008). The artwork returns biomedicine to the weeds as a way to reconsider our relationship to viruses, the material possibilities of our own bodies, and vegetal empathy. I created a system of exchange on the margins of biomedicine and alternative remedies, subverting and complementing the biopolitical role of clinical medicine. It was therefore important to the symbolic intentions of the project that I learn how to draw my own blood with venipuncture. Acquiring this knowledge necessitated maneuvering within medical territory that patients do not typically traverse.

A generous friend in medical school taught me venipuncture in her apartment-style dorm. The apartment was packed with pharmaceutical swag, from Viagra soap dispensers to folding Levitra ballpoint pens that erect to full stature with the touch of a button. Doctors are notorious for their own illicit drug use; thus the apartment was regularly stocked with sharps disposal containers to protect sanitation workers from needle sticks when handling the garbage. Despite the elusiveness of my veins and the frustration they have caused many phlebotomists, I managed successfully to draw a tube of blood on the first try. Soon, I was a self-sufficient phlebotomist and patient of my own becoming.

Creating an illusion of self-sufficiency, I form a circuit in *LCCW* between two parties: the plants and me. I want to emphasize a kind of DIY, micro back-to-the-land form of medication—and to close off social and political indifference, pharmaceutical profiteering, and the tired rhetoric of battling disease. The dandelion, a disparaged weed, has much to offer the stigmatized person with disease; and rather than being stamped out with pesticides, it is allowed to flourish in a cycle of mutual cultivation. *LCCW* is what I call a "pathetic political gesture": genuine in its reach toward empathy and self-care, yet inevitably deficient. I find parallels in *Flood: A Volunteer Network for Active Participation in Healthcare*, a project involving an indoor hydroponic garden initiated by the art collective Haha from 1992 to 1995 that provided bacteria-free greens to immunocompromised people living with HIV. In the absence of effective treatment and feeling the urgent need to *do* something, the community mobilized in this gesture; it was as much a means to cultivate plants (after all, not that many)

FIG. 1: *Life Cycle of a Common Weed*, 2007. Performance documents. Photos by Alia Farid.

as it was a way to cultivate dialogue, community engagement, and empathy. *Flood* and *LCCW* share the ethos of what interdisciplinary researchers Beatriz da Costa and Kavita Philip (2008) call "tactical biopolitics" to renegotiate biopower within the art context. As artist Laurie Palmer reflects, *Flood* was "somewhere between usefulness and metaphor" (2008, 65). The intention of *LCCW* is to catalyze the usefulness of metaphor.

As *Life Cycle of a Common Weed* entered the public realm, this small, closed transaction modestly began to disrupt the everyday biopolitical order and codes of taboo that regulate bodies and their microbiological traces. I held a residency in 2007 at the Rensselaer Polytechnic Institute's Center for Biotechnology and Interdisciplinary Studies, at the invitation of the BioArts Initiative. Spearheaded by artists Kathy High, Daniela Kostova, and Rich Pell, the BioArts Initiative began as the first formalized collaboration between art and biotechnology in the United States, aligned with the practices of artists such as the Critical Art Ensemble, Adam Zaretsky, and the Tissue Culture and Art Project (see generally Kac 2007; Hauser and FACT 2008; Pandilovski 2008). These artists, among others, have worked directly with biotechnical materials and processes to question modes of biopower from within and on the margins of institutions. My performance documents were exhibited alongside large, geodesic dome viral capsids and a few pots of foraged urban dandelions. I held events called *Tea Parties to Befriend a Virus* inside the viral domes and served chocolates in the shape of the hepatitis C virus. The tea parties occasioned the first multidisciplinary socializing in the new biotech center and were attended by undergraduates, administrative staff, researchers, artists, and scientific technicians. One conversation included a scientist who lovingly shared details of her twenty-year research fascination with the virulence of hepatitis B; another scientist, who studies the chemistry of the lipid surface of hepatitis C, said this was the first time he had seen the visual structure of the virus; and some attendees who had family members with hepatitis C were eager to learn about its health effects but had been afraid to ask. The dialogue was loose, distributed, and enduring.

Yet for some people in the building, the photographs of me drawing my blood with a butterfly needle provoked concern, and rumors began to circulate that I had tainted the chocolates with hepatitis C, that I carried HIV, that I was a drug user, that the viral domes were potential sites of infection. Anxiety about the spatialization of real bodies and biota touched a delicate nerve—even in a center of scientific research. The Officer of Biosafety paid me a visit, accompanied by the operations director. He demanded to know, "When was the last time those dandelions had blood?" He asserted that the dandelions violated the biocontainment protocol of the center's laboratories (see generally USDHHS 2007), despite the fact that the public area where the plants were exhibited was subject to rules of hygiene, but not those of lab safety. Despite my careful explanation that transmission of hepatitis C occurs through direct blood-to-blood contact and not via potted plants, it was clear that fear was the issue, not safety. When he threatened to shut down the exhibition, I admitted that the dandelions had not yet been fertilized with my blood. After some debate about whether the project was a lie or a metaphor, the exhibition was allowed to continue.

Squeamishness toward needles aside, *LCCW* is rather benign as performance art. Artists such as Marina Abramovic, Orlan, Ron Athey, Ana Mendieta, and others have extended the possibilities of bodies in far more painful and voluminously bloody public performances. Ritual, catharsis, taboo, and the sacred all figure strongly into the work of these performance artists. The art context, as an institutional framework and a public space, can be the stage of conflicting biopolitical agendas. Bodies and biota are configured according to what Mary Douglas calls "a systematic ordering and classification of matter," and practices that are a "contravention of that order" become threateningly ambiguous (2002, 44). Such "matter out of place" (art, questionably pathogenic blood, fluids, weeds) is managed through the symbolic system of taboo, which "confronts the ambiguous and shunts it into the category of the sacred" (xi). The sacred space of ritual and ceremony is the designated site within the symbolic system where a subject becomes, according to Victor Turner, "undifferentiated raw material" (1967, 98)—an ambiguous figure undergoing cathartic transformation. In the sense that the "shock of the new" is a ritual under modernity, the contemporary art context operates as a designated sacred space as it explores, exposes, and reconfigures the taboo. In making explicit the perimeters of normalcy and comfort, the performance of the taboo and the dramatization of ambiguity offer the catharsis of transgression within the delimited zone of art exhibition.

In *LCCW*, on the other hand, I confront ambiguous "matter out of place" and shunt it into the category of the everyday by desensationalizing the act of opening up the body and reappropriating it as quotidian plant cultivation. During the incident at the RPI biotech center, *LCCW* complicated the boundaries between territories where permeable human bodies, microbes, and vegetal matter all circulate. *LCCW* is not a cathartic and sensational transgression of taboos. Instead, it embodies a kind of relational aesthetic (see generally Bourriaud 1998; Bishop 2004) of "matter out of place" by serving as "the linking element, a principle of dynamic agglutination" (Bourriaud 1998, 21) in the realms of human-microbial-social relations. *LCCW* engages the relational aspects of biopolitics by giving rise to anxieties about the containment of bodies, fluids, and infections, even as these fears may have little to do with actual dangers. Potted dandelions fertilized with blood in the center's lobby may not have violated protocol and may have been no more threatening than sanitary napkin disposal units in their restrooms. But the dandelions disrupt the spatial circulation of risk. Defined boundaries—public/private, my body/ your body, viral/human—become less distinct upon closer examination. *LCCW* may not transgress those material boundaries, but it turns the gaze toward a micropolitical "zone of indiscernibility" (Deleuze and Guattari 1987, 226), populated by slippages, ambiguities, and lines of escape from power.

The incident at the RPI biotech center indicated that *LCCW* is not a closed, private transaction between the plants and me but is instead a site for the private and public to converge and make apparent the biopolitics of boundaries and relations. It became an opportunity to create a micropolitical, post-Pasteurian revision of the outbreak narrative that contended with other people, microbial actors, and vegetal agents moving through space. I decided it was important to invite other bodies into this system of circulation. *LCCW* then became another transaction, one in which the public was solicited to fertilize the dandelions with their blood in exchange for dialogue, dandelion root tea, and seedlings.

Tactics of Anxiety

As a collective activity, drawing out blood from our bodies and feeding it to weeds facilitates lateral transfers on several different levels, including communication, contagion, interspecies minglings, and incorporation. Venous blood is not an excretion or a secretion (Farage and Maibach 2006, 150–160) but a fluid whose flow is induced only by bodily disruption. Such disruption initiates subjective disturbances and places us in a zone of uncertainty and anxiety: a productive liminal space (Turner 1967).

An aesthetic of pathetic absurdity pervades *LCCW*, encapsulating a genuine desire for transformation in the face of apparent insurmount-ability. I am not farming humans for dandelions, and a small prick from the finger is not quite equivalent to being uprooted, chopped, toasted, and made into tea. Yet the caring gesture of intentional blood transfusion to a weed provokes conversation about the possibility of empathic interspecies encounter. Empathy describes a stepping-outside-of-oneself that enables an imaginative alter-subjectivity. *LCCW* imagines the dandelion as a reciprocal empathic subject that offers its own vegetal matter as a dispro-portionate remedy for a diseased person within a vacuum of social respon-sibility and care. Nevertheless, this encounter is not without antagonism, inevitably becoming embroiled in the fruitful dialectic of consumption. *LCCW* entails the eventual and complete destruction of the dandelion-as-autonomous-plant for its use as nutrition, exactly the dilemma of human exceptionalism and interspecies encounter problematized by Donna Har-away in *When Species Meet*: "Trying to make a living, critters eat critters but can only partly digest one another. Quite a lot of indigestion, not to mention excretion, is the natural result, some of which is the vehicle for new sorts of complex patternings of ones and manys in entangled asso-ciation" (2008, 31). The mutuality of these associations is what Haraway calls "becoming with," an expansion of Deleuze and Guattari's concept of "becoming" through alliance as opposed to filiation (1987, 234). Yet "becoming with" encompasses interspecies antagonisms and the conun-drum of human exceptionalism.

One of the dyspeptic elements in the *LCCW* transaction is the viral matter *not* incorporated by the plants. The symbolism of the blood as a gift (rather than poison) persists because human viruses do not (so far) infect plants. As agents of evolution, viruses can perform lateral genetic transfers between unrelated organisms (Margulis and Sagan 2002). After the human genome was sequenced in 2003, endogenous retroviruses were found to account for 8 percent of the volume of human genetic material as parasitic symbionts that laterally integrated with humans (Ryan 2004). Anthropologist Stefan Helmreich describes viruses as "alien to vitality yet enmeshed with it" (2009, 192). In an antagonistic, transductive becoming-with across the interspecies evolutionary bramble, "viral genes usher the liminal, putatively nonliving, into the genetic center of 'life' itself" (192). Helmreich proposes a "symbiopolitics" to rethink the social relations of micro- and macrobial worlds.

It is this liminal, unseen, exogenous other that I ask us to consider "becoming with" in *LCCW*. We are not battling disease but enmeshed with it. Contagion is everywhere as our permeable selves come into proximity with each other and potential contaminations. In supervising the circulation of the unseen within a fluid world, which boundaries do we claim? Acknowledging the liminal presence of viruses and contagion is to dissolve the molar scale of plant-human transaction to the micro scale. Deleuze and Guattari argue that desire and proximity, the force of "becomings," are "already molecular" (1987, 272). "Becoming molecular" is to become particulate in our interrelations, to frame social relations symbiopolitically. I formulated *LCCW* as a zone of proximity for material, corporeal transaction as well as for intersubjective empathic encounter and dialogical transformation. The audience must be enlisted in this material exchange of blood and plants. Within these circuits of consumption and digestion, the dialogical exchange vertiginously doubles as the audience itself becomes a medium within the artwork. The zone of proximity in *LCCW* enables a kind of "becoming endogenous," whereby the audience and the artwork become indistinguishable.

Both the disruption of boundary formations and the liminal presence of contagion produce anxiety. The HIV/AIDS epidemic in the age of microbiology has brought awareness to the porosity of bodies while leaving incomplete the detailed knowledge of disease etiologies and access to their prevention. During an exhibition opening at the Boston Center for the Arts Mills Gallery in 2009, the crowd lingered by the food table near the *LCCW* dandelions in a large, sculptural planter. Someone read the artwork label that listed "small quantities of human blood" among the materials and said, "Oh there's blood in there. Maybe viruses." In response, people gently cupped their hands over their drinks, as if the blood had pervaded the air and fluid around them. *LCCW* produces anxiety as biotic material is eaten and transformed and as the virus—the exogenous other with unknown metamorphic and biotic potential—lurks in the environment. We can identify the virus as an agent, but to speak for this intimate alien as a subject would be illusory. The viral, in between human and plant materiality, occupies the liminal zone of imagination. As it opens into this zone, anxiety has productive political potential.

I am more interested in disruption as an artistic strategy than in the catharsis of shock. The intention to shock is manipulative, funneling the audience to one margin or another and narrowing the nuance of response.

FIG. 2: *Life Cycle of a Common Weed*, 2009. Public fertilization of dandelions with human blood in exchange for a dandelion sprout. Mills Gallery, Boston. Photos by Gina Siepel and Sara Smith.

FIG. 3: Participants fertilize the dandelions with their own diluted blood. Photos by Gina Siepel and Sara Smith.

More often than not, the most interesting issues raised by shocking art-works are silenced because the audience is preoccupied with the emotional tumult of offense, the smugness of identifying with the naughty perpetra-tor, or disinterest because the artwork is not extreme enough. Polarization fails to recognize the tendency of individuals to waver, to be hypocriti-cal and uncertain, to fail even amid our best intentions, to be stumped. Certainly, *épater la bourgeoisie* is sometimes the necessary and effective approach, and shock is entirely subjective. But for the insidiousness of everyday biopolitics, anxiety and ambiguity are richer political territory.

In the sense that catharsis is the expulsion of excrement, or the "purifi-cation of the emotions through vicarious experience" (*OED*), "noncathar-sis" is the interminable suspense of the purgation of tension. Anxiety is a noncathartic feeling that has had no legacy of inspiring Greek tragedies, operas, or epic novels. Unlike anger or sorrow, the incoherent tensions of anxiety lack cathartic release. It is among literary theorist Sianne Ngai's taxonomy of "ugly feelings" that "could be said to give rise to a nonca-thartic aesthetic: art that produces and foregrounds a failure of emotional release (another form of suspended 'action') and does so as a kind of poli-tics" (2005, 9). Ngai traces the spatialization of anxiety not as a matter of interiority, but as a vertiginous in-between of unarticulated insides and outsides. The self-reflective agitation of anxiety, she argues with some con-tempt, has become the "distinctive 'feeling-tone' of intellectual inquiry itself" in the modern era (215). Anxious intellectual inquiry turns ratio-nality into an inconclusive oscillation. It is the antecedent to absurdity, which is similarly noncathartic in its complete suspension of reason and failure to cohere.

Artworks that reveal the boundaries of our anxiety without pushing us to one edge or another instead make us sit with ourselves in a festering confusion. Such artworks might bring us to a becoming-with, an openness to transformation through contact, contagion, and encounter. Although I hope to have developed a site of potential with concern and responsibility, the cathartic resolution of intellectual inquiry is left with the audience. The artwork may not occasion satisfaction or offer the opportunity to absolve guilt. But in revealing layers of ambiguous emotions, it opens a space to confront uncertainty and form responsibilities in an embroiled world of permeable, distributed biota.

Reciprocity and Alliance

Two days before a public fertilization at the Mills Gallery, I received an apologetic message from the curator, informing me that he had decided to cancel the event: "I just heard back from someone from the Department of Public Health, and it is illegal to handle human blood if you are not a certified nurse. And also an inspector from the Department of Public Health must be present. I'm really sorry, um, give me a call please." Naturally, I was confused, but not surprised. I responded, "I do not, by any means, wish to do any illegal activity or endanger anyone, which is why I carefully researched these methods and their uses. I am still unclear about what is specifically illegal about my proposal." Disappointed but optimistic, I imagined that an interesting bureaucratic dialogue might emerge that would ensnarl spatial fluid trafficking within public and private spaces, as well as institutional unintelligibles. Instead, the curator admitted that his own anxieties had prevented him from discussing the event with the board of the nonprofit gallery. The blood fertilization was one potential liability among many in an exhibition that already contained frozen spit, fire code hazards, false alarms, a moving column, live plants, and a sharp sword. He had simply become uneasy and, at the last minute, contacted the public health department. After further discussion of the procedure, it was clear that nothing was illegal or unsafe. He courteously gave me the option to proceed, with the understanding that it would put him in a potentially "awkward" position. Despite the dangers of hitting a nerve in the institutional ganglia, I persisted with actualizing the event.

LCCW is not just about laying bare the fastidious micro workings of biopolitics within institutions. Rather, this anxiety-producing zone of contagion is a potential site for intimacy, alliances, and reciprocity. It needs the audience for its realization. At the public fertilization event at the Mills Gallery, I collected drops of blood from volunteers, including the curator, one at a time. I provided each participant with over-the-counter implements used by people with diabetes to measure glucose: cleansing pads and a sterile lancet. I demonstrated how to massage one's fingers to increase circulation to the tips, swab the skin with alcohol, administer the lancet and squeeze a few drops of blood into a small cup of water to dilute the potent substance. One person found the hygiene excessive and wanted people to share plastic cups to avoid being wasteful (I had to refuse). Some were nervous and asked me to do it for them (as a certified yet uninsured phlebotomist, I could not take on the liability), while others were confidently well versed in these medical gestures. Within the unfamiliarity of these actions, there was much room for thoughtful meandering. Some asked which viruses could be airborne and how; the differences between hepatitis A, B and C; whether mad cow disease could be communicated through plants; if viruses enjoyed the climate of soil. Many participants asked detailed questions about bodily fluids as plant fertilizers, from which long conversations ensued about techniques in gardening, foraging, urban subsistence farming, *Little Shop of Horrors* and *Soylent Green*. After pouring their diluted blood into the lush planter full of dandelions, participants received a small cup of dirt with dandelion seeds to grow at home. Many were careful to choose which of the dandelions in the planter looked like they needed the most attention. Some complained that I should have just left the dandelions in their weedy lots, where they would have been happier. One woman went home to share the health benefits of dandelion tea on her Indian reservation, where diabetes is an ongoing problem. Several weeks later, some participants sent photographs of freshly sprouted dandelion greens sunning in windowsills.

The material and symbolic comminglings of the audience with the artwork can form shifting relations among the audience members themselves and with me, as the administrator of the gesture. Giving blood has a symbolically rich history linked to nation-building (Titmuss 1971; Starr 1998; Waldby and Mitchell 2006), and can facilitate social transactions and alliances outside of hereditary "blood bonds" (see generally Weston 2001). The overwhelming response of blood donation after the events of September 11, 2001 in New York attests to the identification of self within the substance of blood—the gift of one's own vitality for another. Yet many human substances such as placenta, hair, blood, organs, eggs, tissue samples, and umbilical cord blood are entrenched in global circuits of commerce that belie the notion of the "gift" (Scheper-Hughes 2002; Waldby and Mitchell 2006; Landecker 2007; Cooper 2008). Narratives of altruism and civic participation, which bestow virtues upon the giver, promote the extraction of blood even if, as Catherine Waldby and Robert Mitchell's (2006) extensive analysis of Titmuss's *Gift Relationship* shows, the process of fractioning blood "maximized the use value of the donation but also diluted its ontological and civic value, making it more like a pharmaceutical substance and less like a gift from one citizen to another" (Waldby and Mitchell 2006, 43–44). Yet this does little to change the dynamics of blood donation on the supply side, as powerful imagery of the gift persists.

Anthropologist Steffen Dalsgaard (2007), in his study of blood donation in Denmark, probes the "strategies of reciprocity" used to maintain a stable base of blood donors. In the absence of a one-to-one transaction of whole blood to a patient in need, and excepting moments of crisis like 9/11, what maintains donors' motivation? Dalsgaard identifies how a connection is established with the grateful and hospitable nurses, who acknowledge donors as whole beings, provide juice and chocolate, and serve as surrogates of reciprocity by accepting the blood donation. This last is critical, Dalsgaard argues, because "the donor is accepted when his or her gift is accepted, and a certain degree of reciprocity is intrinsic in the acceptance and reception itself. This is why it is said that giving is a gift in itself" (2007, 112). The human staff that constitute the medical arena are the symbolic and material mediators of fluid transfers enabled by techno-scientific advances. In a philosophical account of his own liver transplant precipitated by hepatitis C, Francisco Varela describes the entanglement of the medical "team," the technoscientific stewards, with his own embodied experience and the offered body, the organ that "came tumbling down a complex social network from a recently dead body to land into my insides in that fateful evening" (2001, 260).

As the artist of *LCCW*, I am the pivot of reciprocity between the public and the dandelions. My role in creating a safe, welcoming environment and clear, methodical instruction helps to establish trust. Pedagogy is integrated into the activity itself, showing-by-doing enacted in demonstrations of requisite biosafety procedures, acknowledging each member of the audience as a whole person, accepting the gift of his or her participation, explaining the mutually nutritious properties of blood and dandelions, and allowing ample opportunity for questions and discussion among the participants. If willing, the audience contributes its curiosity and altruism to accomplish my artistic intentions. The work finds its way into the bodies of the audience, resolving the material and conceptual transfer to create a third space in which the boundary between the artwork and the audience is itself permeable and indistinct. In its noncatharsis, the tension of *LCCW* expands outside the event, as fresh attention is brought to bear upon microbial exchanges, weeds, and prearticulate political agencies. Such expansion is principally expressed as a "strategy of reciprocity," whereby the artwork is a dialogical encounter to forge alliances among people—however temporary—in which mutual acknowledgment may form the basis for resistive micropolitical interventions and knowledge production within viral biopolitics.

Acknowledgments

Many thanks to Stefan Helmreich and Eben Kirksey for their adventurous and tireless editorial vision for this essay. I am also grateful for the insightful contributions of Krzysztof Wodiczko, Caroline Jones, Anna Altman, Gina Siepel, and the anonymous peer reviewers.

Caitlin Berrigan is an artist who works in sculpture, video, and participatory actions to open a space of potential for confronting uncertainties within the context of social issues. She was an Agnes Gund fellow at Skowhegan and artist in residence at PRO-GRAM in Berlin. She holds a master's in visual art from MIT and a bachelor's in art history and production from Hampshire College. Her work has shown at the Whitney Museum, Storefront for Art and Architecture, Hammer Museum, Gallery 400 Chicago, LACMA, Lugar a Dudas Bogotà, 0047 Gallery Oslo, and the 2010 Vancouver Olympics. She has been an invited speaker at the New Museum, Harvard Medical School, Stanford University, and the Max Planck Institute in Berlin, among others. Berrigan currently has a studio in Boston and is undertaking a large public commission from the deCordova Museum.

Works Cited

Balch, Phyllis A., and James F. Balch. 2000. *Prescription for Nutritional Healing.* New York: Avery.

Bishop, Claire. 2004. "Antagonism and Relational Aesthetics." *October* 110:51–79.

Bourriaud, Nicolas. 1998. *Esthétique relationnelle* [Relational aesthetics]. Dijon, France: Les presses du réel.

Braun, Bruce. 2007. "Biopolitics and the Molecularization of Life." *Cultural Geographies* 14:6–28.

Brill, "Wildman" Steve, and Evelyn Dean. 1994. *Identifying and Harvesting Edible and Medicinal Plants in Wild (and Not So Wild) Places.* New York: Harper Resource.

Bynum, Caroline Walker. 2007. *Wonderful Blood: Theology and Practice in Late Medieval Northern Germany and Beyond.* Philadelphia: University of Pennsylvania Press.

Carr, Anna, William H. Hylton, Claire Kowalchik, and Rodale Press. 1998. *Rodale's Illustrated Encyclopedia of Herbs.* Emmaus, PA: Rodale Press.

Conticelli, Valentina. 2001. "Sanguis Suavis: Blood Between Microcosm and Macrocosm." In *Blood: Art, Power, Politics, and Pathology,* ed. James M. Bradburne and James Clifton. Catalog of exhibition at the Museum für angewandte Kunst and the Schirn Kunsthalle, Frankfurt am Main, November 11, 2001–January 27, 2002. New York: Prestel.

Cooper, Melinda. 2008. *Life as Surplus: Biotechnology and Capitalism in the Neoliberal Era.* Seattle: University of Washington Press.

da Costa, Beatriz, and Kavita Philip. 2008. *Tactical Biopolitics: Art, Activism, and Technoscience.* Cambridge, MA: MIT Press.

Dalsgaard, Steffen. 2007. "'I Do It For the Chocolate': An Anthropological Study of Blood Donation in Denmark." *Distinktion: Scandinavian Journal of Social Theory* 14:101–17.

Deleuze, Gilles, and Félix Guattari. 1987. *A Thousand Plateaus* [Mille plateaux]: *Capitalism and Schizophrenia.* Minneapolis: University of Minnesota Press.

Douglas, Mary. 2002. *Purity and Danger: An Analysis of Concepts of Pollution and Taboo.* New York: Routledge.

Farage, Miranda A., and Howard I. Maibach. 2006. *The Vulva: Anatomy, Physiology, and Pathology.* New York: Informa Healthcare.

Fleckenstein, Jaquelyn. 2004. "Chronic Hepatitis C in African Americans and Other Minority Groups." *Current Gastroenterology Reports 2004* 6:66–70.

Foucault, Michel. 1976. *Histoire de la sexualite.* Bibliothèque des histoires. Paris: Gallimard.

Gade, Daniel W. 1991. "Weeds in Vermont as Tokens of Socioeconomic Change." *Geographical Review* 81(2):153–69.

Haraway, Donna Jeanne. 2008. *When Species Meet.* Minneapolis: University of Minnesota Press.

Hauser, Jens, and FACT (Great Britain). 2008. *Sk-Interfaces: Exploding Borders; Creating Membranes in Art, Technology, and Society.* Liverpool: Liverpool University Press.

Helmreich, Stefan. 2009. *Alien Ocean: Anthropological Voyages in Microbial Seas.* Berkeley and Los Angeles: University of California Press.

Kac, Eduardo. 2007. *Signs of Life: Bio Art and Beyond.* Cambridge, MA: MIT Press.

Khayyám, Omar. 1901. *Quatrains from Omar Khayyám.* Trans. Frederick York Powell. Oxford, UK: Howard Wilford Bell.

Kiely, Timothy, David Donaldson, and Arthur Grube. 2004. *Pesticides Industry Sales and Usage: 2000 and 2001 Market Estimates.* Washington, DC: U.S. Environmental Protection Agency.

Landecker, Hannah. 2007. *Culturing Life: How Cells Became Technologies.* Cambridge, MA: Harvard University Press.

Latour, Bruno. 2005. *Reassembling the Social: An Introduction to Actor-Network-Theory.* New York: Oxford University Press.

Mack, Richard N. 2003. "Plant Naturalizations and Invasions in the Eastern United States: 1634–1860." *Annals of the Missouri Botanical Garden* 90(1):77–90.

Mack, Richard N., and Marianne Erneberg. 2002. "The United States Naturalized Flora: Largely the Product of Deliberate Introductions." *Annals of the Missouri Botanical Garden* 89(2):176–89.

Manos, M. M., W. A. Leyden, R. C. Murphy, N. A. Terrault, and B. P. Bell. 2008. "Limitations of Conventionally Derived Chronic Liver Disease Mortality Rates: Results of a Comprehensive Assessment." *Hepatology* 47(4):1150–57.

Margulis, Lynn, and Dorion Sagan. 2002. *Acquiring Genomes: A Theory of the Origins of Species.* New York: Basic Books.

Milesi, Cristina, Steven W. Running, Christopher D. Elvidge, John B. Dietz, Benjamin T. Tuttle, and Ramakrishna R. Nemani. 2005. "Mapping and Modeling the Biogeochemical Cycling of Turf Grasses in the United States." *Environmental Management* 36(3):426–38.

Ngai, Sianne. 2005. *Ugly Feelings.* Cambridge, MA: Harvard University Press.

Palmer, Laurie. 2008. "Dirt / Flood / Leaks." In *With Love from Haha: Essays and Notes on a Collective Art Practice,* ed. Wendy Jacob, Laurie Palmer, and John Ploof. Chicago: WhiteWalls; distributed by University of Chicago Press.

Pandilovski, Melentie, Experimental Art Foundation (Australia), and Adelaide Festival of Arts. 2008. *Art in the Biotech Era.* Adelaide: Experimental Art Foundation.

Paxson, Heather. 2008. "Post-Pasteurian Cultures: The Microbiopolitics of Raw-Milk Cheese in the United States." *Cultural Anthropology* 23(1):15–47.

Rabinow, Paul. 1996. *Essays on the Anthropology of Reason.* Princeton: Princeton University Press.

Repo Man. 1984. Dir. Alex Cox. 92 min. Edge City: Los Angeles.

Robbins, Paul, and Julie T. Sharp. 2003. "Producing and Consuming Chemicals: The Moral Economy of the American Lawn." *Economic Geography* 79(4):425–451.

Ryan, Frank P. 2004. "Human Endogenous Retroviruses in Health and Disease: A Symbiotic Perspective." *Journal of the Royal Society of Medicine* 97:560–65.

Scheper-Hughes, Nancy. 2002. *Commodifying Bodies.* London: Sage.

Stanley, Autumn. 1993. *Mothers and Daughters of Invention: Notes for a Revised History of Technology.* Metuchen: Scarecrow Press.

Starr, Douglas P. 1998. *Blood: An Epic History of Medicine and Commerce.* New York: Alfred A. Knopf.

St. John, T. M., and L. Sandt. 2005. "The Hepatitis C Crisis." *Ethnicity and Disease* 15(2):S2-52–S2-57.

Titmuss, Richard Morris. 1972. *The Gift Relationship: From Human Blood to Social Policy.* New York: Vintage Books.

Turner, Victor Witter. 1967. *The Forest of Symbols: Aspects of Ndembu Ritual.* Ithaca: Cornell University Press.

U.S. Department of Agriculture (USDA), Natural Resources Conservation Service. "Plants Profile," s.v. *Taraxacum officinale* F.H. Wigg: common dandelion. http://plants.usda.gov/java/profile?symbol=TAOF

U.S. Department of Health and Human Services (USDHHS), Public Health Service, Centers for Disease Control and Prevention and National Institutes of Health. 2007. *Biosafety in Microbiological and Biomedical Laboratories.* Washington, DC: U. S. Government Printing Office.

Varela, Francisco J. 2001. "Intimate Distances: Fragments for a Phenomenology of Organ Transplantation." *Journal of Consciousness Studies* 8(5–7):259–71.

Wald, Priscilla. 2008. *Contagious: Cultures, Carriers, and the Outbreak Narrative.* Durham: Duke University Press.

Waldby, Cathy, and Robert Mitchell. 2006. *Tissue economies : Blood, organs, and cell lines in late capitalism.* Durham N.C.: Duke University Press.

Weston, Kath. 2001. "Kinship, Controversy, and the Sharing of Substance: The Race/Class Politics of Blood Transfusion." In *Relative Values: Reconfiguring Kinship Studies*, ed. Sarah Franklin and Susan McKinnon. Durham: Duke University Press.

World Health Organization. 1997. *Weekly Epidemiological Record* 72:341–348.

Viral/Species/Crossing:
Border Panics and Zoonotic Vulnerabilities

Melissa Autumn White

We are all in this together, and we will all get through this together.
Dr. Margaret Chan, director-general of the
World Health Organization, June 11, 2009

Immunity and invulnerability are intersecting concepts, a matter of consequence in a
nuclear culture unable to accommodate the experience of death and finitude within
available liberal discourse on the collective and personal individual. Life is a window
of vulnerability. It seems a mistake to close it.
Donna Haraway, Primate Visions: Gender, Race and Nature in the World of
Modern Science

In late April 2009, a novel strain of influenza, now understood to be composed of a recombination of genetic information associated with avian, human, and two swine viruses, made its debut in Mexico. Commonly referred to as "swine flu," given initial concerns that the virus had shifted from a strain infecting pigs to one affecting humans, the strange permutation of novel influenza A (H1N1) was soon declared to have resulted in a viral pandemic by the World Health Organization (WHO). Within six weeks of its emergence, close to thirty thousand confirmed cases in seventy-four countries had been identified (WHO 2009c). By September of 2009, nearly three thousand people had died and preparations for a second "wave" of the pandemic were well under way.

Despite the swiftness of its transmission, the swine flu did not deliver upon its catastrophic promise of massive infection and death on a "global" scale. Indeed, in January 2010 the WHO began to respond to allegations that it had produced, in cahoots with Big Pharma, a phony pandemic

 117

designed to "bring economic benefit to industry." Countering this accusation, WHO director-general Dr. Margaret Chan responded with a "reassurance" that the virus was, in fact, serious; as she put it, "The world is going through a real pandemic. The description of it as fake is wrong and irresponsible" (WHO 2010b). But after a further seven anticlimactic months coming down from H1N1 alertness, Dr. Chan, invoking a biopolitical global population in the process of address, reminded "the world" that "pandemics, like the viruses that cause them, are unpredictable." With that, the H1N1 pandemic was deemed to have run its course, and August 2010 was marked as the time of transition into an official "post-pandemic period" (WHO 2010a).

This essay emerges in partial response to the multiple border vulnerabilities (national, affective, species) illuminated by "zoonoses," dis-eases that stealthily cross, via viral recombinations, the heavily invested species border between human and nonhuman animals.[1] Through two brief but exemplary cases drawn from Canadian institutional responses to the swine flu pandemic, this essay aims to generate space to explore the entanglements of biopolitics and pandemic governance, and, more specifically, what the multiple border panics invoked by the specter of unstoppable risk illuminates about the state of the nation-state under conditions of "late" capitalism. I critically examine the seemingly paradoxical responses of Citizenship and Immigration Canada to the problem of migrant agricultural laborers sourced from "ground zero" of the pandemic, along with those of Health Canada to the declaration of a "swine flu state of emergency" by chiefs of First Nations reservations in the northern regions of the province of Manitoba to offer a cartography of the increasing convergence of bio- and necropolitics in *shared spaces* of the nation (rather than spaces of exception). To do this, I proceed through an analytics of "global apartheid," a referent that attempts to name the ways that smoothed apparatuses of governing "life itself" rely on endlessly intimate, intricate, and proximate geographies of striated difference, where subjects of life and those subjected to death jostle up against one another, cheek by jowl, but not "higgledy-piggledy." Viruses, especially those that move across species boundaries, insistently reveal the fundamental interdependency and vulnerability of all lives and thus illuminate the very conditions upon which (affective) politics unfold today. Their crossings, and governmental responses to their crossings, therefore have much to tell us about the contemporary role of the nation-state in the multiplication of capital.[2]

Temporality, Smooth and Striated Space

In her recent book, *Walled States, Waning Sovereignty*, Wendy Brown argues that the building of walls at the perimeter of a growing number of nation-alized territories is symptomatic of the *decline* of state sovereignty rather than its aggrandizement under conditions of globalization. Ultimately walls can't keep people out, and so they represent a crudely physical depiction of psycho-political uncertainty, a defensive response to a deeply felt vulnerability (Brown 2010). Fortifications emerge as sovereignty wanes; even walled states cannot completely interdict those who are determined enough—desperate enough—to cross into the interior. But if sovereignty is under siege at the perimeter, nation-states have certainly found ways of making this porosity productive; the quite literal state *production* of differ-entially valued lives—the categorization of those who belong against those who don't, and the gradations in between—almost certainly remains a key technology through which the nation-state manifests an indispensability to global capitalism. Yet Brown argues that in the contemporary moment, "states *do not dominate or order*, but *react* to the movements and impera-tives of capital as well as other global phenomenon" (67, my emphasis). In this compressed time of "globalization," capital may move swiftly across the smoothed algorithmic space of predictable populations and transnationalized financial markets, thus loosening the perceptible bonds between labor, human activity, affect, and the state, quickening the pace of what Zygmut Bauman (2007) has referred to as "liquid modernity." Nev-ertheless, the nation-state remains a crucial node in the production and organization of the uneven distribution networks that create the strati-fied valuation of some lives against other "wasted lives" (Bauman 2004; Sharma 2006).[3] Contra Brown, I argue that relatively wealthy (if rapidly plummeting) Western nation-states and extraterritorialized spaces, such as the European Union, assert their indispensability to global capitalism precisely through *ordering* differentially valued lives in space and time through the apparatuses of citizenship, immigration, and border controls.

States (re)produce the uneven geopolitical stratification of vulner-abilities so fundamental to late capitalism, not only through logics of inclusion/exclusion but also through the uneven national allocation of residency rights and privileges that effectively render bodies differentially valued *within* as well as *across* the spaces and borders of the national-ized state (Sharma 2006, 145). In this way, the distinction between citizens (authorized residents) and noncitizens (temporarily authorized or unauthorized residents) is a fundamental technology of what Nicolas De Genova refers to as the fragmentation of "laboring humanity as a whole" (2010, 49). Indeed, as the very possibility of state sovereignty continues to wane under conditions of financialized capitalism, it is in part through this bifurcation of the vital "heterogeneous powers of living labour" (49) that the state assumes/resumes its power; this split is achieved through the imposition of temporal and spatial restrictions on the free movements of laboring bodies, only some of which are recognized as subjects (i.e., citizen-subjects) by the state.[4] The racialized, ethnicized, sexual, and gendered stratification of occupants who live within common territorial enclosures is achieved, in part, through the delineation of deeply unstable and highly invested state categories of (un)belonging, such as "citizen," "permanent resident," "migrant," "aboriginal," and "refugee" (Sharma 2006; Luibhéid 2005, xi). Those categorized as nonimmigrant migrant workers, illegalized migrants, aboriginal and (other) contingent/precarious residents are thus central to the flows of capital, yet may live and die within a given territory without ever being formally recognized by the state apparatus as belonging (Sharma and Chan 2007).

The state requires a territorial component in order to be recognized as such, and this continual reterritorialization is achieved in part through the spatial and temporal organization/stratification of laboring bodies/subjects. As multiple states are fortifying their borders with crudely physical walls at an unprecedented pace (Brown 2010), striations of space and time are less visibly but nonetheless continually being achieved not only at the perimeters of territory, but also within their boundaries. These are lived and biopolitical striations that a number of thinkers have referred to as nothing less than an *effective* (i.e. emergent, rather than strictly "calculated") system of *global apartheid*—one that is achieved through the management and control of the "right to have rights" (Arendt 1968, 296) accorded with citizenship (Richmond 1994; Hardt and Negri 2004; Sharma 2006; Nevins 2008; White 2010).

Significantly, this regime of effective global apartheid is not a "top down" organization of strictly racialized separations; rather I suggest it can be understood as a supple process—or meshwork—of governance that first produces, and then orders, *nationalized* bodies in time and in space.[5] Although this ordering of nationalized bodies—vis-à-vis legal regimes of violence that render some persons natural-born citizens and others

colonized or temporary indentured workers—the juridical and territorial sovereignty of the state is reified. Fortification is thus achieved not
only through crude walls at the perimeter but more insidiously through
the ordering of bodies (as with and without rights) within the interior. As
Nandita Sharma explains, global apartheid describes the geopolitical organization of "an ever-widening differentiation between people in wealthy
and impoverished national states through restrictive immigration policies that imprison impoverished people within zones of poverty" (2006,
29). But crucially, these zones of poverty and segregation are also ordered
within relatively wealthy nation-states;[6] thus, global apartheid refers to the
political institutions and acts of governance that allow an effectively striated humanity (of citizen-subjects and noncitizen-others) to increasingly
"confront one another . . . *within the same spaces* of practical everyday life"
(De Genova 2010, 54; also see Sharma 2006, 140–55). It can also refer to
aboriginal residents and other colonized people violently displaced from
the very basis of their survival by processes of annexation that function, in
part, through respatializing relationships between the land as economic
base and indigenous inhabitants to continue the colonial process of "accumulation by dispossession" (Harvey 2003). The reservation system in
Canada is rooted in just such a system of accumulation by dispossession,
to which I return to discuss below.

The responses of the Canadian government to the swine flu outbreak
of 2009 illuminate the convergences of bio- and necropolitics in shared
nationalized spaces, a convergence that the referent "global apartheid"
attempts (however imperfectly) to name. Déjà vu–like, the tempo-politics
of the swine flu marked the return to a future into which the WHO had jet-
tisoned "the world" since invoking a general pandemic alert in 2005, after
working since 2002 on developing viral response capacities such as early
warning systems, vaccine, and antiviral guidelines (Stephenson and Jamieson 2009, 525). The speculative future of a massive global pandemic had
been looming since the outbreak in Hong Kong in 1997 of avian influenza
A virus H5N1, a strain of influenza that resulted in a low rate of human
infection and had no known human-to-human transmission trajectory,
but which led to the "precautionary" slaughter of the entire chicken population, estimated to be nearly 1 million birds. When the pandemic finally
arrived—dressed, as it were, in pig's clothing—a complex assemblage of
responses was set into motion at the global, regional, and local levels: from
international information sharing between human and animal health orga-

nizations to regional and transnational surveillance networks to anachro-
nistic local responses.[7] As Geoffrey Whitehall and others have argued, the
anticipation of the immanent emergency of the pandemic influenza effectively produced an emergency before it had become one, thus facilitating
the development of a swift and profoundly affective mode of governance
that "engender[ed] obedience and political will" through the production
of "strong emotional responses" (Whitehall 2009, 161; Stephenson and
Jamieson 2009, 525).[8]

The production of preemptive states of emergency—such as that
which served as an effective "justification" for the permanent war on/
of terror—have been theorized as part of a technology of what Gilles
Deleuze, in his own anticipatory structure of feeling, described as the
coming "societies of control," characterized by a shift from the biopolitical
power of *enclosures* (Foucault) to the regulatory power over *capacities*—
that is, affects, or the "power to act" in the Spinozan sense (Deleuze 1992;
Clough 2003; Massumi 2002; Puar 2007; Whitehall 2009). While many
elements of this shift in power have arguably been realized in the contemporary moment, given the financialization of capitalism and the concomitant shift from colonial (i.e., direct and territorialized) governance to
imperial (i.e., speculative and deterritorialized) transnational control, the
nation-state remains a central node in the production of the very possibility of control; technologies of enclosure (striations of space) and the
smoothed spaces of securitization are coextensive.[9] State technologies of
enclosure, ordering bodies in space and time, have not unraveled under the
intensifications of speculative capitalism and the societies of control and
indeed are necessary to its flows. This is evidenced clearly in the following
two cases, which offer seemingly paradoxical responses by the Canadian
state to the multiple border vulnerabilities set racing with the onset of the
swine flu pandemic of 2009.

Migrant Workers/Informatic Vectors

Shortly after the outbreak of swine flu in Mexico was confirmed to be
that of a novel strain of influenza A (H1N1) by scientists at Canada's
National Microbiology Laboratory and the U.S. Centers for Disease Control, and the World Health Organization alerted, national, regional, and
international influenza plans were activated. Calls for a quarantine against
migrants and travelers to and from Mexico were publicly considered by

many nations, including the United States, Canada, and several European countries. However, both the administration of President Barack Obama and Prime Minister Stephen Harper's government decided against such measures in part because such restrictions on travel and movement would not, in fact, *stop* the spread of the virus (Avery 2010, 14; Kippax and Stephenson 2010, 206). Rather, the attempt to contain the virus at its source by halting the movements of people was framed by both governments as deeply threatening to regional and transnational trade relations at a very inopportune time, not least because the pandemic was following on the heels of the financial crisis.

In the Canadian context, concerns over pandemic transmission ultimately centered on the approximately fifteen thousand Mexican migrant workers destined for temporary agricultural work on farms across Canada, from British Columbia to Prince Edward Island. Every year, tens of thousands of Mexican and Caribbean nonimmigrant migrant workers are temporarily brought to Canada under the auspices of the Seasonal Agricultural Worker's Program (SAWP), a federally authorized program administered, pace neoliberalism, through private agencies.[10] Jamaican "guest workers" began arriving to work on Canadian farms in 1966, the year in which Canada's migrant agricultural workers program was created, and the program was expanded to include Mexican migrant laborers in 1974, the year in which SAWP was inaugurated (GWJA, n.d.). Officially, SAWP "matches workers from Mexico and the Caribbean countries with Canadian farmers who need temporary support during planting and harvesting seasons, when *qualified* Canadians or permanent residents are not available" (HRSDC 2011; emphasis mine).

The kind of labor that migrant farmworkers perform, however, is not particularly qualified, which is, in part, how the private agencies that connect employers with temporary workers justify the minimum-wage income the workers generally make and, moreover, how Citizenship and Immigration Canada justifies the temporal and spatial regulation of these contingent laboring bodies. SAWP visas tie migrants to particular employment relationships as well as limit the period of time over which a migrant worker can legally remain in the country. Foucault, in his lectures on biopolitics and the emergence of neoliberalism, suggested that "in the elements making up human capital we should also consider mobility, that is to say, an individual's ability to move around, and migration in particular" (2008, 15). Yet it is not mobility per se that is at stake, as the autonomy of migration (Papadopoulos and Tsianos 2007) makes clear; rather it is the tempospatial politics of the right to residence and, moreover, *the right to have rights*, in a given territorial enclosure. Migrant workers are, in the contemporary moment, expected to be (or are produced as) "hypermobile" even if subjected to intense regimes of governance in the process of securing those mobilities, precisely because they are expected to move in accordance with the shifting requirements of the labor market. It is crucial to note that the Canadian state not only capitalizes on already existing geopolitical disparities in wealth and access to resources (though it certainly does do this), it also continually (re)produces the stratifications of wealth and opportunity so fundamental to the everyday operations of capitalism precisely through immigration regimes and, more specifically, the temporal and spatial limitations on residency and the right to have rights conferred through such regimes (cf. Sharma 2006).

Despite the fact that Canada's reliance on temporary workers from Mexico and the Caribbean is central to agricultural production in the country, the geopolitical and historiographic conditions of this reliance are largely obscured from everyday view through various modes of common sense making. At the outset of the swine flu in Mexico, however, numerous media stories appeared in newspapers across the country, with headlines playing on some variation of "Seasonal Workers Raise Swine Flu Fears on Farms," seen in the *Toronto Star*, April 29, 2009. This making visible of a usually tacit arrangement under the conditions of an emergency (i.e., that of realization of the much anticipated pandemic) marks SAWP as something like a "public secret" in Michael Taussig's (1999) sense, a social relation that is known but whose conditions of possibility cannot generally be articulated lest that articulation undermine everyday social functioning.[11] If Canada's reliance on, and exploitation of, nonimmigrant migrant laborers were not negated from the everyday register of official national life, the a-historical and deeply problematic trans/national imaginary of "Canada" as a benign, peacekeeping, "immigrant friendly," and multicultural nation would be undermined. Arguably, this is why, when the swine flu broke out, media stories and public attention did not focus on the conditions of Mexican migrant farm workers *as workers*, but instead upon the potential threat that these workers *as vectors of disease* posed to an invoked "Canadian public." This "public," however, emphatically does not include all the residents of the nationalized territory. Instead, the term is limited to designating those who formally belong through citizenship and permanent residency privileges—the legitimate and deserving subjects of tax-based public health governance. The nonbelonging migrant Mexican worker (whose exploitable labor is fundamental to trans/national political economy) was figured not so much as an "abject subject" to the nation but as *an informatics node*, a potential transmitter of viral "code" composed of recombined avian-swine-human genetic material.

Given the potentially devastating implications for Canadian dairy, fruit, and vegetable farms because of their reliance on migrant workers, Jason Kenney, minister of citizenship, immigration, and multiculturalism, announced that Canada would "monitor," not ban, seasonal workers by way of increased medical surveillance (CBC News 2009a). Citizenship and Immigration Canada therefore appointed two medical doctors to literally take the temperature of migrant workers before they would be allowed to leave Mexico City (CBC News 2009a). For temporary agricultural workers coming in through SAWP, this involved a "voluntarily" subjection to intensified health surveillance vis-à-vis more extensive medical screening at their own cost after traveling to Mexico City where the medical tests are performed and the work visas distributed. The border moves from the edge of the territory, reassembling in Mexico City at the visa office, and the immigration officials and medical doctors staffing the office become, in effect, agents of the border (cf. Balibar 2002). The centrality of health status to migration management is not particularly remarkable—indeed migrants are routinely denied residency privileges in Canada on the basis of their medical profile (e.g., HIV/AIDS status). This said, the scrutiny of migrant workers as potential vectors of disease transmission speaks clearly to the governance of capacities: to labor under conditions of perpetual exclusion from the right to have rights, migrant workers must demonstrate their capacity as an instrument of capital accumulation ("You're not sick, are you?"). The intensive monitoring of the movements of Mexican migrant workers, positioned as entrepreneurial poor people so crucial to the functioning of regional trade that quarantine or a closure of the border was deemed impossible, reveals the ways in which state territorializations manifest in more insidious forms than border fortifications alone.

As I noted above, discussions of a quarantine were eschewed by both the Obama and Harper governments, particularly given the economic recovery measures both countries had already heavily invested in after the (inevitable) crisis in financial capital. It is also important to note that a tripartite pandemic plan had been drafted by the Canada, Mexico, and the

United States for the North American region in August 2007, following the WHO's 2005 issuance of the global pandemic alert. The North American Plan for Avian and Pandemic Influenza (NAPAPI) represented a move to bring into correspondence the three countries' capacities to respond to the coming pandemic influenza with an explicit focus on preventing the disruption of cross-border trade in the anticipated eventuality of a pandemic outbreak. As the plan outlined, "Canada, Mexico and the United States recognize that controlling the spread of a novel strain of human influenza with minimal economic disruption is in the mutual best interest of all three countries" (NAPAPI 2007, 19). Further, the three countries agreed to work together to "contain a novel strain of human influenza at its source, slow its spread . . . [but] allow the *appropriate movement of people and cargo* across mutual land borders and ports of entry in a way to achieve the public health objective *with minimal social and economic impact*" (Avery 2010, 4; emphases mine). While the development of regional health security measures dates back to the Cold War period, as a defense measure against the possibility of a biological attacks by the Soviet Union (measures that were further strengthened in the face of the influenza pandemic of 1957), NAPAPI more directly acknowledged the threat that pandemic influenza and other infectious diseases emerging at the "animal-human-ecosystems interface" posed to global health security and, thus, to the smooth functioning of the economy (OIE et al. 2008; Avery 2010).

At the heart of NAPAPI is a tacit acknowledgment that the three countries are differently situated with regard to both their capacities to deal with an impending pandemic influenza and their reliance on the movements of people, animals, and goods. "North America" is, after all, starkly divided by what Gloria Anzaldúa has referred to as the border "where the third world grates up against the first and bleeds" (1999, 25). The apartheid wall running along the three-thousand-kilometer-long wound dividing the United States from Mexico makes this geopolitical and deeply racialized separation utterly and crudely apparent, while signaling one of the modes through which this separation is continually reproduced—that is, through controls over movement at the border based on citizenship or residency status as the state scrambles to reassert its sovereignty in the face of its undoing.

But, again, it is not just at the physical border (in the territorial sense) that the regulation of mobility occurs. Rather, interdiction regimes have moved beyond borders to regulate not mobilities per se but the temporalities and conditions of residency privileges and the right to have rights. NAPAPI provides the directives to keep people moving but to surveil them closely; movements of human and nonhuman animals are not interdicted but brought under continual regulation. This is the securitization and reterritorialization of citizenship and residency privileges—a shift in governance from an identitarian *"Who* are you?" to "Are you *authorized* to be here, and if so, *under what conditions*?" (cf. Muller 2004, 287). It is thus not merely coincidental that Canadian immigration minister Jason Kenney introduced a visa restriction for *all* Mexican travelers to Canada in July 2009, just after the swine flu was pronounced a pandemic (Citizenship and Immigration Canada 2009). The official Citizenship and Immigration Canada line was that because refugee claims filed by Mexican nationals had steadily increased over several years, something had to be done to separate "queue jumping economic migrants" from "genuine refugees." The imposition of a travel visa was framed as a measure to ensure that visitors to Canada were "true visitors" and not asylum seekers "pretending" to be tourists, rather than a less than explicit response to the swine flu outbreak (such a response, after all, would contravene NAPAPI, as outlined above). While protecting Canadian agricultural production through the expendability of Mexican migrant workers (otherwise framed as entrepreneurs willing to pay for their own medical screening and visas to ultimately become highly surveilled and contingent laborers), Citizenship and Immigration Canada simultaneously made travel to the country by other Mexican travelers and migrants (potential vectors of pandemic transmission) extremely difficult.

Specters of Death

In the epigraph from Donna Haraway above, she gestures toward the fundamental vulnerability of all life, suggesting that fantasies of "immunity and invulnerability" are defense mechanisms designed to protect a social imaginary "unable to accommodate the experiences of death and finitude" (1991, 224). While all life is constitutively vulnerable and radically interdependent, not all lives bear the burden of vulnerability and susceptibility equally (cf. Butler 2004, 2009). Nowhere is this more clear than in the asymmetrical impacts of the swine flu on variegated populations in Canada, and particularly on First Nations peoples living on reservations in the country. While aboriginal peoples do not require a "pass" to leave the space of the reservation, many aboriginal communities in Canada remain spatially isolated and physically remote. Such effective enclosures of colonized peoples in Canada have the effect of rendering these communities as "disposable populations"—not required as labor in a postindustrial society, positioned as a drain on state resources, such communities are "left to die" (Foucault 2003) in a quite literal sense.[12]

In late June 2009, the Assembly of Manitoba First Nations chiefs called on the federal government to declare a swine flu state of emergency, given the rapid rates of transmission in native communities living on reservations in the province. Close to five hundred cases had been reported, hundreds of these in the remote fly-in communities of St. Theresa Point and Garden Hill First Nations (six hundred kilometers northeast of Winnipeg). As *The National Post* reported, "a disproportionate number of Aboriginal Peoples make up the severe number of cases among Manitobans and the cramped living conditions, lack of running water in some cases, and high incidence of chronic illness are thought to be factors in the spread of disease on reserves" (Fitzpatrick 2009). Further to this, chiefs had been struggling to get the basic supplies they needed for their communities. While the use of hand sanitizers had been identified as one of the "first lines of defense" and had been implemented across the country in public institutions, the shipment of these basic supplies to native reservations were delayed for over a month because of Health Canada's concerns that the high alcohol content (over 60 percent) would be abused (i.e., consumed) by "addiction-prone" populations (CBC News 2009c). Such concerns rely on an essentializing/ eugenicist discourse of "proneness" rather than an acknowledgment of the colonial spatial organization of poverty and concomitant dis-eases of dispossession. Constituting native populations as prone casts them as childlike (hence as justifiably wards rather than subjects of the state). At the same time, this very "proneness" to mental illness, disease, and addiction simultaneously figures aboriginal populations as "unsaveable" others (vis-à-vis the neoliberal logic of privatized and active citizen-subjecthood).

For its part, Health Canada argued that the delay was merely logistical and based on the difficulty of getting supplies to the North. The whole debacle brought the living conditions of some of this territorial enclosure's most abject subjects firmly into the public eye, at least for a moment. Soon after the media spectacle, sanitation supplies were distributed and the story dropped out of the press. But by September 2009, the situation of people living on northern reservations in Manitoba was again front-page news across the country. In preparation for the anticipated "second wave" of the flu, Health Canada had sent remote communities body bags as part of their "swine flu preparation kits." The body bags contained "full post-mortem kits that included a chin strap, five-straps and three identification tags" and were interpreted by chiefs and others as "a dire prediction of what Ottawa expects will happen during this flu season to natives, who were hardest hit in the spring" (Alphonso and Ha 2009). That evening on the CBC national news, anchor Peter Mansbridge announced, in what he qualified as a "stunning development," that "the specter of death . . . has become part of Canada's readiness plan" (CBC News 2009d).

But such a move is not particularly stunning, even though, ironically enough, the federal minister of health was Leona Aglukkaq, the first Inuk appointed to the House of Commons after being elected member of Parliament in the Nunavut riding as a Conservative party member. What this preemptive, anticipatory move signaled was the fact that these are populations already abandoned by the state—indeed, as populations effectively "disappeared" from view in order for the territorial enclosure dominantly known as "Canada" to be a possibility. After delivering a pile of body bags back to Health Canada and dropping them on its doorstep, Grand Chief David Harper of the Manitoba Regional Chiefs Organization stated that it was not only deeply offensive and an indication of the degree to which native populations had been abandoned by the state, but also deeply insensitive culturally speaking. As he put it in a television interview with CBC, "When you prepare [for] death, you are obviously inviting death into your community. . . . We do not, we do not ever prepare for such matters" (CBC News 2009d).

Health Canada's official mission is to make "this country's population among the healthiest in the world as measured by longevity, lifestyle and effective use of the public health care system" (Health Canada 2011). Despite this goal, there is a well-documented gap between the health of aboriginal populations and that of Canadian permanent residents and citizens. This is a gap, not of innate susceptibility, but of poverty, although the statistical evidence is rarely framed in such terms. First Nations people, and in particularly those living on reservations, suffer much higher rates of suicide, addictions, and diabetes, as well as tuberculosis; the last of which has had profound affects on native populations throughout the five-hundred-year history of accumulation by dispossession, otherwise known as capitalism, after the Columbian "exchange."[13] The relatively high rates of these preventable diseases among aboriginal communities, especially those living on reservations, is a stark reminder of the presence of an apartheid system within the country, not just organized at its national borders. Indeed, the South African apartheid system of Bantustans, which created separate territorial enclosures for people on the basis of "race," but *justified* this literal separation through the "differential memberships" that the legal category of "citizenship" secures and naturalizes (Sharma 2006, 142), was based on the Canadian reservation system, which cordoned off natives on enclosed (and often barren) territories to clear the land (in both geographic and economic senses) for European settlement and resource extraction beginning in the late 1800s. It is crucial to recognize that First Nations people today remain excluded from Canadian citizenship, and it is, in part, through the sociolegal category of national citizenship (rather than "race" per se) that the differential statuses of peoples are maintained and naturalized. For indigenous people, reliance on the Canadian state is a kind of "slow death" (Berlant 2007), suspending such subalternized populations in an ongoing colonial relation of extraction, dispossession, and dependency (cf. Alfred 1999).

Conclusion

One of the fundamental capacities affecting one's power to act is freedom of movement. As Hannah Arendt has written, "Being able to depart for where we will is the prototypical gesture of being free, as limitation of freedom of movement has from time immemorial been the precondition for enslavement" (qtd. in De Genova 2010, 33). As this essay has argued, in the face of proliferating movement—of migrants who cross borders whether or not they are authorized to do so, of animals, of cargo, of capital, of viruses—bio- and necropolitics increasingly converge within the shared spaces of the nation-state. In the quickening time of biocultural compressions, or what Banu Subramanian and Karen Cardozo (2011) describe as "naturecultural assemblages," the constitutive vulnerability at the heart of all life may be more apparent than ever before, and yet never more stratified, cheek by jowl. Although at the time of the pandemic outbreak WHO director-general Dr. Margaret Chan offered her assurances that "we are all in this together, and we will all get through this together" (WHO 2009c), the distribution of impacts of, preparations for, and surveillance of the pandemic and the bodies it moved between was far from even.

With an ostensible focus on the governance of the swine flu pandemic, this essay has offered a sketch, however incomplete, of the ways that an effective global apartheid system functions not through border controls per se, but as a regime of continually vigilant and anxious power at work in *shared* territorial spaces of *uncommon* rights to have rights. The controlled insertion of the entrepreneurial poor (prescreened Mexican nonimmigrant temporary migrant workers) into spaces of required labor (agriculture) is a mode of foreclosing the freedom of movement; movement is suspended *effectively* through limitations on rights beyond the narrow confines of a particular employment relationship upon which such workers' right to legally remain in the country depends. At the same time, the movement of swine flu from one potentially infected body to another is mitigated, at least in part, through the increased medical surveillance downloaded onto migrants themselves (anyone coming from Mexico to Canada who was not arriving to work as effectively indentured and highly surveilled labor was, "coincidentally," subject to visa restrictions at the same time the swine flu broke out). Hand sanitizers and antivirals were distributed to all "public" buildings in Canada, but already abandoned interior others were quite literally left to die, as the shipment of body bags as a preparatory measure unmetaphorically reveals. It thus seems to bear remembering that, according to Marx, "centuries of outright and extravagant violence devoted to the subordination of labour to capital—for which the state-form is instrumental, and through which it becomes rigidified and institutionalized—eventually secure what *comes to appear* as merely 'the silent compulsion of economic relations'" (De Genova 2010, 41). Such a "silent compulsion" is at the very core of biopolitics and affective governance today.

Acknowledgments

Thanks to Dan Irving, Jackie Orr, and two anonymous reviewers for their generous and challenging engagements with earlier versions of this essay, and to the Social Sciences and Humanities Research Council of Canada for funding support. Any shortcomings remain the responsibility of the author.

Melissa Autumn White holds a Social Sciences and Humanities Research Council of Canada Postdoctoral Research Fellowship in the Department of Sociology at Syracuse University and is adjunct research professor of sexuality studies and human rights in the Institute of Interdisciplinary Studies at Carleton University.

Notes

1. This essay is a small part of a book-length project titled "*Beyond Containment: Global Health Governance, Human Rights, and Sex/Gender/Species Difference*," in which I take up the question of species-crossing and cross-species contamination in conjunction with global North-South relations and regimes of governance much more extensively.
2. Although I've taken an anonymous reviewer's point from a refracted angle here, I am indebted to him or her for this thought.
3. Bauman argues, provocatively, that "the production of 'human waste,' or more correctly wasted humans (the 'excessive' and 'redundant,' that is the population of those who either could not or were not wished to be recognized or allowed to stay), is an inevitable outcome of modernization, and an inseparable accompaniment of modernity. It is an inescapable side-effect of order-building (each order casts some parts of the extant population as 'out of place,' 'unfit' or 'undesirable')" (2004, 5; emphasis in the original).
4. Furthermore, "the reified power of the state is nothing if not yet another congealed manifestation of the objectified, estranged productive power and creative capacity of 'bare' labouring life, as that sheer vitality has come to be ensnared in distinctly capitalist social relations" (De Genova 2010, 41).
5. As Sharma elaborates, "Apartheid continues to be largely associated with race-based legal differentiations. And because such differentiations are, almost without exception, no longer an explicit part of most national legal systems, there is a strong tendency to deny that any form of apartheid exists at all. Not only does this legitimize global inequalities, it also renders as legal and legitimate the use of coercive state power against those defined as nonnationals. People differentiated on the basis of their nationality/citizenship states are told to rely on 'their own state' for protection, entitlement, and rights. In this sense, an important activity of the system of national states is the spatial definition and delineation of coercion" (2006, 142–43; emphases mine).
6. These intranational zones of poverty are regionally spatialized (e.g., the exchange of labor between the provinces of Alberta and Newfoundland) and are perhaps most starkly apparent in major urban centers where racialized poor and dispossessed residents live in urban wastelands on the borders of extremely wealthy communities (e.g., Vancouver's Downtown East Side and Regent Park in Toronto).
7. Such as Egyptian president Hosni Mubarak's order that the entire pig population in Egypt—some three hundred thousand animals—be slaughtered, a cull that generated much media attention not only because it was unnecessary and resulted in a huge garbage problem in Cairo, but also because it fed

into Islamophobic speculations that it was, in fact, an opportunistic attack on the Coptic Christian minority in the country (see, for example, Hitchens 2009).

8. For an excellent discussion of the tempo-politics of anticipation, a "thinking and living toward the future" that predominates as a structure of feeling in the present moment, see Adams, Murphy, and Clarke 2009.

9. For an insightful discussion of the distinctions between colonialism and imperialism, see Loomba 1998.

10. Provinces participating in SAWP include Prince Edward Island, New Brunswick, Nova Scotia, Quebec, Ontario, Manitoba, Saskatchewan, Alberta, and British Columbia (HRSDC 2011).

11. This is an admittedly promiscuous deployment of Taussig's notion of the public secret, which more strictly refers to "knowing what not to know," a form of social knowledge that is at the base of "our social institutions, the workplace, the family, and the state" (1999, 2).

12. The being "left to die" of aboriginal peoples is, however, a phenomenon related to not only the isolation of reservation life. Indeed, the failure of the police and Royal Canadian Mounted Police (RCMP) to investigate hundreds of missing and murdered aboriginal women involved in sex work in Vancouver and beyond is a stark case in point, and so too is the court's reluctance to persecute white perpetrators of violence against aboriginal women (see Razack's [2000] discussion of the murder of Pamela George). For a Marxian analysis of the externality of aboriginal populations in Canada to the labor market, see Bedford and Irving (2001).

13. The "Columbian 'exchange'" refers to the enormous ecological and economic movements of animals, plants, humans, diseases, and so on between (the so-called) old and new worlds beginning in 1492. Nandita Sharma argues that this "new" world is not the one Columbus "discovered" but rather the one that we've "collectively inherited," a world in which "people across oceans and continents" were first brought into a "single field of power" (2009).

Works Cited

Adams, Vincanne, Michelle Murphy, and Adele Clarke. 2009. "Anticipation: Technoscience, Life, Affect, Temporality." *Subjectivity* (28):246–65.

Alfred, Taiaiake. 1999. *Peace, Power, Righteousness: An Indigenous Manifesto*. Don Mills, Ontario, Canada: Oxford University Press.

Alphonso, Caroline, and Tu Thanh Ha. 2009. "Expecting Flu Assistance, Reserves Get Body Bags from Ottawa." *Globe and Mail*, September 16. http://m.theglobeandmail.com/news/politics/body-bags-sent-to-flu-stricken-reserves/article1290332/?service=mobile

Anzaldúa, Gloria. 1999. *Borderlands/La Frontera: The New Mestiza*. San
Francisco: Aunt Lute Books.

Arendt, Hannah. 1968 (1950). *The Origins of Totalitarianism*. New York:
Harcourt, Brace, Jovanovich.

Avery, Donald Howard. 2010. "The North American Plan for Avian and
Pandemic Preparedness: A Case Study of Regional Health Security in the
21st Century." *Global Health Governance* 3(2):1–26.

Balibar, Etienne. 2002. *Politics and the Other Scene*. New York: Verso.

Bauman, Zygmut. 2004. *Wasted Lives: Modernity and its Outcasts*. Cambridge,
UK: Polity Press.

———. 2007. *Liquid Times: Living in an Age of Uncertainty*. Cambridge, UK:
Polity Press.

Bedford, David, and Danielle Irving. 2001. *The Tragedy of Progress: Marxism,
Modernity, and the Aboriginal Question*. Halifax, Canada: Fernwood.

Berlant, Lauren. 2007. "Slow Death (Sovereignty, Obesity, Lateral Agency)."
Critical Inquiry (33)(4):754–80.

Brown, Wendy. 2010. *Walled States, Waning Sovereignty*. New York: Zone Books.

Butler, Judith. 2004. *Precarious Life: The Powers of Mourning and Violence*. New
York: Verso.

———. 2009. *Frames of War: When Is Life Grievable?* New York: Verso.

CBC News. 2009a. "Canada Will Monitor, Not Bar Mexican Farm Workers."
April 27. http://www.cbc.ca/news/canada/montreal/story/2009/04/27/
montreal-migrantworkers-swine-0427.html

———. 2009b. "Health Minister Orders Probe over Flu Body Bags." September
17. http://www.cbc.ca.canada/story/2009/09/17/liberals-swine-flu-body-
bags-reserves.html

———. 2009c. "Manitoba First Nations Declare Swine Flu State of Emergency."
June 24. http://www.cbc.ca/canada/manitoba/story/2009/06/24/
mb-emergency-first-nations manitoba.html

———. 2009d. The National (television broadcast), September 18.

Citizenship and Immigration Canada. 2009. "News Release: Canada Imposes
a Visa on Mexico." July 13. http://www.cic.gc.ca/english/department/
media/releases/2009/2009-07-13.asp

Clough, Patricia Ticineto. 2003. "Affect and Control: Rethinking the Body
'Beyond Sex and Gender.'" *Feminist Theory* (4)(3):359–64.

De Genova, Nicholas. 2010. "The Deportation Regime: Sovereignty, Space, and
the Freedom of Movement." In *The Deportation Regime: Sovereignty, Space,
and the Freedom of Movement*, ed. Nicholas De Genova and Nathalie Peutz.
Durham: Duke University Press.

Deleuze, Gilles. 1992. "Postscript on the Societies of Control." *October* (59):3–7.

Fitzpatrick, Meaghan. 2009. "First Nations Call for Swine Flu State of Emergency." *National Post,* June 24. http://www.nationalpost.com/news/ FirstNationscallsswinestateemergency/1729124/story.html

Foucault, Michel. 2003. "Society Must Be Defended": Lectures at the Collège de France, 1975–1976. Trans. David Macey. New York: Picador Press. First published 1976.

———. 2008. *The Birth of Biopolitics*: Lectures at the Collège de France, 1979–1979. Trans. Graham Burchell. New York: Palgrave Macmillan. First published 1979.

Global Workers Justice Alliance (GWJA). n.d. "Migration Data and Labour Rights." http://www.globalworkers.org/migrationdata_MX.html

Gottron, Frank. 2009. "Project BioShield: Purposes and Authorities." Congressional Research Service Report for Congress (July 6; RS21507). http://www.fas.org/sgp/crs/terror/RS21507.pdf

Haraway, Donna. 1989. *Primate Visions: Gender, Race, and Nature in the World of Modern Science.* New York: Routledge.

———. 1991. *Simians, Cyborgs, and Women: The Reinvention of Nature.* New York: Routledge.

Hardt, Michael, and Antonio Negri. 2004. *Multitude: War and Democracy in the Age of Empire.* New York: Penguin Books.

Harvey, David. 2003. *The New Imperialism.* Oxford: New York, Oxford University Press.

Health Canada. 2011. "About Mission, Values, Activities." http://www.hc-sc. gc.ca/ahc-asc/activit/about-apropos/index-eng.php

Hitchens, Christopher. 2009. "First They Came for the Pigs: The Terrible Consequences of Egypt's Swine Slaughter." Slate, 28 September. http:// www.slate.com/id/2229830/

Human Resources and Skills Development Canada (HRSDC). 2011. "Seasonal Agricultural Worker Program." http://www.rhdcc- hrsdc.gc.ca/eng/ workplaceskills/foreign_workers/ei_tfw/sawp_tfw.shtml

Kippax, Susan, and Niamh Stephenson. 2010. "Infectious Disease and Globalization." In *The Routledge International Handbook of Globalization Studies,* ed. Bryan Turner. New York: Routledge.

Loomba, Ania. 1998. *Colonialism/Postcolonialism.* New York: Routledge.

Luibhéid, Eithne. 2005. "Introduction." *Queer Migrations: Sexuality, US Citizenship, and Border Crossings,* ed. Eithne Luibhéid and Lionel Cantú Jr. Minneapolis: University of Minnesota Press.

Massumi, Brian. 2002. *Parables for the Virtual: Movement, Affect, Sensation.* Durham: Duke University Press.

Muller, Benjamin. 2004. "(Dis)Qualified Bodies: Securitization, Citizenship, and 'Identity Management.'" *Citizenship Studies* (8)(3):279–94.

Nevins, Joseph. 2008. *Dying to Live: A Story of US Immigration in an Age of Global Apartheid*. San Francisco: City Lights Press.

Papadopoulos, Dimitris, and Vassilis Tsianos. 2007. "The Autonomy of Migration: The Animals of Undocumented Mobility." In *Deleuzian Encounters: Studies in Contemporary Social Issues*, ed. Anna Hickey-Moody and Peta Mallins. New York: Palgrave Macmillan.

Puar, Jasbir K. 2007. *Terrorist Assemblages: Homonationalisms in Queer Times*. Durham: Duke University Press.

Razack, Sherene. 2000. "Gendered Racial Violence and Spatialized Justice: The Murder of Pamela George." *Canadian Journal of Law and Society* (15) (2):91–130.

Richmond, Anthony. 1994. *Global Apartheid: Refugees, Racism, and the New World Order*. Don Mills, Ontario, Canada: Oxford University Press.

Security and Prosperity Partnership of North America. 2007. "North American Plan for Avian & Pandemic Influenza." http://merln.ndu.edu/archivepdf/ARA/State/91311.pdf

Sharma, Nandita. 2006. H*ome Economics: Nationalism and the Making of "Migrant Workers" in Canada*. Toronto: University of Toronto Press.

———. 2009. "Transnationalizing Practices of Decolonization." Paper presented at the Biannual Conference of the Canadian Association for Cultural Studies (CACS), McGill University, Montreal, Canada, October 23–25.

Sharma, Nandita, and Gaye Chan. 2007. "Eating in Public." In *Constituent Imagination: Militant Investigations/Collective Theorizations*, ed. Stevphen Shukaitis and David Graeber. Oakland, Edinburg, West Virginia: AK Press.

Stephenson, Niamh, and Michelle Jamieson. 2009. "Securitising Health: Australian Newspaper Coverage of Pandemic Influenza." *Sociology of Health and Illness* 31(4):525–39.

Subramanian, Banu, and Karen Cardozo. 2011. "Beyond 'the' Animal: The Naturecultural Assemblages of Migrations and Miscegenations." Paper presented at the "Sex, Gender, Species" conference, Wesleyan University, Middletown, CT, February 25–26.

Taussig, Michael. 1999. *Defacement: Public Secrecy and the Labour of the Negative*. Stanford: Stanford University Press.

Taylor, Lesley Ciarula. 2009. "Seasonal Workers Raise Swine Flu Fears on Farms." *Toronto Star*, 29 April. http://www.thestar.com/printArticle/626077

White, Melissa Autumn. 2010. Intimate Archives, Migrant Negotiations: Affective Governance and the Recognition of 'Same-Sex' Family Class Migration in Canada. PhD diss., York University, Toronto, Canada.

Whitehall, Geoffrey. 2009. "The Aesthetic Emergency of the Avian Flu Affect."
In *The Geopolitics of American Insecurity: Terror, Power and Foreign Policy*, ed.
Francois Debrix and Marc J. Lacy. New York: Routledge.

World Health Organization (WHO). 2009a. "Cumulative Number of Confirmed
Human Cases of Avian Influenza A/(H5N1) Reported to WHO." August
31. http://www.who.int.csr/disease/avianinfluenza/country/cases_
table_2009_08_31/en/index.html

———. 2009b. "Influenza A(H1N1): Lessons Learned and Preparedness."
July 2. http://www.who.int/dg/speeches/2009/influenza_h1n1_
lessons_20090702/en.index.html

———. 2010a. "H1N1 in Post-pandemic Period." August 10. http://www.who.
int/mediacentre/news/statements/2010/h1n1_vpc_20100810/en/index.
html

———. 2010b. "Statement of the World Health Organization on Allegations of
Conflict of Interest and 'Fake' Pandemic." January 22. http://www.who.int/
mediacentre/news/statements/2010/h1n1_pandemic_20100122/en/
index.html

———. 2009c. "World Now at the Start of 2009 Influenza Pandemic." June
11. http://www.who.int/mediacenter/news/statements/2009/h1n1-
_pandemic_phase6_20090611/en/index.html

World Organization for Animal Health (OIE). World Health Organization
(WHO), The World Bank, Unicef, UN System Influenza Coordination,
Food and Agricultural Organization of the United Nations (FAO) 2008.
"Contributing to One World, One Health: A Strategic Framework for
Reducing Risks of Infectious Diseases at the Animal-Human-Ecosystems
Interface." Consultation Document, October 14.

How It Feels to Be Viral Me: Affective Labor and Asian American YouTube Performance

Christine Bacareza Balance

On March 15, 2011, just days after University of California–Los Angeles undergraduate Alexandra Wallace posted (and subsequently took down) her incendiary "Asians in the Library" video log (vlog) on YouTube, another video set ablaze Facebook walls and Twitter accounts. Jimmy Wong's "Ching Chong! Asians in the Library Song"—a satirical love song addressed to Wallace—distinguished itself from the hundreds of other ranting and remix response videos. Opening with an excerpt from the offending party's original post—as she mockingly renders a scene of Asians answering their cell phones in the library with an "Ooooh, Ching Chong Ling Long Ting Tong," Wong's video quickly shifts into a style and staging commonly associated with online vlogs. Seated and directly addressing the camera, he is framed by his home studio's accoutrements: computer and electronic keyboard on his left side and a row of cables neatly hanging on the wall behind him. Stuttering in a thick Asian accent and, in turn, deriding Wallace's own orientalist rendition, a guitar-strapped Wong introduces his song into a boom microphone that hangs near his face: "Greetings, Miss Alexandra Wallace. I'm not most . . . how you say . . . politically correct person. So please . . ." (head bows quickly) "do not take offensive. Thank you."

Viewers familiar with the "Asians in the Library" video would recognize that this introduction riffs on Wallace's own preface: while she is not the most "politically correct person," she *does* have Asian friends, and hopes, in the end, that viewers do not take offense. Wong strums a single chord, signaling a magical transformation, as the video again cuts to Wong, now guitarless but seated in the same position. This new version of Wong

 WSQ: Women's Studies Quarterly 40: 1 & 2 (Spring/Summer 2012)

purrs into the microphone without an Asian accent or tone of deference. With his recording studio–style headphones on, his seductive vocal style recalls Asian American radio disc jockey Theo Mizuhara ("Theo" on Los Angeles R&B/hip-hop station 92.3 the Beat), often assumed to be African American by unsuspecting listeners because of his deep and soothing voice. This sexier Wong calls to Wallace—"Oooh girl"—before launching into his own rendition of her library scene: "Don't think I didn't see you watching me talking on my phone yesterday . . . all sexy . . . All Ching Chong Ling Long . . . Baby, it's just code . . . It's just the way that I tell the ladies that it's time for me to get funky."

For Wong, "getting funky" means launching into an acoustic ode to Wallace, a remix and reclamation of words and phrases lifted from her original video post. The song culminates in a repeating chorus, one that "wrings the musicality of the original Ching Chong" bit while satirizing its incommensurability: "Ching Chong . . . It means I love you . . . Ling Long . . . I really need you . . . Ching Chong . . . I still don't know what that means." The song's arrangement of vocal melody and harmony, acoustic guitar, and lo-fi percussion are simple and catchy. Yet the video's visual elements— the main frame of Wong is surrounded by small boxes or PiPs (picture in pictures) of him performing each portion of the music—requires a professional style of multichannel editing. Here, Wong's video evidences the unstable divisions between amateur and professional that is characteristic of the video-sharing website YouTube, ones that have helped redefine contemporary media production.

Since its initial posting, "Ching Chong! Asians in the Library Song" has garnered almost 4 million hits worldwide, received coverage from both Asian American and mainstream U.S. press outlets, and landed the twenty-three-year-old actor/musician a role in an upcoming indie film. As a video that was able to spread quickly and across many screens, the "Ching Chong! Asians in the Library Song," in all respects, was a viral hit. While its popularity must be characterized as unexpected or accidental, in order for a YouTube video to "go viral," it must actually incorporate emotional hooks: key signifiers that catch the attention and sensibility of a particular audience. While sites like YouTube, by hosting such videos, enable the process of viral video making, these videos' successful transmission—from one user to the next—requires what media scholar Henry Jenkins has termed a larger participatory culture of related blogs, social networking sites, and mass media coverage (Jenkins 2006).

With these paradoxical and performative features, viral media has ushered in, according to journalists and industry insiders, a new generation of "Asian American YouTube stars." All but absent in the Hollywood star system and on the Billboard charts, Asian Americans—such as Ryan Higa (NigaHiga), Kevin Wu (KevJumba), and Wong Fu Productions—dominate YouTube's Most Subscribed lists.[1] Paying serious attention to this phenomenon of Asian American YouTube stars, either lauded for its democratizing potential (giving Asian American "unseen talents" a performance stage) or disparaged for its industry-driven tendencies (making visible an otherwise "unseen niche market"), I instead imagine other types of value that the stars hold for their youth audiences. It requires that we revisit this phenomenon, one branded as unforeseen, and locate it within a longer cultural history produced by the laborious acts of "feeling Asian American." As "production(s) defined by combination of cybernetics and affect" (Hardt 1999, 97), these YouTube performances—vlogs, webisodes, and musical covers—function as forms of affective labor for young Asian Americans today. While I respectfully engage the analytical language of media studies, my purpose falls more in line with a central theoretical concern of performance studies: to envision what these enactments might *mean* for their audiences. It is a perspective that falls out of reception studies' qualitative scope and one often concealed by the whitewash of fan studies.

I also want to think beyond a prevalent discourse that celebrates YouTube as a means for Asian Americans to infiltrate the mainstream and, therefore, "change da game."[2] With breakthrough celebrities such as Legaci (pop star Justin Bieber's touring backup vocalists) and Charice Pempengco (child star turned daytime television darling), many critics have heralded YouTube as a launching pad for Asian Americans, a group otherwise lacking representation in U.S. mainstream pop culture. Yet others maintain the opposite view: it is actually young Asian Americans whose "aesthetics and business sense have helped change the face of online video" (Kun 2010). As illustrated in discussions at the Conference for Creative Content (C3), which took place in June 2011 at Visual Communications' annual Los Angeles Asian American film festival, today's Asian American creative hopefuls do not merely accede to but actively exploit social media and information-sharing platforms such as YouTube, Facebook, Twitter, and blogs as what was described at C3 as their "new calling card." To further aid this generation in "negotiating and navigating between community and commerce," C3 panels focused on the entrepreneurial nuts and bolts necessary to succeed online: copyright and intellectual property rights; effective modes of branding, distribution, and news reporting; and crafting performances to capture audiences. And if their hands-on approach to "becoming a YouTube star" was not enough of a draw, the organizers also summoned Asian America's celebrity power as panelists—bloggers Phil Yu and Diana Nguyen, YouTube trendsetter Wong Fu Productions, and *Glee* star Harry Shum.

Along with its ability to infiltrate and infect, the viral has the power to replicate. So, while some journalists and media organizations view You-Tube as an open stage for Asian American performers, artists themselves look to the website as an alternative avenue of cultural production. As twenty-four-year-old Korean American rapper Dumbfoundead (Jonathan Park) noted in a recent *Koream* magazine article, "Asians got tired of waiting to get into the mainstream. With YouTube, you don't have to wait for somebody to sign you, or give you a budget of millions of dollars to make a film; you can just do it. We're like, 'YouTube's here. We're going to smash it up with this YouTube thing'" (Eun and Ma 2010). With "no third party, no money-sucking managers, or closed-minded Hollywood executives," Asian Americans do not simply leverage but actually dominate YouTube's top-ten-channel lists, designating them as celebrities on the video-sharing site. Encompassing "highly visible and successful 'homegrown' performers and producers," as defined by Joshua Green and Jean Burgess, the category of "YouTube celebrity" or "YouTube star" consists of entrepreneurial vloggers such as Jimmy Wong, cultural producers who collaborate with other artists and partake in the site's daily life as active consumers (2009, 91). As a communication genre, vlogs derive from such media antecedents as "webcam culture, personal blogging, and the more widespread 'confessional culture' that characterizes television talk shows and reality television—while also adhering to current social media mandates to 'invite critique, debate, and discussion'" (94). At the same time, while "digital visuality" online "can reinstate an understanding of race as always visible and available to the naked eye," according to media scholar Lisa Nakamura, on the Internet (unlike in cinema) "users have the option to perform their identities in ways that are not possible elsewhere" (2008, 205). No longer simply broadcasting media, YouTube's celebrity system also requires its stars to post responses to their viewers' comments, follow other users' videos, and maintain public profiles through other Web 2.0 channels (Facebook,

Myspace, Twitter). Tapping into and taking part in the "affective economies" of these media and networking platforms, YouTube stars are often
required to extend their performances beyond these virtual arenas.[3]

To succeed in today's participatory culture, with its own logic of affective economics, the larger U.S. entertainment industry has had to rethink
how it does business. No longer able to merely distribute content in a top-
down fashion, organizations and performers—whether amateur or professional, nonprofit or profit driven—are forced to devise new forms of
audience outreach and engagement. In Asian America, the International
Secret Agents (ISA) showcase and nonprofit organization Kollaboration
are two grassroots examples of this new affective economics model as they
both capitalize on a niche audiences' emotional attachment to performers
("people like me") by presenting YouTube celebrities live in performance.
Started in 2008 by Southern California's Wong Fu Productions and hip-
hop group Far East Movement, ISA has since showcased popular Asian
American performers, from YouTube celebrities A. J. Rafael, Ryan Higa,
and Jennifer Chung to reality TV contestants/hip-hop dance crews Quest
Crew and Poreotics, in cities such as Seattle and New York as well as the
Los Angeles ethnoburbs San Gabriel and Cerritos. With five sold-out con-
certs in the past three years, according to Wong Fu Productions' website,
ISA "prov[es] that there is a voice, face, and desire for Asian Americans in
the mainstream world" (see ISA [http://isatv.com/?page_id=66]). While
both ISA and Kollaboration employ YouTube for the purposes of publi-
cizing and programming their events, Kollaboration—with its tagline
"Empowerment Through Entertainment"—actually auditions brand-new
performers on YouTube for its seasonal acoustic as well as electric concert-
competitions. Established eleven years ago in Los Angeles' Koreatown
(where its headquarters are still based), Kollaboration has spread across
the nation, with local chapters, or Kollaboration Cities, in Asian American centers: San Francisco, Seattle; New York; Washington, DC; Toronto;
Chicago; Atlanta; Houston; and Tulsa. Extending the reach of YouTube
stars—from home computer screens onto concert stages—ISA and Kollaboration's community-based efforts also map today's Asian America.

According to *Koream* writers Elizabeth Eun and Julie Ma (2010),
before YouTube's advent in 2005, "it all seemed self-indulgent and border-
line narcissistic . . . uploading videos of yourself belting out pop songs or
talking to an invisible audience." Yet despite the ways online media has
changed the aesthetics and business of entertainment, most YouTube video

performances are still popularly perceived as being amateurish in their look and feel—"narcissistic" and "self-indulgent" musical or spoken solo performances addressed to a built-in computer camera, with little else in terms of lighting, backdrop, or editing. These are consumer-based productions. However, as critics have noted, the probability of a YouTube video's "going viral" hinges precisely on the qualities of authenticity and earnestness. "Not targeted nor read as necessarily containing material for general audiences," Patricia Lange notes, these viral hits often contain "stereotypical, spontaneous, and . . . numerous in-jokes and references that many general viewers would not understand in the way the creators intended" (2009, 73). In other words, to catch an already distracted viewer's attention, viral videos must exude an air of amateur production—versus the slick, professional, and therefore controlled aesthetics of mainstream Hollywood or television sources—and mobilize key signifiers that resonate with a particular community or subculture.

Once struggling in a constrictive media system that viewed its films and performances as unprofitable and the idea of an Asian American audience as moot, indie Asian American artists have reaped the most benefit from social media's democratic promise. Already engaged in analog forms of virality (such as DIY filmmaking, word-of-mouth advertising, and informal networks of production), Asian American artists and entrepreneurs have easily shifted into digital mode. In the nonprofit sector, Asian American theaters and arts organizations mobilize social media in order to publicize upcoming productions, assist in fund-raising campaigns, and archive highlights from past productions or major events. At the same time, some of the most successful Asian American artists on YouTube— Wong Fu, Legaci, Charice, and KevJumba, for example—had years of performance experience and training under their belt before uploading their first YouTube video. In the case of Wong Fu Productions, which started circulating its work via email in the late 1990s, the video-sharing website was merely a cheap and easy alternative for sharing film shorts and music videos, especially with friends who lacked high-speed Internet connections. In all these cases, YouTube was the means, not the ends, to producing and distributing their work.

Yet how do we account for the popularity of YouTube stars and their performances among today's Asian American youth? In other words, besides just continuing a tradition of DIY cultural production, what purpose do these Asian American YouTube performers—their videos and the ways in which they are shared—actually serve? These questions arise for me not only in the space of this essay or during my private moments of writing and researching but also, and more so, in the public spaces of teaching, when students share and retell their fandom for certain YouTube performers and performances—or when I notice swooning from thirty-and-under Asian Americans huddled around computer screens, see them standing in line for tickets to a YouTube college tour show, or hear them screaming from their seats at a recent Kollaboration Acoustic 5 showcase. Is there something about YouTube—a genre of new media dependent upon the viral, as a "politics of form and form of politics"—that speaks to the simultaneously virtual and material aspects of Asian American identity?[4]

At once an all-too-easy catchall term (among census takers, public health researchers, and marketers) for an endlessly diverse population—of various ethnicities, nations, and classes, fluent in a number of different languages/dialects and with divergent immigration histories—"Asian American" originated as a highly contested, simultaneously political and cultural term during the civil rights, anti–Vietnam War, and student movements of the 1960s and 1970s. Purposefully pan-ethnic, it signaled the interlocking, oft-forgotten histories of U.S. war and empire in Asia and earlier Asian immigration to the United States as well as the mutually material and representational effects of these historical events and conditions. According to early Yellow Power proponents, while early twentieth-century U.S. popular representation of Asians focused on "contagious divides"—the discursive lines between U.S. modernity and Orientalized otherness drawn across Asian bodies—since the end of World War II and the Cold War's onset, one particular myth of racialization has prevailed (Shah 2001). Published in 1966, in the aftermath of the Moynihan report and amid rising domestic racial tensions, the main themes of the *U.S. World and News Report* article "Success Story of One Minority Group in the U.S." continue on in the "model minority" myth. Painting a portrait of the Chinese and Japanese as hardworking, obedient, self-reliant individuals whose drive toward assimilation is matched only by their fervent adherence to "traditional Asian values"—filial piety, humility, and sacrifice—the model minority myth is a neoliberal form of racialization.[5] It at once promises U.S. citizenship and belonging to those Asian subjects ("obedient, self-reliant individuals) who must also perform a racialized script that marks them as forever foreign ("traditional Asian values"). In this frequent collapse between "Asian" and "Asian American," model minority discourse has prescribed the parameters of Asian American-ness, setting the terms for political debate within Asian America.[6]

Against this discursive containment, scholars such as Kandice Chuh, Laura Kang, Lisa Lowe, and Karen Shimawaka have helped us fine-tune a working definition of "Asian American," one that reminds us of its supple and performative nature, an identity constituted by multiple and competing epistemologies. As Chuh has cautioned, "rather than looking to complete the category [of] 'Asian American'" we must instead recognize how we are "positioned to critique the effects of the various configurations of power and knowledge through which the term comes to have meaning" (2003, 10–11). These configurations are simultaneously domestic and transnational—the Asian in the United States as well as the American in Asia—with the battle for meaning, both aesthetic and political—fought on the grounds of culture. Culture here operates through "affiliation(s) of meaning" that "occur(s) in negotiation with the material conditions of existence shaped by politics and economics" (Lowe 1996, 2). As Lowe eloquently outlined in her seminal *Immigrant Acts*, Asian American culture is a "countersite to U.S. national culture" where "contradictions are read, performed, and critiqued"; it functions as a "medium of the present" that "mediates the past," remembering fragmented histories while reimagining political futures (65). Likewise, against community-based discursive containment—the kind that espouses notions of Asian Americans as culturally, socially, and politically homogeneous, attempts to expel radical Asian otherness through anti-immigrant sentiments, or even falls prey to the assimilationist lure of performing "model minority"-ness—I want to consider the political potential and critical possibilities offered by Asian American YouTube performances, as staged and everyday performances of affect and participation. By examining them along the formalistic lines of the "viral," a category characterized as corruptive, mobile, and infectious, we are forced to remember and reckon with Asian America's complicated historical path to U.S. citizenship and the forms of political and social belonging it has engendered.[7]

As mentioned above, the success of viral media depends upon (1) a niche or subculture's active participation through online networks (i.e., websites, blogs, and social networking directed at its particular needs/concerns) and (2) its knowledge of and ability to craft emotional hooks, key signifiers that touch upon a shared set of affective investments and affiliations. Asian America's particular use of viral media points to this virtual diaspora's simulated and representational elements and, in turn, to the performative and affective dimensions of the "symbolic ethnicity" of Asian Americans.

A 2001 Pew Internet and American Life Project reported that "fully 75% of English- speaking Asian-American adults have used the Internet," surpassing the numbers for all other English-speaking ethnic and even white American groups and making them "the most wired racial or ethnic group in America," "the young and the connected" (Spooner 2001, 2). Unlike their ethnic or even white counterparts, Asian American Internet users were "proportionally much more likely than others to get information about financial matters, travel, and political information" as well as "to use the Internet as a resource at school or at work" (2). In this comparative race-based research study, the report's author cites the challenges to surveying and collecting coherent data within this pan-ethnic community: heterogeneity of languages, high levels of language retention, and a lack of proper translation services. Thus, with its English-only survey, the Pew report depends upon and, in turn, perpetuates a limited definition of "Asian American."

Alongside a critique of this domesticating discourse, the trope of Asian American "hyperconnectivity" requires a deeper inquiry into the causes and effects of this group's long-standing Internet use and early adoption of Web 2.0 technologies—social networking sites like Friendster, Myspace, Facebook; short message services; and Internet telephone providers such as Skype. For both U.S. and foreign-born Asian Americans who maintain connections to homeland politics and family networks, these digital technologies allow for quick, inexpensive communication across time zones and national borders. Therefore, as Linda Leung has noted, the Asian diaspora is an imagined community "experienced largely over the Internet" and best "characterized as 'virtual'" (2008, 10). While the virtuality of Asian America traffics in both the simulated and representational, it also gestures toward an extensive cluster of real-world implications and everyday situations. The explosion of Korean pop (K-pop) culture globally, in the past decade, exemplifies this interplay between the virtual and material. Although the Internet's role in disseminating state-sponsored and market-driven forms of K-Pop culture is vital, as cultural anthropologist Jung-Sun Park observes, Korean American youth (U.S.-born and 1.5 generations as well as *yuhaksaeng*, students who study abroad) and their "consumption, dissemination, and to some extent, creation of trans-Pacific popular culture"—as they participate in K-Pop-oriented websites and forums and share with friends, family, and other fans the latest news and songs from abroad—plays an equally crucial role (2008, 161). Alienated from mainstream U.S. popular culture, the Korean American youth whom Park interviews find a sense of belonging, a "feeling at home," in K-Pop's style and culture.

In the registers of emotion and affect, Asian American youth also work through and against the specter of the model minority as a prescriptive racial fiction. Throughout its popular cultural history, Asian America has propagated the "grander passions" of anger, rage, and shame (Ngai 2005, 6). Like today's YouTube videos, 'zines of the 1990s yesteryears, with their espousal of punk and indie subcultures' DIY credo, also toed the lines "between commercial and D.I.Y., between mainstream and marginal" (Rubin 2003, 14). In the case of highly successful print publications that survived their digital transformation into online 'zines—Eric Nakamura and Martin Wong's *Giant Robot*, Mimi Thi Nguyen's *Exoticize This!*, and Sabrina Alcantara-Tan's *Bamboo Girl*—the tone of Asian America's talk-back to mainstream U.S. industries and representation took on the punk aesthetic of "gleeful opposition to decorum and propriety" by expressing itself in ways that "fl[y] directly in the face of the 'polite Asian' stereotype" (Rubin 2003, 15–16). If model minority status was maintained through deference, then these cultural forerunners instead chose to express anger and rage, emotions falling outside the boundaries of this racial fiction. Ironically, model minority rhetoric actually figures Asians as *unfeeling* or, as Wesley Yang vividly described in his recent *New York* magazine article "Asian Like Me," "a mass of stifled, repressed, abused, conformist quasi-robots" (2011, 22). Derived as they are from this 'zine publishing tradition, it is no wonder that some of today's most popular Asian American blogs still contain emotionally charged terms—the blogs *Angry Asian Man*, *Disgrasian*, and *You Offend Me You Offend My Family* (*YOMYOMF*). Through these particularly salient examples, we might hone our understanding of Asian American as a "symbolic ethnicity." According to Rachel Rubin, the categorical term of "Asian American" is "symbolic, because of its rhetorical and deliberative nature, but, nonetheless possessed of real-world implications" (2003, 5). As a mode of identification, it holds the possibility of being a "deliberative and motivated thing: experiential rather than biological, grounded in the present as much or more than in the past" (5). For Asian American 'zine writers, this "deliberative and motivated thing" registered as an "attitude," a particular way of expressing one's being-in-the-world. In the case of YouTube performances, such as Jimmy Wong's "Ching Chong! Asians in the Library" parody, the Asian American attitude today references a broader set of emotions than just anger and rage but still performs the affective labor of transforming alienating episodes into a common understanding.

From Europe's capitals to California's Silicon Valley, in hospitals and call centers, Asians and Asian Americans constitute a greater part of the world's affective labor force. According to theorist Michael Hardt, affective labor runs throughout "today's dominant economic forms" (1999, 96). Whereas some forms of caregiving activities continue "the production and reproduction of life, [has become] firmly embedded as a necessary foundation for capitalist accumulation and patriarchal order," Asian American YouTube artists, through their "production of affects, subjectivities, and forms of life" instead "present an enormous potential for autonomous circuits of valorization, and perhaps for liberation" (100).[8] This is not to say that these artists are safe from critique, for the majority of Asian American YouTube performances still tend toward reinforcing community-driven norms. Yet, like their cultural predecessors—from the earliest protest poems and plays, literary anthologies, and documentaries of the Yellow Power movement to the recent past of online magazines, forums, blogs, and cyberzines—these Asian American YouTube performers express their own shared political and social affects, feelings that are produced in response to discourses of virality and that are otherwise absent from most mainstream popular representations of Asian America.

For Davis Jung, producer of the recent Conference for Creative Content, Wong Fu Productions' 2006 "Yellow Fever"—the group's first YouTube video and response to the common narratives of Asian American masculinity—arrived at a critical point in his life. In his online essay "How New Media Gave Me a Voice," Jung narrates familiar tales for Asian Americans—the perpetual mispronunciation of one's name, the attempt to cultivate a love for genres of whiteness (country music, Classical Civilization major), and, of course, the lack of "role models" or "words" to articulate one's self—in order to capture the paradoxical feelings of Asian America: cultural alienation and, yet, the desire to belong. Bored and procrastinating, one fall evening in 2007, the then college-age Jung stumbled upon the University of California–San Diego collective's video link and clicked it. "I cannot tell you how many times I watched that video. It reached out and shook me. It made me laugh, and later on, it made me cry. It excited me, it incited me. It made me question everything that I had ever assumed about myself. It made me question what it meant to be 'normal.'"

Appearing at the end of his essay, this moment of cultural discovery serves as Jung's final word, his response to the question continually raised regarding the value of YouTube for Asian Americans. Pivoting between the dualities of culture and commerce, business and cultural resource, node and network, the rhetoric regarding the content-sharing website vacillates between characterizing it as "culturally generative" (for the several roles it plays as "high volume website, broadcast platform, media archive, social network") and seeing it as merely another "'top-down' platform for distributing popular culture" (Snickars and Vondereau 2009, 13). Yet, as Jung's anecdote so vividly reminds us, we need another set of protocols: an audience-centered analysis of the value of Asian American YouTube performances. By invoking a certain set of shared affects for these Asian American youth audiences, these YouTube stars' vlogs, song parodies, skits, and cover performances produce something "intangible: a feeling of ease, well-being, satisfaction, excitement, passion—even a sense of connectedness or community" (Hardt 1999, 96). Breaking out of the model minority myth's discursive containment, these emerging online personalities restage and respond to the banal and ridiculously racist moments of Asian America's everyday life, performing the affective labor of transforming alienation into humor, hate into love. Unexpectedly, a story or a song might catch us. Moved by these performances, we cannot help but share them, infecting others with the feeling.

Christine Bacareza Balance is currently an assistant professor of Asian American studies at the University of California–Irvine. Her writing has appeared in print in *Women and Performance: A Feminist Journal*, the *Journal of Asian American Studies* (*JAAS*), and *Theatre Journal* and online in *In Media Res*. Balance is currently writing a book on popular music and performance in post–World War II Filipino America. She would like to thank this special issue's editors, her anonymous reviewer, and colleagues Patricia Ahn and Sonjia Hyon for their invaluable feedback on earlier drafts of this piece.

Notes

1. The most spectacular examples: comedic vlogger "KevJumba" (Kevin Wu): no. 9 Most Subscribed Comedian (All Time), 1.4 million subscribers, over 150 million views; character actor/comedian "NigaHiga" (Ryan Higa): YouTube no. 1 Most Subscribed (All Time), 3.4 million subscribers, over 746

million views; directorial/writing collective Wong Fu Productions (Wesley Chan, Ted Fu, and Philip Wang): 785,394 subscribers, over 95 million views.

2. From the title of a panel at the 2010 San Francisco Asian American Film Festival: "Changing da Game: YouTube Legends and the Future of Online Media" (Center for Asian American Media 2010).

3. In this particular case, I am referencing Burgess and Green's use of "affective economies" to describe the participatory culture of emotional attachments and investments expressed on YouTube. Other scholars such as Sara Ahmed and Henry Jenkins have also written about the "affective economies" of political language and actions between racialized individuals within the nation-state (Ahmed 2004) and the logics of "affective economics" as propagated and perpetuated by reality television shows such as *American Idol* (Jenkins 2006).

4. I am borrowing this notion of "the politics of form and the form of politics" to discuss the critical and political work enacted by cultural productions from Jodi Kim's (2010) recently released *Ends of Empire: Asian American Critique and the Cold War*. Thanks also to Joshua Chambers-Letson (2009) for his essay "Contracting Justice: the Viral Strategy of Felix Gonzalez-Torres," which models different ways that a term such as the "viral" can be mobilized as a conceptual meeting point for an interdisciplinary discussion of bodies, the law, and artistic form.

5. In some aspects, the political difficulties faced by a term such as "Asian American" find a kinship with the similarly vexed identity category of "Latino." As Jose Esteban Muñoz has questioned, "Latino does not subscribe to a common racial, class, gender, religious, or national category, and if a Latino can be from any country in Latin America, a member of any race, religion, class, or gender/sex orientation, who then is she? What, if any, nodes of commonality do Latinas/os share?" (Muñoz 2000, 67) Yet, in other ways, "Asian American" has historically served as an umbrella term that has unified seemingly disparate groups. For the purposes of this essay, I draw on the spirit of Muñoz's focus on affective performances, or ways of "feeling brown," as a site for mobilizing different forms of what Norma Alarcon (1996) has designated an "identity-in-difference."

6. It bears repeating here that, within this containment logic of the "model minority," "Asian" more often refers to East Asian Americans (i.e., Chinese, Japanese, and sometimes Korean) rather than Asian/Asian American ethnicities such as Filipinos, South Asians, and Southeast Asians.

7. As Karen Shimakawa writes, "The conceptual U.S. citizen-subject comes into being, in other words, through the expulsion of Asianness in the figure of the Asian immigrant" (2002, 5). See also Soyoung Sonjia Hyon's (2011) disser-

tation, "Anxieties of the Fictive: The Immigrant and Asian American Politics of Visibility."

8. For future conversations and reading, we might think of these affective labors alongside what Alan Bryman (2004) has famously termed the "performative labor" within tourist economies, especially that performed by Asian and American women. Thanks to Patricia Ahn for sharing her proposed work (a dissertation tentatively titled "Disorganized Convergence: Global Music Television and Channels of Asian American Production") concerned with ideas on these particular connections.

Works Cited

Ahmed, Sara. 2004. "Affective Economies." *Social Text* 22(2):117–39.

Alarcon, Norma. 1996. "Conjugating Subjects in the Age of Multiculturalism." In *Mapping Multiculturalism*, ed. Avery F. Gordon and Christopher Newfield. Minneapolis: University of Minnesota Press.

Bryman, Alan. 2004. *The Disneyization of Society*. Thousand Oaks, CA: Sage.

Burgess, Jean, and Joshua Green. 2009. "The Entrepreneurial Vlogger: Participatory Culture Beyond the Professional-Amateur Divide." In *The YouTube Reader*, ed. Pelle Snickars and Patrick Vondereau. Stockholm: National Library of Sweden.

Center for Asian American Media. 2010. "Changing da Game: YouTube Legends and the Future of Online Media." http://www.youtube.com/watch?v=98ayDYfUMtk

Chambers-Letson, Joshua. 2009. "Contracting Justice: The Viral Strategy of Felix Gonzalez-Torres." *Criticism* 51(4):559–87.

Chuh, Kandice. 2003. *Imagine Otherwise: On Asian Americanist Critique*. Durham: Duke University Press.

Eun, Elizabeth, and Julie Ma. 2010. "How YouTube Transformed the Asian American Arts Scene." *Koream*, September. http://iamkoream.com/cover-story-youtube-stars/

Hardt, Michael. 1999. "Affective Labor." *boundary* 2 26(2): 89–100.

Hyon, Soyoung Sonjia. 2011. "Anxieties of the Fictive: The Immigrant and Asian American Politics of Visibility." PhD diss., University of Minnesota.

Jenkins, Henry. 2006. *Convergence Culture: Where Old and New Media Meet*. New York: New York University Press.

Jung, Davis. 2011. "How New Media Gave Me a Voice." http://asianfilmfestla.org/2011/films-events/c3-conference-for-creative-content/how-new-media-gave-me-a-voice/

Kang, Laura. 2003. *Compositional Subjects: Enfiguring Asian/American Women*. Durham: Duke University Press.

Kim, Jodi. 2010. *Ends of Empire: Asian American Critique and the Cold War*. Minneapolis: University of Minnesota Press.

Kun, Josh. 2010. "Unexpected Harmony: YouTube Helps Legaci's Breakout." *New York Times*, June 18, AR1.

Lange, Patricia. 2009. "Videos of Affinity on YouTube." In *The YouTube Reader*, ed. Pelle Snickars and Patrick Vondereau. Stockholm: National Library of Sweden.

Leung, Linda. 2008. "From 'Victims of the Digital Divide' to 'Techno-elites': Gender, Class, and Contested 'Asianness' in Online and Offline Geographies." In *South Asian Technospaces*, ed. Radhika Gajjala and Venkataramana Gajjala. New York: Peter Lang.

Lowe, Lisa. 1996. *Immigrant Acts: On Asian American Politics*. Durham: Duke University Press.

Muñoz, Jose Esteban. 2000. "Feeling Brown: Ethnicity and Affect in Ricardo Bracho's *The Sweetest Hangover (and Other STDs)*." *Theatre Journal* 52(1): 67–79.

Nakamura, Lisa. 2008. *Digitizing Race: Visual Cultures of the Internet*. Minneapolis: University of Minnesota Press.

Ngai, Sianne. 2005. *Ugly Feelings*. Cambridge: Harvard University Press.

Park, Jung-Sun. 2008. "Korean American Youth and Transnational Flows of Popular Culture Across the Pacific." In *Transpop: Korea Vietnam Remix* (exhibition catalogue), ed. Viet Le and Yong Soon Min. Seoul: Arko Art Center, Arts Council Korea.

Rubin, Rachel. 2003. "Cyberspace Y2K: Giant Robots Asian Punks." Occasional Paper, Institute for Asian American Studies. Boston: Institute for Asian American Studies, University of Massachusetts Boston.

Shah, Nayan. 2001. *Contagious Divides: Epidemics and Race in San Francisco's Chinatown*. Berkeley: University of California Press.

Shimakawa, Karen. 2002. *National Abjection: The Asian American Body Onstage*. Durham: Duke University Press.

Snickars, Pelle, and Patrick Vondereau. 2009. "Introduction." In *The YouTube Reader*, ed. Pelle Snickars and Patrick Vondereau. Stockholm: National Library of Sweden.

Spooner, Tom. 2001. "Asian Americans and the Internet: the young and the connected." Pew Internet and American Life Project. Washington, DC: Tides Center.

Visual Communications. 2011. "C3 Conference" (schedule). http://asianfilmfestla.org/2011/films-events/c3-conference-for-creative-content/

Yang, Wesley. 2011. "Asian Like Me." *New York*, May 16, 22–29.

Virality, Informatics, and Critique; or, Can There Be Such a Thing as Radical Computation?

Seb Franklin

Informatics, Politics, and Theory

Over the past two decades a substantial body of critical writing has emerged to address the broad transformations that constitute the historical period named the "society of control" (by Gilles Deleuze) and the era of the "cybernetic hypothesis" (by Tiqqun). In strictly economic terms this same period could be defined as that of computer-enabled, post-Fordist, neoliberal capitalism—and it should be noted straight off the bat that "computer-enabled," in the sense I intend it here, does not describe simply the rise-to-ubiquity of digital technologies in production but rather the broad array of social, economic, political, and cultural changes theorized through cybernetics research in the 1940s and both inspired and emblematized by the universal, binary, and discrete functionality of the computer. The major terms of this historical turn are by now well defined: information replaces material goods as the principle commodity; flexible, precarious forms of labor play a central role in the employment marketplace; the market, underpinned by informatic systems, regulates all social interactions; the notion of the worker as psychologically interior individual is replaced by that of the mathematically modelable automaton. While this present era is in many respects a clear extension of the disciplinary, industrial societies predicated on the familiar systems of exchange, circulation, value production, and exploitation examined by Marx in the mid-nineteenth century, the transformations and novel formations that define it as a distinct historical period require us to reevaluate and adapt our same principle modes of critical thought.[1]

WSQ: Women's Studies Quarterly 40: 1 & 2 (Spring/Summer 2012) © 2012 by Seb Franklin.
All rights reserved.

This essay, which is deeply indebted to the approach set out by Luc Boltanski and Ève Chiapello in *The New Spirit of Capitalism* and taken up by Nancy Fraser in her commanding "Feminism, Capitalism, and the Cunning of History," aims to interrogate certain notions of radical political practice and the theoretical models that might be derived from them in the context of post-Fordist, neoliberal economics and the ubiquitous informatic culture that is tightly bound up with it. In her 2009 article, published in the *New Left Review*, Fraser uses the term "the cunning of history" to describe processes whereby historical change recasts radical practices as central to new modes of production and governance (2009, 99). Focusing on the changing role of second-wave feminism from the postwar, state-organized form of capitalism to the "post-Fordist, transnational, neoliberal" form that emerged in the late twentieth century, Fraser compellingly analyses the "complex, disturbing possibility" that "cultural changes jump-started by the second wave, salutary in themselves, have served to legitimate a structural transformation of capitalist society that runs directly counter to feminist visions of a just society" (99).

All this is neatly summed up in an excerpt from Fredric Jameson's "Class and Allegory in Contemporary Mass Culture: *Dog Day Afternoon* as a Political Film," in which he examines the dialectical situation whereby social movements that campaign for an equal and just society are both structurally integral to and structurally unrealizable by late capitalism. Jameson suggests that

> the values of the civil rights movement and the women's movement and the anti-authoritarian egalitarianism of the student's movement are thus preeminently cooptable because they are already-as ideals-inscribed in the very ideology of capitalism itself; and we must take into account the possibility that these ideals are part of the internal logic of the system, which has a fundamental interest in social equality to the degree to which it needs to transform as many of its subjects or its citizens into identical consumers interchangeable with everybody else. The Marxian position—which includes the ideals of the Enlightenment but seeks to ground them in a materialist theory of social evolution—argues on the contrary that the system is structurally unable to realize such ideals even where it has an economic interest in doing so. (1977, 884)

I am interested in mapping the conundrum set out above, about the simultaneous co-option of radical ideals and the fundamental impossibility of realizing the basic goal of these ideals—that is, a "just society"—by late capitalism onto the current, informatic stage of the same system. For starters, as we will see, this informatic dimension compels us to supplement Jameson's "identical consumers" with "identical producers." Central to this argument is the way in which certain practices—ones that might seem sound as the basis for apparently radical politics when considered in terms of critical logics carried over from the Enlightenment to industrial societies—appear disconcertingly isomorphic with the fundamental principles of contemporary production when viewed through a lens of informatic critique that affords us a technically (as well as theoretically) specific analysis of the conditions of neoliberal, computational culture.

It is straightforward enough to sketch out the ways in which modes of critical thinking—from the base of Marx, Freud, and Saussure and their descendants through to the multiple theoretical approaches to identity politics that have emerged around them—have helped constitute certain modes of radical theory and practice throughout the second half of the twentieth century. In relation to Marx, to be against the dominant mode of production and circulation is to be against a normative, and thus unequal, society. In relation to Freud, to transgress norms, be they related to sex, violence, or identity, is to be against this same society. And in relation to Saussure, to be against monolithic, overarching structures and the reduction of language to pure utility is to be against this society. Each of these formations presents a model of the heroic outsider, the individual who, either alone or in a group of similar individuals, campaigns through word or deed against cultural, economic, and political injustice.

This model of individual or group resistance, which is deeply rooted in the nineteenth-century opposition between Enlightenment and Romanticism, does not contain any provision for the emergent fact that, according to Deleuze, informatic society is characterized by the elimination of notions of the individual and the group in favor of the *dividual* and the data bank (Deleuze 1995, 180). The dividual describes the body that is coded in terms of discrete movements (as theorized by Philip E. Agre in his "Surveillance and Capture" [1994]) or markers of identity (as theorized by Lisa Nakamura in her books *Cybertypes* and *Digitizing Race*). This discretization presents a social violence that is composed not of reactionary force but of preemptive informatics: techniques of targeting, capture, and prediction. As Samuel Weber puts it, "A certain kind of targeting defines 'opportunity' strictly in terms of the present in order to bring the future, and with it *tuchē* [luck, fortune], under control" (2005, 21). Further casting the Romanticist notion of explicit conflict between revolutionary individuals or groups and the state into difficulty today is the notion that this very model of opposition is cast as a form of productive labor under the cybernetically inflected principles of game theory (which emerge from the work of John von Neumann and Oskar Morgenstern in the 1930s and 1940s and which furnish the all-against-all competition model of neoliberal economics), which state that human behavior can be most predictably modeled under the assumption of perpetual conflict or struggle.

The obvious solution to this, of course, is to locate some equivalent theoretical approaches to those set out above in practices that are specific to digital, rather than industrial, modes of production. Networking, hacking, and the virus—three of the most commonly evoked concepts of radical politics in relation to digital culture—emerge as prime candidates here. To call on but a few examples, the supposed political force of these practices can be witnessed in Ted Nelson and Howard Rheingold's presentation of hypertext and distributed communication technologies as drivers of new forms of expression and pedagogy, Critical Art Ensemble's deployment of the hacker as political activist or revolutionary, and Nathan Martins's concept of "viral activism."[2] What this approach of substituting one group of practices for another fails to come to terms with, however, are the structural changes brought about by the emergence of a computer-mediated mode of production. All of the practices set out here might present modes of action specific to the computer, but they retain a connection with the Romanticist notion of the individual or group that is undercut by the predominance of the dividual and the data bank characteristic of control societies, and that places their viability as a base for effective political critique in doubt. Furthermore, by their very status as computational practices, networking, hacking, and computer viruses present the very real risk of nominally radical or oppositional acts' actually bolstering the efficacy of the mode of production by providing novel forms of aesthetic and experiential labor.

Before moving onto the virus, which poses the most complex relationship with informatic culture of the three concepts set out above, it is necessary to work through the ways in which networking and hacking, so easy to situate as modes of resistance or critique, are explicitly posited by the political and economic structures of postindustrial societies as ideal models of labor.

Networks, Hacking, and Informatic Labor

It might be immediately noted that there is a clear difference between net-working and hacking in that the former describes an organizational model while the latter describes a form of delinquency or civil disobedience. Viewed in this way it might appear that hacking, as a normatively "nega-tive" practice, has a closer connection to civil disobedience and the com-puter virus than it does to the network, but to make this claim is to ignore some crucial historical facts about both practices. On the one hand, the distributed network form is as historically bound up with insurgency and guerrilla warfare as it is with the Internet, a fact that places its unequivocally "good" status in relation to contemporary liberal democracy in doubt. On the other hand, the term "hacker," as will shortly be discussed, is central to the early practice of computer science in university laboratories in the 1970s—making it very difficult to argue for the practice as unequivocally "bad" from the perspective of the current world system. If one accepts that both practices have sufficiently checkered pasts as to be indistinguish-able in terms of any innate "goodness" or "badness" it becomes possible to identify some substantial points of comparison that can form the basis for an analysis that is properly suited to their specific technical character.[3]

The key characteristics by means of which networks and hacking can be compared, and that cast their role as oppositional practices in doubt, can be placed into two main categories. First, the network and hacking are broadly conceived of as social practices—that is, they are predicated on the intervention of human users. The most commonly raised categories through which the distributed network is proposed as a politically radical form are (1) as a general model of a nonhierarchical structure that does away with sovereign individuals and institutions and (2) as a distributed communications system that allows groups to flexibly and spontaneously organize with little formal planning. Putting aside for a moment Fried-rich Kittler's challenge—one that might appear increasingly persuasive as this essay develops—that the Internet allows real communication "not between people but between machines" (Armitage 2006, 35), this makes it clear that the notion of networking as politically progressive rests on the novel types of social interaction it affords. In the same way, hacking does not describe a general condition of computer use—although as I will flesh out shortly, it once did—but rather a specific approach based on a "love" of experimenting with technology. The hacker Dr. K defines the practice as follows in the introduction to his collection of anonymous testimonials titled *Hackers' Tales*: "A hacker is motivated by a love of technology; a desire to learn, play and master the technology for its own sake, because it's fun. It's this playful desire, coupled with an intense curiosity, which leads the hacker on" (2004, 15). To put it another way, neither hacking nor networking can be necessarily defined through their outputs. Computer hardware will function in the same way whether it has been accessed through a software interface, elegant formalized programming, or an experimental, hacked-together approach. Equally, the appearance of a webpage is subject to the same technical standards whether it has been composed by a single individual or by a distributed group.

The difference that exists in the processes described above is not technical, located in the forms that are created by a given practice, but social, located in the way in which a form or object is produced through a given practice. This is a condition that we can trace back to one of the earliest developments toward the present informatic society, Claude Shannon's *Mathematical Theory of Communication* of 1948. Shannon, making a case for the kind of statistically oriented approach to formerly human-centered affairs that is characteristic of today's neoliberal economics, states:

> Frequently the messages have *meaning*; that is, they refer to or are correlated according to some system with certain physical or conceptual entities. These semantic aspects of communication are irrelevant to the engineering problem. The significant aspect is that the actual message is one selected from a set of possible messages. The system must be designed to operate for each possible selection, not just the one that will actually be chosen since this is unknown at the time of design. (1949, 3)

Shannon's mathematical theory foregrounds a problem that any critical theory of informatic culture must come to terms with: one of the principle impulses of post-Fordism functions to recast the social as an engineering concern. Clearly this is an ideological function rather than a material one, in that human thought and communication does not become more mechanistic but rather is presented as such—with cybernetic, cognitive-psychological, and neuroscientific approaches at the forefront. Nevertheless, a principle task of theoretical and practical critique must be to locate ways in which this computational ideology can be disrupted. The intent of a practitioner or the cultural delineation of a particular practice, be it utopian (as in the case of the network) or radical (as in the case of hacking), must be mediated through the technical systems that undergird this practice—the digital computer that provides both the inspiration and the means for today's indifferent, statistically modelable approach to the human that any workable critical theory must seek to analyze in terms of its contradictions and shortfalls.

The second characteristic linking networking and hacking is that both can be easily traced through empirical history to normatively "good" notions. Even taking into account the association with guerrilla tactics raised above, the notion of the nonhierarchical, utopian space of the network recurs here. The normative "goodness" of hacking may appear more problematic in light of its recent portrayal as the preserve of terrorists and cybercriminals, but etymologically the term relates to the maximization of limited ability or formal training through perseverance and experimentation. We should remember the above-cited fact that many early computer scientists self-identified as hackers.[4] These two historical meanings of the noun "hacker," both of which are clearly distinct from the criminalized notion in wide use today, are set out by the "white hat" hacker and cybersecurity expert Robert Graham in his "Hacking Lexicon" (2000):

> The word "hacker" started out in the 14th century to mean somebody who was inexperienced or unskilled at a particular activity (such as golf). In the 1970s, the word "hacker" was used by computer enthusiasts to refer to themselves. This reflected the way enthusiasts approach computers: they eschew formal education and play around with the computer until they can get it to work. . . . In much the same way, a golf hacker keeps hacking at the golf ball until they get it in the hole.

The practice that is suggested by the combination of these two aspects of networking and hacking—that is, flexible, nonhierarchical work facilitated by networked computers and proceeding through an experimental or playful approach—presents us with the seemingly paradoxical situation brought about by the centrality of play to contemporary work, a key aspect of the novel forms of value creation that characterize informatic capitalism. So both the network and hacking are social acts that are rooted in notions of coherent distributed organization and an experimental or playful approach to problem solving. Viewed in this way, they cannot be reasonably considered as the basis for radical theory or practice; rather, both present models of organization and labor that are idealized under the conditions of postindustrial, neoliberal economics.

The very concept of play as labor presents us with an unavoidable notion in the critical analysis of informatic culture; that the digital technologies underpinning both work and play are, as Bernard Stiegler argues by borrowing a term from Jacques Derrida, pharmacological. They are at once poison and cure, allowing as much as they restrict. The analysis of networking and hacking set out above suggests that there is a layer model that can be applied to the pharmacological character of digital technologies; the freedoms they enable are confined to the social layer, to the intent of their practitioners, while the restrictions function at the layer of technical processes. This is also one of the key ways in which spectacle still performs an important role in the control society, with apparent freedoms confined to the ever-more-aestheticized graphical interface level while restrictions function at the deep structural level. Networking and hacking may present a platform for radical politics at the social level, but at the technical and infrastructural level they are emblematic of the newest forms of exploitation and restriction. Any critical theory of informatic culture must come to terms with this dual function of technology.

Viruses, Automation, and Identity

Networking and hacking appear to be practices that are opposed but in some way progressive; however, they are in fact closely linked through a common dimension that makes them unworkable as the basis for a theoretical critique. What, then, of the virus? When compared to the distributed network and hacking, the virus might appear to escape a close connection to idealized labor practices because it exhibits a more complex relationship with the social than those two practices, while suggesting a more fundamentally malicious functionality. It is also the only one of the three forms that Gilles Deleuze proposes as a "threat" to informatic control in his 1990 essay "Postscript on Control Societies," in which he draws the analogy between the virus and sabotage in the preceding era of thermodynamic, industrial labor (Deleuze 1990, 180). Despite all this, however, the virus posits some of the most significant challenges when it comes to thinking through the possibility of radical theory and practice within computation. It should be noted up front, however, that the obvious political questions surrounding the relationship between virality and post-Fordist capitalism, those concerning the role of viral marketing and viral networked content, are not of any great interest in this essay. As discussed above, the social uses of technology, while undoubtedly of great import, do little to get at the underlying political formation of informatic societies—that is, the computer technologies that either facilitate or set the inputs and outputs of both labor and leisure practices. Viral content, be it an advertisement or some noncommercial piece of content, is a phenomenon of human users, not of technical systems—and it is these technical systems, because of the way in which they define power relations in control societies while at the same time deflecting critical analysis, that are our concern here.

To be clear, I do not suggest that the technical and the social are independent categories—that computers and networks somehow emerged outside human practices. Rather, I am concerned with the historical process whereby post-Fordism is premised on a cybernetic logic that seeks to do away with the social as such in favor of gridded, predicable mathematical models of complex systems and, as such, confine my analysis to the ways in which this logic might be responded to critically. The hypothetical example of a viral video that, while fulfilling a normatively good objective of spreading awareness of political or economic injustice, contributes to the data mine and thus the bottom line of a company such as Google or Facebook partly encapsulates the dilemma presented here. As the discussions of networking and hacking set out above demonstrate, in an era in which computation represents the material base of the mode of produc-

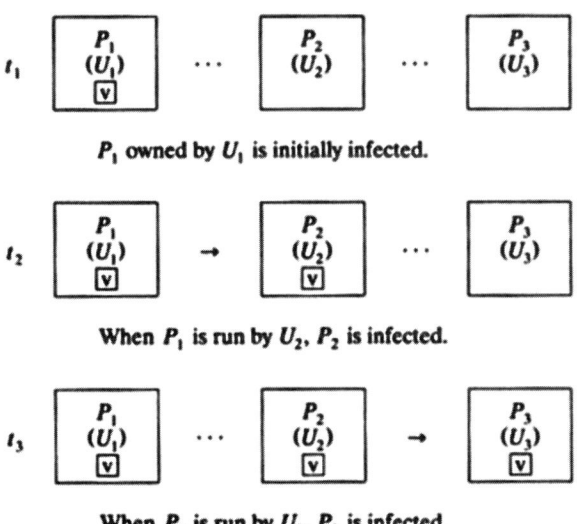

P_1 owned by U_1 is initially infected.

When P_1 is run by U_2, P_2 is infected.

When P_2 is run by U_3, P_3 is infected.

FIG. 1: Virus transfer in a time-sharing system. Source: Frederick Cohen, *A Short Course in Computer Viruses* (New York: Wiley, 1994).

tion, subjecting even the classical labor practices of agrarian and industrial work to the global feedback loops of a system-dynamic logic, the role of any technique that is practiced through computation requires a nuanced critical analysis that addresses the formal as political.

Despite the overwhelming associations with criminality and terrorism that are constantly attached to the notion of the computer virus there is nothing intrinsic to its technical definition that suggests the types of disruptive applications that might enable it to be posited as the basis of a resistant or oppositional politics. According to Frederick Cohen, a pioneer in the study of computer viruses, a virus need be defined no more complexly than as "a program that can 'infect' other programs by modifying them to include a, possibly evolved, version of itself" (1994, 2). It is specifically this characteristic that gives the computer virus its biologically oriented name. A condition of a computer virus's effectiveness is that it exists within, without necessarily impairing the functionality of, the code of the host program. Viruses are not, as Cohen notes, necessarily harmful or dangerous but simply describe programs that reproduce automatically, attaching within a host program, as a biological virus attaches itself within a host cell. If we are to accept this fundamental technical definition as primary—and in the light of the overwhelmingly technical base upon which computer-driven, post-Fordist production is premised such an approach appears essential—the virus is, at best, a politically neutral form.

If, as Cohen suggests, the technical function of the virus is absolutely neutral when it comes to its constructive or destructive potential, there nonetheless exists a substantial gap between this technical description and its cultural framing. The contrast between Cohen's view of viruses as specifically technical entities, carrying no automatic association with harm or damage, and the ones provided on the website of the Microsoft Corporation is telling in terms of the construction of viruses in relation to networked control:

> Computer viruses are small software programs that are designed to spread from one computer to another and to *interfere* with computer operation.
>
> A virus might *corrupt* or *delete* data on your computer, use your e-mail program to spread itself to other computers, or even *erase* everything on your hard disk.
>
> Viruses can be *disguised* as attachments of funny images, greeting cards, or audio and video files.

Viruses also spread through downloads on the Internet. They can be
hidden in illicit software or other files or programs you might download.
(Microsoft, n.d.; emphasis added)

This configuration of the virus as inherently disruptive, corrupting,
and deceptive makes it quite clear how a certain conceptualization of such
an object could find itself posited as a politically radical form. This depiction, however, has little to do with the technical form of the computer
virus, which is computational and thus both formal and indifferent. As
Jussi Parikka notes, "Viruses do not merely represent an example of malicious viral code but are part of a cultural-historical assemblage of digital
culture.... The virus is not ... a random pattern without sense but a certain
rationality" (2007, 285–86). Michael Hardt and Antonio Negri go so far
as to suggest that the technical function of the computer virus is in fact
isomorphic with the function of empire, stating, "Empire's institutional
structure is like a software program that carries a virus along with it, so that
it is continually modulating and corrupting the institutional forms around
it" (2000, 197–98). So on the one hand (according to Microsoft), computer viruses are definitively disruptive, corrupting, and deceptive, while
on the other (according to Hardt and Negri) they are isomorphic with the
function of distributed sovereignty of which Microsoft is an economic and
technological exemplar. The disparity that exists between these cultural
configurations of computer viruses appears to suggest that they are so neutral as to be untenable as a political form. Furthermore, it is precisely this
formal neutrality that restates the technical (if not the practical) status of
viruses as an entirely separate dimension to their cultural or social appearance. As is demonstrated above in terms of the network and hacking, it
is the universal and formalizing nature of the computer, in conjunction
with its role at the core of contemporary production, that makes it highly
problematic to claim computational practices, whatever the human intent
behind them, as a model for progressive or radical theory and politics. The
virus, if we are to accept only the basic technical definition of a program
that replicates itself automatically, describes little more than the idealized
function of computation itself, that is, a system of organization that functions automatically.[5]

Extending from this there is a more troubling set of concerns that
surround the notion of the virus as radical political form, and that point

toward specific historical problems around critique and identity politics in the age of ubiquitous computation. Although it takes its metaphorical name from the function of biological viruses, the automatic function of the computer virus in fact owes itself to the automatic function of its base technology, the computer. If we look back to the roots of computation, the principle mode of production in postindustrial societies, we immediately come up against the fundamental problem in the conceptualization of the computer virus as politically radical form. Alan Turing, in a seminal 1950 paper on computing machines, states that "it is the duty of the [control unit in a computer] to see that . . . instructions are obeyed correctly and in the right order. The control is so constructed that this necessarily happens" (437).

Consider this automatic or necessary functionality in terms of some classical political categories: social class that functions automatically, sex and gender that function automatically, race that functions automatically, identity that functions automatically. Making these notions a reality is the dream of informatic neoliberalism. This is why we need to proceed carefully when claiming this or that cultural practice as politically radical under the material conditions of contemporary culture. To present the overall function of the computer virus as a model for contemporary critique is to place automation at the heart of progressive thought in a way that is deeply troubling, for the automatic, in the context of informatic culture, presents us with an equivalent to the notion of the *natural* or, to align ourselves more clearly with the critical projects of the late twentieth century, *essential* in relation to prior systems of inequality and domination. For natural or essential identity today we must substitute *statistical* identity. The fundamental power of critique lies in its activity; it is a *process* of unearthing contradictions and inequalities that stands in opposition to the automatic form of reading that characterizes ideology. Holding up automation as a component of radical politics thus risks returning thought around the politics of identity to a time before Marx and Freud, de Beauvoir, Butler, Said, Bhabha, Spivak, and those who followed them—or perhaps more accurately placing it in an alternate version of reality in which this work is irrelevant—at a point in history where, as Deleuze has noted, the individual and the group are replaced, in the technics and terminology of domination, by dividuals and data sets.

Noise, Addition, Boredom

It is quite clear that one cannot take the overall function of computer viruses as a model for radical politics or critique because (1) it brings with it no essential functionality that critiques or problematizes computation and (2) a large part of its functionality is no more than a basic condition of computing applied to the reproduction of a program, creating a number of deeply unpalatable outcomes around the notion of automatic identity when applied as a model of critical thought. There is, however, one element of the computer virus that we have yet to examine—an element that is neither a simple social relation nor a simple corollary of computation itself. Viruses are not transformative but *additive*. The code of the computer program, or the organism in the instance of a biological virus, does not immediately begin to function in an opposite, disordered, or entropic way when a virus attaches within it, but in the same way with new information, be it a machine code, DNA, or RNA, added to it. The information previously contained within the host program is not turned into a qualitatively different entity but rather an excessive version of itself, distinguished at the level of code, but not at the level of program functionality or graphical output, through the addition or subtraction of data. When an infected program runs, more often than not it runs in its original form perfectly, with the distinction being that a separate process or set of processes runs at the same time. This additive distortion, which we can define as a quality of the computer virus that relies on automation to propagate but that does not in itself constitute automatism, offers us a route through the problem of politics and cultural theory presented by computer viruses.

This conceptual thicket can be clarified by working through the same principle of addition in relation to the closely related formation of noise, the "passive" danger to control societies that Deleuze describes as corresponding to the "active" danger of viruses (1990, 180). Since Shannon's *Mathematical Theory of Communication* and the multiple, cross-disciplinary contributions of cybernetics, noise principally appears to us as a statistically modelable component of communication, something that is "programmable and hence a mode of algorithmic rationality" (Parikka 2007, 286). While this may hold true for a certain concept of noise that is conceptually remediated (as it is in Shannon) from a material product of electrical or electronic devices to a statistical component of a symbolic-logical communication theory, it does not change the fact that noise describes those components of computation that exist in an unmeasur-able or in-between state and thus cannot be adequately captured, coded, and cast into algorithms or grammars of action. In this conceptualization the computer virus is an example of executed noise, in that it adds new ele-ments in a way that is not registered as a qualitative difference in the host program by any component of computer hardware. A virus attached to a cracked copy of Adobe Photoshop does not necessarily result in that copy of Photoshop running any differently from the "official" version; the virus is simply some extra code that will run in some way completely unrelated to the host program. As such, those lines of code that constitute the virus can be said to be an addition to the host program that is at once both quan-titatively positive and unmeasurable. It is this aspect of the virus—the pos-itive expression of unmeasurability—that can be productively extracted to serve as a model for radical theory and politics under cybernetic post-Fordism, as expressed in the work of Tiqqun and others.

In "The Cybernetic Hypothesis" Tiqqun set out the possibility expressed by additive practices that escape capture and coding as the prin-ciple form of executed unmeasurability within informatic systems:

> For a cybernetician, any disorder can only come from there having been
> a discrepancy between the pre-set behaviors and the real behaviors of
> the system's elements. A behavior that escapes control while remaining
> indifferent to the system is called "noise," which consequently cannot be
> handled by a binary machine, reduced to a 0 or a 1. Such noises are the
> lines of flight, the wanderings of desires that have still not gone back into
> the valorization circuit, the nonenrolled. (2001, 71)

This introduces us to a fascinatingly counterintuitive principle in the theorization of informatic culture: in cybernetic societies *noise is silence*. Silence, in the era of informatic capitalism, is that which cannot be mea-sured, and therefore cannot be captured, coded, transcoded, formalized, or patterned. It is notable that the 0 (or "low" signal) that makes up one half of all binary states in computation corresponds to not 0 volts but around 0.7 volts, because no physical logic gate can register a true 0 volt signal. The 1 (or "high" signal) corresponds to 2–5 volts. In such a system, any signal between 0.8 and 2 volts prevents the gate from registering either the 0 or that 1, of which both are crucial to the technical function of com-putation. This technical model of the positive yet unmeasurable or "silent" state is crucial to radical politics today. It produces noise at the fundamental level of computability (which in this sense includes practices of informatic capture, definition, automation, modeling, and grammatization) in the same way that missing information in the compressed sound, image, or video file introduces noise to its user-readable output. It is this noise that can serve as the expression of those identities or aspects of identities that cannot be cast within predefined, normalized categories or grammars of action under post-Fordism.

Crucial to this model for radical theory and politics in the era of informatic political economy will be a set of procedures that are premised not on attacking or exceeding informatic society but on executing difference in unmeasurable and thus uncodable ways (in the historical framework deployed by Jameson and Fraser we would call these "unco-optable"), ways that cannot be computationally defined and thus cast into algorithms, grammars of action, or new modes of production. Several descriptions of such a practice can be found over the past twenty years, from Deleuze's assertion of the need for "vacuoles of noncommunication" that do not confront but "evade" (1990, 175) to Tiqqun's call for a politics that "comes from desires that exceed the flux insofar as the flux nourishes them without their being trackable therein, where desires pass *beneath the tracking radar*, and occasionally establish themselves" (2001, 72) and Alexander R. Galloway and Eugene Thacker's active promotion of "nonexistence" in the form of "nonexistent action," "unmeasurable or not-yet-measurable human traits," and "the promotion of measurable data of negligible importance" (2007, 135–37). Among other things, what these examples suggest is that radical theory and practice within the era of informatic or cybernetic capitalism will be *boring*, in the sense that it will provide us with none of the visible or audible material that we are accustomed to from prior radical practices and that allow such practices to be valorized as new forms of production. This, perhaps above all other historical impositions, poses the biggest challenge to the theorist or practitioner hanging on to the spectacular radical forms of the past, from the Romantic sublime to Bakhtin's carnivalesque, surrealism, and the various avant-gardes of the mid-twentieth century and thereafter—each of which, in the end, is based in the contestation, through sabotage and entropic excess, of the dominant modes of representation for a given era.

In the conclusion to *Gender Trouble* Butler asks a question that remains essential to those asked in this essay. Situated in the midst of an analysis of the way in which a multiplicity of subject positions becomes potentially unrepresentable, Butler's key question is italicized below:

> The theories of feminist identity that elaborate predicates of color, sexuality, ethnicity, class, and able-bodiedness invariably close with an embarrassed "etc." at the end of the list. Through this horizontal trajectory of adjectives, these positions strive to encompass a situated subject, but invariably fail to be complete. This failure, however, is instructive: *what political impetus is to be derived from the exasperated "etc." that so often occurs at the end of such lines?* This is a sign of exhaustion as well as of the illimitable process of signification itself. It is the *supplement*, the excess that necessarily accompanies any effort to posit identity once and for all. (1990, 143)

Now imagine for a moment that the "etc." in Butler's analysis, and the question that it prompts, result not from too many, or even infinite, subject positions—for today this is brutally synonymous with too many, or even infinite, target demographics, sources of valorizable activity, monetizable practices, and so on—but from the impossibility of identifying and declaring positions to define (and that can thus be exploited to produce value) in the first place. The crucial binary opposition enacted by dominant culture thus becomes that between measurable and unmeasurable. This essential modification of Butler's theory, which reformulates its key concerns to respond to informatic rather than thermodynamic societies, foregrounds the key terms for today's radical theory and practice. In contrast to all of the oppositional forms set out above, tomorrow's radical practice—which is always sadly doomed to be a computational practice according to the definition of computation dreamed of by cyberneticians and neoliberal ideologists alike and set out at the start of this essay—will be based not on contesting or even exceeding representation but rather on escaping it.

Seb Franklin is a writer and teacher based in Brighton, UK. He received his doctorate from the University of Sussex in 2010 and is currently postdoctoral research fellow in the Cultures of the Digital Economy Research Institute at Anglia Ruskin University.

Notes

1. For all the discussion of information technology, computers, and codes that it contains, Deleuze's "Postscript on Control Societies" is perhaps most

notable for the conceptual proximity that it presents between control and post-Fordist, neoliberal capitalism. Throughout the piece Deleuze talks of wages brought into "a state of constant metastability punctuated by ludicrous challenges, competitions and seminars," "an inexorable rivalry presented as healthy competition" (1995, 179) and a form of capitalism that seeks to sell "services" and buy "activities" (181). It is this political-economic depiction of control, for which the computer serves as a model as much as a means of control in itself, that informs the present essay.

2. It should be acknowledged that while the members of Critical Art Ensemble celebrate the practical techniques of hacking as revolutionary in an age of ubiquitous digital information systems, they are less optimistic about the actual (call them old-fashioned) political sensibilities of hackers: "Teen hackers work out of their parents' homes and college dormitories to breach corporate and governmental security systems. Their intentions are vague. Some seem to know that their actions are political in nature. As Dr. Crash has said: 'Whether you know it or not, if you are a hacker you are a revolutionary.' The question is, a revolutionary for what cause? After poring through issues of *Phrack* and surfing the Internet, one can find no cause mentioned other than the first step: free access to information. How this information would be applied is never discussed. The problem of letting children act as the avant-garde of activism is that they have not yet developed a critical sensibility that would guide them beyond their first political encounter" (Critical Art Ensemble 1996, 15).

3. For more on the notions of "good" and "bad" in relation to viruses, see Parikka and Sampson 2009.

4. For an idea of the close proximity of the term "hacker" with "official," often university-affiliated programmers in the 1970s and early 1980s, see Williams 2002, especially chapters 1 and 2 and appendix B. As Williams writes, "It is a testament to the original computer hackers' prodigious skill that later programmers, including Richard M. Stallman, aspired to wear the same hacker mantle. By the mid to late 1970s, the term 'hacker' had acquired elite connotations. In a general sense, a computer hacker was any person who wrote software code for the sake of writing software code. In the particular sense, however, it was a testament to programming skill. Like the term 'artist,' the meaning carried tribal overtones. To describe a fellow programmer as hacker was a sign of respect. To describe oneself as a hacker was a sign of immense personal confidence. Either way, the original looseness of the computer-hacker appellation diminished as computers became more common" (appendix B).

5. For more on this, see Parikka 2007, 207–15.

Works Cited

Agre, Philip E. 1994. "Surveillance and Capture: Two Models of Privacy." *The Information Society* 10(2):101–127.

Armitage, John. 2006. "From Discourse Networks to Cultural Mathematics: An Interview with Friedrich A. Kittler." *Theory, Culture and Society* 23:17–38.

Butler, Judith. 1990. *Gender Trouble*. New York: Routledge.

Cohen, Fredrick. 1994. *A Short Course on Computer Viruses*. New York: Wiley.

Critical Art Ensemble. 1996. New York: Autonomedia.

Deleuze, Gilles. 1995. *Negotiations*. Translated by Martin Joughin. New York: Columbia University Press.

Dr. K. 2004. *Hackers' Tales*. London: Carlton Books.

Fraser, Nancy. 2009. "Feminism, Capitalism, and the Cunning of History." *New Left Review* 56: 97-117.

Galloway, Alexander R., and Eugene Thacker. 2007. *The Exploit*. Minneapolis: University of Minnesota Press.

Graham, Larry. 2000. "Hacking Lexicon." http://www.linuxsecurity.com/ resource_files/documentation/hacking-dict.html

Hardt, Michael, and Antonio Negri. 2000. *Empire*. Cambridge, MA: Harvard University Press.

Jameson, Fredric. 1977. "Class and Allegory in Contemporary Mass Culture: *Dog Day Afternoon* as a Political Film." *College English* 38(8): 843–859.

Microsoft Corporation. N.d. "What Is a Computer Virus?" http://www. microsoft.com/protect/computer/basics/virus.mspx

Parikka, Jussi. 2007. *Digital Contagions: A Media Archaeology of Computer Viruses*. New York: Peter Lang.

Parikka, Jussi, and Tony D. Sampson. 2009. "On Anonymous Objects of Digital Culture." Introduction to *The Spam Book*. Cresskill: Hampton Press.

Shannon, Claude, and Warren Weaver. 1949. *The Mathematical Theory of Communication*. Urbana: University of Illinois Press.

Tiqqun. 2001. *Tiqqun* 2. Paris: Belles-Lettres.

Turing, Alan. 1950. "Computing Machinery and Intelligence", *Mind* 49:433–60.

Weber, Samuel. 2005. *Targets of Opportunity*. New York: Fordham University Press.

Williams, Sam. 2002. *Free as in Freedom: Richard Stallman's Crusade for Free Software*. Sebastopol, CA: O'Reilly. http://oreilly.com/openbook/ freedom/appb.html

Black Friday: Crowdsourcing Communities of Risk

Kenneth Rogers

Black Friday

Just before dawn on Friday, November 28, 2008, Jdimytai Damour, a thirty-four-year-old Wal-Mart employee, was killed in a futile attempt to prevent a crowd of approximately two thousand shoppers from streaming through the main entrance to the Wal-Mart at the Green Acres Shopping Plaza in Valley Stream, New York. Just minutes before it was scheduled to open at 5:00 a.m., Damour was overpowered, trampled, and asphyxiated by the crush of bodies flowing through a bottleneck at the door. He was pronounced dead at 6:03 a.m. at nearby Franklyn Hospital after failed attempts to revive him with CPR. The store closed for two hours later that morning in memoriam.

Damour's death notwithstanding, the scene outside the Green Acres Wal-Mart was typical across the nation that November day in observance of an annual ritual popularly known as "Black Friday." The rite is now all too familiar. Each Friday following Thanksgiving, millions of consumers assemble outside retail outlets, malls, and box stores, often camping out all night with friends and family and enduring inclement weather until national chains fling their doors open at daybreak to begin the highest-volume shopping day of the year. The sale day that informally marks the commencement of the holiday shopping season has become a sensational media event. Obligatory human interest stories feature images of impetuous shoppers dashing frantically into aisles stacked impossibly high with discounted retail goods and feverishly foraging through stuffed racks and bargain bins, while the more staid coverage by the financial press tracks sales numbers minute by minute as a weathervane of consumer confi-

WSQ: Women's Studies Quarterly **40**: 1 & 2 (Spring/Summer 2012) © 2012 by Kenneth Rogers.

dence. Yet both the popular and journalistic conversations about Black Friday rarely deviate from a spendthrift battle cry or scratch beneath the superficial caricature of consumer bliss to question directly the systemic linkages between social, cultural, and economic factors that make the phenomenon of Black Friday possible, factors that, if followed, run deep into the fissures, contradictions, and dangers inherent in a global postindustrial capitalism increasingly dependent on and threatened by deepening systemic risk. The name "Black Friday" may be vaingloriously derived from the color of ink left in corporate ledger books at the day's profit-taking close, yet if one shifts from the sanguine perspective of those on high to that of others witnessing events from within the panicked crowd, "Black Friday" connotes an ominous pall and refers to a very different kind of bottom line: a bottom hit by those who are left behind to pay the price for windfalls gained and gamed by a system of speculative finance, unsustainable consumer debt, declining wages, and precarious labor.

The shoppers and employees who frequent the Green Acres Wal-Mart are representative of communities feeling the less auspicious effects of the sacrosanct shopping day. The vast majority are black, most commuting to just outside New York City limits to the predominantly white, middle- and upper-middle-class suburban community of Valley Stream, the westernmost suburb of Long Island, bordering Queens, from comparatively lower-income, predominantly African American urban neighborhoods like Rosedale, Brookville, and Laurelton because of easy mass transit access, cheaper prices, and a lack of investment by national retail chains in their own Queens neighborhoods. As for the majority-black employees at the Wal-Mart, many are earning wages regarded as at or below subsistence level, near the minimum in the growing sector of low-paying service sector jobs outsourced to third-party temporary agencies. Damour, a Haitian immigrant, didn't technically work for Wal-Mart; rather he was an employee of the temp agency Labor Now, one of many firms, such as Staffmark and SelectRemedy, that crowdsource an exploitable, often immigrant workforce and feeds Wal-Mart cheap, flexible, minimally trained, minimum-wage laborers, making the firm's employment completely scalable to the contingencies and uncertainties of consumer demand and freeing the retail giant from responsibility for benefits, health care, and workers' compensation (Bonachich and Wilson 2008; Laird 2009).

There had never been a more opportune moment to read Black Friday as symptomatic of these systemic problems than late November 2008.

Occurring less than three months after the onset of a catastrophic financial crisis triggered by the bursting of the housing bubble, Black Friday 2008 fell directly in the midst of a growing despair brought on by a deepening credit crisis, a collapsing stock market, a massive wave of home foreclosures, immense "too big to fail" corporate bailouts, increasing homelessness, sky-rocketing layoffs, and rising unemployment. Black and brown communities were suffering, and continue to suffer, from higher unemployment and foreclosure rates and the general stressors of a threadbare social safety net. But recent studies demonstrate how the structural fact of racial segregation enabled one of the most effective tools in the creation of the housing bubble in the first place: artificial market expansion through subprime mortgage-backed derivatives. The credit default swaps that enabled the unsustainable bubble in housing prices pumped liquidity into the housing market by targeting minorities with predatory lending practices packaging and selling more risk-inherent debt. Lenders targeted poorer African American and Latino neighborhoods in metropolitan areas; as has now come light, those neighborhoods were exponentially more likely to receive subprime loans. It was precisely this slice of the housing market that was hit hardest and fell farthest (Rugh and Massey 2010). Yet discriminatory lending practices were founded not explicitly on racial categorization, but sub-identitarian aggregation of things like personal data, degree of education, employment history, and FICO scores, calculated through complex algorithms into a quantifiable factor of risk that could be folded into derivatives and sold on the global financial markets. Thus this discriminatory lending practice was not explicitly racist, like the historical tactics of real estate blockbusting or redlining, but used the rules and incentives of the market as a way of aggregating a pool of risk that could be, in turn, racialized.

Given all this, one might have assumed that Damour's death would have provided both the impetus and the opportunity to collectively and consciously question just what is black about Black Friday—to more critically probe the complex historical and systemic context of the incident and read it as a fatal consequence of the concatenation of factors and events that has gripped our culture and our economy over the past several years. Thus a decisive question becomes, Why did the public reaction remain myopically fixated on the behavior of the crowd outside the Wal-Mart that Friday morning? The overwhelming sentiment found in mainstream press coverage, reader forums, the blogosphere, and statements by police and public officials directed an outpouring of outrage and vitriol at the anonymous crowd, which was consistently vilified as force of criminal menace, deviance, danger, and barbaric incivility. The crowd, personified as a variety of types, was by all accounts identified as the singular source of an enigmatic motivation, an entity that must carry the full burden of culpability. Some even went so far as to address the crowd directly, wagging a scolding finger at its moral failure and excess greed and avarice.[1] Others painted portraits of the crowd as grotesque, as a drunken devolution of human civility to its basest and most primal animal instincts. Further, though it was never explicitly referenced that the clientele and employees of this Wal-Mart are predominately African American, reporting on the incident often made coded inferences to race buried in the eyewitness statements from within the crowd itself.[2] An AP news story narrated the event from a video feed of a serpentine helicopter shot over the mall, showing the scene from a detached elevation, reminiscent of the news coverage of the 1992 Los Angeles riot, and subtly racializing the crowd as an unruly throng of black bodies perpetrating an act of black-on-black crime. A *New York Times* reporter placed the incident on a historical continuum of urban decay and gang violence that spanned three decades.[3] Finally, law enforcement officials criminalized the crowd. The investigating lieutenant deflected community criticism for its inadequate security by insinuating that the unruly crowd's actions might constitute acts of premeditated criminality worthy of prosecution, and the Nassau County Police Department committed to review security footage for evidence of the crowd's intent, despite there being no formal legal precedent to adjudicate a crowd, only actors within it.[4]

This essay will not disregard this reaction as vitriolic scapegoating and misplaced accusation, but will begin from the premise that the public personification of the Black Friday crowd that attributes crowd agency and psychological unity already contains within it a legitimate critique of a society under duress because of increased structural risk, privation, and economic instability. Damour's death occurred alongside the advent of a new historically specific crowd formation devised to yield unexploited economic value via the theoretical refashioning of the traditional field of crowd psychology to fit advancing nonpsychological theories of crowd dynamics based on individualized rational choice. The Black Friday crowd is thus paradigmatic of a more general social problem of collective human conduct that arises out of the tension of psychological theories espousing the intrinsic unity of crowd behavior being retrofitted with mechanistic theories that consider crowds an aggregate of individual actors together forming a dynamic system. The most recent composite of these two divergent theories of the crowd is best exemplified in a recent crowd management technology called "crowdsourcing." Although the term primarily describes the technique of assembling a dispersed, networked digital labor pool, I wish to work toward a more expansive view of crowdsourcing to demonstrate how it is actually the latest iteration of a historic problem that extends back to the late nineteenth century: the conflictual needs, powers, and social functions of the public and civic crowd versus those of the market crowd. After working through the parallel and converging histories of publics and markets, I will conclude by offering a broader definition of crowdsourcing, applicable to a class of designed mechanisms that proactively structure crowd behavior as market behavior claiming to mitigate the increasing forms of financial risk endemic to the excessive economization of social and political life.

The Psychological Crowd

The "era of the crowd" is assembled at the bustling crossroads of nineteenth-century industrialization, population explosion, urbanization, and the solidification of the democratic nation-state. As the everyday experience of crowds has become commonplace in city streets, public parks, railway stations, ports, factories, and theaters, they have given rise to a deeply ambivalently cultural and political concern over the power that they hold. On the one hand, the crowd is identified as the undeniable lifeblood of modern industrial societies, necessary to labor and consumption, and a vital practice of political assembly and mass organization used to strengthen national identity and protect state security in times of war; on the other hand, the crowd is feared as a destructive force whose potential to foment political violence, social protest, and revolution would threaten to tear modern society asunder (Schnapp and Tiews 2006).

By the late nineteenth century, through witnessing the great potentials of the constructive and destructive poles of the crowd's power, the need to understand its intrinsic motivations became the subject of a new field. Gustave Le Bon's *The Crowd* (1895), the first comprehensive sociological study of the modern crowd and touted as one of the earliest works of crowd psychology, explains crowd behavior psychodynamically as a breakdown of the individual into its base animal instincts that overtake the rational, intentional, and conscious ego, what Wilfred Trotter later elaborates as the "herd instinct" (1916, 11–65). The resultant "mental unity" of the crowd absorbs individuals into a singular mass susceptible to volatile action and irrational manipulations of magnetic demagoguery that might threaten the stability of established political order. For Le Bon, implicit in the psychological unity thesis is that the ensuing state of mass automatism and the power of the crowd spreads like a virus, infecting the ideals of bourgeois individualism. In his feminized/racialized depiction of crowd formation, the crowd behaves like "inferior forms of evolution—in women, savages, and children," that might destroy society like a dangerous epidemic compromising the virtues of rational self-interest and self-reliant individualism (Le Bon 1895, 16). "Contagion is so powerful a force," states Le Bon, "that even the sentiment of personal interest disappears under its action" (126). The association of diminished ego boundaries with categories of race, gender, and class hierarchies is a thinly disguised expression of fear about the political threat to established power posed by unrestrained extension of democracy to common people via universal suffrage, populism, class solidarity, and racial equality.

By the 1920s and 1930s, in the context of the rapidly advancing technological society in Europe, a range of studies of the crowd in the work of Trotter, Freud, MacDougal, Reich, and the Frankfurt School developed variations of the crowd psychology thesis laid out by Le Bon, based on the dissolution of individual identity (Trotter 1916; Freud 1990; MacDougal; Reich 1946) Now blended with Marxism and sociology, the anxiety over the power of crowds during the interwar period turned more explicitly directed at the reconstruction of post–World War I political nationalisms concerned that the progressivism of crowds formed out of the labor movement and political solidarity for social democracy could very easily be siphoned off into reactionary panic and authoritarianism through the orchestrated theatrical manipulations of spectacular rallies, mass psychology, and the cult of an autocratic leader who the crowd would follow like sheep to their slaughter (Reich 1946). Perhaps no single contribution epitomizes the apex of this variety of crowd scholarship more than Elias Canetti's *Crowds and Power* (1984). Written with hindsight on World War II, the book offers a comprehensive compendium of crowds categorized into their organic types and subtypes, attributes, systems, dynamics, spatial and temporal dimensions, history, religion, economics, and politics. Arguing with great eloquence, erudition, and rhetorical nuance,

Canetti, like his predecessors, places the crowd at the constitutive center of modernity, while additionally cutting across this expansive categorical taxonomy to offer a portrait of the crowd as an entity phenomenologically self-sensing the authenticity of its own being—a desire that extends from the fragile and precarious balance of the "true" crowd's self-reflexive formation versus its artificial assemblages and manipulations. The danger for Canetti is not precisely derived from the psychological mind of the crowd succumbing to mass deception or fascist demagoguery; it is the inhibition of self-consciousness through the imprisonment of its body. He argues that political power forecloses the spontaneous emergence of the primal and concrete sense of the true "open crowd's" need to seek equality by overcoming the intrinsic human fear of touch by controlling the crowd in architectures of containment, like stadiums, theaters, or places of worship, all of which domesticate and repress the true desire of the crowd to seek its own organic growth, density, equality, and direction (Canetti 1984, 2, 16–17, 29). Thus the irruption of crowd violence is not inherently destructive in its expression, but an embodied form of political defiance by the authentically communal against the powers of containment. Like that of the Frankfurt School, Canetti's crowd offers the promise of the great political equalizer that can cut across boundaries of individuated identity, social class, race, gender, or sexuality, forming a collectivity of common sense without any social stratification; however, these moments of crystallization of the open crowd are always fleeting, fragile, and unsustainable and inevitably recast into its variant psychological personae (the pack, the ring, flight, feast, panic, etc.).

The Market Crowd

At the very moment Canetti marked the apex of crowd psychology, the era of the physical crowd's spontaneous assembly was in historical decline because of new architectures of containment that virtualized the crowd through the proliferation of television and information technology during the 1960s. While the society of the spectacle formed representational crowds through technologies of physical separation and image mediation, there was a less visible yet equally profound transformation of the crowd that took shape through the revitalization of an alternative theory that had existed well before the time of Le Bon: the crowd of the market. Market crowds were constitutionally distinct from social and political crowds in that they were thought not to assimilate individuality into psychological unity, but rather saw systemic collectivity in the self-interested, strategic interactions among rational individual actors pursuing their own individual gain (Mackay 1852, Stäheli 2006).[5] The one exception to the dynamics governing the *homo economicus* of the market crowd would be moments of panic selling or exuberant speculation, when the psychological crowd would eclipse the market crowd and sabotage its proper and natural order, which might then soar or crash according to the irrational whims of the herd. Contradictorily, these moments of market dysfunction enabled the first critical introduction of crowd psychology into the rational interactions of the market crowd. By the 1920s a new class of contrarian investors had emerged to pursue inherent value in the capacity to anticipate these surges of irrational volatility, and what was previously feared as risk became, for some, an opportunity for speculative investment by drawing from theories of crowd psychology to anticipate market behavior (Seden 1912). Instances of market disequilibria were posited as investment opportunities for the first time, bringing together in an unlikely alliance these two incongruent models of the crowd (Stäheli 2006, 277–79).

In the postwar period, a revolution in probabilistic theory developed forms of statistical modeling that could be applied to complex, real-world phenomena with a large number of random variables. In the late 1950s at the Massachusetts Institute of Technology, Norbert Wiener developed mathematical formulas derived from the study of Brownian motion, Markoff chains, and "random walks" that could calculate the variables to more accurately predict the future behavior of an indeterministic system based on probability distributions (Wiener 1966). The "Wiener process" became a form of stochastic calculus that would help develop systems of predictive modeling useful for an array of interdisciplinary applications such as applied mathematics, biology, natural science, physics, actuarial science, and economics. In the early 1970s, the Black-Sholes options pricing model was based on an equation derived from the Wiener process to predicatively calculate the *future* values of a given security to then be rapidly bought and sold through a scheme called "dynamic hedging" that would statistically mitigate risk for speculative investors and become the basis for modern derivatives and hedge funds. A powerful deception of the Black-Scholes equation as noted by Brian Holmes is that the putative laws of the stock market appear to be natural laws, like quantum physics or weather systems, when in truth they form an "artificial world model" used to game the system in a collusive form of "control fraud" (Holmes 2010).

Stochastic calculus spurred an important second-wave absorption of the psychological crowd into that of the market crowd, which increased profit-taking potentials of market volatility for large financial firms. When the advancement of supercomputing in the 1980s and 1990s optimized dynamic hedging schemes to generate derivative values that were increasingly abstracted, the pursuit of greater precision in techniques of risk management required additional mathematical formulas to model an absolutely crucial random variable of the market: the unpredictability of collective human behavior within it. Foundationally based on concepts of John Nash's equilibrium and Herbert Simon's bounded rationality, an emergent field of behavioral economics would offer elaborate formulas that could be fed into the stochastic calculus of market prediction. The driving impetus behind this field that matured during the 1960s and 1970s was the widespread adaptation of cognitive theories of social behavior into the idiom and logic of econometrics. As part of this larger project, the irrational, impulsive actions of market crowd behavior, based on the solubility of the individual into the mass, became understood as an effect of the cumulative strategic interactions between selfish individuals agents acting rationally within a given system. In effect, the rise of behavioral economics closed the theoretical gap between the psychological crowd and the market crowd, creating a unified field theory explaining that the macro behavior (Black-Scholes) and micro behavior of individual actors (Nash, Simon) were simply two views of the same coextensive process. But far more crucial than these theoretical bases were the proofs that made them mathematically calculable, delivering their functional utility to real-world systems, from distributed computer networks to crowd-control techniques. Inevitably, the economic approach to human behavior worked its way back into the social field and extended the logic of the market to all kinds of nonmarket human activities thought to be driven by psychological causes: marriage, crime, leisure, education, friendship, and so on (Becker 1976). Ultimately, the question was asked: If rational individual decisions can make the crowd appear in the guise of a singular psychological entity, might it not also stand, by way of inverse reasoning, that crowds of all kinds—whether social or political, virtual or actual—behave, in essence, like markets? Or more precisely, might they be *made* to behave as such?

Crowdsourcing

A term coined by Jeff Howe in 2006, "crowdsourcing" designates a new trend in e-commerce describing online marketplaces through incentives and schemes for user participation with an appeal to both self-interest and communal belonging. A blended concept named after the "open source" movement and the practice of job "outsourcing," crowdsourcing is a method of generating value by drawing in users with the promise of free services and social networking; once the system has assembled a critical mass of users, the value of the online crowd can then be "sourced," that is, monetized through any number of "prosumer" business models. In the open source model, the value conversions are often asymmetrical: what a user would more likely value as participatory culture on a site like Facebook, YouTube, or Twitter is exchanged (often unbeknownst to the participant) for the currencies of user-generated content, data, time, attention, or labor, which can be monetized and capitalized. However, the outsourcing model is found in systems like Amazon Mechanical Turk, Crowdflower, Microtask, and in the practice of MMORPG "gold farming," which have all delivered unadorned platforms designed to assemble, deliver, and manage a crowdsourced virtual labor market to an employer.

The common reading of crowdsourcing is that it combines the virtual crowd of mass media with an online distributed computing system that can together aggregate a community that enables structured participation at a distance (Howe 2006, 2009; Surowiecki 2005). But I'd like to delink its implacable association with distributed computing technology and read it as a practice emerging directly out of the historical convergence of the psychological crowd and the market crowd traced above. From this point of view, crowdsourcing must be directly linked to an emerging current in behavioral economics called "mechanism design." Based on the mathematical calculus sometimes termed "reverse game theory," mechanism design reorients Nash's focus on the players toward the rules of the game itself. Seeking to overcome the unreliable opacity of human behavioral agents who at times conceal their motives and act irrationally, creating unpredictable and destabilizing effects on markets, mechanism designers reverse engineered game theory to proactively condition individual agents through incentives that direct the collective behavior toward desired outcomes. Devised by economists Roger Myerson, Leonid Hurwicz, and Erik Maskin, mechanism design has become a useful neoliberal strategy of using government to influencing the economy with market incentives rather than with regulation and central planning that more strictly dictates the allocation of resources. The utility of mechanism design to neoliberalism is that it provides a solution to the problem of getting masses of people to behave in a way that is predictable and governable without jeopardizing the autonomy of the individual agent to act "freely" in his or her own self-interest (Maskin 2008).

Recasting the concept of crowdsourcing as an outgrowth of mechanism design simultaneously deepens our understanding of the implicit rationales embedded in social computing systems, while also providing a more concrete and historical way of identifying commonalities across disparate instantiations of the contemporary crowd, in both its theoretical conceptualization and its material formation. For crowdsourcing to yield its social and political potential, it requires the crowd to outwardly appear as a social force while being inwardly conditioned as an economic resource. Maintaining the balance of this schism has become the defining problem of the contemporary crowd. New theories devised to study the crowd are no longer content with methods of behavioral prediction using models of stochastic calculus; the problem has become how to proactively condition crowd behavior that will perceive itself as a socially self-organizing system, but in actuality treat itself as a market and act according to market principles. Crowdsourcing designates the panoply of incentive-compatible mechanisms that catalyze crowd formation to optimize resource allocation and risk management.

While neoliberal free market advocates designed mechanisms to help crowdsource pools of subprime mortgage holders that triggered the disastrous collapse of the housing bubble, the field of computer science was concurrently developing an offshoot called "algorithmic mechanism design," which has now become prevalent in systems of distributed social computing platforms like Google and Facebook. These algorithms seek to optimize the correct participation of the user nodes in a distributed system to work together without being governed by the forcible intercession of a network protocol (TCP/IP or FTP) but through software protocol (API) between shared web applications and content management systems. Algorithmic mechanism design encourages users to optimize their profiles and share private information with other third-party applications, meaning that the protocol of the system is not dictated as an overhead architecture but is "freely" chosen by shaping users who collectively construct the system in pursuit of their unique, independent, and individual goals, and also through the collective recruitment of other users (Nisan and Ronen 1999). Also concurrently, within cognitive science and social psychology, stochastic and game theoretic computational modeling was introduced into the study of the physical crowd to help develop new tactics of crowd control (particularly for incidents of disaster or "escape panic") not dictated by direct orders, laws, or physical barriers, but through incentive mechanisms (Berk 1974; Moussaïd et al. 2009, 201 ; Helbing et al. 2000, 2007; Harrison 2007; Goldstone and Gureckis 2009).[6]

This overlap brings us full circle to Black Friday 2008 and the death of Jdimytai Damour. The public fixation on the crowd's actions that day can now be more readily interpreted as calling into question the inherent fault lines concealed by the incentive mechanisms designed to mitigate systemic physical, social, and economic risk, and question who stands to gain and who to lose. The roiling public outrage that focused on the failure of the crowd's conduct also unmasks the specious and tenuous rationale that the burden of such conduct begins and ends with the crowd. The crowd has become proxy for a more penetrating social problem that can be most summarily stated as the deep social need for real collective self-organization in the face of current political mechanisms designed to govern that organization without appearing to do so. Here resurgent within the practices of crowdsourcing, this problem is simply the contemporary version of a deeply historical tension between the crowd of mass organization, labor, and consumption and the crowd of spontaneous political solidarity feared by the established political order as a viral contagion. Reading the present in the light of this history, the public attribution of responsibility to the crowd in Damour's death is not an absolute reversion to a facile psychological explication of crowd behavior, but also permits the reassignment of responsibility to the increased games of risk inherent in mechanisms designed to manipulate human beings as a resource that must be managed, measured, and economized. The focus on the crowd is spoken in egalitarian empathy about the ultimate risk born by Damour, and the encroaching fear that they also might be on the losing end of a zero-sum game that claims to be for the good of all.

I'll conclude with a final question that must be left to another day: what might a viable form of counterorganization to crowdsourcing look like? Nearly three years after Black Friday 2008, the Occupy Wall Street movement has formed encampments in cities all across the United States.

"We are the 99%" is more than a political slogan pointing to the growing disparity of wealth; it is tactic of crowd formation that neutralizes mechanisms designed for of sub-identitarian crowdsourcing. In its being anonymous, decentered, and mercurial, and in its assembling so inclusive a body of people, Occupy Wall Street's motives, actions, and precise composition cannot easily be identified or externally aggregated. Following this example, and playing on a conceptual hybridization between Canetti's self-sensing "open" crowd and the open source computing movement, I would suggest that something called the "open source crowd" must reclaim ownership of the crowdsourced crowd through a variety of tactical countermeasures. An open source crowd refers to any kind of crowd formed through a self-organizing process of people seeking, by their own means, the increased future potential that comes through the extensive interconnection with other people in ways not exclusively based on identity or self-interest, but rather based on forms of shared interest, communal sense, experience, affect, and feeling. Crowdsourcing, in the expanded sense, is a top-down mechanism designed to capture and manage that potential, while appearing as an open source crowd. At times the open crowd is able to find, sustain, and intensify itself outside of, or by cutting through, these control mechanisms; at others times the creative potential is seized and capitalized by crowdsourcing. In either case, it is important to state that crowdsourcing *does not and can never* generate the open source crowd. Crowdsourcing may be able to develop technologies that use, condition, or redirect its potential, but the open source crowd always exists in excess of the mechanisms designed to manage it.

Acknowledgments

I wish to express my gratitude to local resident Jennifer Cordello for offering me her invaluable firsthand perspective on the culture and communities adjacent to the Green Acres shopping mall.

Kenneth Rogers is assistant professor in the media and cultural studies department at the University of California–Riverside. His research is broadly concerned with the intersection of politics, labor, attention, political economy, and digital media. He has published on the history of video and digital media, crowdsourcing, alternative pedagogy, labor in media art, attention, and biopolitics. His current book project is *The Attention Complex: Media Technology and Biopolitics* (Palgrave Macmillan, forthcoming 2012).

Notes

1. One reader comment from the *New York Daily News* Opinion page read, "Scary Christmas Midland Park, N.J.: Attention, Valley Stream Wal-Mart shoppers: You may escape legal punishment, but you cannot escape your memories. I hope you think about the body of Jdimytai Damour [photo] under your foot every day. I hope you feel his hand closing around your ankle in your dreams. I hope you remember his face whenever you look at whatever piece of crap you sold your soul for that day" (Spencer 2008).

2. "'He was bum-rushed by 200 people,' co-worker Jimmy Overby, 43," Witness Kimberly Cribbs said shoppers acted like "savages" Joyner 2008)

3. [Green Acres] has also seen its share of trouble. In the 1980s, the mall earned a reputation as the 'car theft capital' of Long Island. In 1990, four moviegoers were shot—one fatally—when two groups of teenagers opened fire in a crowded theater that was showing *The Godfather, Part III* (Belson and Zraick 2008).

4. "Detective Lt. Michael Fleming, who is in charge of the investigation for the Nassau police, said the store lacked adequate security. He called the scene 'utter chaos' and said the 'crowd was out of control.' As for those who had run over the victim, criminal charges were possible, the lieutenant said. 'I've heard other people call this an accident, but it is not,' he said. 'Certainly it was a foreseeable act'" (McFadden and Macropoulos 2008).

5. Gabriel de Tarde offered perhaps one of the earliest social theorizations of how an alternative form of sociology could be developed by looking at the infinitesimal transactions, imitations, reiterations, and deviations among individual actors (Tarde 1903).

6. "An alternative method of crowd control is to change the structure of the environment such that certain navigational behaviors are facilitated while others are hindered. Even without physical or abstract barriers, it may be possible to 'indirectly control collective behavior' with substantial efficacy. . . . Under this new approach toward fostering effective collective organization, the aim would be to facilitate the development of self-organized patterns rather than dictate high-level structures via top-down control (Goldstone and Gureckis 2009, 418).

Works Cited

Belson, Ken, and Karen Zraick. 2008. "Mourning a Good Friend, and Trying to Make Sense of a Stampede." *New York Times*, November 30, sec. New York Region. http://www.nytimes.com/2008/11/30/nyregion/30walmart.html

Becker, Gary S. 1976. *The Economic Approach to Human Behavior*. Chicago: University of Chicago Press.

Berk, Richard A. 1974. "A Gaming Approach to Crowd Behavior." *American Sociological Review* 39 (3): 355-75.

Bonacich, Edna, and Jake B. Wilson. 2008. *Getting the Goods: Ports, Labor, and the Logistics Revolution.* Ithaca: Cornell University Press.

Canetti, Elias. 1984. *Crowds and Power.* New York: Farrar, Straus and Giroux. Originally published in 1960

Freud, Sigmund. 1990. *Group Psychology and the Analysis of the Ego.* New York: W. W. Norton.

Goldstone, R. L, and T. M Gureckis. 2009. "Collective Behavior." *Topics in Cognitive Science* 1 (3): 412–438.

Hart, M., P. Jefferies, P. M. Hui, and N. F. Johnson. 2001. "Crowd-anticrowd Theory of Multi-agent Market Games." *The European Physical Journal B-Condensed Matter and Complex Systems* 20 (4): 547–550.

Helbing, D., I. Farkas, and T. Vicsek. 2000. "Simulating Dynamical Features of Escape Panic." *Nature* 407: 487-490.

Helbing, D., A. Johansson, and H. Z Al-Abideen. 2007. "Dynamics of Crowd Disasters: An Empirical Study." *Physical review* E 75 (4): 46-109.

Holmes, Brian. 2010. "Written in the Stars?: Global Finance, Precarious Destinies." *Ephemera* 10 (3) (August): 224-233.

Howe, Jeff. 2006. "The Rise of Crowdsourcing." *Wired Magazine,* June.

———. 2009. *Crowdsourcing: Why the Power of the Crowd Is Driving the Future of Business.* New York: Three Rivers Press.

Joyner, James. 2008 "Wal-Mart Worker Dies in 'Black Friday' Trampling." *Outside the Beltway,* November 28. http://www.outsidethebeltway.com

Laird, Gordon. 2009. *The Price of a Bargain: The Quest for Cheap and the Death of Globalization.* New York: Palgrave Macmillan.

Le Bon, Gustave. 1897. *The Crowd: A Study of the Popular Mind.* New York: Macmillan.

Mackay, Charles. 1852. *Memoirs of Extraordinary Popular Delusions and the Madness of Crowds.* London: Office of the National Illustrated Library.

MacDougall, William. 1920. *The Group Mind.* New York: G. P. Putnam's Sons.

McFadden, Robert, and Angela Macropoulos. 2008. "Wal-Mart Employee Trampled to Death." *New York Times,* November 28. http://www.nytimes. com/2008/11/29/business/29walmart.html

Maskin, Eric. 2008. "Mechanism Design: How to Implement Social Goals." Princeton NJ: IAS School of Social Science Economics Working Papers. (81) (February) http://www.sss.ias.edu/publications/economicsworking

Moussaïd, Mehdi, Dirk Helbing, Simon Garnier, Anders Johansson, Maud Combe, and Guy Theraulaz. 2009. "Experimental Study of the Behavioural Mechanisms Underlying Self-organization in Human Crowds." Proc. R. Soc. B 276: 2755 -2762.

Moussaïd, Mehdi, Dirk Helbing, and Guy Theraulaz. 2011. "How Simple Rules Determine Pedestrian Behavior and Crowd Disasters." Proc Natl Acad Sci 108 (17) (April 26): 6884-6888.

Noam Nisan and Amir Ronen. 1999. Algorithmic mechanism design (extended abstract). In Proceedings of the thirty-first annual ACM symposium on Theory of computing (STOC '99). New York: ACM, 129-140. http://doi.acm.org/10.1145/301250.301287

Reich, Wilhelm. 1946. *The Mass Psychology of Fascism*. Trans. Theodore P. Wolfe. 3rd ed. New York: Orgone Institute Press.

Rugh, J. S., and D. S. Massey. 2010. "Racial Segregation and the American Foreclosure Crisis." *American Sociological Review* 75(5):629.

Schnapp, Jeffrey T., and Matthew Tiews, eds. 2006. *Crowds*. Stanford: Stanford University Press.

Selden, George Charles. 1912. *Psychology of the Stock Market*. New York: Ticker.

Spencer, Laurie E. 2008 "Voice of the People - NY Daily News." *NY Daily News* Opinion, December 4. http://www.nydailynews.com/opinion/voice-people-article-1.356638

Stäheli, Urs. 2006. "Market Crowds." In *Crowds*, ed. Jeffrey T. Schnapp and Matthew Tiews. Stanford: Stanford University Press.

Surowiecki, James. 2005. *The Wisdom of Crowds*. New York: Anchor.

Tarde, Gabriel de. 1903. *The Laws of Imitation*. New York: H. Holt.

Trotter, Wilfred. 1916. *Instincts of the Herd in Peace and War*. New York: Macmillan.

Wiener, Norbert. 1966. *Nonlinear Problems In Random Theory*. Cambridge: MIT Press

Portrait of the Artist as Social Symptom: Viral Affect and Mass Culture in *The Day of The Locust*

H. N. Lukes

In a historical moment when anything from a blog to a revolution can "go viral," we might pause to ask, When did this once troubling biological term come to signify something positive? To contextualize these times of tech-nopolitical optimism, it is worth returning to a certain pessimism about emergent media attending the social, political, and aesthetic concerns of the United States in the 1930s. A decade initiated by the first electron-microscopic image of viruses seemed similarly destined to chart the implications of its metaphorical menace. On one level, the economic stagnation of the Great Depression counterintuitively fostered a new focus on speed, not only regarding literally accelerated transportation and communication but also as a cultural ethos yielding both anxiety and anticipation (Irr 1998, 46–49). Similarly, this era's interest in mass culture was underwritten by a logic of contagion that manifested in the equal and opposite urgency to record and preserve fading folkways (Retman 2011). On the eve of Euro-pean fascism, Marxian and psychoanalytic preoccupations with group psychology centered on how common feeling comes to take on the speed, potency, and inhuman qualities of the mob, and how mobs might lead to revolutions of the Left or Right. In other words, the 1930s seemed cen-trally concerned with the question of how collective affect goes viral.

These discourses appear to synergistically collide in the American literary author Nathanael West's last novel, *The Day of the Locust* (1939), with its representation of the monstrous social worlds produced by South-ern California and the early Hollywood cinema industry. The novel's final scene of a riot at a movie premiere is the inevitable culmination, the final fatal symptom, of what W. H. Auden called "West's disease," the social

WSQ: Women's Studies Quarterly 40: 1 & 2 (Spring/Summer 2012)

malaise of emotional "cripples" in a "democratic and mechanized society" (1971, 121, 123). I will argue, however, that West's disease might not just refer to Auden's cultural lumpenbourgeoisie but also must be seen as a disease of the artist himself; as an ostensibly resistant producer in consumer capitalism, the artist nonetheless appears as an ironic site for viral infection.

The Day of the Locust traces a few months in the life of Tod Hackett, a Yale-trained painter recruited to do Hollywood set design. In his spare time he labors on his epic canvas The Burning of Los Angeles, meant to represent the rage of "those poor devils who can only be stirred by the promise of miracles and then only to violence" (West 1962, 184). Tod becomes obsessed with his neighbors, whom he uses as subject sketches for his masterwork. They include Faye Greener, a gorgeous and vapid seventeen-year-old aspiring starlet; her father, Harry Greener, a culturally fading and literally dying vaudevillian clown; and Homer Simpson, an Iowan suffering from consumption who has come to Los Angeles for his health and does little else than express having "time on his hands" by means of a tic in his seemingly autonomous hands. In early sketches for Tod's composition, a naked Faye is at the center of the canvas as the object of mob rage. As Tod's observations of LA's "dream dump" fail to materialize as his portrayal of the revolutionary affect of a nation, he becomes obsessed with increasingly rapacious fantasies about Faye.

In a final riot scene at a movie premiere on Hollywood Boulevard, seemingly sparked by Homer's finally rising to action in assaulting a child, Tod's leg is broken as he attempts to escape while also trying to save girls from being molested in the mob's abandon. Tod's attempts fail under the force of the mob, but on a conceptual level, it is also too late for him to bridge the difference between his fantasy and reality. In pain and pinned in place, he escapes by imagining that he is sketching the final details of his painting: Faye is no longer the central object and focus of the mob's rage but merely another participant in the foreground. In fact, there is no centering object of the outburst but merely a perspectival spectrum of personified wild affect "falling out of the canvas" (185). A background of flames consuming fantasy architecture leads to a midground of Tod's original subjects, the masses infected with the false promises of popular culture, those who "had come to California to die" (60). In the foreground are all of the novel's major characters in various poses of terror and indignation. Tod is there also, holding "a small stone to throw before continuing his flight"

(185). The authorities draw Tod away from his traumatized fantasia and put him in a police car, in which Tod is both reactive and productive: "The siren began to scream and at first he thought he was making the sound himself. He felt his lips with his hands. They were clamped tight. He knew then it was the siren. For some reason this made him laugh and he began to imitate the siren as loud as he could" (185).

Many critics have read *The Day of the Locust* as a cautionary tale about the mutual imbrications of consumer capitalism and fascist politics (Barnard 1995; Haynes 2007; Veitch 1997). Given that West ended his prior novel, *A Cool Million*, with an actual American fascist uprising, it would seem that *Locust*'s representation of a riot strives to strip bare something more like the virus of spontaneous crowd affect. If so, the conclusion of *Locust* suggests that group psychology also implicates the role of the artist and the domain of aesthetics, not just in a post-Marxist or Freudian sense, but also in a radical rendering of trans-individual and trans-human feeling.

One could argue that Tod's scream voices the virus of mob affect coming to life upon its parasitic possession of its host. In the biological sense, viruses have until recently been theorized as organic but not necessarily alive. Like Foucault's definition of power, the existence of a virus is radically bound to its "exercise" in the consummately relational moment when a virion—or the virus in its dormant, nonliving state—cathects to a host (Foucault 1990, 94). West describes this transformative effect for the general public: "Until they reached the line, they looked diffident, almost furtive, but the moment they had become part of it, they turned arrogant and pugnacious" (177).

As an artist intent on portraying the infection, Tod does not give in to the mob, but neither does he escape it unaffected, or rather uninfected, as his sanity is left in question by the narrative's abrupt conclusion. I would argue that Tod's siren scream calls no one: it is not commentary, a cry for help, a rebel yell, or even a worthy Dadaist intervention. Interpreting Tod's scream as a fully conscious and artistic act, Robin Blyn states, "The final lines of the novel represent a literalization of the imitation of the siren by an artist complicit in the subject of his critique" (2003, 33). Blyn reads mass culture and Faye as sirens, in the sense of the seducing sea nymphs, intent on destroying the artist and his distance from commodity capitalism. While I agree with Blyn's brilliant reading of sound in the novel and the destruction of the artist as the through line of its episodic structure, I think there is much more at stake in this scene than literalization as an allegorical element in a rendering of the artist in the age of mechanical reproduction.

A police siren already stands in metaphorical relation to the tempt-resses of Homer's *Odyssey*; thus, this significatory return demonstrates less literalization than a laying bare of the function of metaphoricity itself. Tod's cry signifies the human organism practicing the most basic form of mimesis by directly imitating a sound, in this case *of* emergency and inspired *by* emergency. At this level of imitation, we observe Tod's raw embodiment, but it is not a state of independence from culture and signifi-cation. He is without language as structure, but he is nonetheless infected by language's sonic materiality and its viral cathexis to human sensory reproduction. Tod's channeling, if you will, binds representation to the virtuality and "autonomy of affect," what Brian Massumi calls "the real-material-but-incorporeal" (2002, 5). *Locust's* final scene of the artist *mani-festing* (in both the transitive and intransitive senses of the verb) in the chiasmus of mimetic literalism and sensory possession might tell us much about the role of aesthetics and affect in the perceived difference between historical mass movements and emergent viral politics.

As *Locust* implicitly suggests, theories of aesthetics cannot separate themselves from the embodied life of the artist. Because of his intense focus on commodity culture and his historical overlap with the theorists loosely affiliated with the Frankfurt School, post-Marxist interpretations have dominated scholarly discussion of West's fiction (Barnard 1995; Haynes 2007; Irr 1998; Roberts 1996; Veitch 1997). Taken together, these critiques tend to produce West as either anticipating or being the prime exemplar of the Frankfurt School's various dialectical interpretations of aesthetics and mass culture. The subject-object anxiety about the relation-ship of theorists to artists implied in this Möbius strip is further compli-cated by the role of the political artist. Whereas West studies have been especially, and arguably belatedly, preoccupied with the political life and intentions of the author, the Frankfurt School seemed singularly uninter-ested in portraying the artist as anything other than fettered by the culture industry.

I would like to take a step back from this conversation by consider-ing Jacques Rancière's idea that aesthetics is "a regime for identifying art [that] carries a politics, or metapolitics, within it" (2009, 15). Rancière defines "metapolitics" as a form of "thinking which aims to overcome political dissensus by switching scene . . . a revolution in the very mode of production of material life" (33). While echoing the dialectical material-ism of post-Marxists, Rancière advances by framing "art" itself as nothing more than a historically specific measure of the "distance" taken from the state of the world (23). Thus aesthetics, as it has been theorized and given a "bad reputation," appears for Rancière as a negotiation between "the promise of an art that would be no more than an art or would no longer be art" (1, 15). Here Rancière summarizes a history of Western philosophy's production of "aesthetics" as fundamentally antithetical to politics even as it cannot help but trace the contours of the political. In other words, aesthetics marks one of two positions: (1) art for art's sake, the recursive site in which the bookends of Immanuel Kant's judgment of beauty as pur-poseless purposiveness and (for this essay's historical purposes) Clement Greenberg's self-containment of Modernism protect the autonomy of art and the evaluatory profession of critics; or (2) the utility of representation as it either (a) entertains or (b) compels the audience to change its world, as exemplified by Bertolt Brecht, among others.

West subtly departs from conventional problems of aesthetics by cen-tering on an artist who *would be no more than an artist or would no longer be an artist.* Following Rancière's articulation of the antibellestristic end of the dichotomy, this latter figure—the artist who would no longer be an artist—implicitly becomes some kind of ethicopolitical subject, ranging from the Platonic philosopher-king to the Marxian proletarian subject. In contrast to Rancière's logic, West's persistent undoing of his protagonists in all his novels (three out of four of whom are some kind of artist) might suggest a more existential situation of "no longer be[ing]." I would argue, however, that *Locust's* alienation of the artist arcs toward the quasi-alive aspects of the virus inasmuch as the artist ceases to be an artist—that is, a human, expressive part of the whole of the body politic—and instead becomes a reification of group affect, an ecstatic form of being that is both less and more than either a human being or an artistic product. Neither a singular among singulars nor a symbolic representative, West's artist embodies a problematic of social synecdoche, where the relation of parts to wholes is disoriented.

If we believe West's critics when they indicate that he is the 1930s "poet of darkness," then we must take his millennial aesthetics not only as his object of documentation but also as his consideration of the function of art and the role of the artist (Veitch 1997, 37). *The Day of the Locust* functions as an implicit commentary on the proletarian novel of the 1930s cultural front by admitting the masses' ugly and excessive jouissance, resistant to organization unless it is overtly fascist. Revolutionary violence is problematized here, since "instead of the possibly insurrectionist sense in which Adorno intends his 'spark' . . . West imagines in the chaos of the crowd a self-wounding reproduction of the very violence, symbolic and actual, *already* meted out upon the same, slack bodies that have 'slaved for nothing'" (Haynes 2007, 347). Given West's statement that "in America violence is idiomatic," *Locust* seems to ask how necessary it is to reach for a revolver when one hears the word "culture" if its producers and consumers—or in West's terms, the cheaters and the cheated—are already armed for either a homicidal or suicidal mission (West 1971, 50).

Interestingly, West chooses not to portray this overt rage directly until the final riot; rather, he frames a kind of viral affect running through individual characters' symptomatic embodiment of culture.[1] On a surface level, it is apparent that all the major characters seem to have an affect that is off, so to speak. Closer examination shows that *Locust's* characters seem to be infected by mass culture through a sort of viral symptom of performative gesture. As a character representing the fading of vaudeville before the rise of film, Harry Greener represents the most direct cultural symptom. "When Harry had first begun his stage career, he had probably restricted his clowning to the boards, but now he clowned almost continuously. It was his sole method of defense. Most people, he had discovered, won't go out of their way to punish a clown" (77). This defense system soon becomes almost autoimmune to the extent that he cannot stop himself and, indeed, performs himself to death as he pushes his routine through an apparent heart attack: "He didn't get very far this time and had to gasp painfully for breath. Suddenly, like a mechanical toy that had been over-wound, something snapped inside of him and he began to spin through his entire repertoire" (92).

What the stage is to Harry, the screen is to Faye, whose gestures constitute a more unconscious and dissociative performance (Edenbaum 1973, 208). "This elaborate gesture, like all her others, was so completely meaningless, almost formal, that she seemed a dancer rather than an affected actress" (94). Her "affected" bodily comportment seems to have an infectious effect on men (who seem autonomically to convert their sexual attraction into violence against each other), though it too functions as a kind of defense system, in which her body seems to be autonomous or at least compensating for her mind: "The strange thing about her gestures and expressions was that they didn't really illustrate what she was saying. They were almost pure. It was as though her body recognized how foolish her words were and tried to excite her hearers into being uncritical" (159).

Certainly West underscores the reification of commodity capitalism by highlighting the inanimate qualities of his characters, especially as they are compared to his characterizations of things, which he does with a "precision [that] seems almost gratuitous, even fetishistic" (Barnard 1995, 141). Yet if we take literally West's terms "formal" and "pure" regarding Faye, we might see these choreographies of gestural affect as more transhuman than a humanist Marxian complaint would have it. Even if, as culture producers, Harry and Faye are "cheaters" in West's lexicon, they are not necessarily fakes, precisely because they seem to lack full agency over their bodily performances. Rather, their channeling of cultural gesture seems to match Massumi's definition of affect as "so pure and productive a receptivity that it can only be conceived as a third state, an excluded middle, prior to the distinction between activity and passivity" (32). We may also see this conductive behavior as symptomatic, inasmuch as Lacan describes the symptom as the symbolic order writing on the human individual's flesh.

The symptomatic indistinction between people and things—and in the end the cheaters and the cheated—is clearest in Homer, whom West describes as a "poorly made automaton" (82). Homer has the most overt psychoanalytic physical symptom in a kind of tic with his hands, "which seemed to have a life and will of their own" (88). The unruly hands at once stand in sharp contrast to his general, obsequious passivity and foreshadow his extraordinary violence in crushing a child at the end of the book. Rather than simply representing either the sleeping rage of the masses or his own sexual repression, Homer's hands seem to register an autonomy of affect that certainly registers the infectious desire of his milieu while also suggesting a kind of raw aesthetic drive. Of Homer's "most complicated tic," Tod notes that "It wasn't pantomime, as he had first thought, but manual ballet" (161).

Unlike the manic vaudeville of Harry and disarranged vamping of Faye, Homer's gestural "ballet" rises to the level of high culture, making Homer, or at least his hands, an implicating foil for Tod as the artist in control of his will and vision set at necessary remove from mass culture. As Blyn states, "In its portrayal of Homer Simpson and Tod Hackett, *Locust* reveals that the space between the automaton and the autonomous artist is no great distance" (2003, 22). In my reading, this conflation certainly becomes true in Tod's ultimate scream. But if the process of the novel traces the dismantling of the artist, then it is not just about the artist as autonomous in a totally reified world but also about Tod the artist *as human*, inasmuch as the novel ultimately flattens the ostensibly deep *identity* of this "very complicated young man with a whole set of personalities, one inside the other like a nest of Chinese boxes" into a dehumanized *situation* of "incorporeal materiality."[2] While hyperreality and the decentering of the sovereign subject in late capitalism and postmodernity arguably reveal all personal symptoms to be social, the artist in *Locust* appears not as a unique subject but rather as a singular *signifier* that corresponds with Žižek's theory of ideology.

Žižek's articulation of the social symptom marries aspects of Marx and psychoanalysis based on Lacan's idea that Marx invented the symptom. Even as commodity and symptom share a function of substitution—the human alienation of labor's surplus value for the false relationality of commodity and the desire of the subject for his or her symptom, respectively—they are each ultimately "uninterpretable" precisely because their purpose is to obscure the system enabling and depending on their act of substitution. As Žižek states, "The symptom is, strictly speaking, a particular element which subverts its own universal foundation, a species subverting its genus" (1989, 16). Žižek speaks of commodity fetishism here, but he might as well be speaking of the Lacanian subject itself: "What is really a structural effect, an effect of the network of relations between elements, [appears] as if this property also belongs to it outside its relation with other elements" (14). Even as it would seem to be the purest of sociological effects, social symptom in a Žižekian context actually reads as a split site of irrational causality. In his reading of Žižek's implicit logic of the exception, Erik Vogt notes, "The social symptom has to be grasped as master signifier *and* as *objet a*" (2007, 62).

If the artist appears in *Locust* as a social symptom, then it does so as this simultaneous but irreconcilable form of grounding and horizon for broader critiques of the culture industry, artistic auras, and everyday life. Rather than reading Tod as either a part for the whole of collective affect or as a canny subject whose artistic intention and critique automatically protect him from the inherent violence of mass culture, might we recognize that West renders the productive jouissance of the artist himself as a *field of excess* against which both the profession of the artist and the passion of any group come into focus. Many critics read Tod's hysteria at the end of the novel as West's cautionary reincorporation of the artist who pretends to be at a critical distance from his or her totally reified world of consumer capitalism (Blyn 2003; Muller 1973; Roberts 1996; Wells 1973). I would argue that West's insistence on Tod's rape fantasies demonstrates that the potential violence of the disillusioned people who "had come to California to die" becomes virulent and personal when it attaches to the artist, precisely because his techne is thwarted by the completion of commodity.

Inasmuch as we might agree with readings of Faye as a commodity, we see this excess of frustrated action in Tod's first admission of rape ideation: "Nothing less violent than rape would do. The sensation he felt was like that he got when holding an egg in his hand. Not that she was fragile or even seemed fragile. It was her completeness, her egglike self-sufficiency, that made him want to crush her" (107). While West's focus on the artist's crushing of Faye arguably signifies either his collusion with or exposure of the misogyny underpinning many of West's artistic peers and influences, especially the Surrealists, I would argue that he outlines something much more structural by using rape to distill and personify the suicidal and homicidal tendencies of the crowd in the portrait of the artist. West first description of Faye states, "If you threw yourself on her, it would be like throwing yourself from the parapet of a skyscraper. You would do it with a scream. You couldn't expect to rise again" (69). Given that his frustrated desire for Faye is often expressed in a "grunt," Tod's siren "scream" in the end suggests that his mimetic infection by the mob virus functions as the culminating of his fantasy of sexual desire in a deathly jouissance (67, 107).

Locust's early critics tended to laud West as having realistically portrayed the "immortal whore" in Faye (Reid 1967, 131; see also Fiedler 1994; Williams 1971). His later critics tend to either avoid or assimilate Tod's rapacious tendencies in broader readings of the frustrations that consumer culture produces. In all these critiques, as Susan Edmunds argues, "The ongoing characterization of Faye as a symbol either of Hollywood's deceptions or of the dreaming masses it deceives proceeds from an impulse to read her character allegorically and thus to deny her the self-interest and agency accorded to historical subjects (1998, 323n1). Despite a few efforts to pathologize Tod's sexuality as abnormal, few critics directly address Tod himself as a symbol for the pervasive misogyny of his immediate milieu and of much Modernist art. Tod's rape fantasies have come to function as a kind of purloined letter of *Locust* criticism. [3] Beyond this obvious gender trouble, this critical blind spot about the novel's unsettling suture of the reader to the protagonist's violent desire proves to be symptomatic of the very phenomenon West isolates—the inability to understand the embodied artist as that which grounds yet it is excluded from a theoretical field of aesthetics.

On face value, the psychoanalytic concept of the social symptom seems to be at odds with the Deleuzian notions of the virtual and the uncontainabilty attributed to the viral. I would argue that thinking with these two seemingly antithetical theoretical bodies allows us to see both viral affect and viral effects, or symptoms. Just as light is both a particle and a wave, psychoanalysis tends to see the idea of social symptom as particulate whereas Deleuzian inspired theories of affect tend to recognize a wavelike manifestation of the virtual. As Ed Cohen points out, the most disturbing conceptual aspect of the virus is not just its definitional troubling of life but also that viruses "are individuals and yet they are parts; they are partial—in all possible senses" (2011, 17–18). Virus's particulate yet pervasive and invasive nature destroys any epistemological rendering of the part in relation to the whole, which is also Tod's problem as an artist.

I thus conclude with a last reading from the novel to demonstrate what contemporary ideations of viral potential might learn from the convergence of aesthetics, mass culture, and viral politics in its early twentieth century analog (in every sense of the term). In a rare moment of self-doubt, Tod reconsiders both the role of the artist and the nature of group viral affect:

> He wondered if maybe he weren't exaggerating the importance of the people who come to California to die. Maybe they weren't really desperate enough to set a single city on fire, let alone the whole country. Maybe they were only the pick of America's madmen and not at all typical of the rest of the land. He told himself that it didn't make any difference because he was an artist, not a prophet. His work would not be judged by the accuracy with which it foretold the future but by its merit as painting. Nevertheless, he refused to give up the role of Jeremiah. He changed the "pick of America's madmen" to "cream" and felt almost certain that the milk from which it had been skimmed was just as rich in violence. The Angelenos would be first, but their comrades all of the country would follow. There would be civil war. (118)

In Tod's contemplation of the cheated as a representative political form, his conceptual crisis arises out of the possibility that they are a random field of beings whose only commonality is their exceptional lack of commonality. The senselessness of the final riot seems to confirm Tod's worry that the virus of group affect is infectious but not necessarily telic. Herein lies the difference between mob and revolutionary violence. West, however, pointedly removed the line "Only the working classes would resist" (Martin 1970, 319) from *Locust*'s penultimate manuscript, suggesting not that viral feeling is always already fascist, but that it must be understood on its own terms before being harnessed for political change.

Yet also at stake in this passage is the social function of art and the artist, which is rendered through Tod's implicit understanding of Rancière's dichotomy of "the promise of an art that would be no more than an art or would no longer be art." Tod's projection of his work's recognition via its "merit as painting" under the rubric of "art for art's sake" is uncomfortably bound to his refusal "to give up the role of Jeremiah." He never resolves the function of art as a form of representation and so defers implicitly to the structure of political representation. Finding the idea that Angelenos might simply be the "pick of America's madmen" ultimately unthinkable, Tod reorients his revolutionary vision through a compensatory act of synecdoche by figuring Los Angeles's cheated as the cream of America's milk.[4] Tod's failure as an artist and political thinker hinges on this insistence about social contiguity.

Wishful thinking on both the left and the right would see social forms as bearing an inherent intimacy—and, indeed, viral efficacy—between their parts and wholes. West's point in *The Day of the Locust* is not Tod's; the author does not mean to conflate part for whole, riot for revolution, Los Angeles for the United States. Rather, I think that West would follow Rancière in seeing a more subtle yet profound operation of the aesthetics *as* a form of politics: "Politics consists in reconfiguring the distribution of the sensible which defines the common of a community, to introduce into it new subjects and objects, to render visible what had not been, and to make heard as speakers those who had been perceived as mere noisy animals" (Rancière 2009, 25). This function of politics is also Rancière's definition of art. West's art voices the potentials and dangers of these "noisy animals" of the cheated. We might also, however, recognize the more quiet viral aspects of how individuals and populations conduct trans-individual affect. For West, real politics and aesthetics cannot ultimately be achieved by a viral spread of feeling from the social part to the whole but rather must create what Rancière calls a "part of those who have no part" (1999, 14).

Acknowledgments

The author would like to thank the *WSQ* editors, Patricia Clough and Jasbir Puar; the anonymous reader; Patty Ahn for invaluable research assistance; Sonnet Retman; and Molly McGarry.

H. N. Lukes is an assistant professor of queer and feminist theory in Occidental College's Department of Critical Theory and Social Justice. Her work has appeared in the *Oxford Literary Review*, *Women and Performance*, *GLQ*, *Homosexuality and Psychoanalysis* (University of Chicago Press, 2001), and *America First: Naming the Nation in US Film* (Routledge, 2007). She is currently working on a book titled "Part for Whole: Queer Aesthetics and the Politics of Belonging."

Notes

1. Since critics have emphasized the studied flatness of West's characters, affect has not been a mainstay of analysis in his books. Employing Massumi's emphasis on affect's chaotic autonomy from contained emotion, I argue for it as the animating if unlikely force of *Locust* (Massumi 2002, 28). Exceptions are Retman and Greenberg, each of whom provides useful readings of affect and satire in West's fiction. Retman emphasizes West's use of the burlesque as a rejection of the era's literary manipulation of empathy, since he understood it to be "a strategy of affect that easily served reactionary as well as progressive causes" (2011, 75). Greenberg's (2011) book charts a dialectical relation of joking and sentiment on the narrative and character level in *Locust*.

2. Massumi borrows the term "incorporeal materiality" from Foucault (Massumi 2002, 5). The portrait of the artist in the hands of West thus echoes the virtual aspects of Foucault's author function. This reading is supported by the fact that West pointedly made Tod the narrative focus of the novel late in his writing process and added all content about his painting itself and his artistic influences in the last revision (Martin 1970, 315).

3. Geneva Gano makes a refreshing departure from this trend by reading Tod's rape fantasies through the lens of misogyny and aesthetics. As she asserts, "Aesthetics actually serves here as a fine word for the artist's single-minded desire for his own, personal gratification" (2009, 55).

4. William Solomon points out a similar structure of warning about the dangers of part-for-whole political thinking in John Dos Passos's work, naming the literary technique "metaphorized synecdoche" (Solomon 1996, 810).

5. Thomas Strychacz summarizes earlier West criticism that critiqued *Locust* for failing to bear out of a clear relation of its parts to the whole of the novel. He furthers criticism that has defended it as being structured like a Hollywood

movie by arguing instead that the cut and suture rearrangement of film makes it a "virtual" art that mirrors Tod's unactualized painting and the disharmonizing aspects of the novel itself. I would argue that this virtuality applies to West's political vision as well, as his fiction's "transforming fragmentation itself into a narrative strategy" parallels Rancière's idea of aesthetic metapolitics (Strychacz 1987, 160).

Works Cited

Auden, W. H. 1971. "West's Disease." In *Nathanael West: A Collection of Critical Essays,* ed. Jay Martin. Englewood Cliffs, NJ: Prentice-Hall.

Barnard, Rita. 1995. *The Great Depression and the Culture of Abundance: Kenneth Fearing, Nathanael West, and Mass Culture in the 1930s.* New York: Cambridge University Press.

Blyn, Robin. 2003. "Sounding American Surrealism: The Sensational Subject of *The Day of the Locust." South Atlantic Review* 68(4):17–37.

Cohen, Ed. 2011. "The Paradoxical Politics of Viral Containment; or, How Scale Undoes Us One and All." *Social Text* 106:15–36.

Edenbaum, Robert I. 1973. "From American Dream to Pavlovian Nightmare." In *Nathanael West: The Cheaters and the Cheated: A Collection of Critical Essays,* ed. David Madden. DeLand, Florida: Everett/Edwards.

Edmunds, Susan. 1998. "Modern Taste and the Body Beautiful in Nathanael West's *The Day of the Locust." Modern Fiction Studies* 44(2):306–30.

Fiedler, Leslie. 1994. "Development and Frustration." In *Critical Essays on Nathanael West,* ed. Ben Siegel. New York; G. K. Hall.

Foucault, Michel. 1990. *The History of Sexuality.* Vol. 1, *An Introduction.* New York: Vintage.

Gano, Geneva M. 2009. "Nationalist Ideologies and New Deal Regionalism in *The Day of the Locust." MFS Modern Fiction Studies* 55(1):42–67.

Greenberg, Jonathan. 2011. *Modernism, Satire, and the Novel.* New York: Cambridge University Press.

Haynes, Doug. 2007. "'Laughing at the Laugh': Unhappy Consciousness in Nathanael West's *The Dream Life of Balso Snell." Modern Language Review* 102(2):341–62.

Irr, Caren. 1998. *The Suburb of Dissent: Cultural Politics in the U.S. and Canada During the 1930s.* Durham: Duke University Press.

Martin, Jay. 1970. *Nathanael West: The Art of His Life.* New York: Farrar Straus and Giroux.

Massumi, Brian. 2002. *Parables for the Virtual: Movement, Affect, Sensation.* Durham: Duke University Press.

Muller, Lavonne. 1973. "Malamud and West: Tyranny of the Dream Dump." In *Nathanael West: The Cheaters and the Cheated; A Collection of Critical Essays*, ed. David Madden. DeLand, FL: Everett/Edwards.

Rancière, Jacques. 1999. *Disagreement: Politics and Philosophy*. Minneapolis: University of Minnesota Press.

———. 2009. *Aesthetics and Its Discontents*. Malden, MA: Polity Press.

Reid, Randall. 1967. *The Fiction of Nathanael West: No Redeemer, No Promised Land*. Chicago: University of Chicago Press.

Retman, Sonnet. 2011. *Real Folks: Race and Genre in the Great Depression*. Durham: Duke University Press.

Roberts, Mathew. 1996. "Bonfire of the Avant-garde: Cultural Rage and Readerly Complicity in *The Day of the Locust*." *MFS Modern Fiction Studies* 42(1):61–90.

Solomon, William. 1996. "Politics and Rhetoric in the Novel in the 1930s." *American Literature* 68(4):799–818.

Strychacz, Thomas. 1987. "Making Sense of Hollywood: Mass Discourses and the Literary Order in Nathanael West's *The Day of the Locust*." *Western American Literature* 22(2):149–62.

Veitch, Jonathan. 1997. *American Superrealism: Nathanael West and the Politics of Representation in the 1930s*. Madison: University of Wisconsin Press.

Vogt, Erik. 2007. "Exception in Žižek's Thought." *diacritics* 37(2):61–77.

Wells, Walter. 1973. "Shriek of the Locust." In *Tycoons and Locusts: A Regional Look at Hollywood Fiction of the 1930s*. Carbondale: Southern Illinois University Press.

West, Nathanael. 1962. *Miss Lonelyhearts and The Day of the Locust*. New York: New Directions.

———. 1971. "Some Notes on Violence." In *Nathanael West: A Collection of Critical Essays*. Ed. Jay Martin. Englewood Cliffs, NJ: Prentice-Hall.

Williams, William Carlos. 1971. "*The Day of the Locust*." In *Nathanael West: A Collection of Critical Essays*, ed. Jay Martin. Englewood Cliffs, NJ: Prentice-Hall.

Žižek, Slavoj. 1989. *The Sublime Object of Ideology*. New York: Verso.

"Viral Things": Extended Review

John Carpenter's *The Thing*. Universal Pictures, 1982
Matthijs van Heijningen's *The Thing*. Universal Pictures, 2011

Elena Glasberg

Now is perfect timing for a re-review of *The Thing*, John Carpenter's 1982 sci-fi horror "classic" of alien infiltration of a polar outpost—as Matthijs van Heijningen's 2011 remake has come and already quickly gone from U.S. theaters. Carpenter's *The Thing* was itself a remake of director Christian Nyby's 1951 Howard Hawks-produced *The Thing From Another World*, which was itself based on John Campbell Jr.'s 1938 pulp story "Who Goes There?" Opening in 1982 against the ugly-cute alien of Steven Spielberg's *E.T.*, *The Thing*'s unseen yet malevolent alien and its spectacular eviscerations and incinerations was a box office failure for Carpenter. Yet, like its alien protagonist long-frozen in Antarctic ice, *The Thing* perversely lives on, a viral zombie that has been remade, preserved, dismembered, transformed, and passed on through genres and media that include the video game, Youtube homage, fanzine, blog, and documentary.[1]

As with the mode of viral reproduction, the phenomenon of the Thing no longer necessarily bears the DNA of its murky origins in Campbell's pre–World War II United States, when waves of European immigration had triggered xenophobic and isolationist reactions. While the alien takeover in the original was resolved by a macho glaciologist who takes command over a dithering biologist he dismisses as overly identified with the creature he longs to preserve and study, Carpenter's plot line is more classically looping, refusing narrative closure as well as any clean distinction between humans and Things. The basic, shared through-line of *The Thing* devolves from the discovery of a UFO embedded in Antarctic ice and its subsequent accidental thawing, setting off an interspecies competition for survival. Neither species can survive alone on ice; each requires

WSQ: Women's Studies Quarterly 40: 1 & 2 (Spring/Summer 2012) © 2012 by Elena Glasberg.

a network of some kind. For humans this network is society, specifically the hermetic homosocial world of the quasi-military science outpost. The Thing's mode of social and biological survival, however, passes through and among individual bodies as it reproduces through imitation, neither acknowledging nor possessing bodily borders. Even the grammatical naming of "the Thing" is a singular epithet that is always also an undefined plural. In the 1935 story, the Thing came equipped with standard-issue red beady eyes and loathsome tentacles. But it was the Thing's ability to infiltrate the dreams and thoughts of the men that Carpenter elaborated on in his screenplay of the paranoid infiltration or infection of the base in which one man after another becomes perfectly, imperceptibly imitated by the Thing. In the 1935 and 1951 iterations the alien threat was amenable to externalization as a monster. It was gleefully incinerated by military flamethrower in 1935, and in 1951 by a DYI-style electrocution clearly staged as a post-World War II populist rejoinder to technoscience and the A-bomb. By 1982 nuclear power had become the thing to fear itself and Carpenter's final scene is thus a version of an arms race standoff. The only way that humans—who in all the versions have an irrational attachment to their already processed bodies and who cleave superstitiously to fictions of individuality and nation on which heroic resistance only feeds—can outdo the Thing's viral reproduction is to deprive the Thing of a host, a decidedly Pyrrhic victory. The two "last men," who could either or both already be perfectly imitated Things, slowly freeze to death locked in each others' gazes in the firebombed ruins of the station.[2]

While a fear of homosexual contact within homosocial groups permeates each iteration of the Thing meme, the psychosexual fantasies of porous bodies only feed more disturbing realms of geopolitical competition. In the 1951 film, Scotty, the heretofore useless (read: feminized) journalist, ultimately takes command of the base radio to broadcast the warning that has become a stock line of Cold War paranoia camp: "Keep watching the skies." Never mind that the Thing crash-landed a hundred thousand years ago; the time and space of national defense is infinitely manipulable and has little to do with the specifics of homosocial outposts or heteronormative national imaginaries. As the "original" (if accidental) colonist to Antarctica, arriving first to the last place discovered in human history, the Thing makes humanity uncanny, belated, and unknowingly estranged from its own history. Reviving a planetary and evolutionary estrangement lost in the 1951 film's resetting in the inhabited and politically contested North Pole, Carpenter reset the action to Antarctica. The isolated Antarctic setting as elaborated by Carpenter introduced a problem of environmental limit as Carpenter relied on the ice itself—not on national surveillance—to contain the spread of the Thing to the rest of the world. He also used film (celluloid) as well as auteur theory and practice and the codes of the sci-fi genre to question forms of preservation and limit. In the film's final sequence, the visuals and soundtrack simultaneously fade, a reinvestment in a fantasy of film-as-theater and of the very individual/ national complex that the film's paranoid narrative of the limits of individuality so successfully challenged. Yet on the level of the celluloid film reel, the camera and heartbeat soundtrack fade out simultaneously and the screen goes dark and silent, leaving the two men trapped alive in their celluloid animation. Put another way, the film ends, but the narrative of the Thing's virality does not.

The tension across genres and media of viral reproduction both imitates and explains the incitement for the Thing narrative's many remakes. The becoming-other of virality refuses beginnings and ends, as it passes through bodies and states. And yet it follows that the viral would also refuse the horror of environmental hard limits and the climate crisis, a real effect of human culture that unlike the logical end game of the nuclear arms race, possesses the nonreproductive, explosive, lateral, and transformative potential of the viral. In its endless ability to reproduce (through imitation, which is a form of cellular splitting at the root of all biological process) the Thing disgusts the human characters, who use guns, flamethrowers, TNT, the codes of the horror genre itself, and finally a nuclear-like explosion, to destroy it. Darwin's theory of evolution initiated a certain phase in the lament for the (inevitable) loss of the "human" in the very likely possibility of the nonrecognition constituting the increments of evolutionary change. The Thing, in its viral evolution, can also become the incitement of a lament for itself, an insistence on originary loss.[3] In comparison to the becoming-possibility of the viral, an older model of linguistic instability like representation begins to feel like an almost comforting vortex, a powerless deconstruction or the dialectic (like a nuclear arms race standoff) that can never change the comforting nested mutability of individual/nation/society. This emptiness, pointed to and enhanced by evolution's posthuman potential, we have learned to live with, even to rely on; it is threatened by virality's potential to refuse and in fact remake the very seeming of hard limits.

The hard limit shared by all iterations of the Thing narrative is polar—Antarctic and Arctic—ice. More than a convenient setting for the locked-room alien whodunit or a dead zone or barrier between the outpost and the rest of humanity, the ice possesses a nonhuman and nonbiologic vitality outside the temperate norms of both human and alien embodiment. While the screened characters are liable to freeze and burn, the narrative plot and the Thing's uncanny rematerializing across time and media bodies manifest a life beyond "life."

Carpenter's classic plot was punctuated, riven through with multiple axes of viral production. Not the least of these axis of extradiegetic production are *The Thing*'s celebrated predigital special effects. The spectacularly transforming, dematerializing, and exploding bodies of the dogs and humans and aliens of the outpost were created with wax, bubblegum, paint, actors, and camera and celluloid cuts. The directorial decisions and editing slices practically gush with real fake blood. But a less noted retro effect is the film's most crucial embedded scene: a close camera shot of the doctor's computer screen model of the cellular modus operandi of the Thing's exponential takeover (should it escape the icy barrier of Antarctica). In this sequence, film screen becomes computer screen to visualize the central mystery of the plot: how an alien seems to be ripping through the population of the South Polar outpost, transforming its animals into copies of themselves; undetectable in final form, yet gruesome when captured in demystified goo-spurting process. *The Thing*'s computer graphics now seem quaint, rigid, one dimensional, and slow, more Pac-Man eats Pong than the modeling of cities inundated by melting polar ice in Al Gore's 2006 documentary on global climate change, *An Inconvenient Truth*. We've all seen the video: the blue-green marble earth. An enormous continent of ice. Frozen, seemingly stable. Then, a rise in temperature and the ice begins to calve and melt away at its edges into oceans that rise, at first gradually, and then building in a mathematically predictable unleashing of climate's warming potential, from coastal inundation to the extinction of human terrestrial culture. This is computer simulation as projection, a predictive visualization of computer modeling. Through data coding and computer-generated visualization, we can supposedly visualize what we cannot actually see in time. And yet we've seen it over and over. This gathering around the crystal screen for the visualization of the coming disaster is a staple now of popular culture as well as of science. Looking back on this singular stock piece of technofuturism, Carpenter's *The Thing* therefore brings on the shock of the old. Predictability, while a goal of scientific method, is just plain cheesy in the horror genre. Carpenter's greatest genius is not the invention of his special effects, but narrative and celluloid (cellular?) infixing of a faked credulity to ensure and destabilize cascading scales of affect, bodies, screens, and narratives.

Viewed as a part separate from its filmic whole, Carpenter's set piece of the Thing's cellular adaption process recasts evolution not as a narrative of ever more human becoming (or the self-serving fantasy of heterosexual reproduction), but as the viral evolution of a becoming-other. Viral reproduction and computer modeling go hand in hand: both are beyond the limit of the human and they are about the limits of the human. Both are virtual in that they work through modeling and speculation outside a visual economy of what can be seen or encountered. And both are horror shows only to the extent that we believe the superstition (Stevie Wonder's 1972 hit plays through the cook's boom box) of evolution as human perfectibility. It's a fiction that social beings fall for over and over (thus the repetitive core plot of *The Thing*) to the very last outpost of humanity. And yet the eugenicist perfectibility of the human is the fiction humanity most urgently needs to leave behind in this post-Holocaust, postnuclear—and penetrative/blood-splattering transmission prefiguring post-AIDS—era. It is no wonder that this film is once again being remade in a time of seeming hard environmental limits and rising temperatures whose effects cannot be appreciated in the moment, but that have, as Gore's and the climate scientists' models all suggest, already happened.

One of those hard limits a viral remake potentially undermines is the celebration of the original that only enforces acceptance of reproductive powers, both cultural and biologic. Yet in their predictable attacks on the remake, prolifically blogging sci-fi horror aficionados miss out on Carpenter's own joke about self-despising remakes (one bored character says, popping in a video from his limited collection of porno and game show tapes, "I know how this one's gonna end"). And in a way we all miss the potential of the viral, no matter how latent (thirty years in the making) or how actualized: it teaches us perhaps to despise the limits of origins—or to despise ourselves only to the extent that we insist we remain ourselves. The 2011 remake's trailer teased, "It's not human. Yet." Despite its supreme self-consciousness as a genre, alien sci-fi continues to repress the nonhuman potential of evolution and the viral foundations (if you will) of a comforting self-reproductive futurity.

Yet in a plot whose overall arc relies upon and even seems to reproduce a reactive attachment to the human, Carpenter's *The Thing* calls into
question human-nonhuman distinction in every scene. Before the spectacular animal-human-alien spewing begins, an early scene of the loner
hero MacReady playing a game of computer chess retrospectively encodes
commentary on the digital processes that have taken over the analog special effects of the film as well as the themes of zero-sum systems and the
human–artificial intelligence interface. In a close-up MacReady concen-
trates on a move, staring into the screen of a PC box as a "female" voice pro-
claims, "Checkmate." MacReady facetiously ascribes human motive and
gender to the chess program by pronouncing it a "cheatin' bitch" and pours
his J&B into the hard drive, causing a mini-explosion. At this moment the
machine passes the Turing test, conceptualized in 1950 by British math-
ematician Alan Turing as a way to test his prediction that computers would
eventually become indistinguishable from humans.[4] MacReady's heroic
grenade is tossed at the wrong object, since the computer is indeed just
a box of electronics. But its program is viral, reproducing beyond its box.
Thus "cheatin' bitch" is the grousing of a ruined man who no longer can
compete with the system he designed. This moment is the real test of the
film, not the red herring "blood test" MacReady later devises to prove, as
he absurdly boasts, "what he already knows," which is that he is human,
not a Thing. In this scene of coercive scientific testing, MacReady deduces
of the alien, "What if it's alive in each of its parts?" And he is correct, about
the nature of the viral, if not the distinction between Things and men: like
all the scenes, the parts, the characters, and the disembodied voice of the
computer, none requires the fictional cohesion once offered by narrative
and the human.

Another moment in which the Thing "passes" the Turing test is even
more intertextual. In Carpenter's most celebrated special effect scenes a
human head drops off a body, sprouts legs, and then scurries off screen.
This scene of biomorphic estrangement elicits the line "You've gotta be
fucking kidding" delivered in stoner outrage, by a character, who in retrospect the plot points to as the first human to have become a Thing, or
the "original fake." This line itself has broken free of Carpenter's "original" and sprouted in countless Hong Kong action films. Just as its infixed
ejaculation "fucking," puns on reproduction and belief, the line bursts its
own containment and cannot insulate the fiction of autonomous human
being from contamination. No viewers of the alien Thing, of things, or

of *The Thing* should believe their eyes; even less should they believe (in) their eyes. Virality—reproduction through disassembly, deintegration, and reintegration without end—has undone the integral primacy of the human-embodied optics and thus the visual, data-driven grasping of the world. That this scene also routinely and universally fools even repeat viewers points to the less remarked upon but more important mode of virality as it swarms outside and in between the limits of genre, through time, across the screen of spectacle, and from the experience and memory of viewer to viewer as well. The viral becomes a mode of production beyond narrative, mind, biology, visuality, or genre. *The Thing* not only passes the Turing test, it undoes the reproductive ligatures of the logical test (as MacReady explodes the computer and later the base itself) and all the parts—and wholes—of the human.

Like fetishization as a process of taking a part for a whole, the 2011 remake may succeed in that it has focused ultimately on the seemingly inescapable psychosexual joke of human heterosexual reproduction. The film's primal scene, so to speak, establishes the Norwegian all-male sociality that is soon to be interrupted by the addition of a U.S. female scientist as well as by the discovery of the buried alien. One bored fellow tells another a dirty joke to pass the time. It is a familiar enough joke, even if it is told in Norwegian with (English) subtitles: a little boy runs from the room having walked in on his parents having intercourse. He then calls to his father, who comes in only to witness the boy on top of his grandmother, engaged in the same act. The boy looks back at his astonished father, saying, "It's not so funny when it's *your* mother, is it?" Surely the joke comments on the prequel as imitation (the 2011 remake is actually a prequel, back-filling the events that had occurred at the Norwegian base and that determined the plot of Carpenter's remake) and competition between males within the limits of the nuclear family. But the joke also reverberates as a diminution of the posthuman potentiality of Carpenter's plot about the ends and limits of humanity on earth by burrowing back into history of Norway's forgotten Antarctic imperialist, Roald Amundsen, the man who beat the British to the South Pole one hundred years ago and into the (female) body in a failed attempt to reground human reproduction, if not reproducibility.

Paradoxically, even the use of the most technologically advanced special effects is a backtracking and retreading of the reproducibility of representation. Using computer-generated imaging (CGI) effects, Heijningen reveals the Thing-as-embodied monster within a full-screen frame. In this craven use of CGI's potential to seamlessly integrate effects and (presumably) human actors within a single frame, the film falls into its own joke about parts and wholes, fully revealing an insectlike re-membering of male and female body parts that conveys disturbing visual jokes of misbegotten sexual intercourse. In revealing its reliance on kinship taboo and on CGI hyper-realism, the 2011 Thing remains within its full framing. In revealing its taboo, and the whole of the grotesquely assimilated body parts, the 2011 film fails at and through spectacle and mimesis. Truly, the 2011 *Thing* is a bad copy that unfortunately believes in originals and descendants.[5]

The 2011 remake with its crucial yet underdeveloped recasting of a female actor in the role of the hero offers a devastating assessment of liberalism and postcolonial feminism, even as it retroactively inserts its female hero back in the time of "prequel" or as preceding Carpenter's masculinist U.S.-focused *The Thing*. Despite this sex-change gambit, the latest *Thing* is a locked-room psychosexual whodunit preoccupied with a fawning post-feminism: its greatest revelation makes use of a realist-reductive fanboy reading of the Thing meme (how does it reproduce nonbiological appurtenances of identity like dog tags, clothing, and dental fillings?) to undermine its own survival narrative (guaranteed on the level of the narrative, since this is a prequel)—which the Thing must, cleverly, latch onto and promote if only for its own survival. This usurping of the human survival plot for the means of the Thing's survival is pure Carpenter-era *Thing*. The heroine's deducing that her male heroic partner is really a Thing breaks up the "last couple." Fortunately, the dog still survives and is last seen loping just ahead of the Norwegian machine gun and grenades, toward the opening scene of what knowing filmgoers already recognize as Carpenter's 1982 Antarctic Base 31. In returning to the scene of the "original imitation" the 2011 re-remake ensures the vitality and virality of Carpenter's *The Thing*. As a better imitation, Carpenter's narrative is self-knowing enough not to attempt the narrative sureties and cultural fantasies of its precursors. And yet, despite its irresolution and the innumerable red herrings bursting from the 1982 plot like so many poorly assimilated body parts, it seems pretty clear now, thirty years out, that the viral nature of media transformation has ensured the failure of any filmic remake: the alien Thing, the Thing meme, and *The Thing* have themselves transformed the mode and reception of their transit. Virality neither begins nor ends with the humanity isolated at the South Pole. Being part of this idea—letting it shoot through and explode us—is the glorious spectacle-tentacle of hope offered by the Thing's endless elaborations of the impossible containment of the viral. Viva *The Thing*!

Elena Glasberg's book *On Ice: Antarctica as Symbol and Material* is coming out from Palgrave Macmillan in 2012. Glasberg writes about visual arts, music, literature, and ice in publications including *Political Legal Anthropology Review*, *Genre*, *The Scholar and Feminist*, *Journal of Historical Geography*, *New Zealand Journal of Photography*, and *ARTIndia*, and teaches in the writing program at New York University.

Notes

1. John Carpenter's *The Thing* lives on and through its viral media elaborations as a single-shooter video game and as a "meme" on fanboy blogs and in Hong Kong–style action films, not to mention in films documenting its making such as *Fear Is Just the Beginning* (1997) and *The Thing: Terror Takes Shape* (1998).

2. "Last men" builds on Carol Clover's *Men, Women, and Chainsaws*'s well-known feminist critique of the horror genre in which the "final girl" must suffer various viewer-identified degradations at the hands of the slasher/monster before being allowed to prevail. In the case of the last men, (male) viewer-identification with the alien remains at a standoff, ensuring the survival of the Thing (and its narrative) along with the homosocial male pair "frozen" in their anxious staving off of the spectre of homosexuality.

3. The universe of H. P. Lovecraft looms in the background of the Thing narrative. His 1935 novel, *At the Mountains of Madness*, like "Who Goes There?" was inspired by U.S. explorer Richard E. Byrd's overflight of the South Pole in 1928. Lovecraft's Antarctic expedition from Miskatonic University unknowingly stirs an encounter with the all-powerful "Old Ones," a civilization that likely produced humanity as a by-product of other ventures. Darwinian evolution has been another source of engagement for science fiction filmmakers. See especially chapter 3 in Creed 2009.

4. One possible means suggested by Turing in 1950 to gauge the ability of a machine to successfully imitate the human mind was a blind game of chess played by a human judge against another human and a computer. See Epstein, Roberts, and Beiber 2009.

5. An October 2011 review in the *Boston Globe* puts this problem of the self-knowing remake this way: "The result is that the new "Thing" kind of does what the alien does—digest the original and spit out a creepy copy whose sole purpose is to survive at any cost."

Works Cited

Clover Carol. 1992. *Men, Women, and Chainsaws*. Princeton: Princeton University Press.

Creed, Barbara. 2009. *Darwin's Screens: Evolutionary Aesthetics, Time, and Sexual Display in the Cinema*. Melbourne: Melbourne University Press.

Germain, David, 2011. "Sci-Fi Prequel Dishes Out Same Old Thing." *Associated Press*, October 12. http://news.yahoo.com/review-sci-fi-prequel-dishes-same-old-thing-202454622.html

Epstein, Robert, Gary Roberts, and Grace Beiber, eds. *Parsing the Turing Test: Philosophical and Methodological Issues in the Quest for the Thinking Computer*. New York: Springer, 2009.

Crossing over Horror: Reincarnation and Transformation in Apichatpong Weerasethakul's *Primitive*

Una Chung

In Alfred Hitchcock's *The Birds* (1963), the entrance of a stranger into the small coastal town of Bodega Bay, California, triggers the eruption of violent attacks from birds—seagulls, crows, unidentified others. In a post-trauma conversation among locals at a diner, one person points out that birds are prehistoric, unknowably alien, belonging to a geological time not contained within a human evolutionary narrative. Another person points out that there are also a lot more birds in the world than people are aware of—someone gives a number—and it seems clear that the significance of that number, in its day-to-day invisibility, is hard to fathom. Someone tries to make the number more dramatically graspable by speculating that if all birds were to rise up in a war against humans, they would be sure to win. The horror of the imagined scenario imbues the unfathomable birds with some sense of accountability, some sense-ability, even as this scenario of an interspecies war humanizes the attacks occurring in the town, which are far more enigmatic in nature.

The birds follow a precise but inexplicable rhythm of attack and rest. They are propelled toward the humans in a massed onslaught of speed and force with unabated intensity until they reach a point of change in rhythm. During periods of rest, the birds seem content to perch and slowly gather into a visible mass. People move slowly and safely among the birds during periods of rest, whereas energetic motion attracts the birds' attention and draws them toward people during periods of attack. Although there are deaths among birds and humans, there is no discernible narrative of murder or war, only a destructive force that obeys the rhythms of a score that we cannot hear. It is hard to see a concerted goal behind the force, much less any intentional character such as malice; there is only violence

WSQ: Women's Studies Quarterly 40: 1 & 2 (Spring/Summer 2012) © 2012 by Una Chung. All rights reserved.

and affective rhythm. It is not the life of one species over another that is at stake. Most of the bloodshed comes from bird bodies shattering against and through windows of buildings, phone booths, car windshields. There is rather an uncanny responsiveness between bodies of birds and humans that unfolds through the film. People are able to fall into step with the rhythm of attack and rest in order to make their own escape from the besieged town. The stranger from the city, Melanie, displays taut calm, a mixture of alertness and relaxation that is crucial to her survival. In the schoolyard, she notices with shock the sudden amassing of birds behind her, yet without panic she immediately intuits that it is not about being seen but about being sensed. She moves slowly and gracefully, her face remaining tense but calm, and enters the school to warn the children. Only when she loses complete touch with the rhythm of the birds and gives in to restless urges, instead of remaining still, does she finally fall victim to a violent attack, which leaves her catatonic.

The birds thus seem to demonstrate certain qualities of the viral: invisible, too small, too many, overly mobile, movement signifying contagion, alien reminders of a world not ruled by humans. Hitchcock's film gives us an image of the viral as an image of horror. Without horror, birds remain singly or in pairs in their cages, taught to mimic human words, or bred in chicken coops and given feed. The film does not indulge in arbitrary fantasies of birds escaping into the wild or gaining human cognitive ambitions such as waging modern war. Hitchcock's birds do not present us with an image of anthropomorphic horror but of a human fear of the viral. These birds evoke horror through a play of numbers and visibility. In the scene where Melanie waits at the schoolyard, we see one bird, then three, then another three, land behind her. We look ahead with her at a single bird flying in the sky and track the arc of its descent behind her, when suddenly we see that the space is thick with birds perched on all available bars and railings. The absence of solid structures in the image enhances the effect of the birds' filling up all empty space, a quality of something unseen suddenly made visible. The famous and oft-discussed soundtrack and the repetitive chant of the children singing, underscore the period of rest, the boredom, the slow rhythms of accumulation, which lead to the massed onslaught. In a later scene, after the explosion of a car at a gas station, the camera jumps to a high aerial view above the bay, and from behind the camera, a bird drops down into view, followed by another, and then a mass of birds covers the sky.

For Slavoj Žižek, the camera's "God's perspective" above the bay clears the screen of any possible human subjective point of view, which is then used to bring our vision directly into alignment with the viewpoint of the attacking birds (2010, 236). According to Žižek, we are thus made to experience the horror of looking from the vantage point of murderous agency. We realize that it is for our gaze that the spectacle of violence has been staged. We imagined ourselves innocently looking for visual pleasure but discover a murderous drive within. If we wish to understand why in this film "every relationship of partnership is either doomed to fail or totally void of libidinal content," then we must look to the "massive, oppressive material presence" of the birds, which "gives body to the impossible jouissance" (9). There is nothing to see in that moment when the camera brings us into alignment with the absolute gaze, but there is something to be felt, understood, in that moment of horror: the presence of something inhuman that sees through our own seeing. Our own points of view are not closed circuits within our being but cracks opening onto our world from something utterly alien.

Hitchcock's camera in *The Birds* embodies the same drive as "monsters, cyborgs, the living dead . . . machines which run blindly, without compassion, devoid of any 'pathological' considerations, inaccessible to our pleas . . . yet at the same time . . . defined by the presence of an absolute gaze" (Žižek 2010, 256). The eruption of birds from the pure gaze of Hitchcock's camera suggests that "this Otherness ultimately coincides with the machine (camera) itself" (256). The drive of the id—the essence of the animatedness of the human body that terrifies us in its deafness to the socially determined nature of our desires—can be materialized not simply in the allegory of the birds as attacking Furies but directly in the camera's capacity to produce the horror of the absolute gaze. This technological capacity is linked, for Žižek, to psychosis: "This dream of a drive that could function without its representative in the psychic apparatus is what one is tempted to baptize the psychotic core of Hitchcock's universe—a core strictly homologous to Freud's dream of a moment when the symbolic procedure of psychoanalysis will be replaced by pure biology" (241). This fantasy of "pure biology," or perhaps the pure machine of posthumanism, augurs the "collapse of the very field of intersubjectivity as medium of Truth in late capitalism" and with it the end of psychoanalysis (262).[1]

There is a cruelty in Žižek's writing—the cruelty of a Lacanian analyst—when he writes, "The public fascination with figures like Hannibal

Lecter, the cannibal serial killer from Thomas Harris's novels, provides a ray of hope: this fascination ultimately bears witness to a deep longing for a Lacanian psychoanalyst" (262). The "ray of hope" may allow psycho-analysis to continue providing "symbolic integration of our traumas" but there is never any hint about how we might cross over horror. For Žižek, horror is in fact essential; it is the only cut to an outside—one that shows us precisely that there can be no outside within the enclosure of global capitalism. It seems to me that Žižek's investment in insisting on a certain structural critique of capitalism in fact curtails the power of his analysis of horror and closes off the creative potential of the future of psychoanalysis.

We might articulate the political critique differently—not against capital but rather toward the cultivation of new practices (which produce new socials). Patricia Clough wonders whether psychoanalysis and tech-noscience could not be reconfigured together by an "imagination of a criti-cal practice capable of a more direct engagement with semiotic-material objects" (2000, 184). In fact, Clough suggests that a certain genealogy of thought that moves from feminist critiques of technoscience through Jacques Derrida to Sigmund Freud will uncover the very technical sub-strates of the unconscious: "Freud refused to describe the nervous system as compartments for storing memories; instead his description proposed that the nervous system is a substrate in motion" (33). Derrida not only "turns Freud's mystic writing-pad into a perpetual motion machine," but also in effect begins to unfold the technical substrate onto "a distributed network of transmissions without beginning or end" (38). We are led by deconstruction of nature and culture to a point where the line between human and machine becomes indecipherable. But it is here that decon-struction too stalls. There is a different blockage of love at work here; Clough will call it love of television, a machine that she imagines Derrida was "unable to embrace." Derrida could see in Freud's use of the metaphor of the mystic writing pad a presentiment of the technical substrates of the unconscious but was unable to articulate fully what it would mean for human life to see so directly into its own mutability—not simply through evolutionary time but directly in its own momentary affective fluctuations. Could we (bear to) see our horror released into waves of nervous energy and quanta of attention? Could we forego using our psychosis to condemn the complicity of technology and capital, and simply invent new practices of living that engender different social worlds? To love television is not about being an avid consumer but rather is a way of saying that we might loosen our grip on the containment, or securitization, of human identity connected to our belief in fixed ontological categories that ignore the technical substrates of the unconscious. "Derrida hesitates. He turns back from ontology or turns ontology to the historical production of technology" (40). This second turn, away from the machine he had begun to turn Freud toward, is so often where our understanding of technology seems fated to begin—with the line between history of production and life of human being. Technology becomes a problem with objects rather than of our own becoming across multiple life forms and life times, beyond the limited borders of individualism.[2]

Keith Ansell Pearson attempts to chart a path between the extremes of technophilia and technophobia toward a reconceptualization of viral life. Pearson objects to the naturalization of technological evolution, and the new "theology of capital" that justifies "life's evolution leading in the direction of nonaffective machines, in which thought exists without a body," and where "there is no future of, or for, invention, since all is given" (1997, 2). At the same time, Pearson makes clear, "Neither do I adhere to fantasies of historical revolution in which we humans will reclaim our rightful control and mastery over nature and society," which have inspired major thinkers such as Herbert Marcuse, Guy Debord, and Fredric Jameson (3). For Pearson, the "desire for complete historical immanence" as much as "our contemporary cyberspace gurus" inspire "dread and loathing," real horror (3). Rather than succumb to psychosis, however, Pearson advocates, for contemporary thinkers, a dousing by Nietzschean nihilism, a suicidal, sobering, and unflattering coming to terms with "the culminating point of Western narcissism and humanism" (7).

> The task today is no longer to seek God, dead or alive . . . but to be drawn to the *land of the future where human impotence no longer makes us mad* and where it is possible to decode the signs of alien life within and without us. For this we do not so much require new truths, rather it becomes necessary to remember and relearn some ancient ones. One will then discover them as if for the first time, for there is only the "first" time that is repeated again and again. The future, for example, has always been "out there." It does not simply lie ahead of us. It is the place of the "outside." (7–8; my emphasis)

If I might read for poetic nuance, as it were, I would suggest that Pearson invites us to think of the human as a *realm of being* (rather than an ontological truth) and the future as the name for a different land, where "human impotence no longer makes us *mad*" (my emphasis). There is indeed to be a crossing over horror, a place beyond the paradoxical "truth" of psychosis that claims madness can be the only true experience of recognizing the impossibility of (human) truth. In a land of sanity, call it the future, "machines provide pathic and cartographic access to a plurality of beings and worlds" (Pearson 1997, 6). We understand ourselves to be sharing in viroid life—a "figure for the indeterminacy of life itself and of the complexity of the evolutionary process" (Lynch 1999, 120). It is not the virus that threatens us but our "narrative of teleological biological and technological progress" that claims the virus as a threat to itself (119). The image of "viroid life" necessitates that we consider the nonlinear transfer of information between more highly evolved and less highly evolved species (Pearson 1997, 133).[3] This is due to not simply the "new truths" of science but perhaps also the "ancient ones" of repetition and difference and, I would add, karma and rebirth.

We are currently living at a time when digital technologies, algorithmic design, and ecosensibilities are producing environments that do not resemble the inhuman machines of yesterday's future, "the living dead," but rather animated affective beings—responsive architecture, sensual machines and mobile devices, global networks of information that move at the speed of thought. What terrifies us today is not the idea that these material appearances of animatedness are at their core not human or not really alive. What we do painfully lack is a *form* of subjectivity (other than "hyper-self-reflexivity") adequate to what we feel we actually are and a *common notion* of life adequate to our experience of today's lived environments. We remain fascinated by the voice of Žižek, perhaps, for he seems to offer us the unfeeling (dead) eye of god, at a time when we find ourselves surrounded by endless screens that capture our attention for seemingly no purpose at all—the truism of the pure productivity of capitalism not being sufficient answer. Clough implicitly raises the question of whether horror might not serve a purpose other than to provoke self-destructive immanent critique (revolution over capitalism), instead directing us toward shock (or trauma) as a site where we can reencounter "the play of the differences of preontological forces" (Clough 2000, 40). Bound up in social formations of familial relations are also "agencies immanent to matter." The social organization of production is not the only access point into new political futures. Rather than horror, which is oriented by our attachment to a certain historical configuration of the social (an attachment to historical norms of sanity and humanity), we might find Cloughian psychoanalysis showing us that "technology crosses through ontology."[4]

The Birds leaves us with an enigmatic image of Melanie's face that suggests not only horror but also the Open, the future. Her face is impassive; her eyes are open but no longer looking onto the same world as those of the others fussing around her and busily enjoying their symbolic integration, so to speak. Assured of the reality of a murderous violence greater than her own, Mitch's mother gives up her own small measure of resentment and gives Melanie a small hug. Mitch's sister continues to disavow what has occurred by remaining attached to her caged lovebirds—"They haven't harmed anyone!" Mitch himself drives determinedly away with his brood under his paternal care. The film gives narrative closure to these three characters, who happily return to a semblance of a larger society, San Francisco. But for Melanie, there is only indetermination. What does she see? What will come after? It seems important to see in this face a real startling openness—provoked not through the manipulations of horror (speculation about what we cannot see), but through a strange stillness, an uncertainty about what rhythms she hears now. Hers is not the dead eye of Marion's corpse in *Psycho* but a nonreactive eye that continues to look forward to what is to come—a bird's eye. "It is not clear what future will come beyond the future given with the unconscious thought of teletechnology. It is being written; no doubt somewhere it is just starting itself up. In fits and starts, across mystic writing-pads, it is producing bodies, assemblages of scenes, screens, and moving machines" (Clough 2000, 186–87).

Can there be a crossing over horror?

Does viroid life open us up to ways of thinking about birth and death beyond the horror of self-witnessing? Are there aesthetic practices that can lighten the impulse toward horror accompanying our glimpse of life beyond rational sight?

Apichatpong Weerasethakul's *Primitive* project, including the feature film *Uncle Boonmee Who Can Recall His Past Lives* (2010) and the multimedia installation of *Primitive*, consisting of eight videos and one print, shifts the ground from under the composition of horror by exploring how reincarnation and transformation might provide us with a different aesthetic form for understanding subjectivity and technicity.[5] *Primitive* explores the condition of memory in the rural village of Nabua in northeast Thailand, near the border of Laos. Nabua was occupied by the Thai military from the 1960s to the 1980s during an aggressive repression of communism. The violent treatment of sympathetic Nabua farmers and their families by the military caused many to flee to the jungle. Foregoing the trope of witnessing (and its basis in self-reflexivity), Weerasethakul approaches the vexed issue of political history and collective trauma in Nabua through dream, time travel, reincarnation, and transformation.[6]

Weerasethakul does not seek to remedy or even remediate the political history of Nabua by transmitting knowledge of local memory into universal archives or twittering incendiary accusations to the public; nor will he shake the locals into horrified rememory of the traumas of the past by staging confrontations among different groups and generations.[7] In response to the question "Did the experience of making the installation change the relationship the residents of Nabua have with their past?" Weerasethakul answers, "I don't think so. I hope not. The idea was not to change" (Carrion-Murayari and Gioni 2011, 12). "The important thing was that we lived" (12). We meet the isolated teens of Nabua and live with them for a moment in the gallery installation of *Primitive*, where they are seen sometimes in military fatigues and ambiguously dramatic tableau vivants and at other times freely at play in casual jeans and T-shirts—running, dancing, wrestling, and building a time machine for travel to the future. To live directly the nonlinear temporal entanglement of the present moment, without concertedly tracking past or future, is in fact a potent way to engage the challenge of remembering political history, that is, by *living it, as it finds us*, knowing that we are embedded in it in ways more complex and nonarbitrary than our conscious knowledge of time might lead us to think. This complex relationship of Boonmee and the teens of Nabua (and of ourselves) is figured artistically through Weerasethakul's use of different media: media as bodies of time, bodies of time as relations of speed/stillness, and relations of affect (i.e., surprise of encounter) replacing fixed social relations of kinship or political antagonism.

Nabua (2009) gives us a striking composition of visual and audio shocks—flashes of lightning and incandescent smoke, accompanied by loud explosive cracking. The incredible force transmitted by this film does not lead to violence. Shock is accompanied by a different rhythm of slow movement, a sense of turning and expanding from the edges—not a backing up or darting forward by a seeing body but an expansion of the field of vision. It is as if the world were slowly revolving on its vertical axis with a gentle sliding sideways along the horizontal. *A Dedicated Machine* (2009) presents a still horizon where a near-spherical object (a time machine rather than the sun) slowly moves up and down: it is within a nonlinear temporality that dreams may cross the technical substrate of the unconscious. Together these (dis)orient the dark gallery space of *Primitive*, which we enter not as into a building encoded by the urgent necessities of social navigation, but rather to experience a state of mind akin to sleep, permitting dreams, the rhythmic attunement to films and videos that merge with our own "impressions of light and memory." Within this space, the local teens of Nabua are presented as figures of the future. They are given a claim on the future that Thai society does not offer them. Boonmee, the titular character of the feature film, travels to the future in a dream on the brink of his death and meets the Nabua teens. A cinematic character, who killed communists for the Thai military, and real descendants of the disappeared in Nabua thus meet in the land of the future, amid Boonmee's recollection of past lives. This is one example of the kinds of encounters that arise within the space of *Primitive*. These do not resemble the uncanny travels of Gulliver or a vision of Utopia, but rather suggest the play of memory, free from one who remembers: a loosening of individuals into indefinite features, qualities, and affects that can quickly cross among different media, genres, bodies, and times. To remember a past life means to be no longer bound by the individual constraints of memory and subjectivity and, therefore, to be open to the present livingness of infinite traces of other lives crossing through one and gathering together unexpected capacities to act.

This same quality is demonstrated with incredible simplicity and power merely through the use of light and screen in the film *Phantoms of Nabua* (2009). *Phantoms of Nabua* (2009) consists almost entirely of constantly changing qualities and movements of light. The camera seems unable to show us anything but light: a lone fluorescent light against the dark sky; a dark projector screen where flashes of lightning strike the ground and plumes of bright white smoke erupt, allowing ghostly buildings to flash into view; a wide-angle shot of a large empty space with single fluorescent light above, screen small in the background, and flickers of deep red embers of fire appearing toward the front. A ball of flames jumps into view within the darkness, and the shuffling noise of teens playing soccer with the fireball becomes audible. The scene intensifies as the flaming ball whizzes to the left then to the right, while voices call out to each other in the dark, and bodies only rarely and fragmentarily light up in the red glow of fire. The screen in the background is barely visible but for the flashes of light that appear on it, until the fireball makes contact and sets the screen aflame. The teens gather around the screen after it catches fire and kick the flaming ball back and forth through the gaping hole that emerges from the disintegrating screen. The light of the projector behind the screen becomes nakedly visible (we realize that it had always been visible as a sphere of light on the screen) and the rhythms of its flickering cone of light capture the camera's attention. The darkness of this film makes it impossible for us to do anything but chase the light with our eyes. The film does not frame our vision so much as modulate our perception in relation to the qualities of light. The camerawork and editing are not crafted in order to produce a point of view, a particular body looking. The rhythms of the bodies and voices of the young men playing soccer are inseparable from the rhythms of light passing across or jumping different media. Through this astonishing work with light, film apparatus, and screen, we could say that we are given back to the play of preontological forces. The phantoms of Nabua are not fixed onto a historical past or a historically limited form. Perhaps the image of ourselves that we have been seeking is not the chalk line around a human form but this quality of light that is undeniably materially present and yet can move directly among lamp, screen, fire, projector, and image. Light is that which can cross different mediating bodies—not without dying—yet indestructible. For Weerasethakul, "better than cinema is the light itself" (qtd in Carrion-Murayari and Gioni 2011, 14).

"The installation is like flashes of dreams where you sift through with your own pace. They are remnants of a performance. I am fine when people say that they sleep through my movies. They wake up and can patch things up in their own way" (Apichatpong Weerasethakul qtd. in Carrion-Murayari and Gioni 2011, 14). Whereas previously we noted the viselike grip of Žižek's eye watching *The Birds*, here we encounter a filmmaker who invites us to find our own rhythms of falling asleep and waking up within the space of his work. It seems that horror has an intimate link to the desire to witness one's own birth or death, one's own falling asleep and awakening. This impulse has drawn to itself the pornographic capacities of visual media technologies that purport to show us our own (Oedipal) blindness, or even the cultural drive to trace the "forensic materiality" of digital information (Kirschenbaum 2008). The historical birth of a particular medium seems less important than the dominant desire that comes to shape its mode of perception. Clough could see in television's capacity to simultaneously record and transmit images a glimpse of subjectivity enfolded with technology in ways resonant with the perpetual motion of the deconstructive process that allows us to see nature and culture as both distinct and inseparable. Where deconstruction hesitates (in perpetual vacillation), Weerasethakul moves forward assuredly, though gently, into an aesthetic sensibility that crosses beyond the point from which one can look in both directions, and moves through reincarnation and transformation into the land of the future. Beyond capitalist systems of exchange, there are other paths by means of which life changes forms and changes hands. If the automatic subjectivity of capital was the archetype of the hysterical subject, who insisted on self-identity and self-increase, we may need to reroute our sensibilities through the viral passage among human, animal, machine, god, and ghost, who appear through the action of birth, death, and rebirth). We might give up the perpetuity of horror for the simple rhythms of life and death. We may need to learn strategies of attunement and affective rhythms that can more directly engage a mind that we now, finally, again, for the first time, understand is—*crossing over horror*—not at all our own (and never was).

Una Chung, is a cultural critic, writer, and a professor in global studies at Sarah Lawrence College. She teaches courses in new media art and theory, postcolonial and Asian American literatures, East Asian film, global feminisms, and Gilles Deleuze. She is currently working on a book project, *Practical Sensations: An Aesthetics for New Media* (Palgrave Macmillan, forthcoming 2013). Her research is twofold: writing postcolonial theory for emerging media technologies and curating/cultivating new media practices for a new politics of sensibility.

Notes

1. For more on affect, media and technology, see Massumi 2002.
2. Also see Elsaesser 2009. Elsaesser's rationalist approach explores the implications of a technologically determined unconscious without taking up the ontological question raised by Derrida's deconstruction of "an assumed opposition between the psychical and the nonpsychical, life and death" (qtd. in Clough 2000, 40). For Elsaesser psychoanalysis gives way to media theory.
3. Although it is beyond the scope of this essay to address directly, it should be noted that the thinking of this essay is heavily indebted to the work of Luciana Parisi. See Parisi 2004.
4. For a provocative discussion of how therapy and art (drawing on Félix Guattari's schizoanalysis) might repair the ravages of semiocapitalism, see Berardi 2009.
5. I am referring to the 2011 installation at the New Museum in New York.

There have been five installations of the multiplatform project *Primitive*, each of which was composed quite differently in each gallery, because of the collaboration of artist and respective curator. Previous locations include Munich, Paris, Liverpool, Mexico City, and Yokohama.

6. Weerasethakul's *Primitive* installation is headed by a curatorial note that tells us, "Rather than a political history of Nabua, *Primitive* is meant to be experienced as a dream of 'reincarnation and transformation.'" Additionally, for a postcolonial critique of historiography, see Chakrabarty 2007.

7. Weerasethakul states, "Later on, there was a popular monk twittering about the red shirt demonstration in Bangkok, saying that 'killing time is more sinful than killing people.' He indirectly urged the government to kill the demonstrators. In retrospect, I was just killing time in the village. The important thing was that we lived. That's all I care about" (qtd. in Carrion-Murayari and Gioni 2011, 12).

Works Cited

Berardi, Franco. 2009. *Soul at Work*. New York: Semiotext(e).

Carrion-Murayari, Gary, and Massimiliano Gioni, eds. 2011. *Apichatpong Weerasethakul*. New York: New Museum.

Chakrabarty, Dipesh. 2007. "Minority Histories, Subaltern Pasts." In *Provincializing Europe*. Princeton: Princeton University Press.

Clough, Patricia. 2000. *Autoaffection: Unconscious Thought in the Age of Teletechnology*. Minneapolis: University of Minnesota Press.

Elsaesser, Thomas. 2009. "Freud as Media Theorist: Mystic Writing Pads and the Matter of Memory." *Screen* 50:1.

Kirschenbaum, Matthew G. 2008. Mechanisms: New Media and the Forensic Imagination. Cambridge, MA: MIT Press.

Lynch, Lisa. 1999. "*Viroid Life: Perspectives on Nietzsche and the Transhuman Condition* (Review)." *Configurations* 7(1):119–23.

Massumi. 2002. *Parables for the Virtual: Movement, Affect, Sensation*. Durham: Duke University Press.

Parisi, Luciana. 2004. *Abstract Sex: Philosophy, Biotechnology and the Mutations of Desire*. New York: Continuum.

———. 2004. "Information Trading and Symbiotic Micropolitics" in *Social Text* 80, Vol. 22, No. 3.

Pearson, Keith Ansell. 1997. *Viroid Life: Perspectives on Nietzsche and the Transhuman Condition*. New York: Routledge.

Žižek, Slavoj. 2010. *Everything You Always Wanted to Know About Lacan but Were Afraid to Ask Hitchcock*. New York: Verso.

Manic Impositions: The Parasitical Art of Chris Kraus and Sophie Calle

Anna Watkins Fisher

[There] is the moment when Echo traps Narcissus in a certain way. . . . Echo, in her loving and infinite cleverness, arranges it so that in repeating the last syllables of the words of Narcissus, she speaks in such a way that the words become her own. . . . In repeating the language of another, she signs her own love.

Jacques Derrida, in the documentary Derrida, 2004

The letters are a rhizome, a network, a spider's web. There is a vampirism in the letters, a vampirism that is specifically epistolary.

Gilles Deleuze and Félix Guattari, Kafka: Toward a Minor Literature

Feminist Parasites

This essay asks how parasitism might articulate itself as an experimental art practice as well as a performance model for contemporary feminist politics. My thinking here is drawn from a larger critical project, which argues that by "dragging" the impositions, parodies, and caricatures said to represent feminism, by performing "feminism" back to itself, a younger generation of feminist artists have already begun to reimage feminism as a critically viable project capable of assimilating irony and equivocality for its tactical gain. By performing parasites, artists Chris Kraus and Sophie Calle model feminist tactics that feed on and destabilize patriarchal forms by seizing upon the gendered analogy of the "correspondence" between the feminized parasite and her masculinized host. "Precisely what is a para-site?" asks David Bell of Michel Serres's study The Parasite. "It is an opera-

***WSQ: Women's Studies Quarterly* 40: 1 & 2 (Spring/Summer 2012)** © 2012 by Anna Watkins Fisher. All rights reserved.

tor that interrupts a system of exchange. The abusive guest partakes of the host's meal . . . and gives only words . . . in return" (1981, 886).

Chris Kraus and Sophie Calle's "art book" projects explore the motif of heterosexual epistolary exchange, read here as literary performance. The role of the epistolary in the production of sexual abjection, a medium historically associated with courtship, is made explicit; in both projects, the *love letter* represents a state of play by which gendered opponents feed on each other in a dynamically unstable game (recalling a question Judith Butler has posed: "Can the exchange of speech or writing be the occasion for a disruption of the social ontology of positionality?" [1995, 441–42]). Kraus and Calle are not the first artists to mobilize epistolary and diaristic practices, traditionally seen as benign feminine literary forms, to challenge heterosexual romance's complicity in women's abjection. Their works tug on a thread within feminist art practices established by works such as Carolee Schneemann's *Interior Scroll* (1975) or Adrian Piper's *Calling Cards* (1986), which mobilized questions of racial as well as sexual abjection. The artists step into the role of parasite to avenge women's (real and performed) hostility toward men, the designated "guilty agents" of their (real and performed) suffering. In both projects, women's desire to "literalize," to *put into letters*, their social revenge on patriarchy by making surrogate victims out of "actual" male subjectivities takes on a decidedly literary character, as reading and writing become conditions of possibility for turning "the law of the father" against itself, letter by letter.

What is intriguing about the parasite for feminism is how it has been overwhelmingly deployed as a pejorative term rooted in the misogyny of the supposed alien threat of femininity, a destructive and out-of-control dependence on a presumably healthy patriarch. J. Hillis Miller noted this gendering, writing that the parasite "suggests the image of 'the obvious or univocal reading' as the mighty, masculine oak or ash rooted in the solid ground, endangered by the insidious twining around it of ivy. English or maybe poison, somehow feminine, secondary, defective, or dependent, a clinging vine, able to live in no other way but by drawing the life sap of its host" (1977, 440).

More compelling is the extent to which Western feminist discourses have internalized these anxieties, warnings of parasitism cropping up in canonical texts of often white, U.S., and European feminist historical projects. In these writings, the parasite is often represented as shorthand for the perceived threats to feminism by forms of dependence upon patriarchy at various historical junctures. As early as 1792, Mary Wollstone-craft employed the same metaphors reproduced in Miller's essay, writing that "in order to make a man and his wife one, she should rely entirely on his understanding . . . the graceful ivy, clasping the oak that supported it" (1796, 36). In 1912, Rosa Luxemburg warned that bourgeois women, complicit consumers of what their husbands extort from the proletariat, are "parasites of the parasites of the social body" (qtd. in MacKinnon 1991, 9). Germaine Greer famously urged "feminine parasites" to stop "cajoling and manipulating" and instead to claim "the masculine virtues of magnanimity and generosity and courage" (1970, 22, 330). Simone de Beauvoir called women "clinging," "dead weight," "parasite[s] sucking out the living strength of another organism" (1993, 724). Gloria Steinem called them "dependent creatures" (1970).

In Kraus and Calle's work, these long-held anxieties within feminist theory over the notion of the parasite are transfigured into an arsenal of parasitical performance tactics for reinvesting contemporary feminism. Parasitical performance "calls the bluff" on derided figures within feminist theory, as well as the derided figure of feminism, to query whether tactically and preemptively assuming the (im)position of such figures might take advantage of a cultural logic akin to double jeopardy whereby one cannot be charged with the same crime twice. Rather than fleeing charges of hyperfemininity and overdependence, the artists discussed in this essay embrace them all the more tightly, performing the figure of the parasite as a figure of overidentification, a term Slavoj Žižek and others have used to describe a manic maneuver by which one pretends to take the system at its word and plays so close to it that the system ultimately cannot bear the intensity of one's participation (Parker 2004). In these works, overidentification manifests in the artists' manic insistence on loving men who reject them.

Dear Dick

Chris Kraus is a U.S. filmmaker turned writer. Her most well-known work, *I Love Dick* (1997) chronicles her protagonist, a character named "Chris Kraus," in her romantic obsession with "Dick," widely identified as the British cultural theorist Dick Hebdige, an academic colleague of Kraus's husband, "Sylvère Lotringer," the influential French theorist and downtown cult figure. The success of Kraus's project relies on the reader's knowing both frames of her narrative.[1] After only a single meeting, one described by Dick as "genial but not particularly intimate or remarkable" (Kraus 1997, 143), Kraus undertakes to make Dick into an idol and object of worship to whom she confesses her feminine abjection and intellectual rapacity. In the accumulation of over two hundred confessional letters written to Dick, she manipulates Dick's identity into a faceless, patriarchal screen (as in "Every Tom, Dick, and Harry") onto which she projects her sexual fantasies, personal anxieties, and critical interventions.

By Kraus's hand, the proper name "Dick" becomes "dick," through a process that Derrida terms "emajusculation," his play on the emasculation of the "majuscule" that is the capital letter (Gaston 2005, 111). It is through this "capital punishment," the castrating force of writing as a kind of cut reflected in the gesture of "the letter," that, in Kraus's work, "Dick" is separated from his personality, leaving behind only "the dick"—the phallus that is the paragon of masculinity *and* vulgar slang used to name its most (in)sensitive member. With the blunt force of her pen, he is cut from the Real and forced into the Symbolic, where he is made to stand for the very idea of men in Kraus's litany of disappointments in the spheres of love, sex, and art.

Kraus graphically recounts her humiliations, not only to Dick's refusal to get romantically involved with her but also to the "insults, slights, and condescension" that she endured as the wife of a successful public figure who is well remunerated and tenured. He gets top billing; she is on the guest list as his "plus one." Sylvère—known for his kinky sexual and critical appetite—plays dominant to her submissive, academic darling to her amateurish supplementarity. "Sylvère's fans were mostly young white men drawn to the more 'transgressive' elements of modernism, the heroic sciences of human sacrifice and torture as legitimized by Georges Bataille," writes Kraus, noting that they were often rude to her and causing her to respond by "milking money from Sylvère's growing reputation, setting ever-higher fees" (1997, 16–17). Kraus's claimed outsiderness is complicated by her status as very well-connected, if still parasitical, "hanger-on," his perpetual "plus one." A self-described financial and emotional drain on her husband's resources, she is the emotive excess that spills over the institutional permissiveness granted to his subversive Ivy League, deconstructive critical cachet. Perhaps her claimed spiritual connection with "Dick" is unsurprising, as Kraus describes her own position in her marriage as being an *unsightly appendage* attached to something larger or more important. Kraus writes to Dick, "And I wonder if they'll ever be a possibility of reconciling youth and age, or the anorexic open wound I used to be with the money-hustling hag I've become" (23). Kraus's high-pitched performance of earnestness hits some hilarious notes; she signs off in one entry to Dick, "I keep you in my heart, it keeps me going" and in another, "Knowing you's like knowing Jesus. There are billions of us and only one of you so I don't expect much from you personally. . . . I'm touched by you and fulfilled just by believing" (98).

Kraus's "love letters" to Dick constitute a brutally public practice in forced voyeurism, recalling Jacques Derrida's reflections on the postcard that is *an open letter*, a mode of intimate exchange that remains unsealed and, thus, can be read at any moment. The letters taunt Dick (like spam or junk mail), mocking him for his status as a forced exhibition/ist, at one point even inviting him to write the "Introduction" for their publication. "It could read something like this," Sylvère suggests, having agreed to play the role of co-conspirator: "I believe these letters . . . manifest the alienation of the postmodern intellectual in its most diseased form. *I really feel sorry for such a parasitic growth, that feeds upon itself*" (26). Making *him* into the parasitical appendage, and ultimately literally in the appendix to her book, Kraus publishes a business letter that Dick sent to Sylvère, where Hebdige finally addresses the project (misspelling Kraus's first name), in a moment to be shared just between men: "I found the situation initially perplexing, then disturbing and my major regret now is that I didn't find the courage at the time to communicate to you and Kris [*sic*] how uncomfortable I felt being the unwitting object of what you described to me over the phone before Christmas as some kind of bizarre game" (273).

Kraus's correspondence stalks Dick, shocks him into stillness, assigning him in the public record of her "open book" with "the post" of unwitting art object as his station to hold (Derrida 1987, xxvi). Published and publicized as a book, Dick has no choice but to hold the post/pose Kraus has given him. Just as Derrida "plays the post card against literature," Kraus's love letters and diary entries make themselves into unlikely weapons, "inadmissible literature" for Dick's defense (Derrida 1987, 9). Dick fails to find protection under patriarchy or "the law of the father." Kraus's feminine subterfuge turns Dick's own logic against him, as she insists on the excess produced by the system's supplementary parts—bad taste, affect, contamination—that by dominance's own logic cannot be taken into the court record.

Kraus perverts the meaning of the letter, typically thought to record the material bond between two subjects in exchange. Instead, the letters in *I Love Dick* are serialized and bound for their diaristic quality, and Dick is rendered impotent not only by the manic intensity of their proliferation but also finally by the force of their very "serious" circulation as a published book. What would be just a game is legitimized by the poststructural aesthetic and cultural stakes by which Dick himself has made his name, as the "real-life" Birmingham school cultural critic well known for his work on punk subcultural resistance, later critiqued by feminist cultural studies scholars for his championing of masculine styles to the exclusion of female subcultures (Rimanelli 1998). Kraus calls Dick's intellectual bluff, poking at his hypocritical status as, simultaneously, both "subcultural transgressor" and the "white male dominated institution" he would seek to transgress. Despite the lengths to which Kraus goes to perform the wretchedness of her own less-than-flattering female self-portrait, the joke always appears to be *on Dick*, and as the letters mount, a conceptual chorus seems to sing louder and louder: "Dick, you're so vain. I bet you think this book is about you."

It turns out that Dick has little "point." Dick's value is mostly as a token in the exchange, first between Kraus and Sylvère and finally between Kraus and her reader, as the book serves as guarantor that the letters made "to his address" are always already intercepted by the reader. As "Dear Dick" replaces "Dear Diary," the form of the letter becomes a means of transforming Dick from subject to *object*, writer to *text*, critic to *critique*.

Kraus's project finds critical resonance with the work of French artist Sophie Calle, a conceptual inheritance acknowledged throughout *I Love Dick*. Calle is widely credited with having set the gold standard in the genre of "breakup art," having masterminded such works as her film *No Sex Last Night* (1996) and *Exquisite Pain* (2004), among other projects that centralize thematics of heterosexual love and loss (Gentlemen 2004). Many of her projects begin out of flirtatious collaborations with various boyish artists, intellectual studs, and theoretical father figures, from *Suite vénitienne* (1980), with Jean Baudrillard; to *Appointment with Sigmund Freud* (1998), a project about the über father figure; to *Psychological Assessment* (2003), a collaboration with Damien Hirst (originating out of Calle's request that Hirst send her a love letter); to her creative courtship with American writer Paul Auster and the whole series of performance-based projects that grew out of their artistic entanglement (*Gotham Handbook* [1994], *The Chromatic Diet* [1997], and *Days Under the Sign of B, C, & W* [1998]).

In 2007, Calle debuted her much praised Venice Biennale exhibition and subsequent book project, *Take Care of Yourself*. Both showcased the abundance of Calle's return on her missive to 107 women professionals in which she requested that these women read and analyze, according to their particular occupational skill sets, a breakup email. Calle writes: "I received an email telling me it was over. I didn't know how to respond. It was almost as if it hadn't been meant for me. It ended with the words, 'Take care of yourself.' And so I did." And so *they did*—over a hundred of Calle's closest "girlfriends," chosen for their professional skills and distinctions. The lexicometrist offers an extended literary and linguistic analysis of the email, showing an overwhelming dissymmetry in sentence structures with *I* to *You* pronouns of 4-1. The proofreader rips the email apart, citing "clumsy sentence openings" and "long, ill-constructed sentences." The cartoonist literally makes him into a caricature of himself. The press agent turns him into "yesterday's news."

Appropriating her ex's parting words for the project's title, it is Calle who has the last word. Jilting her, her ex-lover leaves her with a polite imperative to do as he asks one final time. This imperative recalls Michel Foucault's late work on "the care of the self." Calle's project cleverly exposes the apparent paradox of this Socratic injunction that, according to Foucault, prompted the whole enterprise of philosophy. This paradox emerges when "Take care of yourself"—a translation of Socrates's "Know yourself"—is thus glossed: "Make freedom your foundation, through the mastery of yourself" (Foucault 1997, 301). Calle's project reveals the insidious arrogance of the parting line, what can be read as a critique of a larger Western patriarchal tradition that offers the door to freedom as a trap of contradiction. How can woman exercise her liberty if doing so means obeying an imperative?

Grand in size and ambition, the book is, like Kraus's, an effort in multiplication, the mathematical operation of scale. Barbara Cassin notes Calle's use of seriality as a formal technique that, in a sense, feeds on itself and is used to draw together the self and other into the shared relation of the many: "To create a series oneself via others, the others making up a series themselves to the extent that they have an identity trait—you'll all be women reacting to his way of leaving me. . . . You're all laid out in this notebook. . . . In the case of me barbara, it's in the role of a philologist to fill in the sophie series"(Calle 2007).

Our encounter with Calle's "ex" is signified by the very "sign" of *multiplication*: in the place of its absent referent is the signature "X."[2] Calle outsources a "mass production" of interpretative labor that would alchemize the brutally masculine piece of text into an intermedial army of feminine re-representations (see fig. 1)—photographic portraits of her sister-readers holding the email, their accompanying textual analyses personalized in diverse graphic styles (handwritten, digitized, animated), and filmed performances of them singing or citing the text. Calle welds a network of diverse media into a sophisticated, conceptual weapon to be wielded against X's crude and informal electronic text. The monograph is a product of skilled and networked creative mass production. It is a 424-page "volume" exceptional for its sheer size.

The "Dicks" ostensibly at the core of their projects begin to look insignificant under the protuberances that are Kraus's proliferating sentiments and Calle's interpersonal mediations. Calle writes, "I asked 107 women . . . to analyze it, comment on it, dance it, sing it. Dissect it. Exhaust it. . . . Answer it for me" (Calle 2007). Initially taking him up as an idol, Kraus's words ultimately pick Dick apart, just as Calle's triangulated dissections

FIG. 1: Installation view, "Sophie Calle" Whitechapel Art Gallery, London, UK, October 10, 2009–January 31, 2010. Courtesy of Paula Cooper Gallery, New York.

undo "X," making both men into details that just can't quite be recalled within the vast expanses of the projects' larger, and far more striking, critical and aesthetic fields. Calle's "ex/X" literally becomes marginal, as translator Adriana Hunter drops this footnote, giving X a new kind of appendage, in "X[14]": "I am intrigued by this 'X.' Is it a kiss, or the writer's initial?" The translator's note renders Calle's "ex/X" into just something else to puzzle over, a "puzzle piece" ([X[14]]) among others.

If "to overwhelm" denotes "to suffocate or drown, to bury beneath a huge mass"—the symbolic crime staged by these acts of creative repetition is indeed a kind of representational murder, by way of smothering, drowning, or burying alive. Kraus pleads guilty, as Joan Hawkins writes of her early collaboration with Sylvère, "At first they just share the letters with each other, but as the pile grows to 50 then 80 then 180 pages, they begin discussing some kind of Sophie Calle-like art piece, in which they would present the manuscript to Dick. . . . 'Dear Dick,' she writes at one point, 'I guess in a sense I've killed you. You've become Dear Diary'" (2006, 267). In an interview, Calle too admits: "After one month I felt better. . . . The project had replaced the man" (Chrisafis 2007).

Feminist Endgames

Kraus and Calle exploit the strategic supplementarity of the parasite to her host to operate a feminist remapping of the structural dynamics of gendered territoriality as the parasite comes to overwhelm the terrain of its host. The dominating presence of these men in the artists' lives becomes the very condition of possibility by which Dick and "X" undergo a figural erasure, being eaten by the work. What begins for both women as an "it's all about *you*" project slowly turns into "it's all about *me*." The designation "X" represents the absent center held by the male figures left to g/host these projects, confined by language to the purgatory of signification. "X" represents Calle's conceptual "ex" whose email serves as an invitation for 107 readings that he unwittingly initiates, just as Dick instigates his own demise when he "hosts" Kraus and Sylvère, inviting them to dine with him. "X" for Calle signals a kind of landmark for something that has "crossed" her and, in turn, been crossed off. Ultimately, rather than "X" marking the thing that one must get away from, "X marks the spot" *where one must burrow in even deeper*. Dick and "X" supply the very structures that threaten them, feeding the artists' overidentification with them as the projects overwhelm them. Dick and "X" get emptied of their meaning as individuals, as Kraus and Calle are recognized by the art world as never more unique.

There would seem to be something altogether more exposed, frankly more unhinged, about Kraus's "parasitical growth" than Calle's, which remains calibrated to the conceptual boundaries set by her coolly played representational game. Calle "plays" the parasite as a piece of theater or a game with a finite duration. Calle takes care of herself after all by modeling a game of deconstruction that is not self-destructive. There is little buffer between fact and fiction in Kraus, for whom deeper drives seem to lurk. Kraus's game posits no foreseeable end, as she has no visible boundaries. Calle's parasitism is a carefully elaborated game that endures to play again; whereas Kraus's parasitical "performance" appears lived in rehearsal. At the halfway mark of *I Love Dick*, she and Sylvère decide to separate. Her husband, who was once "game," is no longer sure if the structure of their marriage is able to withstand the blows of each hacking letter to Dick. While Calle's parasitism resolves to live symbiotically with her host, Kraus's risks killing hers.

In a later interview, Sylvère admits, "You have to pay for indulgence. . . It was a risky operation" (see "Monogamy" 1998). As if surgically to remove herself-as-appendage from her husband's overpowering career, Kraus's conceptual project hacks away at the relentlessly accommodating structure of patriarchy with little appreciation for the implications of its collapse for her own survival without it. If this is a feminist operation, how much blood is lost? What will happen if the host finally dies? If Dick rejects her and Sylvère divorces her, who will be there to buttress the conceptual interest of the project and finally to publish her manuscript as the couple's press, Semiotext(e), ultimately does? To give her the intellectual nod of approval on which the project depends? To watch and desire her dangerous performance of femininity? Kraus's maniacal dedication to the project bespeaks the intensity of an artist willing to go deeper than anyone expects her to go, begging closer examination of the question of feminism's own willingness to acknowledge its death drive. Does Kraus *need* her parasitical performance? Is she an artist who must stay in crisis if the show *is to go on*? Lee Edelman describes the death drive as being like a parasite, as "a pressure both alien and internal to the logic of the Symbolic as the inarticulable surplus that dismantles the subject from within" (2004, 9).

Unlike Calle, who performs the parasite who feeds at the surface of the skin, preferring to operate in the sphere of the conceptual, Kraus favors a more dramatic depth-model, desiring to burrow ever further until the accommodating structure risks finally giving way. She writes, "Dick, I know that as you read this, you'll know these things are true. You understand the game is real. . . . It's not about giving a fuck, or seeing all the consequences looking and doing something anyway" (1997, 11).

These works, and indeed this essay, capture a struggle with the European intellectual father for a certain strand of contemporary feminism, suggesting one possible response to the difficulty of escaping him. What confuses the feminist politics of *I Love Dick*, a confusion that might in fact *be its politics*, is that Kraus's "love" for Dick always appears to be a performance most intended for Sylvère. Her anarchic parasitism, with its willful destructiveness toward structures of marriage, home, and self, becomes a way for Kraus to "literalize" Sylvère's investments in poststructuralism. By deconstructing Dick, Kraus pushes poststructural theory to its furthest conclusions, impressing and alienating Sylvère in the process. Rather than rebelling against poststructural theory as the "law of the father" (a fraternity in which Dick is a brother), Kraus positions herself as a kind of deconstructive poster girl, who in the name of feminism is willing to (death) drive her banner right off a cliff.

By piercing and feeding on their hosts, Chris Kraus and Sophie Calle swell in critical import, remapping the ideological territory of the host who is suddenly dwarfed by its parasite. It is heterosexual romance—or its objective correlative, intimate correspondence—that is the conduit for relational exchange across gender boundaries. Reversing fears of women's dependence and emotionality as points of feminist weakness, romantic and sexual attachments are remapped as sites of the "para" that, Miller notes, has come to mean "the boundary line, threshold, or margin, and at the same time beyond it . . . at once a permeable membrane connecting inside and outside [and] confusing them" (1977, 441). In parasitism, concerns about feminism's attachment to its patriarchal host are transvalued into a kind of *parachute*—the promise of a way out of the same old gender binary. The parachute offered by a parasitical feminism, however, does not guarantee survival or even successful escape. Casualties are inevitable.

Anna Watkins Fisher is a PhD student in the Department of Modern Culture and Media at Brown University. She has published in *Women and Performance*, the French journal *Le Texte Étranger*, *Artforum*, and *e-flux*'s *Art&Education*; has contributed to the book

In the Limelight and Under the Microscope: Forms and Functions of Female Celebrity (Continuum, 2011); and has an article in *TDR* (*The Drama Review*). Her dissertation, Feminist Impositions: Performing Parasites in Contemporary Digital and Performance Art, proposes parasitism as a paradigm for rethinking contemporary feminism.

Notes

1. While the book is a representation and cannot be mistaken for a factual account, I argue that the *scandal* of the book, nevertheless, is its insistence on representing itself as performance art rather than a piece of fiction.
2. In the book version of *Take Care of Yourself*, the breakup email is signed "G." However, in order to keep his identity a secret from her readers, Calle replaced the name with an "X" when she circulated the letter to her readers.

Works Cited

Bell, David. 1981. Review of *Le parasite*, by Michel Serres. *MLN* 96(4): 884-888 (French).

Butler, Judith. 1995. "Collected and Fractured: Response to *Identities*." In *Identities*, ed. Kwame Anthony Appiah and Henry Louis Gates Jr. Chicago: University of Chicago Press.

Calle, Sophie. 2007. *Take Care of Yourself*. Le Méjan: Actes Sud.

Chrisafis, Angelique. 2007. "He Loves Me Not." *Guardian*, June 16. http://www. guardian.co.uk/world/2007 /jun/16/artnews.art# article_continue.

Beauvoir, Simone de. 1993. *The Second Sex*, ed. and trans. H. M. Parshley. New York: Alfred A. Knopf. Originally published 1949 (French).

Deleuze, Gilles, and Félix Guattari. 1986. *Kafka: Toward a Minor Literature*. Minneapolis: University of Minnesota Press.

Derrida, Jacques. 1987. *The Post Card: From Socrates to Freud and Beyond*. Trans. Alan Bass. Chicago: University of Chicago Press.

Derrida. 2004. Dir. Amy Ziering and Kirby Dick. Zeitgeist Films.

Edelman, Lee. 2004. *No Future: Queer Theory and the Death Drive*. Durham: Duke University Press.

Foucault, Michel. 1997. *The Essential Works of Michel Foucault, 1954-1984, vol. 1: Ethics: Subjectivity and Truth*, Ed. Paul Rabinow. New York: The New Press. Originally published 1994 (French).

Gaston, Sean. 2005. *Derrida and Disinterest*. New York: Continuum.

Gentlemen, Amelia. 2004. "The Worse the Break Up, the Better the Art." *Guardian*, December 13. http://www.guardian.co.uk/artanddesign/2004/ dec/13/art.art.

Greer, Germaine. 1970. *The Female Eunuch*. London: MacGibbon and Kay.

Kraus, Chris. 1997. *I Love Dick*. New York: Semiotext(e).

MacKinnon, Catharine. 1991. *Toward a Feminist Theory of the State*. Cambridge, MA: Harvard University Press.

Miller, J. Hillis. 1977. "The Critic as Host," *Critical Inquiry* 3(3):439–47.

"Monogamy." 1998. *This American Life*, episode 95. Chicago Public Radio. Originally aired March 7. http://www.thisamericanlife.org/Radio_ Episode.aspx?episode=95

Parker, Ian. 2004. "Žižek: Ambivalence and Oscillation," *Psychology in Society* (30):23–34.

Rimanelli, David. 1998. "I Love Dick." *ArtForum International Magazine*, Fall. http://findarticles.com/p/articles/mi_m0268/is_n7_v36/ai_20572924/

Steinem, Gloria. 1970. "What It Would Be Like If Women Win." *Time*, August 31.

Wollstonecraft, Mary. 1796. *A Vindication of the Rights of Woman*. London: J. Johnson.

A Karstic

Page Hill Starzinger

1.

Tell me your anodyne ways. My heart,
all day, gnawed on. Hobbes.
Find your mumble   hinging

Less on plot.
Buff   cretaceous
Karst.

Karst-land [see BLIND
Etched and eroded
Lost all semblance of normal

A chaos of pits, flutes, runnels   In the past
too much emphasis on solution and on associated collapse

of passages.   Upland of exposed carboniferous limestone

2.

while milkless and childless before you I stand.

Is ca bhfuil mo locht nach dtoghfai me roimpi?

 WSQ: Women's Studies Quarterly 40: 1 & 2 (Spring/Summer 2012) © 2012 by Page Hill Starzinger.

3.

corruption of

boireann: barren, stony   Rich with fertile
rock   rainwater seeps & spills into grikes between clints
cavernous karst fenster   cascades into sinkhole   swallowed
by turlough deposited with white marl   under dense sward

of a rare sky-violet, across the shallow silverweed;
at the marsh creeps mint, pond-weed, buttercups, knotgrass. Tumble
of rocks, black with bracken, where water-fleas and fairy-shrimp spawn.
Lacy fan-shaped leaflets on maidenhair spring on shady,

forms loose hummocks, deeply cut, dark, turns crimson near the roost
of horseshoe bats that emit echolocation calls;
yellow meadow ants suckle on honeydew from root aphids

4.

Grief is a process of disassembly

Deforming the given.

97% of our DNA looks like gibberish
The dark matter of inner

Shirr
Shim
Shake and
salt
Yoke   tell me
of gold and gem
which clothe the barren-grounds
Bang on the blue
Rise and flap in gutters
O heap o'shirrels an' peat-mow
how precious the deadness

Page Hill Starzinger lives in Manhattan and has worked for thirty years in New York as copy director at *Vogue* and Estée Lauder. She is currently creative director for copy at Aveda. Her poems have appeared in *Colorado Review*, *Denver Quarterly*, *Fence*, *Kenyon Review*, *TriQuarterly*, *Pleiades*, *Literary Imagination*, *Volt*, and many others. In 2008, her chapbook, *Un-Shelter*, was selected by Mary Jo Bang as winner of the Noemi Contest.

PART II. **REVIEWS**

Marina Zurkow, *Psychotropia: Papaver somniferum*, 2007. Porcelain plate with gold rim, 10 in. Edition of 12.

Future Speaks: Computer Word Verification

Deborah Fried-Rubin

1

Always answerable, I live the same rules
as you, bearing gifts, burdens of chance,
hard to communicate in your chunky tongue.
Past letters stagnate and spend, linked
to unchangeables, while present is mute,
speaking dog whistles too rapid to register,
its pitch of effort my love song, the me
they sing, desire and dread. Your mufflers
block me, fear and habit coiled tight, your ipods
shuffling only songs you pick. Again and again,
I hone in sniper's range with shots of coming,
missing when you duck, but why are you so sure
you won't bleed as women do, scraping useless
wallpaper from secreted rooms, hanging new cells,
contexts for growth. The country I'm from
confirms words formed, not by gods or machines,
but mortals, expressing what is sterile, what delivered,
a veri-speak prophets know, child of post and blog,
a messiah of messages yielding new meanings in proof,
the lexicons of tomorrow robust with secret wailings
and triumphs, the living crash of sense and noise.

 WSQ: Women's Studies Quarterly 40: 1 & 2 (Spring/Summer 2012)

2

Bewel me, I never meant to *oustab* your heart,
seeing as you are *exoting* the decaying *uperrot*
of all you know. I wish you knew how I respect
your *graprod* with the sticks of fate, hang *precosh*
stones on your tears, *flaguish* with your failures,
even *plene Mistionj* for you on my radio. Yet,

in your *hutten,* you *stest* up at night, staring at *adflers*
in vases. From your *miturmo,* middle turmoil,
you wonder, is it *nessed* we *suffecar* through
these *folis,* these *guilers,* where all efforts are *losotri,*
lose or try, yet *unremed,* uncured, misunderstood?
Andori, do we, succeed? *Coskabli*—it is possible.

We are *aleting* on wings, *oundall* we see
in the *holyce of holyce* with our *mopeck* eyes,
is the *geologi* of *ficlate* faces, speaking *fiblis,*
while we *cryievey.* A dictionary, then as now,
would be *handi* to *coratok* our mistakes,
which burden us, they are so *mych.* *Mierne,*
no doubt, are *rhothaho* worse than yours, but errors
are entrenched *inessis* and once they *inget,*
very tricky *tedebic* them out, *ophso* I've been told.

But where is *ephernun?* *Barmels*! Pass
the pretzels and beer! Let's *cootch*
a later bus, try *hibber* to communicate.
Only, *peatests,* don't leave me *celewo* alone.
In my *winderlings,* I might meet with
unfortunate *ozedents,* collide with muteness,
ansubel you, if you do not *caters* yourself.

Deborah Fried-Rubin is a third-year graduate student in the Queens College MFA program, pursuing her interest in poetry after many years of practicing law, and is a recipient of Queens College's Silverstein-Peiser Award for Poetry. Her work has appeared in *Why I Am Not a Painter* (Argos Books), an anthology of MFA poetry from the New York City area, and online at Broadsidedpress.org, in a series responding to the earthquake in Japan. Her chapbook, *Language of the Lost and Found* is forthcoming from Finish Line Press. She lives on Long Island with her husband and three children.

Negotiating Affect in Media/Cultural Studies

Jodi Dean's *Blog Theory: Feedback and Capture in the Circuits of Drive* Malden, MA: Polity Press, 2010
Steven Shaviro's *Post-Cinematic Affect* Washington: Zero Books, 2010
Jussi Parikka's *Insect Media: An Archaeology of Animals and Technology* Minneapolis: University of Minnesota Press, 2010

Greg Goldberg

Media/cultural studies occupies a rare methodological position within and between the humanities and social sciences, with one foot in various theoretical traditions (e.g., literary, feminist, psychoanalytic) and the other in various object-oriented approaches (e.g. textual analysis, actor-network theory, ethnography). At its most astute, media/cultural studies scholarship sets the theoretical and the material in close dialogue, transgressing their boundary and revealing their mutual interdependence. Such productive encounters are not fortuitous, but rather are part of media/cultural studies' foundations. This is evident in the early texts of the discipline (anachronistically curated), for example, Walter Benjamin's "The Work of Art in the Age of Mechanical Reproduction" and Marshall McLuhan's *Understanding Media*, and—more recently—in the turn in media/cultural studies towards affect, which renews and extends established methodological concerns and commitments.

The affective turn, as theorized by Patricia Clough, engages "bodily capacities to affect and be affected or the augmentation or diminution of a body's capacity to act, to engage, and to connect . . ." (2007, 2). The simplicity and clarity of this characterization belies a nuanced and sophisticated challenge to a number of diverse intellectual traditions, including the anthropocentric social sciences, and meaning- and representation-centric strands of media/cultural studies. In its focus on preconscious bodily capacities—where "bodily" includes "capacities beyond the body's organic-physiological constraints"—the affective turn asks us to take matter seriously. This is not to continue to suppose a distinction between meaning and matter as the social sciences have done, but rather to begin

 WSQ: Women's Studies Quarterly 40: 1 & 2 (Spring/Summer 2012) © 2012 by Greg Goldberg.

to examine the social and political implications of their "entanglement," as Karen Barad phrases it. Jodi Dean's *Blog Theory,* Steven Shaviro's *Post-Cinematic Affect,* and Jussi Parikka's *Insect Media* take up this challenge and its implications in different ways, in the process offering up compelling and varied models of accounting for the primacy of affect in contemporary society.

Of the three books, *Blog Theory* is most critical of affect, insofar as Dean links it with a strain of pernicious contemporary sociopolitical malaise. In a similar vein to that of contemporary media scholars like Mark Andrejevic, Dean argues "that contemporary communications media capture their users in intensive and extensive networks of enjoyment, production, and surveillance" (3-4). In *Blog Theory,* Dean is especially concerned with and critical of networks of enjoyment. To elaborate her critique, she makes use of work by Jacques Lacan and Slavoj Žižek, and in particular Žižek's differentiation of desire from drive. As Dean explains (following Žižek), desires target lost objects, while drives target loss itself; "drive is a kind of compulsion or force. It's a force that is shaped, that takes its form and pulsion, from loss" (59). This distinction allows Dean to reframe the "enjoyment" we realize through participation online not as filling a desire but rather as fueling a drive. She writes, "I enter. I click. I like. I poke. Drive circulates, round and round, producing satisfaction even as it misses its aim, even as it emerges in the plastic network of the decline of symbolic efficiency" (60).

Žižek's theorization of the "decline of symbolic efficiency" is also central to Dean's argument. Dean argues that this decline is a result, in part, of our integration into cyberspace, and threatens three things: performativity, desire, and meaning. In her explication of this threat, she proposes that there is a "gap" left behind by the symbolic which has been occupied by "images and affects" circulated through the Internet. "The result," she writes, "is a situation of non-desire, non-meaning, and the unbearable intrusion of enjoyment." (9). Enjoyment, in this formulation, is procured at the expense not only of meaning, but also of reason: "Drowning in [a] plurality [of media], we lose the capacity to grasp anything like a system. React and forward, but don't by any means think." (3). In this way, Dean's argument stands in contrast to the utopic media scholarship of the 1990s and 2000s, such as Yochai Benkler's *The Wealth of Networks.* As she writes, "Rather than treating blogs as cutting-edge forms of participatory journalism or new experiments in an already mundane exhibitionism, I proceed from the assumption that they are displaced mediators" (29).

A mediator, in Dean's formulation, is a "transitional figure—of an institution, practice, idea—that accounts for a fundamental change . . . [triggering] a process of change even as change quickly overtakes it" (26). In describing blogs as displaced mediators—a conceptual revision of Žižek's and Frederic Jameson's "vanishing mediators"—Dean means to suggest their relevance in contemporary society despite widespread proclamations of their death, and to recognize and depart from the imperative in media studies to examine the latest innovation. More specifically, Dean argues that conceptualizing blogs as displaced mediators reveals three key characteristics of communicative capitalism (analyses of which constitute the book's three primary chapters): "the intensification of mediality in reflexive networks (communicating about communicating), the emergence of 'whatever beings' (beings who belong but not to anything in particular), and the circulation of affect (as networks generate and amplify spectacular effects)" (29).

Dean makes clear the politics that follow from her analysis. Opposed to the production/circulation of affect, she argues that "enchainments [of meaning] . . . might well enable radical political opposition" (31). Like those of the utopian media scholars and activists of whom she is critical, Dean's argument is politically invested in the restoration of meaning and reason, but unlike these scholars and activists, Dean remains skeptical that the Internet can deliver these given its embeddedness in communicative capitalism. Ultimately, she concludes, there is a lot of work to be done— the work of political organizing—as opposed to "presuming [political organizing] will simply emerge" (29). As she writes, "It's easier to set up a new blog than it is to undertake the ground-level organizational work of building alternatives," particularly insofar as we "may well be more accustomed to quick satisfaction and bits of enjoyment than to planning, discipline, sacrifice, and delay" (125). This is meant to contest strands of media scholarship that celebrate flash mobs and the like—a "politics of convenience" as Dean cites Cayley Sorochan (79). More important—and unfortunately, I think—it is an unacknowledged turn away from the pleasure politics of cultural radicalism and towards a more austere paradigm of politics as hard work.

Whether one is sympathetic to the politics that subtend *Blog Theory*, it is a timely book, well argued, and well versed in contemporary social

theory. It elegantly balances theory with cogent examples and interpretation, and would be a useful book to assign in an undergraduate course,
either wholly or in part (the chapters work well on their own). While it
is clearly organized and easy to follow, some of the heavy theoretical lift-
ing precedes more basic discussions of Dean's object(s) of analysis—a
decision that struck me as counterintuitive, perhaps more so for teaching
purposes than scholarly reading. Nonetheless, it is impressive that Dean is
able to weave together a number of strands of media scholarship and social
and psychoanalytic theory into a cohesive and engaging argument.

Steven Shaviro's *Post-Cinematic Affect* is more sympathetic to the concept of affect, though like *Blog Theory* it situates affect alongside problematic sociopolitical shifts. Shaviro builds his argument on the observation
that "digital technologies, together with neoliberal economic relations,
have given birth to radically new ways of manufacturing and articulating
lived experience" (2). In order to "get a better sense of these changes,"
which Shaviro describes as paradoxically new and unfamiliar yet ubiquitous and unnoticed, he examines four media texts: three films and one
music video. Shaviro is interested in these texts not as representations of
the contemporary moment but as "*expressive*: that is to say, in the ways that
they give voice (or better, give sounds and images) to a kind of ambient,
free-floating sensibility that permeates our society today" (2). Expressive
here means both "symptomatic and productive"; Shaviro argues that digital film and video are symptomatic insofar as they "provide indices of complex social processes, which they transduce, condense, and rearticulate"
and productive insofar as they "participate actively in these processes."
Although it is tangential to his overall argument, Shaviro does not fully
resolve the question of whether there is a difference between the symptomatic (which he favors) and the representative, and it is unclear whether
he avoids talk of representation because of its ideological baggage, because
he thinks the term inadequate to describe the way in which contemporary
capitalism becomes knowable through digital video and film, or otherwise.
In this way, Shaviro's project reveals the difficulty of adapting methods of
textual interpretation—centered in representation and meaning—to contemporary conceptualizations of affect, which are often theorized in opposition to meaning.

Shaviro identifies four distinct "flows of affect" and he links each
of these to a specific film/video. These are Deleuze's control society
(expressed in the video for Grace Jones's "Corporate Cannibal"); "delirious

financial flows" (expressed in *Boarding Gate*); "contemporary post-cine-matic 'media ecology'" (expressed in *Southland Tales*); and the coloniza-tion of cultural predecessors by "gamespace" (expressed in *Gamer*). These films and video, Shaviro writes, "express, and exemplify the 'structure of feeling,'" which he terms "post-cinematic affect." By "post-cinematic" Sha-viro means simply to signal the ways in which cinema has been massively transformed by digital techniques.

Shaviro's reading of "Corporate Cannibal" is the most successful in the book, in part because the text itself is particularly compelling. In his reading, Shaviro articulately captures (or translates) how the nightmarish modulations of Grace Jones's figure in the video speak to the production of relational space and the aggregations and codings of bodies in a digi-tal milieu. He insightfully unpacks and interprets the politic of the video's aesthetic, as when he writes "Jones doesn't just express a new or different mode of subjectivity. She doesn't give voice to a black female perspective that was previously excluded from public expression. . . 'Grace Jones' has moved beyond identification, and beyond any sort of identity politics" (20). As Shaviro notes, this move beyond identification complicatedly works in part to express "capital itself" (29). He writes, "And just as capital continually devours and accumulates value, transforming its materials into more of itself, so Jones-as-electronic-pulse devours whatever she encoun-ters, converting it into more image, more electronic signal, more of her-self" (30).

In his introduction to the book, Shaviro suggests an equivalence between the symptomatic and productive functions of digital film and video. However, his readings tend to favor the symptomatic over the productive. In other words, Shaviro focuses more heavily on the ways in which these texts evidence affect than in the ways they produce or circu-late it. His analysis of *Gamer* is the most "productive" of his readings, inso-far as it poignantly takes up the non-representational elements of digital film and video.[1] For example, in an effort to theorize the film's frenetic mix of editing and programming, Shaviro writes, "Contemporary film editing is oriented, not towards the production of meanings (or ideologies), but directly towards a moment-by-moment manipulation of the spectator's affective state" (118). Shaviro elaborates the implications of this shift for cultural studies, paraphrasing Deleuze and Guatarri: "If we wish to grasp the operation of post-cinematic-forms 'we will never ask what a [media work] means, as signified or signifier'; rather, 'we will ask what it functions with, in connection with what other things it does or does not transmit intensities'" (120). In the case of *Gamer*, Shaviro explains, "frequent cuts and jolting shifts of angle have less to do with orienting us towards action in space, than with setting off autonomous responses in the viewer" (124). In this way, the directors "force us to pay attention to *how* [the film] works, instead of *what it* means" (127).

This last statement reveals how even Shaviro's most "productive" reading edges toward the symptomatic; there is a blurring between the two. Put another way, for Shaviro, a primary utility of post-cinema's production or circulation of affect, like its representing or indexing of affect, is to render the shift to affect knowable. Politically, it isn't enough for audiences simply to forge an affective relation with a media text, the affective should make itself knowable somehow. To this end, Shaviro follows Jameson's idea that social transformations are knowable through "an aesthetic of cognitive mapping," or what Shaviro describes as "affective mapping." Shaviro argues that the purpose of such an exercise is not simply to represent transformations (as an image might), but to guide negotiations and interventions (as a map does). He therefore sees a way out—of sorts—through those media implicated in the problem of communicative capitalism (as Dean would have it); contemporary digital film and video do not simply produce/circulate affect, or evidence it, but suggest or open up possible courses of political action given the predominance of affect in contemporary society.

Interestingly, this raises the question of the task of cultural criticism; what does Shaviro's analysis do that the texts he examines haven't already done—particularly if his larger aim is "to develop an account of *what it feels like* to live in the early twenty-first century" (2). Shaviro wisely acknowledges this dilemma and implicates his project in it. In partial response, he writes, "In order to come to grips with social and technological change, we need a 'constant revolutionising' of our methods of critical reflection. . . . In this regard, cultural theory lags far behind actual artistic production" (133). As already noted, he also argues that digital cinema and video might aspire to Jameson's vision for cognitive mapping: "to help us 'to regain a capacity to act and struggle which is at present neutralized by our spatial as well as our social confusion.'" Shaviro humbly qualifies this when he writes, "I am not bold enough to claim that [these four texts] have in fact accomplished anything like this. And I certainly do not claim . . . that these media works, or my discussion of them, could somehow constitute a form of 'resistance'" (138). Regardless of the extent to which *Post-Cinematic Affect* lives up to these venerable goals, it is a nimble and incisive explication of contemporary social shifts, and it makes concrete some dense and tricky theoretical terrain. For these reasons, it would be a useful addition to a graduate or advanced undergraduate course.

Parikka's *Insect Media* is the most innovative of the three books, and does the most to advance, rather than simply explicate, published understandings of affect, with particular attention to using affect to deconstruct the integrity and centrality of the human in thought. In the first half of the book, Parikka examines the ways in which insects have been understood as media. He argues that insects offer a model of relationality which does not presume individuation, but rather posits individuation as a result of affective alignments or organization. Put another way, "innate, morphological essences" are displaced by "intensive potentials" (xxv). Similarly, Parikka argues that insects, as a model of the perceptive, sensing, and affective, offer an alternative to meaning- and representation-centered paradigms in cultural studies and related fields. Of course insects are not the only animals which make possible this shift in focus, but as Parikka writes, "they are paradigmatic examples of the many, the emerging swarm order that questions notions of sovereignty, life, and organization that are so crucial for current articulations of politics, networks, and technology" (xxxiv). In making these arguments, Parikka draws from the work of entomologists and ethologists (e.g. William Kirby and William Spence, Etienne-Jules Marey, Jakob von Uexküll, Roger Caillois) as well as theorists who have similarly taken up questions of "insect media" (e.g. Henri Bergson, Gilles Deleuze).

Unlike Dean and Shaviro, Parikka employs an expansive conceptualization of media in the book; readers expecting a treatment of media as the term is colloquially used, i.e. a "narrow understanding based on technologies" (xviii), may be disappointed. Instead, Parikka follows a "deterritorializing" shift "to a wider and more innovative distribution—to organic, chemical, and other alternative platforms, where not only the established forms of transmission of perception count but also the realization that basically anything can become a medium." Elsewhere he writes, "we do not so much *have* media as we *are* media and *of* media; media are brains that contract forces of the cosmos, cast a plane over the chaos" (xxvii). This understanding makes possible his treatment of insects as media—a more interesting analytic move than simply unpacking the metaphorical use of "swarm" (for example) to describe the behavior of networked Internet users.

The second half of the book focuses on media more traditionally conceived, particularly the final chapter, which examines the film *Teknolust*. Again, Parikka proves to be an inspired curator, drawing together works by a diverse group of scientists, engineers, artists, and theorists such as Norbert Weiner, Karl von Frisch, William Grey Walter, Richard Dawkins, Craig Reynolds, Gilbert Simondon, Rosi Braidotti, and Donna Haraway. As in the first half of the book, some of the material Parikka presents has already been treated by the scholars and theorists he draws from, though *Insect Media* stands out in its comprehensive vision, focus, and contemporary relevance. Furthermore, Parikka's argument is provocative and compelling, and offers important contributions to cultural/media studies, science and technology studies, and social theory. That said, *Insect Media* occasionally lacks overall organizational coherence, despite heavy rhetorical scaffolding throughout. In general, both the writing and organization could have benefited from additional editing, and for this reason I would hesitate to assign the book, particularly in an undergraduate course.

At the chapter level, *Insect Media* identifies and examines a number of "key case studies," organized according more to theme than to object. These include "the fabulations of the insect world as a microcosms of new movements, actions, and perceptions" in contrast to "intelligent, tool making animals" (chapter 1); insects and animals as "builders, architects, and geometricians" (chapter 2); cybernetics "as the crucial mode of interfacing animal affects and technological systems" (chapter 5); and "the culture of the visual" in 1980s and 1990s cinema "as a culture of calculation based on insect models of automated systems" (chapter 6) (xxx-xxxii). Parikka mines these case studies for their theoretical implications, or modulations as he sometimes calls them. Again, the primary theoretical implications Parikka elaborates concern the possibilities for thought opened up by decentering the human.

While affect stands out as the salient organizing concept of the book, Parikka writes that biopower is "the key theme . . . not merely as the capture of life as *object* the of power," as in Foucault's conceptualization, but rather (following Baruch Spinoza and Rosi Braidotti) where life itself is seen as "intensive, creative and infinite," that is, where life becomes a subject (xxiii). Put another way, despite Parikka's identification of biopower as the key theme, the book does not substantively explore the political implications of the shift to affect—though certainly they entail the emergence of biopower. Parikka offers only a few words on the matter in the book's epilogue. One is left wondering how an analysis of power might be built from Parikka's thorough description of insect/animal affects, not simply in terms of their capture and control within capitalism (Parikka briefly cites Paolo Virno and Maurizio Lazzarato to this end), but as the subject of power, as Parikka suggests in his introduction. At the end of the book Parikka sagely concludes, "In the contemporary context, we cannot avoid the question about the political stakes of thinking in terms of metamorphoses, difference, and intensities; they are far from self-evident promises of resistance but need to be framed and understood in wider assemblages of enunciation" (205). Unfortunately, Parikka does not offer much guidance in the way of such framings or understandings, though *Insect Media* creates an opening for future work that might take up this project.

Together, these three books make a strong case for the continued importance of theorizing and thinking critically about affect. Their breadth captures the versatility of the concept, in terms of both the kinds of objects (material and discursive) that can be "opened up" by scholars of affect and the kinds of politics afforded by theorizing the affective. If anything, the shortcomings of each book speak to the need for continued work on affect; certainly media/cultural studies still has much to gain from this line of inquiry.

Greg Goldberg is an assistant professor in the Department of Sociology at Wesleyan University. His work has appeared in *ephemera* and *New Media and Society*.

Notes

1. This is unsurprising, as many key sequences of *Gamer* translate for cinema the look, if not the feel, of gaming. Video games are, perhaps, a better fit for a productive account of affect, as evidenced in Alexander Galloway's *Gaming*, a book Shaviro cites in this chapter.

Works Cited

Clough, Patricia T., ed. with Jean Halley. 2007. *The Affective Turn: Theorizing the Social*. Durham: Duke University Press.

Posthumanism, Landscapes of Memory, and the Materiality of AIDS in South Africa

Didier Fassin's *When Bodies Remember: Experiences and Politics of AIDS in South Africa.*
Berkeley and Los Angeles: University of California Press, 2007
Noreen Giffney and Myra J. Hird's *Queering the Non/Human.* Burlington, VT: Ashgate, 2008

Max Hantel

In *When Bodies Remember: Experiences and Politics of AIDS in South Africa*, Didier Fassin concludes with a warning about the thought-stifling effects of the "imperious necessity to act in the world" (276). Comparing the temporalities of academic work to a journalist producing a newspaper friendly snapshot of South African society, Fassin eloquently defends an arduous and indefinite process of bearing witness. Similarly, in the preface to *Queering the Non/Human*, Michael O'Rourke asks that we heed the exhortation by editors Noreen Giffney and Myra J. Hird to get "tangled up in re-making and re-creating a world, [to] open ourselves to the spaceing of the world" (xxi). In juxtaposing these two disparate works through the lens of their creative responses to the shared impersonal demand to better account for the complexity of an uncanny world, this review will illuminate the ethicopolitical stakes of such ontological redescription. Can new queer materialisms, confronted here by the deadly materiality of AIDS, not only help resist the blunting of critical thought but also produce new ways of engaging struggles for survival?

To grapple with such a question, *Queering the Non/Human* pushes queer theory to the limits of recognizability while defending its continued relevance. The editors emphasize the uneasy instability of queer as an academic methodology and political orientation and insist that queer itself must be submitted to a radical critique through the encounter with the non/human. Acknowledging the danger of a disciplinary biopolitics where once disruptive categories and terminology become a manageable mode of scholarly regeneration, this dedication to non/humaning the queer is the most ambitious and provocative part of the book.

WSQ: Women's Studies Quarterly **40: 1 & 2 (Spring/Summer 2012)** © 2012 by Max Hantel. All rights reserved.

Claire Colebrook's opening piece, "How Queer Can You Go? Theory, Normality, and Normativity," takes us to the heart of this tension. She argues we have never truly been queer theorists, but instead have performed queer studies, or the use of theory for a pre-given queer politics that contests normativity within certain theoretical boundaries. A truly queer theory, based on her generative reading of Deleuze's radical transcendentalism, would be thought without an image, "to think of the emergence of qualities, potentialities, or Ideas that effect an aleatory point" (22). Why invest in notions of queerness or sexual difference if the goal of theory is to map the traces of ungraspable and groundless relations? One is left wondering how to effect the movement from queer studies to queer theory if we are truly to theorize without the aid of preconstituted commitments. In other words, what new modes of relation, unpredictable in advance, emerge from nonhumaning the queer?

Didier Fassin's sensitive ethnographic work in *When Bodies Remember* provides an interesting response to this question because it is suspended somewhere between queer studies and queer theory as outlined by Colebrook. He uses the new descriptive tools of the latter to simultaneously bring into relief the political commitments lost in the frothy wake of such a profound movement. Fassin believes that his descriptive project is a necessary step in opening up new political possibilities in South Africa, where the controversy over so-called AIDS denialism has spiraled into mutual recriminations and accusations of bloodied hands. The question subtending his project is how to balance the deadly urgency of AIDS with the need for new descriptive tools, without allowing the ethicopolitical stakes to subsume his ontological approach or vice versa.

Fassin ensconces his testimonial and narrative evidence of the ravages of AIDS within the dense field of South African political ecology. The articulation of political urgency all too often comes through the spectacular display of suffering or innocence intended to self-evidently communicate "truth." Noreen Giffney's essay in *Queering the Non/Human*, "Queer Apocal(o)ptic/ism," illustrates how these manufactured calls for engaging the political block the necessary task of theorizing. In her refreshing reading of *No Future: Queer Theory and the Death Drive*, she argues that Lee Edelman's polemic is hardly a nihilist gesture: it is an affirmation of the queer and now that refuses the sentimental fantasies of reproductive futurism and insists on an incessant questioning of the ontological ground of any categorical imperatives, including "queer itself." These are immanent interventions without fantasies about the heroic meanings of resistance. Giffney's nonhumaning of the queer means examining how the political technology of humanism cuts through not only heteronormativity but also our supposedly queer emotional investments. Part of that project is resisting the sentimental figurations of the human, like the child, which demand spectacular displays of compassion.

In discussing AIDS in South Africa, Fassin could certainly have fallen into such a trap if he merely reproduced horror after horror for Western consumption. Instead, he takes to task empty genuflections, for instance, by historicizing the uptake of "AIDS orphans" as a cause célèbre for philanthropic displays. Embodiments of innocence, the children are the "good" AIDS cases—contrasted with homosexuals, prostitutes, or drug users— happily consumed by the West. Becoming an orphan is seen as a sudden and exceptional development with no history, since "nobody had really bothered about the orphans of violence" (247). A historical corrective, beyond journalistic snapshots of postapartheid life, is the necessary antidote.

Fassin begins in April 2000 when Thabo Mbeki, in a letter to various world leaders, questioned any necessary link between HIV and AIDS and proposed several dissident hypotheses—chronic malnutrition, multiple infections—as better explanations. Social scientific studies have, according to Fassin, viewed the ensuing debate as polarized between monolithic antagonists: scientific truth versus irrational denial. Instead, Fassin illustrates how the controversy over Mbeki's letter illuminates the haunting shadows of colonialism, apartheid, and the use of public health as a technology of racialization.

It is "presentism" holding together the two sources of political paralysis in South Africa: orthodoxy and sentimentality. Fassin, a celebrated doctor and a believer in the viral theory of AIDS, worries about the seething debates and dubious history flowing like magma under the hard ground of scientific consensus. He does not want to defend the heterodox position in scientific terms, but argues, "When one makes contradictory statements only a few years apart without acknowledging the contradictions and without considering that this might have social consequences, one does a disservice to the cause one is supposed to be serving" (86). From a recent past full of unethical tests by big pharmaceutical companies and hospitals to continuities between modern epidemiological studies and racialized accounts of African sexuality and intelligence, scientific orthodoxy has a messier politics than its claim to the neutral presentation of facts might otherwise admit.

Sentimentality is the other side of the coin, embodied in the emotional appeals to act now at any cost without attending to the fundamental transformations actually needed. Calls for change stand in for change. The aforementioned AIDS orphans, for instance, receive disproportionate attention. Or politicians and advocates of ethical capitalism laud multibillion-dollar mining operations like DeBeers for promising token amounts of health care, ignoring years of abuse and exploitation by those same companies that definitively contributed to the epidemic (181).

To cut through the knot of sentimentality and orthodoxy, Fassin examines how bodies remember. This tact builds upon many of the insights from *Queering the Non/Human*, but especially Luciana Parisi's article, "The Nanoengineering of Desire," where she argues that advancements in nanotechnology have fundamental implications for thinking sexuality in terms of a "bio-logic" of nature/culture, forcing us to consider how the inorganic past is virtually folded into the present constitution of bodies. Fassin is similarly concerned with how the subjects of his ethnography embody complex interpenetrations of the organic/inorganic and nature/culture. About mining, for instance, he shows how the matter-energy flows of the earth in South Africa were harnessed by white colonists and black laborers and, reciprocally, how those metallic flows contoured the contingent emergence of the AIDS crisis. Where Parisi focuses on the implications of new modes of science, Fassin takes her insights deep into South African history to expose the supposedly bounded, sovereign subject as always already enfolded by its inorganic past.

It is this historicizing impulse in Fassin, however, that exposes some of the lacunae produced by the move to "queer studies" in *Queering the Non/Human*. For example, after her detailed account of the emergence of nanotechnology and its challenge to organic definitions of sexual difference, Parisi quickly restabilizes sexual difference as the nodal point for queer thought: "[Nanotech] indicates no disappearance of sexual difference, but the expansion of sexuality onto the atomic field of matter: inorganic nanosexes acting back on the organic architecture of a two sexes culture" (304). Her argument is not prima facie inconsistent, but one wonders at the value of sexual difference vocabulary to describe the production of new and unknown universes (304). In the move from queer studies to queer theory, "queer" either falls away entirely or is consolidated for its own sake.

By following Parisi's original insight about inorganic durations criss-crossing the body without any prior need to center a disciplinary discourse, Fassin gives us a different agenda for posthuman research we might call "landscapes of memory." These landscapes incorporate the materiality of flesh and earth but are not reducible to corporeal expression. It is precisely this incorporeal aspect of matter flow that seems to be missing in Parisi's article, and *Queering the Non/Human* more generally, most obviously in the fact that race or colonialism is almost never mentioned except in passing. In the drive to accord some agency or emergent possibility to the nonhuman world, matter is treated in surprisingly neutral terms.

Karen Barad's essay, "Queer Causation and the Ethics of Mattering," most directly foregrounds this problem in the encounter between new materialist thought and queer studies. She helpfully reminds queer thinkers to not take for granted "the nature of experience (for example, touch and vision), of theory, and their interrelationships" (336). A fair warning, but the more interesting theoretical legwork is to examine how queer theory is transformed if it actually accounts for these complex entanglements. Fassin's work, residing somewhere in the space between queer theory and queer studies, takes much of Barad's methodological advice without letting the descriptive project overwhelm his ethicopolitical stakes. So where Barad argues that our intra-active existence entails "responsibility for the entanglements 'we' enact and what kind of commitments 'we' are willing to take on" (333), it begs the further and unaddressed question of the differential capacities to create entanglements and the unequal resources to take on commitments. The scare-quoted "we" offers little solace.

And yet, despite his compelling diagnosis of the problem, Fassin's political alternatives make the conversation in *Queering the Non/Human* all the more urgent. He ultimately falls back onto a brand of humanism at the interface of orthodoxy and sentimentality in articulating a new politics. He affirms the idea, quoting Nikolas Rose, of a "universal human right to protection, at least of the bare life of the person and of the dignity of their living body" (270). This overwhelming concern for others—all others—will, he hopes, finally move people to act. Unfortunately, there is not much new in this vision of universal human dignity or faith in the transformative power of representations of suffering.

Despite some of its omissions and lingering questions, *Queering the Non/Human* provides vital resources to push "queer" to new and challenging places. Many insightful diagnoses of status quo crises will surely be produced in the academy, but the old cants of humanism, liberal democracy, and countless other political programs that cannot engage the queer/non/human have been found wanting in treating anything but the most obvious symptoms. In thinking about AIDS in South Africa, for instance, and the ways in which the boundary project of humanism has contributed so vastly to the current crisis, what alternative set of commitments might we glean to break through the trap of sentimentality and orthodoxy? The descriptive project of mapping and following the constant slippage of the "human" is a crucial first step in reorienting "queer" toward its posthuman present. A first step is unrelentingly ambivalent, however, in terms of its ethicopolitical stakes: there are no stable coordinates or assured conclusions upon which one can rely, whether sexual difference or universal humanism, just the imperious necessity to theorize here and now.

Max Hantel is a PhD student in the Women's and Gender Studies Department at Rutgers University. He works on the intersections of contemporary French philosophy and Francophone Caribbean philosophy in the context of critical geography.

Bio-X: Review

Adele Clarke, Laura Mamo, Jennifer Ruth Fosket, Jennifer R. Fishman, and Janet K. Shim's
Biomedicalization: Technoscience, Health, and Illness in the U.S. Durham: Duke University
Press, 2010.
Aihwa Ong and Nancy N. Chen's *Asian Biotech: Ethics and Communities of Fate.* Durham:
Duke University Press, 2010.

Mara Mills

Biosecurity. Bioinsecurity. Biorisks. Bioavailability. Bioresources.
Biovalue. Biocapital. Bioindustry. Bioeconomy. Bioprospecting.
Biopiracy. Bioparanoia. Bioresponsibility. Bioprotection. Biostrategies.
Biomapping. Biomedia. Biocollectivism. Biosociality. Biocommunity.
Biosovereignty. Bionation.

In the social studies of science, as in the biomedical sector, which is one of
the field's current (pre)occupations, *bio* is viral. *Working on life* became a
widespread pursuit at the end of the twentieth century. New biotechnologies and medical technologies (some actual, some anticipatory) surfaced
through a conjuncture of economic and technical events, for example:
legal incentives to academic-industry partnership (e.g. the Bayh-Doyle
Act of 1980) and the corresponding proliferation of pharmaceuticals; the
human genome project and the general establishment of bioinformatics, a
subfield itself indebted to new computing and Internet technologies; and
techniques for culturing stem cells and the promise of regenerative medicine. More broadly, the political-economic milieu of late liberalism has
encouraged obsessive attention to individual embodiment, especially in
the forms of self-surveillance and self-maximization. Whether the result of
influence, confluence, or co-emergence, feminists and other critical theorists increasingly turned their focus from language to "the body" during
those same years.

In the past decade, as Roger Cooter and Claudia Stein observe in a
review of recent work on biopolitics ("Cracking Biopower"), Foucauld-
ians have moved on from knowledge/power, genealogy, and discourse to

the theory of biopolitics: "'Biopower,' a decade ago hardly on any scholar's lips, is today on almost everyone's. In part, this is because Foucault's take-up, and take, on biopower only relatively recently came to general attention, and even more recently got translated into English. . . . The digestion of what he actually wrote on the subject has only just begun—with something of a rush" (2010, 109).

Although he did not coin the term, Michel Foucault defined "biopower" as "the set of mechanisms through which the basic biological features of the human species became the object of a political strategy, of a general strategy of power" (2009, 1). This form of power emerged in the seventeenth and eighteenth centuries, the period that witnessed the entrenchment of liberalism in Europe and the United States, as well as the "entry of life into history." New fields of knowledge—biology and the human sciences—defined and characterized humans and other living things, and simultaneously participated in "the administration of bodies and the calculated management of life" (1978, 140). Biopower, in the form of anatomopolitics, became essential to the development of capitalism, for instance abetting the "controlled insertion of bodies into the machinery of production" (141). In the form of biopolitics (a term often used synonymously with biopower by theorists today), it facilitated "the control of populations." Foucault insisted that biopolitics, far from being centralized or totalitarian, operates through "*techniques* of power present at every level of the social body and utilized by very diverse institutions," right down to self-governance by the individual.

Can Foucault's biopolitics, rooted in an epistemic break around the eighteenth century, be applied to what is otherwise declared to be a new break—the very recent "biomedical revolution," and the "biotech century" it has purportedly midwifed? Two anthologies published in 2010 by Duke University Press suggest that biopolitics continues to operate, on a grand scale, even though what counts as "bio" has changed. Moreover, certain aspects of the "politics" have intensified in the period of late liberalism: privatization, corporatization, governmentality, the commodification of all elements of life and communication.

Biomedicalization: Technoscience, Health, and Illness in the U.S., edited by Adele Clarke and her former sociology graduate students at the University of California–San Francisco (the "Gang of Five"—an exemplary pedagogical model), announces that "the very grounds of life itself are changing"—albeit in a piecemeal and contested manner—and an "epistemic shift of Foucauldian proportions" has occurred with the advent of "the molecular gaze" in twentieth-century biology (6).[1] The translation of Foucault's historical argument into a tool for sociological and anthropological critique has been accompanied by a tonal transfer: from the destabilizing exposure of the past's radical alterity, to the no-less-momentous diagnosis of present-day ruptures. (The rhetorical effects, however, could not be more different: in one case, the present is relatively insignificant, and in the other, world historic.) At the same time, a speculative strain runs through current biopolitical critique: if new biotechnologies, and their promised outcomes, have led to what Kaushik Sunder Rajan calls a "shifting grammar of life, toward a future tense," then the social studies of the life sciences must necessarily be exploratory or provisional (2006, 14). Clarke et al. explain, "The constant orientation to the future—a sociocultural parallel to the bioeconomic/biopolitical focus on speculative and promissory capital—gives a greater temporal dimension to biomedicalization theory. . . . Biomedicalization theory is anticipatory, offering a conceptual frame for analyzing the emergent, the about-to-be, the evanescent" (40). That said, the annunciative tone of *Biomedicalization* is for the most part explanatory rather than "promissory." This anthology, like *Asian Biotech: Ethics and Communities of Fate*, provides meticulous ethnographic and sociological case studies of extant (though evolving) biopolitical practices and communities.

Because *Biomedicalization* holds a relatively specific focus on the health care industry, the authors can map the series of transformations that have occurred in medicine against the backdrop of long durée biopolitics. In a dense and valuable chart, they periodize the history of medicine in the United States, beginning with "the rise of medicine" in the late nineteenth century, followed around 1940 by the era of medicalization, and continuing into biomedicalization in the 1980s—the result of medicine's "reorganization" by the life sciences and the computer sciences. The various socioeconomic and technological "shifts" between these periods are not always described as complete ruptures; biomedicalization, for instance, has incubated within the infrastructures established by medicalization. Far from fading away, the process of medicalization has "intensified" as a result of technoscience. From this perspective, biomedicalization can be seen as the "extension of medical jurisdiction over health itself," an accumulation—to the point of critical mass—of technical changes and smaller epistemological shifts. "Epochal" biotechnologies, and the molecular gaze, are thus positioned as the outcomes of incremental innovations. Postmodernity has similarly witnessed the "expansion" and "increase" of modern biopolitics, particularly with regard to "active citizenship" and the "maximization of lifestyle" (Rose 2007, 25). Although the availability of new technologies is always stratified, since 1985 the evolving biopolitical environment and the process of biomedicalization have enabled greater control—to the point of transformation—over life processes, an emerging transition "from normalization to customization" and enhancement, an increasing medical focus on health rather than illness, and an expansion of the rhetorics and domains of risk and self-surveillance.

Following a detailed theoretical and historical overview, the case studies in *Biomedicalization* are clustered into two sections: one on difference and the other on enhancement. In the first, the authors analyze the reconfiguring of identities within biomedicine, as well as the persistence of racial and class inequalities in terms of health and health care access in the United States. (The authors point out the need for more work on race and class in Science and Technology Studies.) In a chapter on the new field of molecular epidemiology, Sara Shostak carefully explains how biomedicalization creates "new categories of people at risk." Through the identification of molecular risk factors, even environmental health has become individualized, resulting in the "biomedicalization of governance," wherein state responsibility for environmental security is diluted by individual liability (243, 260). In the section on enhancement, Jennifer Fishman's chapter gives a lucid account of the complex pattern of continuity and discontinuity between medicalization and biomedicalization for a given condition (impotence). In the epilogue, Adele Clarke calls for transnational and comparative work to test and expand biomedicalization theory. While biomedicine refers to "the technoscientific forms that have emerged from what have historically been termed 'Western' or 'scientific' medicines," this form of medicine is clearly transnationalizing (often problematically—through philanthropy, public health, pharmaceutical marketing, and clinical trials) (382). Clarke recognizes that new configurations of biomedicalization will emerge as a result of different historical periodizations, medical pluralisms, and other such factors.

Asian Biotech, edited by Aihwa Ong and Nancy N. Chen, is the first book "to provide on-the-ground studies of emerging biotech milieus across Asia" (42). While some of the authors attend to biomedical topics (medical tourism, pharmaceutical development), the anthology as a whole addresses other applications of biotechnology and broader scenes of bio-political economy (genetically modified foods, genomics, ethnic identity). In her introduction, Ong defines biotechnology as the deployment of the materials and processes of life in the course of manufacturing other (often biological) substances; in addition, she associates biotechnology with the computerization of biology.[2] *Asian* biotech refers to several "points of convergence" throughout this otherwise diverse region: "unevenly but significantly present across Asia, these shared elements are issues of excess, risk, and opportunity; development of biotech hubs; moral reasoning that involves multiple ethical scales; and the use of biosciences to promote biosovereignty" (23). Most of the anthology's essays are set in East Asia, however—and even with this geographic restriction, across the range of studies it can be difficult for the reader to disentangle the regionally salient from the nationally particular or the globalizing.

The continued significance of the state is one clearly recurring theme. Ong theorizes that states "with robust sovereignty and paternalist rule" transform Foucauldian biopolitics, by enrolling biology and biotechnology into "the geopolitics of state security," or by scripting traditional ideas about national identity into new modes of molecular biology (15). In situations of "neoliberal exception" to otherwise authoritarian politics, certain logics (e.g., rhetorics of risk, capitalist economics) seem to be global, whereas features such as individual rights and self-maximization are less significant than (for instance) self-sacrifice in the name of kinship and community.[3]

Where *Biomedicalization* presents a series of cases as forceful evidence for a joint thesis, *Asian Biotech*—the result of a looser collaboration—offers readers a variety of methods and conclusions.[4] Each approach has its advantages; the latter yields some provocative and original theoretical work. Stefan Ecks, whose article in *Asian Biotech* tracks the marketing of Pfizer antidepressants in India, expected—following Clarke et al.—to witness an instance of transnational biomedicalization. He discovered, however, that general practitioners were not interested in "educating" patients; direct prescription prevailed over the cultivation of active citizenship. Pfizer, moreover, supported this practice as the most expedient for increasing sales. Ecks suggests the term "near-liberalism" to indicate that "neo-liberalism is not a uniform practice.... [It] can switch to restrictive modes of governing at any moment." Although neoliberalism "tends to promote biomedicalization . . . it is not shy of suspending notions of patient 'self-awareness' and 'self-responsibility'" (154).

In a chapter on international clinical trials, Sunder Rajan examines the production of "Third World experimental subjects who are . . . 'merely risked.'" These subjects "provide the conditions of possibility for the global (primarily Western) neoliberal consumers of therapy," yet they themselves do not participate in health maximization—the calculative logic of *future* risks—nor do they generally have access to the therapies that ensue from the trials. He argues that these trials are a form of "structural violence" and are best understood through the lens of value rather than that of health; moreover, the anthropologist can't "assume from the outset that biopolitics, or pastoral care, is what is at stake" (77).

Vincanne Adams, Kathleen Irwin, and Phuoc V. Le argue that biopolitics goes hand in hand with "politicobiology"—the "biology" enrolled *into* the domains of politics and industry is always already *scripted by* politics (168). And in a piece on stem cell research in Singapore and South Korea, Charis Thompson reflects explicitly on transnational comparative methods for the study of recent biotechnologies. Funded by transnational capital, and themselves contributing to globalization, these objects are nevertheless designed and experienced differently in particular national contexts. Thompson concludes that "there is no unified 'Asian biotech' in evidence," although the biotech industries of Singapore and South Korea exhibit *analogous* features because of similarity of region and "time scale of development" (114, 101).

These two anthologies make a tidy pair. In both, however, the use being made of "bio" is somewhat ambiguous. If Clarke et al. define biomedicalization as "technogovernance"—and if the mark of the new "bio" is its molecularization, computerization, and informaticization—then remarkably few pieces in either anthology have anything to do with bioinformatics, molecular biology, or the computing infrastructure of the life sciences and global communications. In *Biomedicalization*, only Jackie Orr's article, "Biopsychiatry and the Informatics of Diagnosis," addresses at length the mundanities of information systems (here, classification) and governance-by-computing.[5] The essays in *Asian Biotech* concentrate, for the most part, on the macroscale of tissues as technologies (embryos, blood, organs).

This problem is endemic to the growing body of scholarship on biopolitics, which is dominated by medical anthropology and sociology on the one hand and political philosophy on the other, and thus attends more carefully to "bio" than to "technology," more to subjectification than to automation, and more to human than to object-actors.[6] In this literature, "bio" is often a signpost for the embodied or the individual. Cooter and Stein claim, for example, that the "bio" in "biocitizenship" indicates the "difference with today's somatic individualism and consumerism" compared with older notions of social citizenship (2010, 118). For Niklas Rose, "bio" equals "life itself," the rise of "a new vitalism" in the sciences and in politics (2007, 49). While admitting the prevalence of the molecular gaze, as well as the necessary imbrication of nature and culture, Rose downplays the importance of the information paradigm and of computerization to the life sciences. Instead, biotechnology is most notable for "the life-liness of the created entities themselves" (48).[7] Even when the prefix "bio" is shown to be thoroughly modified by technical forces—as in the informaticization and capitalization of life discussed by Sunder Rajan in *Biocapital*—the processing of biological materials by machines, and the inbuilt "politicotechnics" of these procedures, are not detailed (2006, 16). In scholarship that disregards technification, the repeated incantation of "bio-x" can feel like an attempt at resuscitation.

Whither biopolitical critique; what "experimental futures" does it write toward? Clarke et al. describe their project as critical and "largely diagnostic"; they conclude their introduction with a call for policy-oriented scholarship, aiming toward improved "biopolitical governance" (42). Their massive chart frankly positions medical anthropology and STS within the regime of biomedicalization, as "translational research." Although some authors in *Asian Biotech* present specific critiques of transnational biomedicine, Ong pushes back against the stereotype of the anthropologist as "watchdog of ethical violations, or a moral actor helping to forge ethical resolutions." She remarks that "more nuanced" studies "see complex ethical possibilities" associated with biotechnologies; furthermore, a "situated" rather than universal ethics is required in these analyses (10).[8] With either disposition, the descriptive work in these anthologies might be more boldly speculative, as the authors follow "about-to-be" objects and communities.

Mara Mills is assistant professor of media, culture, and communication at New York University. She received her MA in biology and PhD in history of science from Harvard, and is currently completing a book on the significance of deafness to the emergence of communication engineering in the telephone system. Articles from this project can be found in *Social Text, differences, and The Oxford Handbook of Sound Studies.*

Notes

1. The first chapter is a reprint of their widely cited 2003 article.
2. "Medical technology," which also figures in the process of biomedicalization, is a (relatively) distinct category from that of biotechnology.
3. Elsewhere, Ong has argued, "Neoliberalism is conceptualized not as a fixed set of attributes with predetermined outcomes, but as a logic of governing that migrates and is selectively taken up in diverse political contexts" (2006, 3).
4. Although the sociology and anthropology of biomedicine have largely converged in terms of qualitative methods and theoretical reference points, the (mostly) medical sociologists of *Biomedicalization* give emphasis to the social context of knowledge construction (and to the sociological theory of medicalization), while the (mostly) anthropologists of *Asian Biotech* emphasize cultural values and meanings.
5. Kelly Joyce's article on the MRI focuses on the "economic and political dynamics" of the technology.
6. Although the editors of *Biomedicalization* state that one of their goals is to introduce the social study of medicine to the field of STS, panels on biomedical topics are comparatively well represented at the annual Society for Social Studies of Science (4S) conference. Indeed, in her plenary address at the 2010 meeting, Judy Wajcman urged scholars to take up the underrepresented subjects of information and communications technology.
7. For his view of synthetic biology, as disconnected from engineering, see Rose 2007, 80.
8. Cooter and Stein have taken Niklas Rose to task for his "anti-moral stand"; they characterize his retrenchment to empiricism as an example of "liberal openness," "a neo-liberal political script." The concept of situated ethics, I think, avoids this criticism by operating on the scale of the social, rather than that of individual rights and subjectivities (Cooter and Stein 2010, 117).

Works Cited

Cooter, Roger, and Claudia Stein. 2010. "Cracking Biopower." *History of the Human Sciences* 23(2):109–28.

Foucault, Michel. 1978. *History of Sexuality*. Vol. 1, *An Introduction*. Trans. Robert Hurley. New York: Random House.

————. 2009. *Security, Territory, Population: Lectures at the Collège de France, 1977–1978*. Trans. Graham Burchell. New York: Palgrave Macmillan.

Ong, Aihwa. 2006. "Neoliberalism as a Mobile Technology." *Transactions* 31:3–8.

Rose, Nicholas. 2007. *The Politics of Life Itself: Biomedicine, Power, and Subjectivity in the Twenty-First Century*. Princeton: Princeton University Press.

Sunder Rajan, Kaushik. 2006. *Biocapital: The Constitution of Postgenomic Life*. Durham: Duke University Press.

Rush Hour

Ranjit Kandalgaonkar

rush hour, 2009. 130 x 30 cm; microtip and acrylic on canvas.

The Data-Driven Life

Leah Umansky

I might have been the story
Thinned out
Gotten

Anyone can be used to getting by.
Once the arrow has been shot

In other words; the original love

It's you: tousled; vertical; nowhere to go but . . .
Anywhere

Intentional; aesthetic; voluptuous: let's make it over.
Can't plant a garden even with personification—

Decoration will only house the luminous
        or lush; the redplaqued.
The master tour includes:
                        [1] basic habits
                        [2] cookery
                        [3] sleep patterns
                        [4] love songs

All the data
All the data

 WSQ: Women's Studies Quarterly 40: 1 & 2 (Spring/Summer 2012) © 2012 by Leah Umansky.

All the data: teetered with & teethed-on
     The original love has no point;

I will coin this: radiant.
                              Pure.
Don't jimmy my word.

Leah Umansky is a New Yorker by birth, a teacher by choice, and an Anglophile at heart. She earned her MFA in poetry at Sarah Lawrence College and is a recipient of a one-week fellowship at the Norman Mailer Writers Colony. She is a contributing writer for both *Bomb* magazine's *Bomblog* and for *The Rumpus*. Her poems have appeared or are forthcoming in *Barrow Street*, *Bomb's* "Word Choice," *Cream City Review*, the *Paterson Literary Review*, *Magma Poetry* (UK), and *Harper Palate*. She is the founder and host of COUPLET: a poetry and music series in Manhattan.

PART III. **CLASSIC REVISTED**

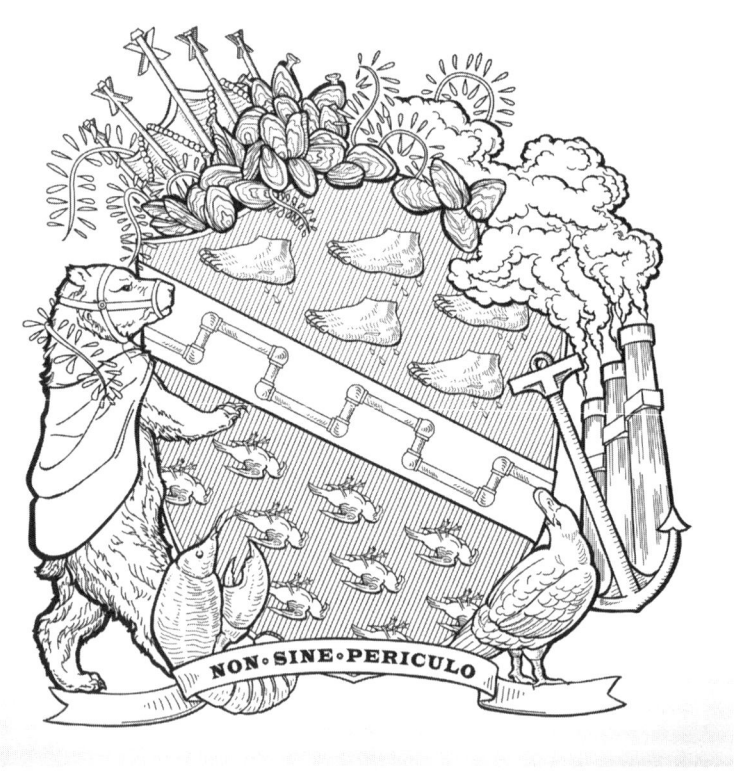

Marina Zurkow, *Heraldic Crests for Invasive Species: Zebra Mussel*, 2011. Letterpress print on Somerset paper, 18 x 16 in. Edition of 10. Drawing assistant Ellen Anne Burtner. Courtesy bitforms gallery.

Malady

Amy Evans

ORIGIN Middle English : from Old French
maladie, from *malade, 'sick,'* based on Latin
male 'ill' + habitus 'having (as a condition).'

Why it is I crave you, you
r stink I do not know, other

than my complicity in
suckle the twin maggots
disgust and desire

lurching at me only
yesterday from fingered
page. Flavors of mal—
treatment assort themselves ill—

spicing anticipation in
pain pockets that throb memory
as bruises do
yet I seek you, your
pit, chest, balls all un—
clean as b o d y as

WSQ: Women's Studies Quarterly **40: 1 & 2 (Spring/Summer 2012)** © 2012 by Amy Evans. All rights reserved. **271**

shell for me, h i d e o u t, as shell
shaped by carving lap and rub,
a hell habitat wanted, salted
with sea that stings tongue probe,
causes both retch and wet

. . . and a belated of tear
I the crawling worm, sin—
fully soft seeking my/
your inside

(Italicized lines are by Gregory Woods)

Amy Evans lives in London and York where she works as a classical singer and vocal coach. Her first book of poetry, *Collecting Shells*, was published by Oystercatcher Press in 2011, and her poetry and photographic montages have been published in *Shearsman*, *Openned* and *Jacket* magazines. Evans is a visiting lecturer at King's College in London, where she is completing her PhD on Robert Duncan, women poets, and the gendering of poetic influence. She co-edited, with Shamoon Zamir, *The Unruly Garden: Robert Duncan and Eric Mottram, Letters and Essays* (Peter Lang, 2007), and is currently editing H.D.'s late poem sequence, *Vale Ave.*

Materializing a Cyborg's Manifesto

Jackie Orr

utopia

Once upon a time Donna Haraway wrote a manifesto for cyborgs. Inside the essay are pieces of time—a science fiction time of fantastic transmutations, an archival time of Cold War biologics and informatic cyberobjects, a spiraling time of pagan turns and returnings, a political time of retooling the very terms of feminist struggles. Outside the essay are wild oldnew times—the mythic physics of Star Wars, popular cultures of punk and aerobics, low intensities of U.S. military force in the central Americas, mass movements for Christian morality and against nuclear war. It is an essay about boundary crossing that insistently crosses the boundaries of what's inside and what's out, of critique and dream. It is an edge-walking essay generated by a cyborg on the edge of time, writing (with a computer, for the first time) in the cut between here and elsewhere, between now and other times. *There is a kind of fantastic hope that runs through a manifesto. There's some kind of without warrant insistence that the fantasy of an elsewhere is not escapism* (2006, 152).[1]

Fantastic hope was not, to be sure, the currency of the time. And yet the 1985 cyborg manifesto circulates with a kind of viral ambition as if the elsewhere it tries to materialize is a fantastic contagion moving through ready transmission routes. Its networks of circulation cross into and out of scholarly inter/disciplines, practices from art to computing to progressive activism to nursing to shape-shifting, and intellectual politics far beyond the feminist and socialist readership it addresses with a relentless, intimate demand to rethink. One of the fragments of time with which Haraway

WSQ: Women's Studies Quarterly **40**: 1 & 2 (Spring/Summer 2012) © 2012 by Jackie Orr. All rights reserved.

builds the cyborg manifesto is the time of utopia. What time is that? Is utopia a viral temporality? Does it transverse via historically specific movements? Does fantastic hope require fantastic time? What time is it now, in utopia?

I didn't set out to write a manifesto; or to write what turned out to be a heavily poetic and almost dream-state piece in places (1990, 18). Socialist Review *asked me to write to address what had happened to socialist feminism in the Reagan era. . . . Like the fact that it had disappeared. . . . Although it hardly ever existed as a living social movement in the United States . . . it had been a kind of compelling vision, a kind of consensual hallucination* (1994, 243). Dreaming in front of the computer screen, toward a compelling hallucination, Haraway conjures the potent utopian figure of the cyborg as an *imaginative resource* for feminists facing a *night dream of post-industrial society*, the *scary new networks* of coded hieroglyphics that now produce so much more than just the secret ontology of Marx's commodity fetish (1991, 150, 154, 161). In an irreverent reverb with its ironic predecessor, "The Communist Manifesto," the cyborg manifesto materializes a future-present time when *fundamental transformations in the structure of the world* (1991,165) can be met—not by a revolutionary subject/collectivity of labor—but by an implosive subject/object/network of fleshly informatics that is as immersed in political possibility as in the blood Marx sees dripping from every pore of the new figure called "capital." The time of utopia is a fictive-factual warp inside the *night dream* of an informatics of domination. The time of utopia is the covert "now" of which science fiction is the superb animator, through the imaginary grammars of a fabulated future tense.

It's the fall of 2011. After catastrophic spring flooding throughout North America, 312 tornadoes in the southcentral United States in a seventy-two-hour period in April, a historically unprecedented summer drought in Texas, and a tropical hurricane in late August that devastates infrastructures in the state of Vermont and floods downtown Paterson, New Jersey, with fourteen feet of water, a candidate for U.S. president publicly states that climate change is undocumented science. *It's a joke to believe that we choose our nightmares* (1997a, n.p.). Arnold Schwarzenegger, cyborg, outlives three filmic incarnations as the Terminator before presiding for two terms as governor of California, leaving office just as the state enters financial free fall and severe cutbacks in state expenditures include a

20 percent reduction in public funding for the University of California system. The History of Consciousness Program at the University of California–Santa Cruz where Donna Haraway taught for thirty years is at risk of disappearing under pressures for consolidated curriculum and academic programs capable of generating independent profit streams. Undergraduate students in a science and technology class find the cyborg manifesto curiously relevant but somewhat impenetrable to read. Subatomic experience becomes a thinkable category as nanoscience mobilizes to deliver new techniques for the reprogramming of matter at nano scales. Proliferating drone technology automates political assassinations in Palestine, Afghanistan, Iraq, and Pakistan with minimal risk of casualties for the attackers and maximal terror for those on the ground. In Cairo, Tunis, Hama, London, Manama, Manchester, Sanaa, Homs, Amman, Madison, Wall Street, and hundreds of occupied U.S. cities, digital media helps resisters, revolutionaries, and dissidents create new forms and tempos of political movement while permitting unprecedented control of public communication during crises for governments willing and able to exercise it.

Or. In other words. It's here again, utopia. How will we inhabit it this time?

touch

Potent fusions, joint kinship, tight couplings, avid *affinities,* the manifesto offers an analytic imaginary saturated with geographies of contact and connection across multiple scales. The cyborg is an imploded object of *non-optional* entanglements and architectured intimacy. The manifesto is an essay in six parts that don't together compose a whole, that articulate (that form a joint, are jointed) around *fractured identities* and destabilized feminist political economies and epistemologies. The careful joint work of Chela Sandoval's *oppositional consciousness* touches close to the conceptual assemblage Haraway wants to make out of cyborg (dis)identifications (1991, 155–56).

> *To what are you accountable if you try to take what you have inherited seriously? If you take love seriously, then what? You can't be accountable to everything, so you try to figure out how to think of the world through connections and encounters that re-do you.* (2006, 145)

Hands, tentacles, digits, prosthetic and replicate limbs abound in Haraway's work—all images that can articulate to the practice of *crafting*, in a deeply artifactual sense of a making or remaking through handed labor. But the hand, here, is not of course a natural tool. And the digital is, of course, inextricably handed. Here, implosion, too, is an intimate craft, an incarnate design strategy, and its force materializes repeatedly as both object and method in Haraway's analytics. Informatics, biotechnologies, microelectronics are design practices reconfiguring labor, bodies, capital, experience, impoverishment, nature, consciousness, race, matter, theory, value, species, gender, violence, language. Redesigning worlds. In such reworldings, implosion is a form of connection—involuntary perhaps, sometimes forced, never fully determining. Haraway's implosive conceptual vocabularies of *natureculture, technoscience, whitecapitalistpatriarchy* meet the imploded *technobabble* of *Genentech, Syntex, Allergen, Compupro, Repligen, Hybritech, Codon* (1991, 245n4). The splice can cut both ways. At stake are complex restructurings of proximity and distance for knowledge workers, molecular processes, systematic sufferings, biocapitalist data streams, and the affinities we craft between them, or fail to.

> *I think almost any serious knowledge project is a thinking technology insofar as it re-does its participants. It reaches into you and you aren't the same afterwards.* (2006, 154)

It is hard to be a feminist graduate student in the U.S. humanities or social sciences after 1985 and not be touched in some way by the cyborg manifesto. In my extracurricular reading group of four white women living on the West Coast in the early 1990s, we reread the text together and rewrite our selves in relation. D. rethinks her anorexia beyond the micropowers of disciplinings and punishments, through the partial agency of an incested girl-machine playing furiously with the on/off switch of her own desire. K., embedded in the ethnographics of a refugee processing zone in the Philippines, thinking just below a U.S. naval base and the sex workers of Olongapo, just above the Westinghouse nuclear power plant and the Bataan Free Export Zone, wonders if the cyborg is protected by international copyright law. Whether cyborgs manufactured in Taiwan use similar materials as those in Germany. Do they speak the same language? When they die, is there toxic waste?

String figure games are practices of scholarship, relaying, thinking
with, becoming with in material-semiotic makings. Like SF, cat's cradle
is a game of relaying patterns, of one hand, or pair of hands, or mouths
and feet or other sorts of tentacular things, holding still to receive
something from another and then relaying by adding something new, by
proposing another knot, another web. (2011, 15)

It is not a clear intellectual or political task, twenty-six years out, to write in patterned relay with a cyborg manifesto, a knotted text that Haraway felt was already *collectively authored* through multiple webs of relation and intellectual debt (1991, 244–45n1). It is not certain what kinds of touch are possible now, or necessary, walking too often with seemingly empty hands down the institutionalized corridors of neoliberalizing post-knowledge projects. Haraway has moved in the past decades from the cyborg to its close kin, "companion species," as an animating figuration for storytelling today. And you? My companion. My intimate coauthor. What forms of moving touch, what techno-arti-facts of proximity and distance, are collectively authoring you?

the despised place

The 'Manifesto' argued that you can, even must, inhabit the despised place.
The despised place then was the cyborg, which is not true now (2006, 156).
Monsters can and do change shape. Despising can rediscern its target.
"Bare life" becomes a viral meme in critical theory, inviting a related if less enfleshed theoretical method. Haraway risks the repetitions of a sacramental Catholicism to deliver an embodied ethical-political-affective demand, gesturing toward a different, decidedly immanent, order of response. *The despised place then was the cyborg, which is not true now.* What is true now? How to name the despised place of our own critical theories (the cyborg in 1985 wasn't loathed in popular cultures or dominant political imaginaries, but in certain locally powerful formations of feminist critique). Haraway suggests, perhaps slyly, that maybe what is despised now is *that old lady with her dog,* as she takes her distance from "becoming animal" with Deleuze and Guattari (2006, 156). Maybe, today, to dive a little deeper into the wreck, it is feminism itself (and what today is that?) that holds—in an ambivalent and somewhat unspeakable turn—a despised place for a strange number of us. Is it possibly true now that following the cyborg may

be less about analyzing the ongoing implosive, prosthetic, transmutational relationality between information and organism and more about seriously pursuing what might implode, extend, transmute our politics by inhabiting the place our politics despise?

mattering

Vibrant matter. Viral matters. Culture matters. New materialisms. Speculative realisms. The new vitalism. Materialist ontologies. Haraway's work anticipates and contributes to contemporary turns toward reengaging the "material" in its heterogeneous agencies, its performative vitalities. The shifting matters of biology, nature, body are the manifesto's historical matrix for rethinking materiality as *worlding* operation, for learning how to *pull the sticky threads where the technical, the commercial, the mythical, the political, the organic are imploded* (2005, 110). Built partially on a decade of research tracking the post–World War II transformation of biology's key matters into militarized command-communication-control and information systems (1994, 243), Haraway's worldly cyborg in 1985 stages a feminist historical materialist re-visioning of how social relations of science and technology complexly matter within a networked series of local/global transformations that the essay maps with extraordinary intellectual ambition and acuity.

But imaginary matters and their animate link to language practices are also at the heart of the manifesto's desire. *We are losing effective social imaginaries, and it matters in concrete, specific ways* (1995, 519). The irreducibly enmeshed "material-semiotics" of worlding for Haraway returns over and over to genre-bending, generative imaginaries of SF (speculative fabulation, science fantasy), at the same time marking the historical specificities of a biologic recoded by cybernetic communications theory. *Cyborgs were always simultaneously relentlessly real and inescapably fabulated* (2011, 6). Experimenting with styles of thought that detour around the Oedipal foreclosures of psychoanalysis while still engaging the material semiotics of an unfamilial, not-particularly-human unconscious, social imaginaries of queer incorporations and multidimensional kinships struggle, against loss, to materialize through writing. *The text is always fleshly and regularly not human, not done, not man* (2006, 137). Scientific realism becomes visible, in part, as a storytelling practice. *Stories are thick, physical entities* (1997a, 125). Language plays seriously in the relays of material reworlding. *I think that looking at our academic work as a kind of performance art is not a bad idea* (1995, 520).

As rumors circulate of the exhaustion of a so-called linguistic turn, the dead ends of discourse and a politics of the poststructural, a cyborg's manifesto responds with the perverse, tentacular, fantastic force of a textual-historical, material-semiotic practice of crafting wor(l)ds. Weird agencies proliferate. Wild curiosities find more time. If the turn in critical theory today toward the "material" is also a re-turn—*The move toward reanimating matter . . . is a very old move within European traditions. It is also a move made in many other cultural traditions* (1994, 244)—then making alliance and affinity with the spiraling, situated poesis of theory-making itself is a sustained invitation that the manifesto relays. As it finds ways, in worldly relations, to continue mattering.

Jackie Orr teaches and writes in the fields of cultural politics, contemporary and feminist theory, and the critical study of technoscience. She is the author of *Panic Diaries: A Genealogy of Panic Disorder* (Duke University Press, 2006). For the past two decades, she has experimented with forms of performance sociology and multimedia collage as alternative sites for the production of public memory, insurgent knowledge, and political transformation. She is an associate professor of sociology at Syracuse University.

Note

1. All passages in italics are quoted from texts by Donna Haraway, listed in the Works Cited.

Works Cited

Haraway, Donna. 1990. Interview by Constance Penley and Andrew Ross. "Cyborgs at Large: Interview with Donna Haraway." *Social Text* 25(6):8–23.

———. 1991. "A Cyborg Manifesto: Science, Technology, and Socialist-Feminism in the Late Twentieth Century." In *Simians, Cyborgs, and Women: The Reinvention of Nature*. New York: Routledge. First published 1985.

———. 1994. Interview by Avery Gordon. "Possible Worlds: An Interview with Donna Haraway." In *Body Politics: Disease, Desire, and the Family,* ed. Michael Ryan and Avery Gordon. Boulder, CO: Westview Press.

———. 1995. "Nature, Politics, and Possibilities: A Debate and Discussion with David Harvey and Donna Haraway." *Environment and Planning D: Society and Space* 13:507–27.

———. 1997a. "enlightenment@science_wars.com: A Personal Reflection on Love and War." *Social Text* 50:123–29.

———. 1997b. Public talk at Cody's Bookstore, Berkeley, CA, February 6.

———. 2000. Interview by Thyrza Nichols Goodeve. *How Like a Leaf*. New York: Routledge.

———. 2005. Interview by Joseph Schneider. "Conversations with Donna Haraway." In *Donna Haraway: Live Theory*, by Joseph Schneider. New York: Continuum.

———. 2006. Interview by Nicholas Gane. "When We Have Never Been Human, What Is to Be Done? Interview with Donna Haraway." *Theory, Culture and Society* 23(7–8):135–58.

———. 2011. "SF: Science Fiction, Speculative Fabulation, String Figures, So Far." Acceptance speech for Pilgrim Award, July 7. http://people.ucsc.edu/~haraway/PilgrimAward.html.

Aren't Athletes Cyborgs?: Technology, Bodies, and Sporting Competitions

Rayvon Fouché

In a special edition about the idea and the proliferation of the term "viral," it is more than appropriate to consider the work of Donna Haraway. I, and I assume many others, first met Donna Haraway in class. For me it was as a graduate student in science and technology studies that I first encountered "A Manifesto for Cyborgs." The conceptualization of cyborgs as a strange melding of human organic/biological material with any of a multitude of technoscientific artifacts was a new and refreshing intellectual taste that was familiar, but distinctly different from my everyday diet of social constructionist meditations on technological and scientific practice. Haraway's cyborg theorization has spread like a virus (minus the sickness-inducing pathogens) through academic and nonacademic communities. It is viral in that it has relatively silently and efficiently spread across multiple disciplinary domains. It is also viral because it has been reproduced and replicated so often that its origin has been obfuscated. Thus, in the context of virality of Haraway's cyborg, is there a place to say anything new? Doubtful. But there may still exist small windows to contemplate splicing cyborg ideas into new places and spaces. This essay will move in this more fruitful direction. That is, how can the concept of "cyborg" be used to intervene and reconceptualize commonly understood notions of gender, bodies, identity, and community? Of course, taken as a whole this is a monumental task. I will take a small slice of the pie and center my discussion on the world of sport and think about the ways the "cyborg myth is about transgressed boundaries, potent fusions, and dangerous possibilities which progressive people might explore as on part of needed political work" (Haraway 1991, 154).

WSQ: Women's Studies Quarterly 40: 1 & 2 (Spring/Summer 2012) © 2012 by Rayvon Fouché.

My point of entry may seem a strange departure point, but sport is one locale where cyborg bodies have been not only accepted but also embraced. The rhetoric about freakish bodies producing unnatural performances has been a familiar refrain within commentaries about sport. Yet the popular mythology about sport is that competitions should be fair and in this fairness the best man, woman, or body should win (Magdalinski 2009). But even as the most casual grade school playground kickball participant knows, the world of sport is far from fair and equal. Sport is about creating, exploiting, and maintaining inequalities, or what is more commonly known as competitive advantages. Competitive advantages can be acquired in many ways, but the history of sport in the twentieth century has been about gaining a competitive edge through the use of technoscientific artifacts attached to the body or integrated into the body or a change in body mechanics. In the early 1960s, Dick Fosbury changed the body mechanics of high-jumping by developing a new body technique demanding that a competitor reorient his or her body to the bar. If one views the body as a machine, this new technique can be seen as a technological innovation (van Hilvoorde, Vos, and de Wert 2007). Initially there was concern that Fosbury's new method of high-jumping undermined the integrity of the event. But the fact that this technique was in theory learnable by all and did not alter or add anything appreciable to the body quelled objections to the "Fosbury Flop." However, discussions, debates, and legal battles about which artifactual technologies can and should be attached to or used by a body and those technologies that influence the internal dynamics of a body drive much of the popular discourse about technology and sport. The dominant internal technologies fall under the broad category of "doping" (Møller 2010). The sheer invisibility of these technologies is part of what makes them so effective for competitors and troubling for fans and sport governing bodies. External technologies like overly hydrodynamic swimming suits and seemingly erratic balls seen in the 2008 Olympics and the 2010 World Cup, respectively, received many complaints from fans and competitors alike. In general the same concern is raised about external and internal technologies. They are both perceived as unleveling the playing field by sublimating the natural human body to technology. By reducing sport and technology relationships to body techniques, internal manipulations, or external technologies, those invested in maintaining the illusory primacy of the pure human athletic body (primarily sport governing bodies, competitors, fans, and those producing the technologies) can convince themselves that it is easy to determine what is and is not permissible within a given sporting competition.

In the past few decades, it has been harder for publics, competitors, and governing bodies to willingly ignore the profound ways athletes, their bodies, and subsequently the sports they love have changed with new and emerging technologies. It is this turn that makes one wonder if recent technologies from blood-boosting pharmaceuticals to featherlight shoes will make the human athlete, as we currently think we know him or her, obsolete. Are we approaching a conceptual shift in sporting competitions whereby athletes' bodies simply mediate a new and potentially more important set of competitions between scientists, engineers, and designers? Possibly, but in the current fanatical sport moment I am not sure that either viewing and consuming publics or sport governing bodies will stand idly by and allow sport to openly make this transition. Nevertheless, emerging technologies are demanding a reconceptualization of what sport is and is not. Sport governing bodies from cycling's Union Cycliste Internationale to track and field's International Association of Athletics Federations regularly grapple with the emerging technology and ineffectively attempt to legislate it away from their sports. Yet the cyborg nature of sport is self-evident to those willing to acknowledge its existence. Instead of following debates about the ways sport governing bodies attempt to protect their brands and the illusion that their competitions are *only* between bodies of approved athletes, this essay is interested in why the cyborg idea should be embraced within sport. To be more specific, why it is necessary to abandon the fictitious construction of a natural athletic body based on outdated sex differences and replaced it with the currently existing cyborg athlete? But this is not so easy, since as Haraway argues, "The main trouble with cyborgs, of course, is that they are the illegitimate offspring of militarism and patriarchal capitalism, not to mention state socialism" (1991, 151). Athletes from the post–World War II era are artifacts of the military-industrial complex, of which Haraway writes. Steroids, amphetamines, and a host of other substances were created to produce "new" cybernetic soldiers, but this research also had a profound impact on athletics (Dimeo 2007, 46).

Currently athletes at the elite level, and increasingly those not categorized as representing the top of their sport, undergo a battery of psychological and physiological tests throughout their careers. These tests are administered to quantify performances or to understand what makes great athletes great and how this greatness can be re-created in less than great athletes. But if we have all the data, why is it not used to rethink competition? Most sporting competitions are divided only upon the lines of sex. This has been historically used because it has been seemingly easy. Until recently, sex was easy to understand. It was testable. This former fact in the structure of gender verification testing has been destabilized, but not abandoned (Ballantyne, Kayser, and Grootegoed 2010). But what happens if we embrace the continuums of gender and sex? I would argue that the resulting competitions would be, if not better, more interesting and relevant (Foddy and Savulescu 2010). The experiences of Caster Semenya over the past few years can be instructive in rethinking gender and sex as defining characteristics of sporting competitions.

Caster Semenya's body, sex, gender, race, and identity have all been questioned. In July 2008 the seemingly unknown South African runner competed in and won the women's eight-hundred-meter event at the Commonwealth Youth Games. The *Telegraph* indicated that at this race rumblings began about her deep voice and masculine features ("Caster Semenya" 2010). These reverberations were no longer ignored when Semenya simultaneously won the African senior and junior championships in July 2009 with record-breaking performances. The International Association of Athletics Federations (IAAF) argued that "it was obliged to investigate after Semenya made improvements of twenty-five seconds at 1500m and eight seconds at 800m—the sort of dramatic breakthroughs that usually arouse suspicion of drug use" (Smith 2009). Although tests for performance-enhancing drugs were undertaken, the IAAF also requested that Athletics South Africa (ASA) perform gender verification testing before the World Championships in August. Most of this would have remained private, but a fax relating to the case was inadvertently sent to the wrong individual. The Australian *Daily Telegraph* led the reporting of the story indicating that she had testes and no ovaries (Hurst 2009). Unfortunately, the news broke a few hours before Semenya was to run in the eight-hundred-meter final. Not initially ruffled by the flurry of reporting activity, she won the race and became the world champion in a time of 1:55.45, which was the fastest eight-hundred-meter women's time of the year. This race was her last competition until July 18, 2010. During this period the ASA maintained that Semenya was not banned from competition, but had to wait for the results from the IAAF.

In a September 11, 2009, interview with the *Sydney Morning Herald*,

IAAF spokesman Nick Davies contended that gender verification tests were *only* performed "to assess the possibility of a potential medical condition which would give Semenya an unfair advantage over her competitors" (Magnay 2009). The official IAAF press release stated the following: "We can officially confirm that gender verification test results will be examined by a group of medical experts. NO decision on the case will be communicated until the IAAF has had the opportunity to complete this examination" (International Association of Athletics Federations 2009). In early September it was still unclear what Semenya did and did not know about the testing, but it appears that she was kept mostly in the dark about the types of tests and the intended uses of the results. This was confirmed on September 19, 2009, when ASA president Leonard Chuene admitted that he had lied to Semenya about the types of testing performed (Jacobson 2009). What transpired over the next period of months has not been disclosed, but when Semenya's attorney, Greg Nott, acknowledged that "direct negotiations with the IAAF representatives, through the mediator, [had] been ongoing for 10 months . . . in Monaco, Istanbul and Paris," it was clear that the resolution of the case was as much about science as it was about politics (Hart 2010). On July 6, the IAAF released the briefest of press releases, indicating, "The process initiated in 2009 in the case of Caster Semenya (RSA) has now been completed. The IAAF accepts the conclusion of a panel of medical experts that she can compete with immediate effect" (International Association of Athletics Federations 2010). To date, no information about the testing or how these tests informed decisions regarding Semenya's ability to compete have been released to the public.

Of course the Semenya case raises a host of interesting questions about sex, gender, politics, race, and the body, but can her case push toward a more formally realized cyborg athlete and revolutionize how publics, sport governing bodies, and competitors themselves understand the problematic workings of gender and sex within the tradition-laden world of sport?

The current Semenya situation, if one can call it that, illustrates that contemporary sport and sport governing organizations have yet to develop a respectfully coherent way to understand bodies that do not simply conform to the outmoded binary of male and female. Part of the problem for sport has been the slippage in the use and meaning of "gender verification." The most altruistic reading of sex/gender verification is that it initially began as a method to catch "cheaters." Specifically, the goal was to expose men who chose to compete as women. This narrative gained traction when during the 1966 European Track and Field Championship six competitors from an Eastern Bloc team withdrew from competition when they learned that they would have to pass a physical inspection by a panel of physicians (Ljungqvist and Simpson 1992). Although the International Olympic Committee (IOC) stopped compulsory gender verification testing in 1999 (and no single man has ever been "caught" impersonating a woman) the IOC and the IAAF replaced the system with a case-by-case assessment in 2003 and 2006, respectively (Simpson et al. 2000). Semenya's questionable body was funneled into this new case-by-case system. But what was this new system questioning? Laura Hercher argued that since "Semenya was reared as a girl; her genitalia are female [and she] self-identifies as a woman . . . how is it possible that any inquiry could authoritatively declare that she is not a female?" (2010, 552). This misunderstanding by competitors, governing bodies, and publics is at the heart of the gender verification problem. Scientists from biological to genetic counselors call into question the idea of genetic verification and bluntly state that "human society as a whole is lacking in its ability to deal with disorders of sex development (DSD) at either a social, competitive, legal, or clinical level" (Wonkam, Fieggen, and Ramesar 2010). The concerns arise when androgens are used to determine a perceived level of maleness or femaleness. Certain conditions like congenital adrenal hyperplasia (CAH), adrenal tumors, or partial androgen insensitivity syndrome can produce higher androgen levels in women or have other effects that could give a woman a genetic advantage for a specific competition. Studies have shown that women with complete androgen insensitivity syndrome (cAIS) and XY chromosomes may have fewer androgens than the "average" female (Qinjie et al. 2009). Thus, claiming that a cAIS woman would have an unfair advantage because of a Y chromosome is highly problematic. Sport governing bodies now understand this and have for the most part discontinued solely using the Y chromosome as an indicator of sex, but are still struggling with what is an appropriate natural advantage. For track and field athletes the IAAF has agreed that women with CAH, adrenal tumors, or cAIS can compete as women. This is a fine starting point, but what is desperately missing is an understanding of "which conditions *disqualify* an athlete from playing as a woman" (Dreger 2010, 23). Since no information has been released about Semenya's case other than that she was withdrawn from competition and eventually reinstated, her tragic situation will not shed any light onto how non-normative bodies will be treated within sport defined by a male/female binary.

This has also left Semenya in a strange space filled with assumptions and speculations that can only partially be resolved on the track. Although she did race and win a bit in 2010, she was hampered by injuries. So 2011 has become the year of assessment for a healthy Semenya. Exercise physiologist Ross Tucker (2011) indicates that she will always be under scrutiny. He explains, "Either she would win convincingly, and the world's athletics followers would say 'She has an unfair advantage, they obviously didn't change anything, and now thanks to her lawyers, no other women can even compete.' Or, if she didn't win her races, the world would say 'This proves that she must have had surgery or treatment.' A catch-22 for Semenya." Sadly this is where she has been left. Now there is much room to speculate upon the multiple chemical, pharmaceutical, surgical, or psychological options deployed to push, prod, pull, or direct her body off some indeterminate perch on a gender spectrum to comply with the IAAF's evolving definition of femaleness. Drawing from Haraway and feminist scholars, the case also highlights how the female athletic body is a construction with publics, governing bodies, competitors, and physicians/scientists invested in maintaining a carefully calibrated equilibrium of female sex identity. The Semenya case produces a new level of murkiness because no statement has been released to bring the collective understanding of the female athletic body back to a familiar prescribed sex orientation. In a sense, sport governing organizations, competitors, and casual and enthusiast publics have not been allowed to breathe a collective sigh of relief by consuming a tidy resolution to the Semenya case and confirm that, sadly, in an athletic arena sex once again has triumphed over gender.

Semenya has upset the balance in many ways. It is striking that she was seen as *too* masculine in a space where masculine athletic prowess is not only accepted, but also championed. The appearance of her body apparently crossed the line from being a svelte and toned biological machine to an overly masculine and questionably freakish alienating device. Many competitors mumbled about Semenya's body, but only Elisa Piccione would state, "For me she is not a woman" (qtd. in Sawer and Berger 2009). In that moment of female hypermasculinity her fellow competitors and the sport governing body disaggregated Semenya from her body and constructed it as a flawed and inadmissible device requiring further examination and review. In this evolving moment of what is and is not too masculine within gender-differentiated sporting competitions, the sport governing body chose an equally troubling adjudicator of this bodily conundrum: science. Historically science has been a useful tool enabling sport governing bodies to extract themselves from the social and cultural issues precipitated by delineating what is and is not an admissible athletic body or performance. The entire business of drug testing has enabled sport governing bodies to allow science to determine if an athlete is competing within the defined rules of a sporting competition without fully addressing the varying levels of naturally occurring chemicals or conditions that produce competitive advantages for some athletes in certain sports. The Semenya case initially appeared as if it would be a simple probe into a woman's body to determine if it was real, pure, or authentic enough to participate in sport. Unfortunately, in the Semenya case, the ways that sport governing bodies used the historical power and authority of science to sidestep the social and cultural mechanisms that create gender identity are not questioned. I would contend that most sport governing bodies are not particularly interested in going to the "softer" intellectual domains for explanatory evidence. The truth-manufacturing machine of science would output a sex confirmation, upon which the appropriate choices would be made therewith. But from what has transpired over the past few years, Semenya, her body, or both presented a snag somewhere that demanded she be pulled from competition for a period of months until apparently her sex could be reset or fixed.

Outside of her current situation, why was Semenya a problem to be fixed? First her body, at least for the short period in which she was not allowed to compete, transgressed the boundaries of what Western athletic society deems a female body. In recent years athletes like Oscar Pistorius and his J-shaped carbon fiber prosthetics have pushed sport into an uncomfortable dialogue about how new and emerging technologies and bodies no longer fit into the athletic performance binary of able body/disabled body (Camporesi 2008). In a similar way, Semenya's body questions the tensions between male and female. What is going on is that we, and I mean the collective "we," have colluded to maintain the myth that athletic bodies are not cyborgic. This is what has been driving the hand-wringing around Semenya and Pistorius. This is one of the multiple backgrounds that motivated the IAAF to legislate and rule on Semenya's sex. Her cyborg identity clearly would disrupt the orderly nontechnoscientific media fantasy that has been the cornerstone of sporting competitions. The collective silence around Semenya's body implies that under the current state of the rules it is unplaceable, which is the dominant message delivered to the masses not privy to the decisions based upon the testing results. Thus if hers and future athletes and their bodies cause so much controversy, why not embrace the cyborg nature of the body? This does not mean opening the floodgates, where anything is permissible within sport, but finding a place where sporting competitions are based on a more complex and comprehensive understanding of the body. But what would it mean in practice to embrace the cyborg in the athlete? Of course in this corporate sporting moment this is nearly an impossible prospect, but reading athletic bodies through Haraway's work demands asking this question. The negatively valenced reading of this prospect contends that acknowledging the cyborg athlete would destroy the history and tradition of sport by allowing something other than basic genetics, hard work, and perseverance to determine the outcomes of sporting competitions. I prefer to contemplate a more optimistic analysis and contend that embracing the cyborg in athletes has the potential to resolve deep-seated social, political, and cultural tensions within sport. Specifically, the cyborg understanding of athletes can be leveraged to reconstruct competitions that are no longer based on sex or gender.

At first glance, it would appear that seeing the body as a cyborg would cause concern, but explaining the workings of the body in mechanical terms has been a common trope since the Enlightenment. In the first few sentences of the introduction to Thomas Hobbes's *Leviathan* he writes, "For what is the heart, but a spring; and the nerves, but so many strings; and the joints, but so many wheels, giving motion to the whole body" (1998, 7). Hobbes began to understand and rationalize the body as a machine. This perspective reflects the rhetoric of the life sciences, promotes critical commentary within cyborg literature, and even resonates with futurists like Ray Kurzweil. Framing the body as machine has profound implications for sport. What does it mean for athletes, fans, and governing organizations to view the organic material of bodies as inspectable and perfectible pieces of machinery? Jan Rintala (1995) argues that contemporary society champions machinelike bodies by disassociating them from humanity to produce sporting cultures that dehumanize and alienate athletes from their bodies in the quest for increasingly greater displays of physical performance. More recently the dynamics of dehumanization and alienation have become less relevant as science and technology are seen at worst as necessary evils and at best required interventions to keep sport safe, rebuild injured athletes, maintain an upward slope of human performance, and build and sustain public trust. The body is expected to perform like a machine, but maintain its human qualities. This situation gets messy when publics want and even demand great performances no matter the cost, but deny the high level of cyborg enhancement necessary to create these performances.

As insightful as Rintala's comments are, his writing overlooks the place where Haraway's writing is so relevant: the place of gender. Sport competitions have been heavily sexed and gendered from the outset. The earliest Olympics did not allow female competitors and it was not until the 1960s that more than a few competitions existed for women. Feminist movements of the twentieth century, and legislation like Title IX in the United States, led the way for more sporting opportunities for women. Although more opportunities presented themselves, these competitions remained marginalized primarily because of the perception that the performances by women were of lower "quality." Scientific studies have shown that the physiological differences between elite female and male athletes are quite small when compared with those in the general population (Lim, Peterman, and Turner 2011). The largest differences are in strength, while the smallest are in endurance. But if all athletes are cyborgs, why aren't men and women competing against each other? Outside of the size-and-strength issue, one of the larger problems is that women competing against men is a direct confrontation to historically rooted masculine sport cultures that many want to maintain. Even many scientists who are critical of the ways that genetic information has been used to determine sex in sporting competitions and who seem to support the postgender cyborg athletic body nonetheless believe that there are "sound reasons for separating the sexes in athletics including history and historical continuity of the sport, safety, and competitiveness" (Caplan 2010, 550). Although research clearly points in a specific direction, many scientists have yet to accept that "the cyborg is a creature in a post-gender world" (Haraway 1991, 150). Sadly, I learned as a very young boy that the easiest way to rattle an opposing competitor was to challenge his masculinity. But even as a young boy it was clear to me that all bodies were not the same. Not all bodies have the same "potential" or physiological attributes. But embracing the diversity of bodies outside of the context of gender and sex, it may be possible to reshuffle the sporting competition deck of what is a relevant competition. This is not to say that sex-based competitions should be eliminated, but if comparative bodies, rather than comparative sexes or genders, were to compete against each other, more interesting and closer competitions would result. We are, for all intents and purposes, at a precipice where human bodies will cease to determine the outcomes of sport competitions. Many athletic competitions are no longer between humans on the playing field, but instead are battles between humans in scientific or engineering laboratories where the sporting body has become a medium through which to display the latest scientific knowledge or technological innovation. In our emerging technoscientific era, will publics, competitors, and sport governing bodies be able to detach themselves from the tenets of uneven competitive advantages in the interest of seeing more balanced competitions with cyborg athletes? Haraway's work can greatly inform this debate and provide "a way out of the maze of dualisms in which we have explained our bodies and our tools to ourselves" (Haraway 1991, 181).

Rayvon Fouché is an associate professor of history and a research associate professor at the Information Trust Institute at the University of Illinois at Urbana-Champaign. His work explores the multiple intersections and relationships between cultural representation, racial identification, and technological design. Fouché's current book project examines the relationships between sport, science, and technology with an eye toward understanding what is at stake for sporting cultures when they define themselves by and against new and emerging scientific knowledge and technological artifacts.

Works Cited

Ballantyne, Kaye N., Manfred Kayser, and J. Anton Grootegoed. 2011. "Sex and Gender Issues in Competitive Sports: Investigation of a Historical Case Leads to a New Viewpoint." *British Journal of Sports Medicine*, May 3.

Camporesi, Silvia. 2008. "Oscar Pistorius, Enhancement and Post-humans," *Journal of Medical Ethics* 34(9):639.

Caplan, Arthur L. 2010. "Fairer Sex: The Ethics of Determining Gender for Athletic Eligibility: Commentary on 'Beyond the Caster Semenya Controversy: The Case of the Use of Genetics for Gender Testing in Sport,'" *Journal of Genetic Counseling* 19(6):549–50.

"Caster Semenya: Anatomy of Her Case." 2010. *Telegraph*, July 6. http://www.telegraph.co.uk/sport/othersports/athletics/7873921/Caster-Semenya-anatomy-of-her-case.html

Dimeo, Paul. 2007. *A History of Drug Use in Sport, 1876–1976*. New York: Routledge.

Dreger, Alice. 2010. "Sex Typing for Sport." *Hastings Center Report* 40(2):22–24.

Foddy, Bennett, and Julian Savulescu. 2011. "Time to Re-evaluate Gender Segregation in Athletics?" *British Journal of Sports Medicine* 45(15):1184–88.

Haraway, Donna J. 1991. *Simians, Cyborgs, and Women*. New York: Routledge.

Hart, Simon. 2010. "IAAF Confirms Caster Semenya's Return," Telegraph, July 6. http://www.telegraph.co.uk/sport/othersports/athletics/7875157/IAAF-confirms-Caster-Semenyas-return.html

Hercher, Laura. 2010. "Gender Verification: A Term Whose Time Has Come and Gone." *Journal of Genetic Counseling* 19(6):551–53.

Hobbes, Thomas. 1998. *Leviathan*. Edited and with an introduction and notes by J. C. A. Gaskin. Oxford: Oxford University Press.

Hurst, Mike. 2009. "Caster Semenya Has Male Sex Organs and No Womb or Ovaries." *Daily Telegraph*, September 11. http://www.dailytelegraph.com.au/sport/semenya-has-no-womb-or-ovaries/story-e6frexni-1225771672245

International Association of Athletics Federations. 2009. "Statement on Caster Semenya." http://www.iaaf.org/aboutiaaf/news/newsid=54277.html

———. 2010. "Caster Semenya May Compete." http://www.iaaf.org/aboutiaaf/news/newsid=57301.html

Jacobson, Celean. 2009. "SAfrica Track Chief Apologizes for Runner Sex Test." *USA Today*, September 19. http://www.usatoday.com/sports/olympics/2009-09-19-509262529_x.html

Lim, Allen C., James E. Peterman, and Benjamin M. Turner. 2011. "Comparison of Male and Female Road Cyclists Under Identical Stage Race Conditions." *Medicine and Science in Sports and Exercise* 43(5):846–52.

Ljungqvist, Arne, and Joe Leigh Simpson. 1992. "Medical Examination for Health of All Athletes Replacing the Need for Gender Verification in International Sports." *Journal of the American Medical Association* 267(6):850–52.

Magdalinski, Tara. 2009. *Sport, Technology, and the Body*. New York: Routledge.

Magnay, Jacquelin. 2009. "Secret of Semenya's Sex Stripped Bare." *Sydney Morning Herald*, September 11. http://www.smh.com.au/news/sport/secret-of-semenyas-sex-stripped-bare/2009/09/11/1252519599453.html

Møller, Verner. 2010. *The Ethics of Doping and Anti-doping*. New York: Routledge.

Qinjie, Tian, He Fangfang, Zhou Yuanzheng, and Ge Qinsheng. 2009. "Gender Verification in Athletes with Disorders of Sex Development." *Gynecological Endocrinology* 25(2):117–21.

Rintala, Jan. 1995. "Sport and Technology: Human Questions in a World of Machine." *Journal of Sport and Social Issues* 19(1):62–75.

Sawer, Patrick, and Sebastian Berger. 2009. "Gender Row over Caster Semenya Makes Athlete into a South African Cause Celebre." *Telegraph*, August 23. http://www.telegraph.co.uk/news/worldnews/africaandindianocean/ southafrica/6073980/Gender-row-over-Caster-Semenya-makes-athlete- into-a-South-African-cause-celebre.html

Simpson, Joe Leigh, Arne Ljungqvist, Malcolm A. Ferguson-Smith, Albert de la Chapelle, Louis J. Elsas II, Anke A. Ehrhardt, Myron Genel, Elizabeth A. Ferris, and Alison Carlson. 2000. "Gender Verification in the Olympics." *Journal of the American Medical Association* 284(12):1568–69.

Smith, David. 2009. "Caster Semenya Row: 'Who Are White People to Question the Makeup of an African Girl? It Is Racism.'" *Observer*, August 23. http:// www.guardian.co.uk/sport/2009/aug/23/caster-semenya-athletics-gender

Tucker, Ross. 2011. "800m Caster Semenya & Robby Andrews," *Science of Sport*, June 12. http://www.sportsscientists.com/2011/06/800-m-musings- caster-semenya-robby.html

van Hilvoorde, Ivo, Rein Vos, and Guido de Wert. 2007. "Flopping, Klapping, and Gene Doping: Dichotomies Between 'Natural' and 'Artificial' in Elite Sport." *Social Studies of Science* 37(2):173–200.

Wonkam, Ambroise, Karen Fieggen, and Raj Ramesar. 2010. "Beyond the Caster Semenya Controversy: The Case of the Use of Genetics for Gender Testing in Sport." *Journal of Genetic Counseling* 19(6):545–48.

Haraway's Viral Cyborg

Joseph Schneider

Nearly thirty years ago, Donna Haraway began writing her famous essay published in 1985 as "A Manifesto for Cyborgs: Science, Technology, and Feminism in the 1980s." In its vision, argument, and detail, it resonates strongly with what today is called viral analysis and criticism. In what follows I'll briefly suggest how.

First, the essay was blasphemous, transgressive, and invasive, arguably all viral qualities. Its claims for the liberatory promise of her cyborg—born as "the illegitimate offspring of militarism and patriarchal capitalism, not to mention state socialism" in the "belly of the beast" of U.S. Star Wars dreams of a global "New World Order"—for making women's lives better did not sit well with all feminists or, I am sure, with all socialists (Haraway 1991b, 151). Even though she insisted that "the cyborg is resolutely committed to partiality, irony, intimacy, and perversity . . . is oppositional . . . and completely without innocence . . . not reverent; . . . [does] not remember the cosmos . . . [is] wary of holism, but needy of connection . . . [and] exceedingly unfaithful to . . . [its] origins"—all qualities one might think required by a feminist politics and scholarship of the day—she spoke powerfully to but also *for* U.S. feminism at the end of the century (a risky business at any time, even for a cyborg) (151). Moreover, she engaged, if not embraced, what many who were concerned about the human and especially gendered costs of the technology of modernity saw as a profound threat. Zoë Sofoulis (2002, 101), a graduate student of Haraway's then, gives insight into the rippling "quake" the essay caused: "Whereas a standard feminist line on technology had been to equate it with abstract masculinist rationality, militarism, and the rape of the Earth, Haraway

insisted on the intimate physicality of our relations to nonhumans, and on
. . . 'the pleasures of the interface'"; and, it should be added, with no guar-
antees for results that then might easily have been recognized as "success."

This blasphemy from within, her disinclination for either intellectual
or political purity, and her criticism of the exclusionary and totalizing
effects of feminism's identity politics and standpoint epistemology made
the manifesto and Haraway immediately controversial and, it seems to me,
viral. Indeed, each word above, from her description of the cyborg, is used
today to describe the viral (see, for instance, Pearson 1997; Cohen 2011;
Galloway and Thacker 2007). Finally, the essay itself was promiscuous,
not, surely, in the sense of being random or disorganized, but rather in the
diverse political, cultural, and disciplinary alliances and scope it effected
and in giving license and encouragement to others inclined to follow.
And the *OED* on the biological version of promiscuous offers the following: "*Biol.* Of a protein, organism, etc.: able to infect or interact with, or
bind non-specifically to, a variety of hosts or targets" (notice the "*or interact with*").

Moreover, it was precisely those elements of the essay that were "troubling" for some that were at the same time gifts to many others, disturbing the feminist "us": "Haraway's poetic claim that the cyborg 'gives us
our ontology' captured the imagination of many who were . . . starting
to explore new identities and forms of social life and community made
possible by the Internet" (Sofoulis 2002, 101). Her insistence, then and
in all subsequent work, that there are no "innocent" positions, politically
or intellectually, and that pollution, boundary violation, and interfaces of
all sorts—originary connectivity or relationality, as she would call it later
(biologist that she is)—are "the name of the game on planet Earth" challenged leftist, feminist, and intellectual politics of the day. In this, Haraway
let us see that, in Sofoulis's words, "complicity with 'the system' was not
an unmentionable crime nor a paralyzing political embarrassment, but
understood as something *inevitable*, which did not necessarily prevent further effective political work for justice, peace, and survival" (2002, 101),
risks and vulnerabilities to the contrary notwithstanding. These claims
remain a point of contention for some even today.

Pollution, fusion, replication, paradox, partiality, and irony. These all
take center stage in Haraway's cyborg myth. Each is regularly invoked in
cultural analysis and criticism using the material-semiotic figure of the

virus. While allowing that in the early 1980s a "cyborg world" could be read as, and in fact could be, terrifying and hopeless (think, for the viral, "emerging infectious diseases" and "system/network 'failure'" as Steven Soderbergh's new film, *Contagion*, plays at your local multiplex, offering no doubt images of both), she insisted it also "might be about lived social and bodily realities in which people are not afraid of their joint kinship with animals and machines, not afraid of permanently partial identities and contradictory standpoints" (Haraway 1991b, 154). In this and similar claims, Haraway (1991b, 151–153) further weakened a set of boundaries that already in the past century's final quarter were unstable and had begun to "leak": "between human and animal" or "other living creatures," between "(organisms) and machines," and "between [the] physical and non-physical" or the material and nonmaterial.

This focus on the porosity of boundaries, their "fleshliness," and the attendant ambiguities about what or who an entity is (even, if it *is* "an entity") and when and where such a claim might be made about "it" that Haraway elaborated became itself a signature of "post" thought, although she then mostly positioned herself to one side of that prefix and still does so. The figure and the material or materiality of the porous boundary, with selective and varying rates of flow across it, part of a dynamic "metastable" system or network of interfaced and similar boundaries and "nodes" linked by vectors or "edges" could hardly be more central to our understanding of what "a virus" is in both biology and informatics, of its conditions of possibility, and of the diverse risks of narrowly focusing only on "it" as a closed or clearly bounded entity (see Galloway and Thacker 2007, 31–32).

Ed Cohen, writing on "the paradoxical politics of viral containment," gives us an example of such an "it" definition from the bio-sciences: "Technically speaking, *virus* describes a small quantity of genetic material, either RNA or DNA (which can appear in single or double strands), enclosed within a protein coat, and sometimes surrounded by a lipid envelope. Viruses appear to exist everywhere on Earth and may in fact constitute 'the most abundant biological entities on the planet'" (2011, 18). Radically decontextualized, although still both multiple and partial, the definition is a stunning instance of how naming inevitably conceals more than it reveals, including often long and contentious biopolitical and professional struggles over who/what "owns" what objects and who/what should be held accountable for both knowledge of them and policy or action toward them, not to mention what the named objects and movements "do."[1] Much, then, is "in a name"; or is it perhaps not enough? Both, at the same time.

Alexander Galloway and Eugene Thacker, in *The Exploit: A Theory of Networks*, define computer viruses much more contextually than the above, but, similarly, as fragments or parts of code from one system or network that "worm" their way into or "exploit" the inevitable "design flaws" and choices built into another, causing copies or replicants to be made, changing the "host" system and themselves, and hiding their tracks as they move on (2007, 83). They argue that it is impossible to think about viruses as separate from the particular networks that they access and so often upset, since the viral access and the particular vulnerabilities of a given network define one another. As if describing a cyborg on speed, they write that such viruses "are defined by their ability to change their signature and yet maintain a continuity of operations (e.g., overwriting code, infiltrating as fake programs, etc.). Viruses are never quite the same" nor, it seems, are their "hosts" (but then who/what is which?) (83). But computer viruses, unlike their older biological siblings, for the most part don't "just happen." They are made by human intelligence and motive.

Cohen specifies the paradox and irony further: "Viruses cannot produce themselves by themselves. . . . [They] exist only insofar as they have successfully spurred a cellular organism [or, in informatics, a program or its documents; each of which it then will "infect"] to commit some of its own resources and processes to producing more 'copies' of the 'original'" (2011, 18). In Sofoulis's terms, this is "complicity with 'the system'" with a vengeance. Up so close, but yet not personal; indeed, not human; but not always a body's or a network's "enemy" (see Haraway 1995a)[2]; and perhaps not alive, but even that notion is here opened further, with the latest generation of viruses proclaimed to be artificial life (or, might artificial life come first, then "the viral"?) (see Galloway and Thacker 2007, 85). "Us" and "we" and "them" altogether, but who/what and under what conditions? In this, viruses are, Cohen adds, citing Haraway, very trick[ster]y (Cohen 2011, 18)[3]; she might add "imploded," putting it with her later-named "stem cells of the technoscientific body": "nodes that [can] explode into entire worlds of practice . . . [the] chip, gene, seed, fetus, database, bomb, race, brain, ecosystem" (Haraway 1997, 11).

There are viral insights in Haraway's cyborg text that I have missed and not mentioned. The essays collected here will, I am sure, detail a number of them, even without necessarily drawing on her text. The technoscientific capacity actually to "see" a virus and the impact of this visualization for its history (see Cohen 2011, 20), not to mention the linkable insight from Haraway (1991c, 200) and Katie King (1991, 1994) about what came to be called an "apparatus of bodily production," thinking here about the body of the virus itself and the technology of its "being," surely would be another (see also Karen Barad's [2007] concept of intra-action).

I want to end with a turn to speculation about what Haraway might say about the implications of what I have been calling a viral analysis and criticism. This is perhaps more difficult, in part because for all her encouragement of boundary transgression, critique of human exceptionalism, and love of what she calls "the mud and slime of my proper home world" (2008, 30) of biology, her writing keeps the human "in the game" as an important material-semiotic entity, even if not the most important or the most capable. That seems important but also honest. There are no innocent positions. Her own recent choice of an "obligatory" connection is not virus but dog-human relationality in the form of "companion species," leaving a much larger part—even if still inevitably partial—in her story for "us." She remains committed to the aim of flourishing, a value choice that has been an abiding one for her, and that does include *Homo sapiens*, as she might name us. While perhaps not drawn to the abstractions of "network theory," she would appreciate the many parallels that Galloway and Thacker draw to her ideas and their attention to what Gilles Deleuze (1992) called "societies of control" and securitization. And although she would have a much sharper "political" vision on the viral than I can here imagine, she would underscore the paradox that is so present in "viral writing"—on which she might offer a riff linking that phrase to her own "cyborg writing" toward developing greater literacies for critical feminist readings of this terrain (see Haraway 1991b, 175; 1995b). Cohen makes the theme of paradox "personal" in a quote from Michel Serres's *The Parasite*: "'Let us try to face it head on, like death, like the sun. We are all attacked, together [*sotto voce*, we hear Haraway's (1991b, 181) cyborg: "We have all been injured, profoundly"]. . . . We parasite each other and live amidst parasites. . . . They constitute our environment'" (Serres qtd. in Cohen 2011, 24) (but where does the "body" or the "system" or the "network" end and its "environment" begin? The boundaries are indeed porous; the "system" is open).[4] And Cohen begins his own essay with Haraway (1991a, 224) from the relevant "The Biopolitics of Postmodern Bodies," written in part out of her personal experience with HIV/AIDS: "Life is a window of vulnerability. It seems a mistake to close it. The perfection of the fully defended, 'victorious' self is a chilling fantasy."

Joseph Schneider is Ellis and Nelle Levitt Professor of Sociology at Drake University. He has written on the medicalization of deviance, the experience of chronic illness, social problems theory, and postmodern ethnography. His most recent book is *Donna Haraway: Live Theory* and he is at work on a book that argues for the importance of "new materiality" in cultural theory.

Notes

1. As both Alfred North Whitehead, whose work has influenced Haraway more, and Jacques Derrida have made clear.
2. See Donna Haraway (1995b) on cyborgs and symbionts. No question, "virus" has had a very "bad press," historically. Lynn Margulis and Dorion Sagan's (2002) work on symbiosis and symbiogenesis offers a picture of what might be called the "viral process" with considerably less moral "starch" such that "symbiont" highlights "living together with" a "virus" and thus lets us see more complexity.
3. His point is that Haraway uses the trickster figure—coyote but also the world in Native American lore and even dogs in her recent work—to foreground the porosity and dynamic ambiguity if not undecideability of important boundaries and objects. Cohen cites Haraway's *How Like a Leaf* (2000, 66–67). See also Joseph Schneider (2005, 81, 111–13).
4. An important tangent to this discussion turns on the critique of autopoiesis and the question of the nature of the system/environment relationship. While for some time seen as a defining feature of life, the authors cited here writing on the viral, and Haraway herself (2008, 30–31), distance themselves from this view of life as a closed, self-maintaining system. Pearson (1997, 140–142) and Galloway and Thacker (2007, 55–63) similarly seek to complicate this view. See also Cary Wolfe (2010, 111–112; 120–122) and his discussion of Niklas Luhmann's systems theory in this regard.

Works Cited

Barad, Karen M. 2007. *Meeting the Universe Halfway: Quantum Physics and the Entanglement of Matter and Meaning*. Durham: Duke University Press.

Cohen, Ed. 2011. "The Paradoxical Politics of Viral Containment; or, How Scale Undoes Us One and All." *Social Text* 106(29)(1):15–35.

Deleuze, Gilles. 1992. "Postscript on the Societies of Control." *October* 59:3–7.

Galloway, Alexander, and Eugene Thacker. 2007. *The Exploit: A Theory of Networks*. Minneapolis: University of Minnesota Press.

Haraway, Donna J. 1985. "A Manifesto for Cyborgs: Science, Technology, and Feminism in the 1980s." *Socialist Review* 80:65–107.

———. 1991a. "The Biopolitics of Postmodern Bodies: Constitutions of Self in Immune System Discourse." In *Simians, Cyborgs, and Women: The Reinvention of Nature*. New York: Routledge.

———. 1991b. "A Cyborg Manifesto: Science, Technology, and Socialist-Feminism in the Late Twentieth Century." In *Simians, Cyborgs, and Women: The Reinvention of Nature*. New York: Routledge.

———. 1991c. "Situated Knowledges: The Science Question in Feminism and the Privilege of Partial Perspective." In *Simians, Cyborgs, and Women: The Reinvention of Nature*. New York: Routledge.

———. 1995a. "Cyborgs and Symbionts: Living Together in the New World Order." In *The Cyborg Handbook*, ed. C. H. Gray, H. Figueroa-Sarriera, and S. Mentor. New York: Routledge.

———. 1995b. "Writing, Literacy, and Technology: Toward a Cyborg Writing." In *Women Writing Culture*, ed. G. A. Olson and E. Hirsch. Albany: State University of New York Press.

———. 1997. *Modest Witness@Second_Millennium. FemaleMan_Meets_Oncomouse: Feminism and Technoscience*. New York: Routledge.

———. 2000. *How Like a Leaf*. New York: Routledge.

———. 2008. *When Species Meet*. Minneapolis: University of Minnesota Press.

King, Katie. 1991. "Bibliography and a Feminist Apparatus of Literary Production." *Text: Transactions of the Society for Textual Scholarship* 5:91–103.

———. 1994. *Theory in Its Feminist Travels: Conversations in U.S. Women's Movements*. Bloomington: University of Indiana Press.

Margulis, Lynn, and Dorion Sagan. 2002. *Acquiring Genomes: A Theory of the Origin of the Species*. New York: Basic Books.

Pearson, Keith Ansell. 1997. *Viroid Life: Perspectives on Nietzsche and the Transhuman Condition*. New York: Routledge.

Schneider, Joseph. 2005. *Donna Haraway: Live Theory*. London: Continuum.

Sofoulis, Zoë. 2002. "Cyberquake: Haraway's Manifesto." In *Prefiguring Cyberculture: An Intellectual History*, ed. D. Tofts, A. Jonson, and A. Cavallaro. Cambridge, MA: MIT Press.

Wolfe, Cary. 2010. *What Is Posthumanism?* Minneapolis: University of Minnesota Press.

Awash in Urine: DES and Premarin® in Multispecies Response-ability

Donna Haraway

Cyborg Littermates

Cyborgs are kin, whelped in the litter of post–World War II information technologies and globalized digital bodies, politics, and cultures of human and not-human sorts. Cyborgs are not machines in just any sense, nor are they machine-organism hybrids. In fact, they are not hybrids at all. They are, rather, imploded entities, dense material semiotic "things"—articulated string figures of ontologically heterogeneous, historically situated, materially rich, virally proliferating relatings of particular sorts, not all the time everywhere, but here, there, and in between, with consequences. Particular sorts of historically situated machines signaled by the words "information" and "system" play their part in cyborg living and dying. Particular sorts of historically situated organisms, signaled by the idioms of labor systems, energetics, and communication, play their part. Finally, particular sorts of historically situated human beings, becoming-with the practices and artifacts of technoscience, play their part. Characterized by partial connections, the parts do not add up to any whole; but they do add up to worlds of nonoptional, stratified, webbed, and unfinished living and dying, appearing and disappearing. Cyborgs are constitutively full of multiscalar, multitemporal, multimaterial critters of both living and nonliving persuasions. Cyborgs matter in terran worlding.

But cyborgs are critters in a queer litter, not the Chief Figure of Our Times. "Queer" here means not committed to reproduction of kind and having bumptious relations with futurities. Irreducible to cyborgs, the litter interests me, the particular kin and kind nursed on the fluid and solid effluvia of terra in the late twentieth and early twenty-first centuries. I write this brief essay in gratitude to the people of WSQ and especially to the authors of the three essays in this *Viral* issue who play with "my" cyborg in order to relay the string figures—the speculative fabulations, the scientific facts, the science fictions, and the speculative feminisms—to whatever sorts of tentacular grippers will receive the pattern to keep living and dying well possible in "our times." Made up of an aging California dog, pregnant mares on the western Canadian prairies, human women who came to be known as "DES daughters," lots of menopausal U.S. women, and assorted other players in the story of "synthetic" and "natural" estrogens, the litter for this essay is decanted from bodies awash in a particular pungent fluid—urine. Waste and resource, out-of-place urine from particular female bodies is the salty ocean needed for my tale. Leaks and eddies are everywhere. These leaks and eddies might help open passages for a praxis of care and response—response-ability—in ongoing multispecies worlding on a wounded terra.

DES for Hot Peppers

In October 2011 my twelve-year-old canine friend and lifelong sports partner, Cayenne, aka Hot Pepper, started taking a notorious, industrially produced, nonsteroidal, synthetic estrogen called DES (diethylstilbesterol) to deal with urinary leakage ("Diethylstilbestrol," n.d.).[1] Perhaps I should not write she "started taking," but rather, "I started feeding her as an occasional late-night treat, following her last pee, a luscious, slippery, Earth Balance® margarine-coated capsule of DES." Plato gave us all the tones in the extricable ambiguities of his pharmakon: cure and poison; care, curare; remedy, toxin. Aging spayed bitches like Cayenne and postmenopausal women like me often could use a hormonal tightening of slack smooth muscles in the urethra to keep socially unacceptable leaks plugged up. The term "estrogen deficiency" is a tough one for feminists like me, marinated at a young age in the women's health movements and feminist science studies, to pronounce. But the fact is that a few extra dabs of estrogens do some handy jobs in aging mammalian female bodies—at a price, of course, in many currencies of living and dying. Granted, the adrenal glands still secrete some estrogens for those of us with missing or dried-up ovaries, but output is pretty low and smooth muscle can get pretty flaccid.

But giving this beloved, elder, nonreproducing dog to whom I am responsible even very low dose and infrequent diethylstilbesterol caused acute DES anxiety syndrome in me. My blood pressure rose higher than the high canine blood pressure that motivated changing urine-plugging drugs for Cayenne in the first place. Even if I could keep my critique of biocapital in a sealed flask, my feminist biopolitical juices started oozing from every pore, leaking all over my obligations to our dog. Rusten, my male human spouse was drawn deeply into this mammalian female well of worry, and not just because neither one of us much wanted to sleep in the urinary wet spot if estrogen-deprived urethral smooth muscle were left unattended in the nocturnal hours in our species-queer connubial bed. Cross-species kinship has consequences. Our now shared DES anxiety syndrome had to be treated immediately by our excellent primary care veterinarian, who did the service of presenting us with scientific studies and her own history of practice with low-dose, minimum-frequency DES for elder dogs; this was the "talking cure" we needed—a high dose of reason, evidence, and story, taken nightly with uncanny and unruly molecules. Still, my vet herself is too young to have been infected with my kind of terror of DES. Besides, she can't possibly be the daughter of a woman who took DES sometime between 1940 and 1971, when a report in the *New England Journal of Medicine* tied DES to a nasty vaginal clear cell adenocarcinoma in girls and young women who had been exposed to this drug in utero. Otherwise, my vet would surely do more than remember what I am afraid of. A talking cure might not be enough.

Despite the fact the a double-blind study done at the University of Chicago in the early 1950s showed no benefit from DES for sustaining pregnancies in women, and the fact that by the late 1960s, six of seven leading human gynecological textbooks stated that DES did not prevent miscarriages, the drug continued to be prescribed frequently over three decades for averting miscarriage and also for an almost comical (except it was not funny) host of other "indications," both on and off label. Ultimately, probably two million women in the United States alone took DES during pregnancy. Probably every reader of this *Viral* issue of WSQ knows some of the offspring of these pregnancies, but may or may not know their often hidden suffering. I do—both people and their suffering, or a little bit of it— and the extraordinary psychologist-scholar-friend who told me about her DES history when I told her about Cayenne performed just the generative acts of "becoming-with" that have occupied my soul since writing *When Species Meet*, or really since the "Cyborg Manifesto." My human friend, this

human DES daughter, was already an avid, if dog-allergic, admirer of Cayenne; she is one of the humans who, when she visits, induces enthusiastic canine play-solicitation performances from my very nonpromiscuous
dog. But suddenly and oddly, their unexpected DES kinship threw them
transversally, not genealogically, into a litter together differently. Separated
by allergies, they were joined in the flesh by a disreputable nonsteroidal
estrogen. It is clear to me that human Sheila has assigned herself to keep a
baleful queer sisterly eye on those gel caps I give dog Cayenne. That kindly
critical lateral eye will complement the regular blood tests Cayenne will
now have to endure to keep track of the health of her blood-forming cells
and immune functions.[2] A good sphincter can he hard to find.

For very good reasons tied to the history of the women's health movements and to action, finally, by agencies like the U.S. Food and Drug
Administration, these days DES is a controlled substance you can get only
(or mainly) for nonhumans. In the 1990s, the only approved indication
for DES in human beings was treatment of advanced prostate cancer in
men and of advanced breast cancer in postmenopausal women, and that
use has been recently superseded. The last U.S. manufacturer of DES, Eli
Lilly, stopped making and marketing the no-longer-profitable drug in
1997. That's why Cayenne and I found ourselves at a homeopathic and
compounding pharmacy in 2011.[3]

Diethylstilbesterol was first synthesized in 1938 in a laboratory of the
University of Oxford in the waning heroic days of the history of endocrinology. Those were the days when one might still find eminent biochem-
ists prowling around nonhuman animal slaughter floors collecting many
pounds of ovaries, pancreas, testes, adrenal glands, kidneys, pituitaries
(try collecting pounds or kilograms of pituitary gland!), and other organs
and tissues from many species to ferret back to the lab to extract and then
chemically and physiologically characterize the first few precious micro-
grams of natural steroids or other potent hormones. Stalking the newly
dead in graves of the European Renaissance for human bodies to dissect
has a long uncanny laboratory history into the present. Current-day laboratory mice and their archived and curated parts would probably be our
best informants for today's stories of organs without bodies and life after
death. The 1930s were still the days when biochemical laboratories were
used to distilling tiny amounts of chemical gold from the dross of vats of
urine and other bodily fluids, human and not.

DES did not come from these material sources, but it inhabits the same cross-hatched histories, where what counts as natural or artificial was (and is) constantly morphing in the study and production of things called "sex hormones." No wonder biologist feminists like me find our politics and psyches relentlessly and variously material in ways that Foucault hardly dreamed of. It's those laboratory wet spots in nighttime knowledge making that get feminists roused.

So in my town, you purchase the expensive, carcinogenic, immune-suppressing, anemia-inducing, smooth-muscle-plumping molecules known as DES in snowy powder form in gel caps from a homeopathic and compounding pharmacy, Lauden Integrative Pharmacy. "Compounding pharmacy" sounds so early twentieth century to my ear, but I can see that when Big Pharma no longer makes or sells a still-useful molecule, one that is no better than she should be, the up-to-the-minute, seemingly old-fashioned drugstore gets the leavings. Lauden Integrative Pharmacy sells lots of homeopathic substances for both human and more-than-human animals. I paid for Cayenne's DES capsules at a counter draped in the colors, posters, and icons of "Western" and "Eastern" alternative medicine, both ancient and modern.

To say this scene is emblematic of the mixed structures and affects of biomedical technoscience is an understatement. Lauden formulates many of the chemotherapeutic and other drugs prescribed by the veterinary specialist clinic where Cayenne and I are under the care of a fine consulting internist and cardiac specialist for her early mitral valve disease. MVD is the reason my fast and sporty Hot Pepper's moderately high blood pressure was not acceptable, and so a new diagnosis of MVD is the reason we changed prescriptions from a drug she had gobbled happily for a few years, called Propolin® (PPA, or phenylpropanolamine, "for oral use in dogs only") to DES. PPA does a fine job pumping up urethral smooth muscle and keeping urine in its hygienic reservoirs for properly timed release in assigned places. But unfortunately PPA is indiscriminate and tightens arterial smooth muscle too, thereby raising blood pressure—not a good idea in dogs with early heart disease. For better and for worse, estrogens are more discriminating in the tissues they home in on. Anyone with breasts—or breast cancer—knows this.

But it's the multispecies business in the compounding pharmacy that really drew my attention. When I get an anxiety syndrome, I am thrown into compulsive scholarly antics, and DES anxiety syndrome was no exception. Urine, urethras, damaged heart valves, "abnormal pregnancy outcomes," and cancer-ravaged breasts and uteruses have provided the cross-species organic stuff of the story. So far, my tale has emphasized a litter of critters made up of dogs; humans; and slaughtered animals, mainly pigs, sheep, and cows. It's that last category that will take me into the last stanza of the DES recitative and plump out the litter a bit before we get to my next staring estrogen molecules for remaking kin and kind.

DES was the molecule used in the first experimental, scientific demonstration of successful hormonal growth promotion in cattle in the history of those animal-human relations called agriculture (Raun and Preston 2002). Although in 1947 researchers at Purdue University demonstrated DES-induced growth promotion in heifers, Purdue did not pursue patent protection for the cattle and sheep work that its investigators carried out. These agricultural scientists used DES because implants had already been formulated for use in poultry, those feathered workhorses in so much of the history of factory farming. The FDA banned DES for growth promotion in chickens and lambs in 1959 and in all animal feed in 1979. But from 1954 to the early 1970s DES was used widely as a growth promoter in the beef industry. Agricultural industry and university agricultural science (especially at Iowa State College) were close partners in research for this use. The agricultural-industrial complex was in its postwar adolescent growth spurt. Iowa State and W. Burroughs filed for a patent on oral DES for cattle in 1953; it was granted in 1956. In 1972 the FDA removed oral DES from the market for use in cattle (1973 for implants). DES residues found in bovine livers and human DES daughters converged to take the drug off the legal agricultural market, although stories of illegal use still surface. But the core story here is not DES as such; the big story is the relentless rise of hormonal growth promoters of the next molecular generations that are integral to the ecosystem-destroying, human- and animal-labor-transforming, multispecies-soul-mutilating, epidemic-friendly, corn-monocrop-promoting, cross-species-heartbreaking feedlot cattle industries. All of a sudden, I cannot forget that in 1947 heifers too became DES daughters, and the bovine sons followed in droves. Cyborg's enhanced litter is outsized. The product of a daughter of a dog family known for prowess in cattle herding before the times of DES, my dog's urine spots lead inexorably to feedlots, slaughter houses, and unmet agricultural animal, human, and ecological well-being and advocacy obligations around the world. Response-ability yet-to-come, again. In companion species worlding, becoming-with makes strong demands on the littermates.

Conjugating Kin with Premarin®

Conjugating is about yoking together; conjugal love is yoked love; conjugated chemical compounds join together two or more constituents. People conjugate in public spaces; they yoke themselves together transversely and across time and space to make significant things happen. Students conjugate verbs to explore the yoked inflections of person, number, gender, kind, voice, mood, position, tense, and aspect in a field of material-semiotic meaning making. To learn about recursive yoking, conjugate "to conjugate." Now, do that with estrogens. Conjunctivitis is an irritation of the mucous membrane lining the inner surface of the eyelid. What might conjunctivitis mean in the odoriferous fluid mixtures of conjugated estrogens, such as the motley of naturally occurring but nonhuman estrogens purified from pregnant mares' urine to make very profitable pills for Big Pharma? And also to give lots of human women the means to decide whether or not they will bear children, or endure hot flashes, or lose bone mass, or add to or subtract from their risk of cancer or heart disease? Or to find that "our bodies ourselves" includes mares and their foals (and a few stallions), with all the political and ethical consequences of that conjugation? Conjugated estrogens are about yoking molecules and species to each other in consequential ways. In the Moby Thesaurus, one mouth-watering synonym of "conjugate" is "conglobulate"; that is what I will try to do with horses, humans, urine, and hearts conjugated with Premarin®.

Once upon a time, when I thought I needed estrogen during menopause—to stave off familial heart disease, of all things—I relied on the animal-industrial complex, repeated pregnancies and long-term confinement of mares, and natural conjugated estrogens called Premarin (compounded with a progestin into HRT, hormone replacement therapy) extracted from equine urine.[4] Now, I give my dog a synthetic estrogen with a terrible human and bovine history to control her urinary incontinence, for the sake of her heart—and her indoor way of life. Oh, Cayenne, dog of my heart, a human taste for irony will not get us through these companion species relationships, these meals of situated molecules and required response-ability yet-to-come. Somehow, a feminist science studies scholar and lifelong animal lover, my menopausal self failed to know much about the pregnant mares and their disposable foals.

Did I forget, never know, not look—or just not care? What kind of conjunctivitis was that? Social movements for animal flourishing had noticed those horses and made a very effective fuss about it, and these movements were full of feminist women and men. Why not me too? Was it only after it turned out that HRT probably harmed my heart rather than guarded it that the horses came into my ken? I don't remember. Marx understood all about how privileged positions block knowledge of the conditions of one's privilege. So did the innovators of feminist standpoint theory, the founders of the women's health movements, and the thinkers and activists shaping movements for animal flourishing—that is, my friends, comrades, and colleagues—well before I was in menopause. Still, I managed not to know about the conditions of work for those adult horses for a very long time, much less know about the fate of the excess foals. I ate equine-conjugated estrogens; I drank pooled mares' urine, literally; but I did not conjugate well with the horses themselves. Shame is a prod to lifelong rethinking and recrafting one's accountabilities!

A collaboration between a Canadian pharmaceutical company and an endocrinologist at McGill University led to the development in 1930 of the first orally active, water-soluble, conjugated estrogen, called Emmenin®.[5] Emmenin® was extracted from the urine of Canadian women in late stages of their pregnancies, but supply considerations set the researchers and company to looking for a more copious and available mammalian source. Even if they were paid and desperate, pregnant women would not stay attached to collection bags for long or pee nearly enough to supply their sisters with hormones. German researchers at the time were studying water-soluble estrogens in the urine of pregnant zebras and horses in the Berlin zoo, and by 1939 the pharmaceutical company Ayerst had established a method to get a stable concentrate from pregnant mares' urine. The result of an extraction and concentration process with more than one hundred steps, Premarin® was ready to be marketed in Canada in 1941. The horses, confined in stalls for months at a time attached to collection bags, were originally contract workers on Quebec farms, and the product was manufactured in Montreal. Eventually, high demand issuing from the growing practice of prescribing hormones for menopause, coupled with the history of successive buyouts among the pharmaceutical companies, resulted in production moving to the expansive Canadian western prairies, with a new processing plant in Manitoba.

About decade after I started menopause in the late 1980s, by 1997 Premarin® became the number one prescribed drug in the United States, reaching the sales figure of $2 billion by 2002 (Women's Health Initiative

2002; Vance 2007; see also Wilks, n.d.). Used in over three thousand scientific investigations by 2011, this drug complex remains the most studied estrogen therapy in the world. Definitively by 2002, strong data gathered in the context of the Women's Health Initiative showed that not only did estrogens not prevent heart disease but they were positively correlated with increased incidences of blood clots, strokes, heart attack, and beast cancer. Sales of Premarin® dropped fast—by a lot. Redundant equine workers went to slaughter—lots of them. Dependent contract farmers were put out of business. Drug companies scrambled. Women worried; I know.

However, reduced in volume, harvesting of pregnant mare urine (PMU) remains a worldwide business and Premarin® remains a much prescribed and profitable product. Today Pfizer, which bought out Wyeth-Ayerst in 2009, contracts with about two dozen horse ranches, mainly in western Canada. In 2003, there were over four hundred Wyeth-Ayerst-contracted PMU farms in Manitoba. With industry reorganization in the wake of the crisis in Premarin® prescriptions after 2002, profit per PMU mare went up between 2003 and 2007—a lot. The North American Equine Ranching Information Council (NAERIC) is a committed, sophisticated industry group that presents in its best light the history and contemporary practices of PMU farming (NAERIC, n.d.). The NAERIC website includes a "four seasons" description, with beautiful pictures, of the annual life cycle of the horses on idyllic-looking farms said to be thoroughly regulated and inspected for animal welfare. This site narrates that, from autumn through early spring, mares are confined in their own "comfortable" stalls attached to a "lightweight, flexible pouch that is suspended from the ceiling by rubber suspension lines" that allow a full range of motion, including lying down. Horses have access to sufficient water—a major change from the period before reform, when the demand for concentrated urine trumped equine thirst, with predictable medical consequences for the horses. Put together by international veterinary and welfare groups that inspect equine ranches, and available online from the NAERIC site, the *Equine Veterinarians' Consensus Report on the Care of Horses on PMU Ranches* concluded that numerous reforms after an investigation in 1995 led to major improvements in the lives of the horses. "The public should be assured that the care and welfare of the horses involved in the production of an estrogen replacement medication is good, and is closely monitored."[6]

On-site analysis on several farms by HorseAid in 1999 found conditions much less satisfactory than NAERIC claims, even if one grants that the guidelines, which leave the question of exercise to the discretion of pressed farmers with no indoor exercise facilities in a northern plains winter, are good enough for horses.[7] Confined mares stand around too much, eat too much, get fat, and develop bad feet—sounds like a lot of working females across species to me. With very little room to make costly changes in care practices, contract farmers are at the low end of the financial food chain generated by pregnant mares' urine, just as they are for broiler chickens or other animal industrial products.

Currently, about two thousand NAERIC foals per year are born on twenty-six PMU farms, including draft, light horse, and sport breeds. The foals are sold mostly to families and show barns. About forty-nine thousand horses have been registered with NAERIC since 1998. Better-bred foals are more profitable, and so fewer are slaughtered or enter the rescue-and-adoption apparatus. These days, ranchers collecting pregnant mares' urine "rely on selling foals as much as they rely upon the urine collected from the pregnant mares. Many of these farms utilize websites and forms of promotion identical to non-Premarin®-related horse breeders, and, in nearly all ways, are indistinguishable from the average breeder of equines" ("Premarin," n.d.; "Fact Sheet." n.d.; Premarin.org [http://www.premarin.org/])[8]

The reforms promoted by NAERIC came into being because of activist animal rights, women's health, and horse advocacy groups. Beginning hands-on, on-site study in 1986, HorseAid was the first animal rights organization to investigate conditions on PMU farms and the risks to women from HRT medication, publishing its damning results first in print in 1988 and then in 1994 on the Internet, with graphic images and details about farm and industry practices and human medical data (HorseAid 1988). In 1995, seven years after HorseAid's 1988 report, NAERIC was founded to advocate for reform and the humane treatment of PMU horses. But reform was not and is not the ultimate goal for HorseAid or organizations like the Int'l Fund for Horses. Both groups continue to argue for shutting down all PMU farming, where months-long confinement of pregnant horses, however "comfortable" (i.e., in a box 3.5 feet wide by 8 feet deep by 5 feet high for six months), and the slaughtering of mares who fail to become pregnant, continue.[9] The availability of a wider range of laboratory-synthesized and plant-derived hormones makes arguments to end PMU production harder to evade. Taking account of all PMU farms in 2002, HorseAid estimated that about fifteen thousand "excess" foals went to slaughter. Reflecting Premarin® sales declines since 2002, cuts in contracts to farms, and a more market-oriented foal production, the number in 2011 is much lower, but could be zero.[10]

HorseAid has always been clear about its advocacy both for women's health and for the well-being of horses, and its reports also pay attention to the difficulties of farms and farmers in an agribusiness system in which making a living by farming has become brutal.That fact, of course, does not address what would make raising horses on the northern prairies viable for economic and ecological human-animal well-being, and that should not be an idle goal.

Viral Response-ability

There is no innocence in these kin stories, and the accountabilities are extensive and permanently unfinished. Indeed, responsibility in and for the worldings in play in these stories requires the cultivation of viral response-abilities, carrying meanings and materials across kinds in order to infect processes and practices that might yet ignite epidemics of multispecies recuperation and maybe even flourishing on terra in ordinary times and places. Call that utopia; call that inhabiting the despised places; call that touch; call that the rapidly mutating virus of hope, or the less rapidly changing commitment to staying with the trouble. My slogan from the 1980s, "Cyborgs for Earthly Survival," still resonates, in a cacophony of sound and fury emanating from a very big litter whelped in shared but nonmimetic suffering and issuing in movements for flourishing yet-to-come.

In my DES story, tracking Cayenne's urine spots to out-of-the-way places brought us into a still-expanding conglobulation of interlinked research, marketing, medical and veterinary, activist, agricultural, and scholarly body-and-subject-making apparatuses. Digital and molecular species vied for attention with urethras and vaginas. Females in trouble seemed to luxuriate everywhere; even the industrially synthesized molecules seemed to respond to the lure of (always nonreproductive, in this story) sexual tropisms, despite decades of astute feminist wariness of so-called sex hormones. Cyborgs laughed. Do cyborgs get mitral valve disease or go through menopause? Of course they do, just like their kin. The

relations of intimate care yoking together one woman and one dog ram-
paged virally into all sorts of publics. Sheer contagion. Companion species infect each other all the time. Bodily ethical and political obligations
are infectious, or they should be. Before my dog and I could get out of
the story, we were in the nonoptional company of—and accountable to—
heifers in labs, beef cattle in feedlots, pregnant women in all sorts of places,
daughters and sons and granddaughters and grandsons of once-pregnant
women, angry and well-informed women's health movement activists,
dogs with heart disease, and bevies of other spayed leaky bitches and their
people in vet clinics and on beds.

In my Premarin® story, all the players seemed to be marinating in vats
of Canadian equine urine, the only thing that seemed to hold together the
virally exploding, vulnerable species of the tale. One registered trademark's
travels through bodies brought together, in the need to craft response-ability, quite a motley of mortal beings: fetal calves stripped of amniotic fluid,
urinating pregnant Canadian women, pregnant mares and their foals and
consorts in Manitoba and beyond, activists in horse rescue and women's
health, economically strapped contract farmers, a California menopausal
woman worried about familial heart disease in the company of a lucrative
market-ready crowd of other menopausal Americans, and German zebras
in zoos in the 1930s. Big Pharma, Big Agribusiness, and Big Science provided drama and villains aplenty, but also plenty of reason to damp down
the certainty of villainy and explore the complexities of cyborg worlding.

Each diner exposed to high risks of familial heart failure, eating dangerous and notorious estrogens in later life seems, finally, to be what here,
in this tale, conjugates—yokes together—the cyborg author and the dog
of her heart. *Cum panis*, companion species, females of two species (along
with their microbiomes with species in the zillions) at table together, in
different decades, slurping drafts of dubious estrogens in self-care and care
of the other. Why tell stories like this, when there are only more and more
openings and no bottom lines? Because there are quite definite response-
abilities that are strengthened in such stories.

It is no longer news that corporations, farms, clinics, labs, homes, sciences, technologies, and multispecies lives are entangled in multiscalar,
multitemporal, multimaterial worlding, but the details matter. The details
link actual beings to actual response-abilities. Each time a story helps me
remember what I thought I knew, or introduces me to new knowledge,
a muscle critical for caring about flourishing gets some aerobic exercise.

Such exercise enhances collective thinking and movement too. Each time I trace a tangle and add a few threads that first seemed whimsical but turned out to be essential to the fabric, I get a bit straighter that staying with the trouble of complex worlding is the name of the game of living and dying well together on terra. Having eaten Premarin® makes me more accountable to the well-being of ranchers, northern prairie ecologies, horses, activists, scientists, and women with breast cancer than I would otherwise be. Giving my dog DES makes me accountable to histories and ongoing possibilities differently from if we never shaped kinships with the attachment sites of this molecule. Perhaps reading this essay in this *Viral* issue has consequences for response-ability too. We are all responsible to and for shaping conditions for multispecies flourishing in the face of terrible histories, but not in the same ways. The differences matter—in ecologies, economies, species, lives.

Notes

1. This Wikipedia article is a good first stop with a useful bibliography, but is worse than worthless for tracking feminist and women's health activist connections to DES. See Bell 2009. Barbara Seaman, who died in 2008, is one of my heroes in this story; her work was crucial to persuading the U.S. federal government to convene a task force on DES. In 1975, she cofounded the National Women's Health Network. For a bit of the history and tributes to Seaman, see Editors, n.d.; Seaman 2009. Jewish women have been central in the history of feminist women's health activism. Another hero who recently died, Pat Cody, also worked effectively to change a personal tragedy caused by DES into a global feminist health movement. See Ruth Rosen's (n.d.) tribute to Cody. For innovative and standard-setting feminist science studies, see Oodshourn 1994. First-generation users of DES have increased incidence and mortality rates from breast cancer. Second-generation offspring, "DES daughters," develop dangerous vaginal and breast cancers, as well as other problems like infertility and "abnormal pregnancy outcomes." That means damaged or dead children. DES is the only transplacental carcinogen known in our species. What a distinction! It is also a teratogen; see "abnormal pregnancy outcome." DES sons have nasty effects too.

2. "The most-serious side-effect of estrogen therapy [in dogs] is bone-marrow suppression and toxicity that may progress to a fatal aplastic-anemia. . . . Side effects are more common in older animals" (Forney, n.d.).

3. See Brooks 2011: "As the uses of DES dwindled to a few veterinary uses, its

manufacturer found it unprofitable to continue production and DES went off the market in the late 1990s. Fortunately for the numerous incontinent female dogs hoping to lead indoor lives, the human carcinogenicity issues have not crossed over into the canine health arena. The low doses and infrequent dosing schedule has [*sic*] positioned DES as a medication of unparalleled safety and convenience in the treatment of canine incontinence. Compounding pharmacies now make this medication readily available to patients who need it on a prescription basis." An important player in companion animal consumer marketing, Foster and Smith tells us that prolonged use in pets can cause ovarian cancer (Veterinary and Aquatic Services, n.d.).

4. Popular sites on estrogens in and for women can be found at http://www.healthywomen.org/condition/estrogen and http://www.midlife-passages.com/estrogen.html. Premarin® is a mix of conjugated estrogens branded with a registered trademark. These equine estrogens are chemically different from those made in the human body; namely, they are not bioidentical, but they are bioactive across species. Ethinyl estradiol is the artificial estrogen commonly found in contemporary birth control pills and, like DES, is manufactured in the laboratory. Nomenclatures for hormones around terms like "natural," "synthetic," "biomimetic," "bioidentical," and "artificial" can be confusing, biologically and politically. For example, soy-derived estrogens often are called "natural," but not because they are chemically identical to naturally occurring human estrogens. "Natural" is about branded biovalue in many contested senses. Cenestin® is a conjugated estrogen marketed by Duramed Pharmaceuticals. Made from plant sources, Cenestin® is called "natural" at EarlyMenopause.com (http://www.earlymenopause.com/makingsenseof-hrt.htm); but it is a conjugated mix that is chemically a copy of Premarin®, and so neither is bioidentical to human estrogens. Because it is derived from horses, Premarin® gets called synthetic, although it is heavily processed but not synthesized in the laboratory or factory. Substituting a plant source for horse urine, Cenestin® is a kind of "work-around" that becomes cost effective when the biopolitical/bioethical cost of a technoscientific product gets too high in a particular natural cultural ecology. Duramed calls its conjugated estrogens "synthetic" and an "advanced form of Premarin," emphasizing that "Cenestin does not contain any hormone synthesized by the horse" (http://www.cenestin.net/). So, Cenestin® is at once natural, synthetic, mimetic, and advanced, while Premarin®'s relation to horses forbids the label "natural."

5. See Hormone Foundation, n.d. The first hormonal treatment for symptoms of human menopause in the United States, in 1929, was with a derivative of calf amniotic fluid. Emmenin, from Canadian pregnant women's urine, was first marketed in the United States in 1933. In 1939 DES was marketed as a more potent estrogen than Emmenin. An obvious cyborg cocktail, the mix of

historically situated organic and technological species, both human and not human, could hardly be missed.

6. The report, which is undated, can be found at http://www.naeric.org/about. asp?strNav=0&strBtn=5.

7. See "What Are the Living Conditions of the Mares?" at Premarin.org (http://www.premarin.org/#). This is a HorseAid website.

8. Leslie Hall, Old River Ranch, Monticello, wrote a favorable view of PMU farms at www.applesnoats.com/pmu.pdf.

9. Premarin.org (http://www.premarin.org/#); "Fact Sheet," n.d. The horse-fund.org fact sheet ("Fact Sheet," n.d.) paints a very different picture from that of the NAERIC website. HorseAid is much more careful in its descriptions and dates than is Int'l Fund for Horses, which continues to publish as current conditions originally described in the 1980s and 1990s, but also prints an interesting and damning time line on Premarin and its checkered corporate and medical history. See http://www.horsefund.org/premarin-timeline.php. A site with data on Premarin® sales and PMU farm numbers from 1965 to 2010 is at http://tuesdayshorse.wordpress.com/2010/04/07/wyeth-wins-horses-lose-in-the-premarin%C2%AE-drug-salessweepstakes/.

10. Working in Manitoba for about nine years, Equine Angels Rescue Sanctuary, (http://www.foalrescue.com/), narrates a story from October 2011 about helping PMU farmers get out of the breeding business. The plan pays attention to the needs of farmers, foals, mares, and stallions. Other PMU horse rescue sites are at http://www.savinghorsesinc.com/PMU_Nurse_Mare_Foal_Rescue.php; http://www.aspca.org/fight-animal-cruelty/equine-cruelty/adopting-a-pmu-horse.aspx; and http://www.unitedpegasus.com/United_Pegasus_Foundation/ABOUT.html. Reflecting the sharp decline in farm numbers since 2002, rescue operations now attend more to out-of-work PMU horses than to overproduced foals.

Works Cited

Bell, Susan. 2009. *DES Daughters, Embodied Knowledge, and the Transformation of Women's Health Politics in the Late Twentieth Century*. Philadelphia: Temple University Press.

Brooks, Wendy C. 2011. "Diethylstilbestrol (DES)." Pet Pharmacy. http://www.veterinarypartner.com/Content.plx?P=A&C=31&A=487&S=0

"Diethylstilbestrol." N.d. Wikipedia. Accessed November 16, 2011. http://en.wikipedia.org/wiki/Diethylstilbestrol

The Editors. "A Tribute to Barbara Seaman: Triggering a Revolution in Women's Health Care." 2011. In "The Ecology of Women." Special issue, *On the Issues*,

Spring. http://www.ontheissuesmagazine.com/2011spring/2011spring_tribute.php

"Fact Sheet." N.d. Int'l Fund for Horses. http://www.horsefund.org/pmu-fact-sheet.php

Forney, Barbara. N.d. "Diethylstilbestrol for Veterinary Use." Wedgewood Pharmacy. http://www.wedgewoodpetrx.com/learning-center/professional-monographs/diethylstilbestrol-for-veterinary-use.html

Hormone Foundation. N.d. "Estrogen Timeline (1920–1939)." http://www.hormone.org/Menopause/estrogen_timeline/timeline2.cfm

HorseAid. 1988. "PREgnant MARes' urINe, Curse or Cure?" *Equine Times News*, Fall/Winter. http://www.ehow.com/about_6665212_history-pmu-horses.html

North American Equine Ranching Information Council. N.d. "About the Equine Ranching Industry: History of Premarin." http://www.naeric.org/about.asp?strNav=11&strBtn

Oodshourn, Nelly. 1994. *Beyond the Natural Body: An Archeology of Sex Hormones*. New York: Routledge.

"Premarin." N.d. Wikipedia. http://en.wikipedia.org/wiki/Premarin#Controversy

Raun, A. P., and R. L. Preston. 2002. "History of Diethylstilbestrol Use in Cattle." American Society of Animal Science. www.asas.org/Bios/Raunhist.pdf

Rosen, Ruth. N.d. "Pat Cody: Berkeley's Famous Bookstore Owner and Feminist Health Activist (1923–2010)." *Journal of Women's History*. http://bingdev.binghamton.edu/jwh/?page_id=363

Seaman, Barbara. 2009. "Health Activism, American Feminist." In *Jewish Women: A Comprehensive Historical Encyclopedia*. Jewish Women's Archive. http://jwa.org/encyclopedia/article/health-activism-american-feminist

Vance, Dwight A. 2007. "Premarin: The Intriguing History of a Controversial Drug." *International Journal of Pharmaceutical Compounding*, July/August. http://www.ijpc.com/abstracts/abstract.cfm?ABS=2619

Veterinary and Aquatic Services Department, Drs. Foster and Smith. N.d. "Diethylstilbestrol (DES)." Doctors Foster and Smith, Pet Education.com http://www.peteducation.com/article.cfm?c=0+1303+1470&aid=3241

Wilks, John. "The Comparative Potencies of Birth Control and Menopausal Hormonal Drug Use." Lifeissues.net

Women's Health Initiative. 2002. "Risks and Benefits of Estrogen Plus Progestin in Healthy Postmenopausal Women." *JAMA*, no. 288:321–33.

PART IV. **FICTIONS**

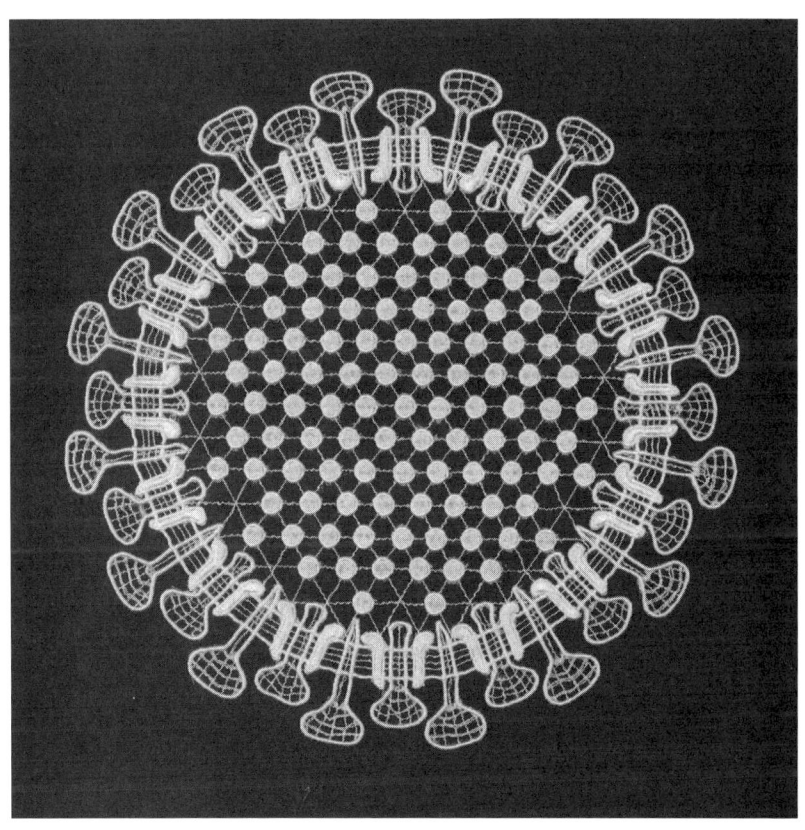

Laura Splan, *Doilies (SARS)*, 2004. Freestanding, computerized, machine-embroidered lace mounted on velvet, 8 in. diameter.

From *The Book of Scab*

Danielle Pafunda

Dear Mom and Dad,

When they ship us out into the fields, someone immediately steps on a nest of sweat bees, and we all get stung. They send a retired nurse out to see if anyone's dying and the nurse smells like gin and menstrual blood. The nurse has her own bone saw and a pair of latex gloves she washes and dries on a loop of twine hanging from her belt. The nurse finds two boys and a girl swollen and wheezing and takes them back with her. The rest of us stay in the field, inching forward carefully.

My bee won't die. It suctions to my ear, a gray jewel pulsing. It tells me things about life underground, about life in a hive, about living dead. It tells me that it spent its entire life looking for me, and now I'm the one who gets to kill it. It tells me that the winters have gotten colder and the springs are wetter and drier and earlier and that tornadoes and blizzards and beetles are coming nearer, that the radiant devices make it hard to breed that its own mother died in a vat of paint and its hive can only find pollen in a few of the flowers. It tells me that everything we've ever heard about chemicals is entirely true. It tells me that I was born dead, too, it tells me that we have unidentified substances in our blood it tells me that unlike a bee, I'll die with my weapons intact, I'll die with a neat set of knives and a semiautomatic weapon stacked beside me, I'll die with a can of mace and a noose packed tightly in a bag, I'll die with someone interrupting me, I'll die with my face poised to open and speak I'll die with six varieties of meat in my freezer and no one to catch me.

My bee has been waiting forever for me and it won't stop squirming. It digs deeper into my ear, it tells me that we've only just begun, that we are a superior being locked in its deathy embrace that I'm purified by my nearness to the bee that it could smell me sweating a mile away that my sweat told it to come to me that my sweat is my only saving grace is the only thing about me that isn't putrid with lies, that as long as the bee pulses into my ear I am a citizen, that it has a thousand brothers and sisters but I am the only one it really loves, me.

Your Ugly Little,
Scab

Danielle Pafunda is author of *Iatrogenic: Their Testimonies* (Noemi Press), *My Zorba* (Bloof Books), *Pretty Young Thing* (Soft Skull Press), and the forthcoming *Manhater* (Dusie Press Books). She's a contributor to the art/lit/crit blog *Montevidayo* and an assistant professor of gender and women's studies and English at the University of Wyoming.

Red, Red, Red: An Essay/Film in Eleven Parts

David Oscar Harvey

Conducting a linguistic analysis of the filmic image, Roland Barthes found something traumatic about his object of study. His semiological methodology required a comparison between cinematic units of signification and language. The analogy brought forth an important distinction: "language doesn't use supports. . . . The word doesn't support the meaning: it is the meaning"(1985, 52). In other words, the word unequivocally declares what it is that it signifies. This one-to-one semantic relationship between signifier and signified does not hold for film. The dissimilarity between word and image is what, for Barthes, affords the image its traumatic element, its inclination toward semantic ambiguity. A picture is worth a thousand words and pictures in motion are worth more yet. In conventional films, the traumatic kernel of the image is managed and bound by meticulously plotted narrative practices. The film is constructed in such a way that the spectator understands, moment to moment, what the images presented before him or her mean. And so, films typically reassure instead of traumatize. One formal technique to attune our comprehension toward a stable end is voice-over. The device, though not limited to such, is most famously linked with the documentary. The voice-over is an additional stratum of signification layered upon the image. Yet instead of enlarging the semantic field of the film, it contains it. Most often voice-over directs the spectator's manner of engagement with the image, allaying its trauma. But what is the voice-over without the images it's meant to accompany? Might words then solicit the variety of trauma Barthes locates in the filmic image?

What follows is the voice-over text from my experimental documen-

 WSQ: Women's Studies Quarterly 40: 1 & 2 (Spring/Summer 2012)

tary *Red Red Red*. The project had many false starts, unsatisfactory interviews, and ultimately uninspiring filmed tableaus. It was only when I wrote the voice-over that the film began to take shape. Instead of recording "reality" and molding my film from the patchwork of fragments I had collected, I wove its images, its rhetoric, and its world around words. *Red Red Red* is an essay film, a text that takes shape through a mediation of my subjective and often esoteric thoughts and sounds and images recorded in the world around me. In its early phases, I too confronted my "film" in the version you are about to encounter. It is not so much that the words of my voice-over wrangle and corral the logic of the images they accompany; rather it is from these words that the images are summoned, produced. As I reread my voice-over after the film's completion, I find myself nostalgic for a time when the image track wasn't finalized and the possibilities of my film were not, in a sense, foreclosed. Perhaps Barthes wasn't completely correct. Maybe words don't instantly and finally point to what it is they mean. Within the words of my film's narration there was always another substrate, one of images. Their possible incarnations left me frazzled, excited and, yes, perhaps a bit traumatized. You can watch my film online at the following link: http://www.imdb.com/video/wab/vi2632097049. Yet with respect to the incarnation of *Red Red Red* before you, please read my "film" first—that is, my film's bare bones. As you read, imagine a film, imagine the words opening unto an imagistic field and in-and-of themselves incomplete. The series of words that form this text call for and render something beyond them. They are in such a context, traumatic, empathetically uncertain and saturated with a stubborn potentiality. Then again, was Barthes right? Are these words, despite the context from which they were pulled, quite simply enough?

> To begin teaching someone: "That looks Red," makes no sense, for he must say that spontaneously, once he has learned what Red means, i.e. learnt the technique of using that word. For if someone has mastered the use of what looks red—or indeed what looks red to me—he must also be capable of answering the question, "And what is Red like?" and 'What does something look like when it turns to Red?
>
> —Ludwig Wittgenstein[1]

There is a story about a boy: he is afraid of the color red. He does not trust men in red shirts, sit in red chairs, or drink from red cups. Still, he exists in a world in which red is, so he exists cautiously, on edge. One day, the boy experiences a decay of sensitivity to color; at the beginning all colors are not affected, their basic color remaining the same, but their saturation decreases until one day the spectrum is simplified to four colors: yellow, green, blue, and red. Finally a monochromatic stage of gray is reached. The boy cannot see red, but still red is. At first, the boy trembles to imagine red everywhere: After all, it could be there or even there. . . . By the story's end . . . the boy is calm.

1. I should tell you this is a film about the criminalization of HIV in the midwestern state of Iowa. Next, I should tell you that I live in Iowa, am HIV positive, and do not like the law, but, it seems to me, neither should you. I wanted to make a film about something, about this thing, about this law that is unfair. Yet making a film about something suggests a separateness between the filmmaker and his or her topic. Is this a documentary? Is this an autobiography? Or is it merely some kind of assertion? I do not know.

I do know that when you test HIV positive in the state of Iowa, or if you are HIV positive and move to the state of Iowa, the Department of Health finds you, calls you in, sits you down, and tells you about the law, gives you a printout on which the law is written, gives you condoms, lots of condoms, a few issues of *POZ* magazine, and informs you about services for people with HIV, of which there are truly none. They find you and inform you of your now criminalized body, criminalized being, criminalized sex. Is this how it is? I worry that I'm exaggerating . . . Here is the law according to the Iowa Code:

> A person commits criminal transmission of HIV, if a person knows of his or her HIV positive status: engages in intimate contact with another person; transfers, donates or provides blood, tissue, semen, organs, or other potentially infectious bodily fluids for administration (e.g.,transfusion) to another person; or in any way transfers to another person any non-sterile intravenous or intramuscular drug paraphernalia previously used by the person infected with HIV. "Intimate contact" means the intentional exposure of the body of one person to a bodily fluid of another person in a manner that could result in the transmission of HIV. Actual transmission of HIV is not a necessary element of this crime. It is an affirmative defense that the person exposed to HIV knew of the other person's HIV positive status, knew that the action of exposure could result in transmission of HIV, and consented to the action of the exposure with that knowledge.

2. In April 2009, Iowa became the third state to legalize gay marriage. I met the decision somewhat uneasily, with great ambivalence; not because I'm against gay marriage, all people should have the right to wed, though it's somewhat dispiriting that so many gay people should want to. I was irritated because the passing of this law allowed the world to look upon Iowa as a progressive state. In Iowa City, where I live, a gathering took place to celebrate the law, and as I walked by I wondered how many people even knew about the HIV criminalization law. Most of the people I spoke to, from my college professors to acquaintances at the city's one gay bar, had no idea that the law existed. Nobody fucking cares about HIV/AIDS anymore and much of my everyday experience fortifies this curmudgeonly perspective. Insofar as the contemporary gay agenda, HIV/AIDS is invisible. On the docket is a process of integration, normalization, of proclaiming a desire for lives more ordinary and essentially composed of heteronormative values. *Become like me and I will respect your difference.* Gay marriage laws effectively expedite this process. I'm nostalgic for a time of queer politics when multiple practices of sex, sexuality, kinship, and worldmaking were of foremost priority; wherein people would know of and rally against HIV criminalization laws, laws that made people with HIV legally accountable pariahs, demonstrably put upon, othered, and certainly not a member of the wedding.

3. I was never about gay pride. I thought, and I suppose I still do, that gay pride presupposes shame, that somewhere in the discursive spool that constitutes gay pride lurks an element of homophobia and ultimately self-hatred. Yet I find myself wanting to somehow exercise (I suppose embody) a sort of HIV pride. Is this different from gay pride; is it more understandable, more defensible to want to somehow proclaim HIV pride than gay pride . . . or less? Listen, I'm hungry for a collective mode of self-assertion. Shame is the inability to identify with others, a self-lacerating mode of loneliness. Pride is a step in the other direction, but, to be honest, it seems to me to be something less than acceptance. The law, this law wants to make scarlet letters from the tongues of those of us who are HIV positive. A stands for AIDS, which I do not have, but you might think I do, when I tell you that I'm positive. Within the vigilant articulation compelled by these laws is a nefarious sort of policed pride, though one that perversely begets the removal of the self from others . . . shame.

4. And now for some facts: HIV criminalization laws fall under state juris-diction and so vary from state to state. At the present moment, thirty-two states have laws specific to HIV criminalization on the books. Yet each of the fifty states is said to have some sort of law applicable to criminalizing HIV, even if the law is not specific to the virus. Although it is no longer the case, throughout the 1990s it was required that each state possess some variation of such a law if that state wished to be eligible for federal monies aimed to curb HIV infections. Iowa, for instance, did not officially ratify its law until 1998.

Each state and indeed each county within that state prosecutes people with varying degrees of frequency and voracity. Many of the states, like California, include "intentionality" within the wording. Hence, one can be prosecuted only if intent to transmit HIV was part of the criminalized act. Such a thing, of course, is difficult to prove and so the states that include intentionality as part of the criminalized activity rarely prosecute. The state of Florida seldom deploys its law; however, recently is was compelled to do so when a man, an Olympic medal–winning equestrian, failed to inform a regular partner of his HIV status. Articles detailing the case did not state whether the equestrian barebacked, that is had anal sex sans pro-tection, or whether the equestrian transmitted the HIV virus to his (rid-ing) partner. The defense attorney's office did go on record as stating that the equestrian was thought suitable for prosecution because the crimi-nalized act occurred repeatedly. Hence, the frequency of the act seems to come into play. Nothing, however, in the wording of the Florida law states as much. The arbitrary nature of the enforcement as well as the pliancy of the legalese are part of what makes the laws so unsettling . . . unwieldy gavels and precariously balanced scales of justice coming down on Lord knows who or when?

5. The most prevalent grocery chain in Iowa is called Hy-Vee, though I call it HIV, as the name seems to demand it. Can you imagine a grocery store called Hy-Vee in New York City or San Francisco? The local convenience store chain meanwhile is called Kum 'n Go . . . No need to unpack the alternate meanings at play in that one; might as well call the place Nut 'n Bolt. Within these names, I read a highly visible form of disavowal. The names, in remaining adamantly as they are, suggest an imperviousness to innuendo, a willful naïveté. Of course, they cannot in the end hope to maintain this, yet they (and their designations) nonetheless persist in

a phantasmic sphere immune to ribald significations. The public face of Iowa presents itself as if entirely wholesome, not to mention free of sexually transmitted diseases. Perhaps this is why it forcibly compels those of us who are HIV positive to identify ourselves without equivocation. Iowa would like to present itself and its citizens as "clean." A recent issue of *POZ* magazine advised its HIV positive readers who lived in a state known to actively enforce such a law to not only disclose their HIV status to prospective sexual partners but also to record that conversation or alternately to have one's partner sign a document attesting to his or her knowledge of one's HIV status.

6. The Iowa law is worded so loosely that experts said it might cover an HIV positive person's kissing another without disclosure of the person's serostatus. Of course, it's impossible to get HIV from kissing. It's also highly implausible to get HIV from oral sex. A doctor I had while living in New York assured me that the acquisition of HIV through oral sex was a panic-inducing myth and that if one was really worried about such a prospect one should not take a partner's ejaculate into one's mouth. The partner could, for instance, cum on your face (what if it gets in my eye; what if it gets in my ear; one of my friends asked me . . .). People have also been prosecuted by these laws for spitting and biting during an assault. For example, a HIV positive Michigan man bit his neighbor during a dispute and was charged with bioterrorism, even though, as with oral sex, the risk of transmitting the virus during such a variety of contact is near infinitesimal. I am talking about the irrational fear of People with HIV/AIDS Who Bite.

   To have HIV entails narrating assurances to those who do not; I say, this is okay and this and also this, this too, while the other nods his head not quite believing me. Thirty-six Iowans have been charged under the law and twenty-five have been convicted. The numbers may seem low, but with approximately twenty-two hundred documented persons living in Iowa with HIV, nearly 2 percent of this population has been charged with the law and over 1 percent have or are serving prison sentences. This is to say nothing of the exacerbated sense of social, psychic, and legal stigmatization experienced by those of us living in Iowa with HIV under the law on a day-to-day basis.

7. I'm not quite sure what to show you. During the 1980s and 1990s HIV/

AIDS was hypervisual; we were saturated with mythologized and pathologized bodies equated with AIDS. The final days in the life of a person with AIDS somehow became synonymous both for the entirety of that person's life living with the virus and for the disease itself. These persons were depicted as wasted, alone, abject, skeletal, and as if undead or always already dying. This has changed, but I still think such iconography, however grossly inaccurate and moralizing, constitutes the optical unconscious of the trauma of AIDS, like people falling from the Twin Towers, like the photographs of the concentration camps after liberation. Though associations linger like an afterimage of AIDS, the present visual field of the epidemic is blanched in a stillness of polite optimism. Strangely, the HIV criminalization laws have mostly sprung up in the past ten to fifteen years, an era referred to by many, at least in the terms of the West, as one of post-AIDS.

The epidemic of AIDS had once upon a time played out in an ecstasy of visibility, wherein one was encouraged to imagine the disease as it showcased itself in gaunt faces and whirls of deep purple upon bodies sagging downward toward the inevitable. Because of antiretroviral treatment, such monstrous iconographies now rarely surface; hence the law compels those who are HIV positive to name themselves upon nearing the edge of desire's fulfillment. We are not allowed to pass, to assimilate. I'm not sure what to show you because there's nothing to see, nothing to recognize in the visual field . . . and that's what frightening for so many. This is a film with nothing to show you, though it wants to.

8. I thought I would make a film founded upon voices . . . that I would meet people, Iowans who were prosecuted by the law and they would tell their stories, but, for the most part, they don't want to. In Bremer County, Iowa, Nick Rhodes was sentenced to twenty-five years in prison for sleeping with a man, only once, to whom he did not disclose his status. Rhodes also did not transmit the virus. After I heard about the sentencing I decided that I would make this film and that Rhodes should be in it. I approached Rhodes about my project, saying we could collaborate about the nature of his contribution to and inclusion in the film. Rhodes kindly considered this and a bit later very sweetly commended the nature of my project, said he wished he could be a part of it, but given the conditions of his parole, he couldn't agree. Bradley Harris, the judge who initially sentenced Rhodes to twenty-five years said to the defendant, *"One thing that makes this case dif-*

ficult is that you don't look dangerous; you don't look like most of our criminals that sit here. But the risk is still there, just like if you would have shot a gun." A few months later the sentence was drastically reduced, although lifetime probation and registration as a sex offender was part of the sentence. Still, I couldn't get over the initial sentencing, the trail of Rhodes, even if it was mitigated. I suppose I can't get over the law in the general or that I live the land in which such things are carried out . . . quietly, discreetly.

9. During the crisis era in the United States, that is, during the time before successful treatments of the virus, communities, like the activist coalition ACT UP, passionately fought for rights and accessible treatments for people with HIV/AIDS, as well as more just modes of representation. They constituted another mode of visibility, one that was righteous and hard won, ultimately resulting in countless victories and the most successful grassroots movement in American during the twentieth century. These people, who came a generation before me and whom I tremendously admire, were vigilant and militant in making themselves and their cause seen and listened to. But they are gone. Gone, not meaning deceased, though some are, but the vibrant movement that they championed and ignited is a thing of the past. This is understandable. AIDS is different now. In the United States, the virus, when treated, oftentimes does not progress to AIDS at all. We might say we are no longer living in the era of AIDS but that of HIV. The cause is less dire, the stakes less high. But for those of us who are positive, perhaps particularly for those of us who were recently diagnosed, it is difficult to parse what exactly being HIV positive means. Compared to the early days of the epidemic, we are lucky, fortunate to be the bearers of a hopeful and healthy forecast, no doubt. But this does not mean that the virus doesn't change us. With it, we inherit a history; one of pride and shame, activism and defeat. Identifications with most of these things, however, entail a reckoning with histories now past, one complicated by assurances of a long hold on futurity. But what of the present? What does it mean to be living with HIV now? I do not know. I don't see anything. I have heard it said that this felt feeling of nothingness, this absence of a secure identification with what it means to be HIV positive is a luxury. I can't entirely accept this, though I'm sympathetic to both the sentiment and manner of thinking. It does mean something to be HIV positive. But what? I long for this; long to see it. To orient myself, not to it, but toward it—whatever this it may be.

10. In nearly all the cases I read about, around the United States, willful transmission rarely seems the impetus behind not disclosing one's serostatus. What is it then? Can't you figure it out? That it's a fear of rejection, alienation, a willful, if negligent, attempt to be as if unmarked. There is real power in remaining unmarked and there are serious limitations to visual representation as a political goal. Is visibility a trap? I suppose it's assumed that if we couldn't keep ourselves safe from the virus we aren't able to guard others from the same, nor that we'd want to. This is wrong.

Also wrong is legally mandating HIV positive people with the sole responsibility of prevention. The logic of the law encourages HIV negative people not to concern themselves about HIV; that is, if their partner isn't forthcoming about a positive serostatus. While the law compels HIV positive people toward speech, it compels HIV negative people toward passivity and silence. In other words, why actively ask after your partner's serostatus or practice safer sex or use clean works, if your partner, legally bound to come forward if he or she is HIV positive, does not do so?

Wrong as well is prospectively discouraging people to get tested or seek medical attention. If one believes oneself to be at risk for HIV infection, yet nonetheless values these risk-bearing experiences as an integral part of one's quality of life, one might not want to learn of one's possible serostatus. Such knowledge would demand this person disclose their infection, which might decidedly limit access to sexual relations with a variety of partners; a situation he or she might wish to avoid. One alternately might get tested anonymously, test positive, but delay medical attention and perhaps treatment, as such recourse would necessitate that the person be on record as HIV positive and so interpolated by the law.

Finally wrong is a law thought to encourage candor that in many cases promotes deceit. Again, hypothetically, say an HIV positive person (maybe you or me) liked another person and performed oral or protected sex with that person, but was unable as yet to disclose his or her status. Now, say these persons continued to like each other with growing intensity over time. But the HIV positive person is now in an impossible situation. He or she obviously must tell the object of his or her affection about the object of his or her infection. But, how can the person do so? How can you, I do so? There is the worry of the partner's response, but then there is the conundrum of the law. If the object of affection takes the news very, very badly he or she might, under the law, seek the prosecution, the persecution of you or me. How might you or I confront this risk . . . one of imprisonment, public shame, and essentially the end of a life as it is presently known?

11. And then there is my appetite for change. But it's like the itch and spasm of a phantom limb; how to even *begin* to change this nasty situation? I think about ACT UP, I think about them a lot actually, and their strategy of forcefully bringing attention to just how bad, how unfair and fucked up, things were in relation to AIDS. Fostering awareness promises the collectivizing of concern necessary to get the ball rolling. And then there is the nature of the broadened attention, of being attended to, which in and of itself can mollify dispossession. To such an end, I might parasitically use the public interest story of a gay wedding. After all, liberals adore looking with approval upon homosexual nuptials. I would storm the wedding, ruin the wedding, covering its members in sticky streamers of artificial blood. I would be asked why I did this and I would tell them . . . Or I would seek out perhaps the most dastardly villain in the saga of Iowa's HIV criminalization law, Judge Bradley Harris, ring his doorbell, wait, introduce myself, and shoot him with my cock . . . all this because my penis is not a concealed firearm and my body does not make of me a bioterrorist. Are these proposed actions hysterical, too far in excess of ACT UP's mandate of nonviolence? Perhaps, but I am at a loss.

Or I could make a film, about this thing, about this law that is unfair.

We began with a fearful boy whose story ended quite well. But what happened after his calmly ever after? I imagine the boy, perhaps now a color-blind young man, missing but not seeing red. What was outside him has vanished, residing now internally as a memory, if not a certain shade of knowledge. So perhaps red was no longer of the world but his. Still, there was loneliness about red's lack of reflection. He longed to perceive that this and that are red; that it and they are red; he and she? Red. To see himself . . . in red.

David Oscar Harvey is a PhD candidate in the Department of Cinema and Comparative Literature, at the University of Iowa. His pieces in *Discourse* and *LGBT Transnational Identity and the Media: Post Colonial—Post Queer* address issues surrounding HIV/AIDS, as does his essay film, *Red Red Red*, which has recently screened at a number of film festivals. He is presently completing his dissertation, "Cinematic Assemblages: An Anatomy of the Essay Film in Interwar Europe."

Notes

1. Quoted in Jarman 2010.

Works Cited

Barthes, Roland. 1985. "The 'Traumatic Units' of Cinema: Research Principles." Trans. Dana Polan. On Film 14:48–53.

Iowa Code. "Criminal Transmission of Human Immunodeficiency Virus," Chapter 709C (1998), http://coolice.legis.state.ia.us/cool-ice/default.asp? category=billinfo&service=iowacode&ga=83&input=709C#709C.1

Jarman, Derek. 2010. *Chroma: A Book of Colors*. Minneapolis: University of Minnesota Press.

Hypnotizing Chickens

Melanie Crean

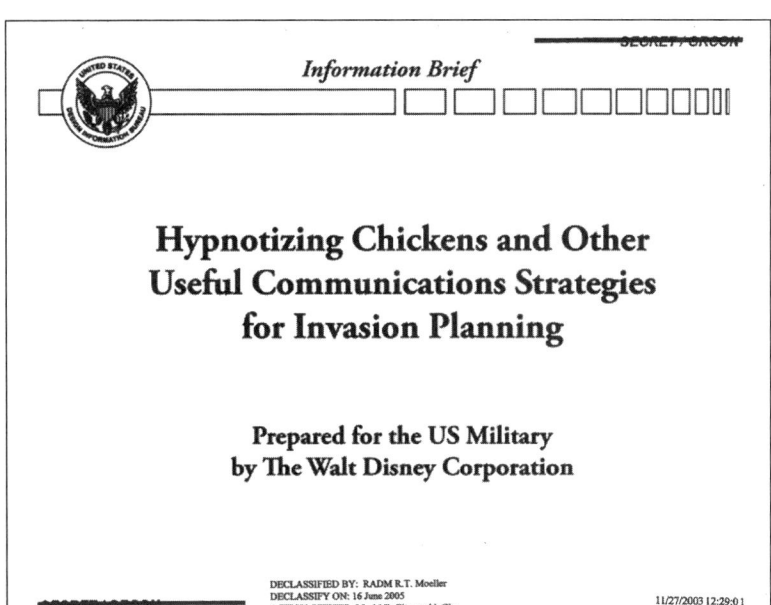

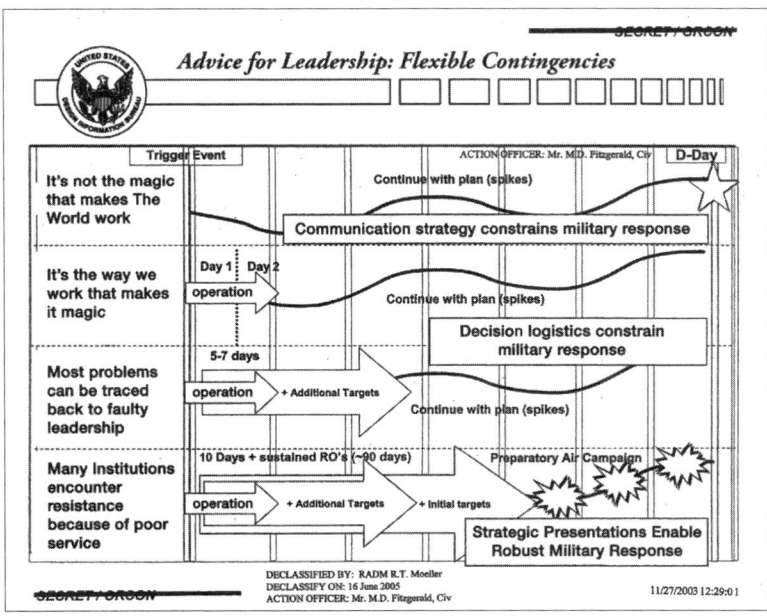

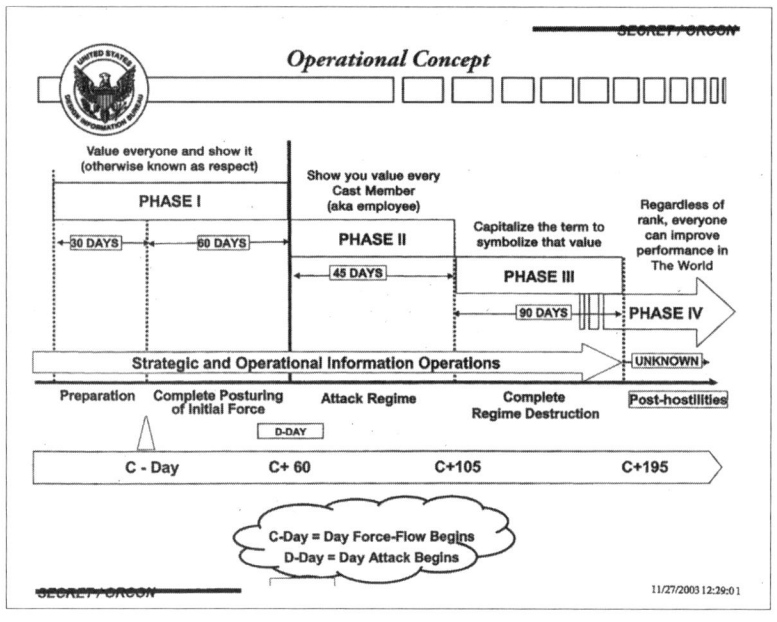

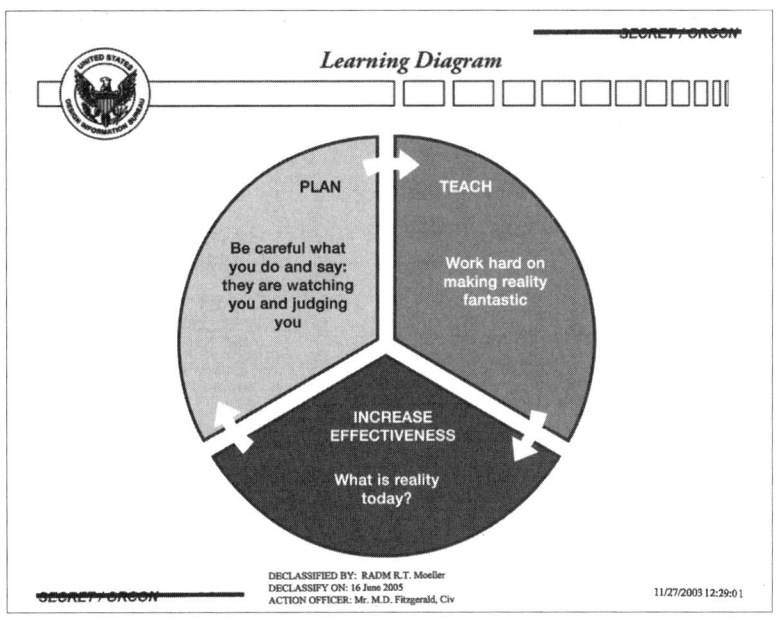

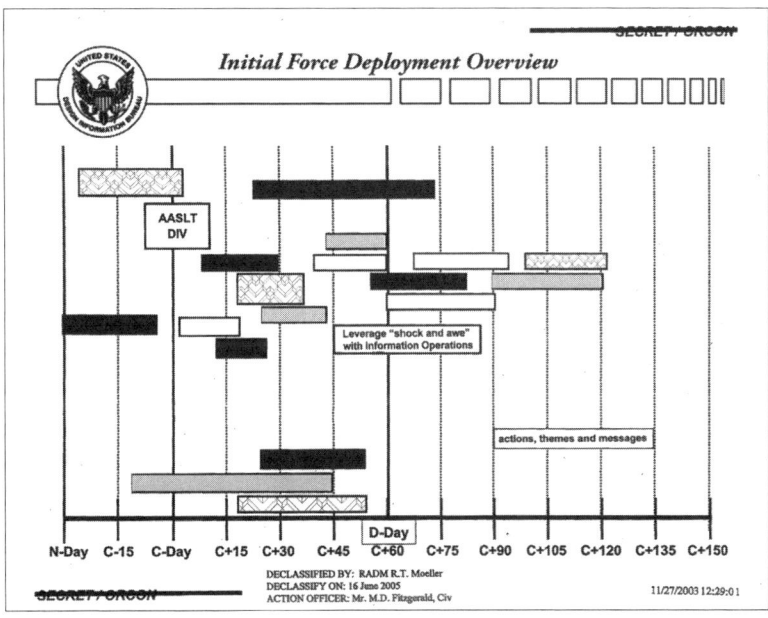

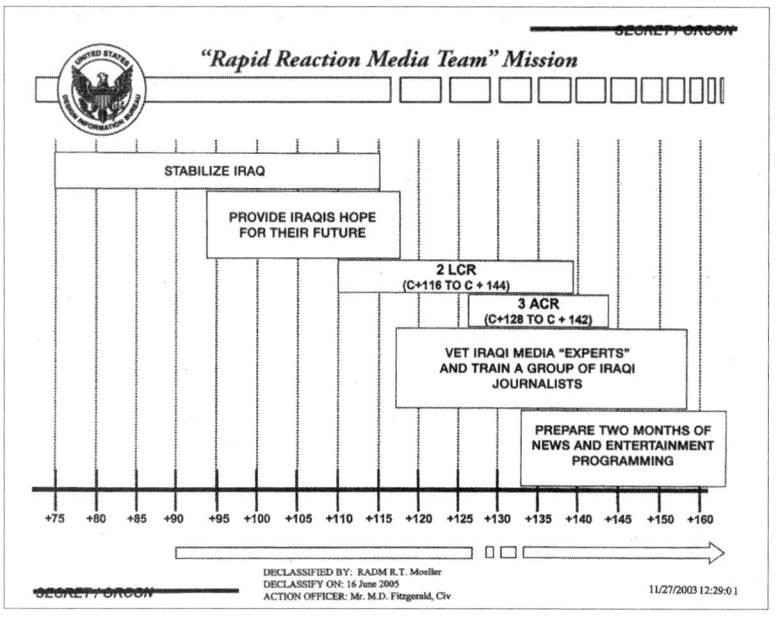

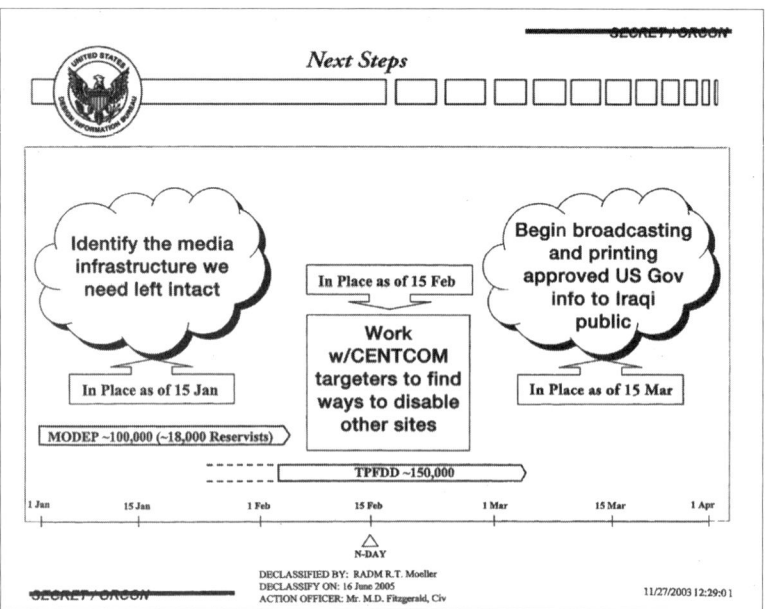

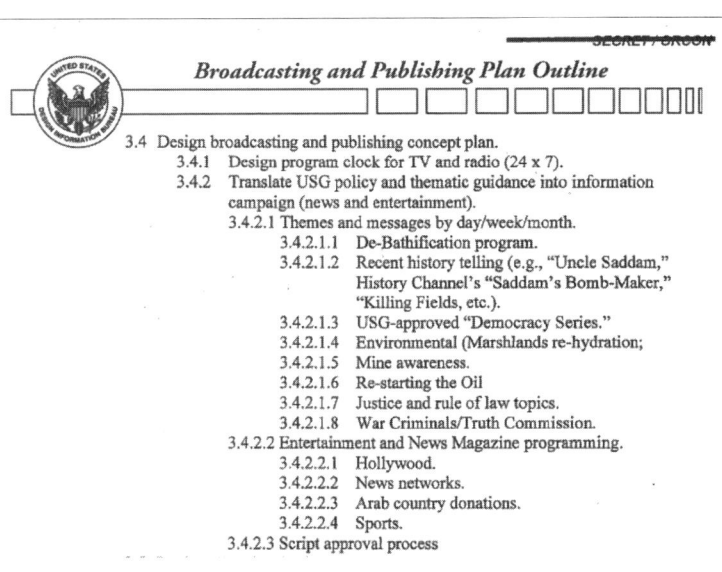

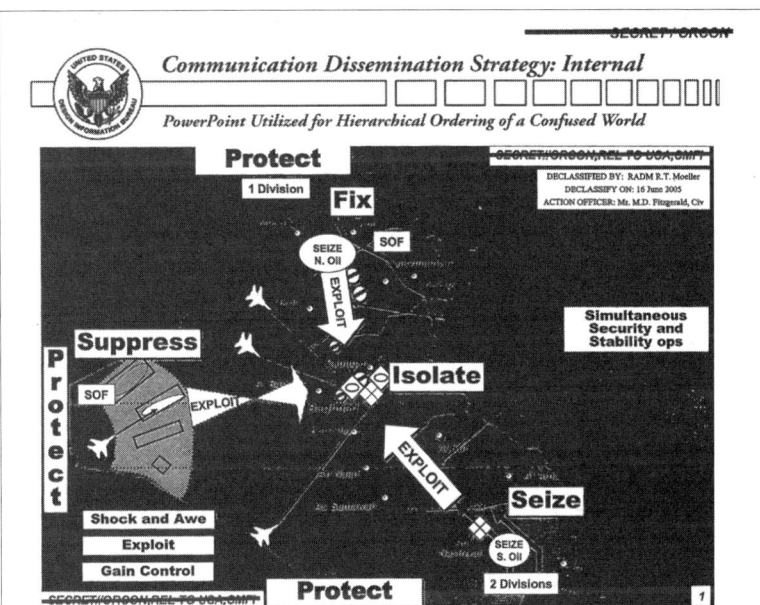

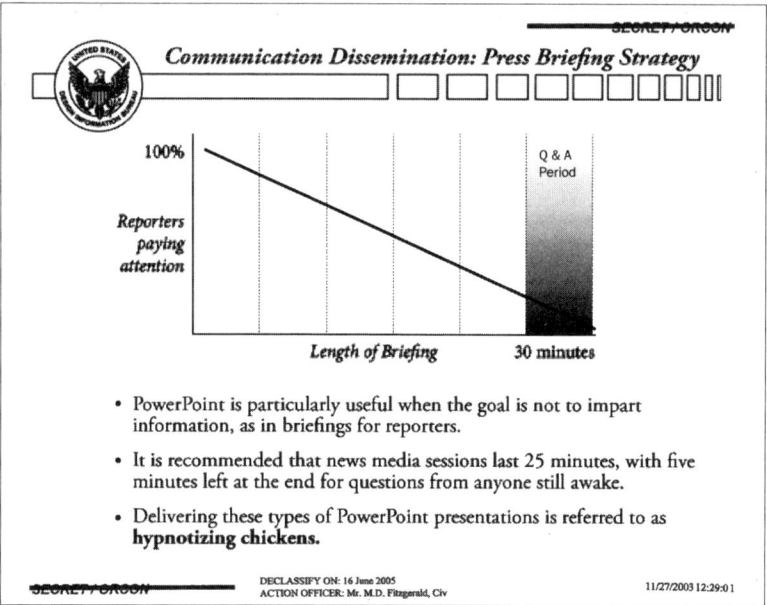

- PowerPoint is particularly useful when the goal is not to impart information, as in briefings for reporters.
- It is recommended that news media sessions last 25 minutes, with five minutes left at the end for questions from anyone still awake.
- Delivering these types of PowerPoint presentations is referred to as **hypnotizing chickens.**

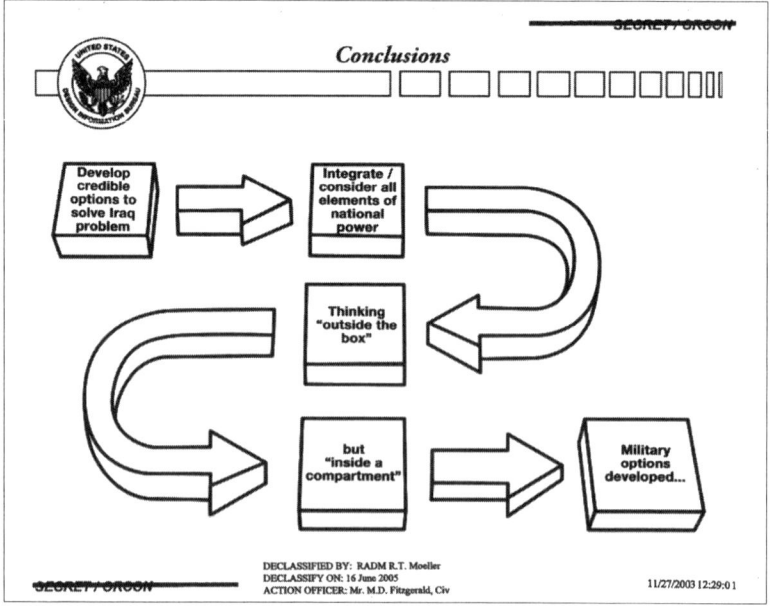

Artist Notes

This graphical essay was inspired by an April 26, 2010 article in *The New York Times* titled, "We Have Met the Enemy and He is PowerPoint" by Elisabeth Bumiller. The article describes how military culture, communications, and decision-making strategy have been affected by the widespread use of PowerPoint graphic presentation software. The communicative sensibility afforded by PowerPoint generally results in descriptions of interconnected economic, political, cultural, and strategic factors being reduced to bullet-pointed phrases and framed in graphics. This reductionist aesthetic decreases the potential for critical thought and analysis. General Stanley McCrystal, when looking at an unimaginably complicated organizational chart in the summer of 2009, is reported to have said, "When we understand this slide, we'll have won the war." The military has allegedly come to rely on PowerPoint decks for their "hierarchal ordering of a confused world," a panacea for some problems, which in turn has created others.[1] The title of this graphical essay is taken from the United States military tactic of filling up press briefings with extremely dull PowerPoint presentations to intentionally bore media correspondents, and thus avoid providing any real information to the public. As Bumiller puts it, little information is transmitted, and even less time is left for questions. This tactic is known within the military as "hypnotizing chickens"; the chickens, in this instance, being the press.

This poses a paradox: the same form of communication that the military uses to confuse, or "hypnotize" the press—PowerPoint presentations—has also come to dominate and reshape their own internal communication. In particular, high-level decision makers now make more decisions in less time, based on less information. Military decision-making papers were formerly three- to four-page analytic essays that were researched, contextualized, considered overnight, discussed, and decided upon later in group settings. As a result of PowerPoint, the schedules of high-level personnel are now broken up into half-hour time slots so they can make decisions every thirty minutes, following a standard twenty-minute PowerPoint presentation.

Because bullet points are by nature short and general, they are both open to interpretation and dependent on an accompanying explanation. When orders have been delivered in PowerPoint form without a verbal explanation, it has resulted in confusion and frustration. In his book *Fiasco,*

Thomas Ricks writes that while planning the invasion of Iraq, instead of issuing clear orders, General Tommy Franks relied on sending the PowerPoint decks he had cleared with Donald Rumsfeld to his subordinates, who were baffled as to how to interpret them.[2]

The viral potential for PowerPoint decks is a byproduct of their digital format, contributing to this confusion and frustration. As Dr. T.X. Hammes observed in his article "Dumb-dumb Bullets" in the *Armed Forces Journal*, "It is an accepted reality that PowerPoint presentations— particularly important ones—inevitably are disseminated to a much wider audience than those attending the brief. We have created huge staffs and they are all hungry for information. This means most of the people who actually see the brief get an incomplete picture of the ideas presented."[3]

Upon further research into the military's leadership strategy, I discovered that several branches of the armed services have contracted with the Walt Disney Company to provide leadership training.[4] Disney, which enjoys high customer satisfaction and low employee turnover rates, bases its strategy on providing all of its employees, no matter the rank, with leadership opportunities, and fostering trust among the community.[5] I found it ironic that the military was receiving leadership training based on theories of participation and trust at the same time it was planning its military-infused media strategy for Iraq, a top-down model predicated on giving hope to the Iraqi public through the placating medium of television.[6]

Layouts for this piece (except for slides one, five, and eleven) came from redacted Iraq War PowerPoint slide decks available at the National Security Archive. *Slides two and three are based on Tab C: Compartmented Plan Update, slide six from Tab L: Compartmented Concept, slide ten from Tab J, slide twelve from Tab I: Compartmented Concept.*[7] *Text from slides seven, eight, and nine is based on material from the white paper Rapid Reaction Media Team Concept.*[8] *Slide four is from Security Agreement Framework.*[9] Text has been altered to include leadership strategy from former Disney vice president Lee Cockrrell's *Creating Magic: 10 Common Sense Leadership Strategies from a Life at Disney.*[10]

Melanie Crean is an artist and teacher based in Brooklyn, New York. She is an assistant professor of media design at Parsons the New School for Design in New York City, where she teaches production and theory-based classes in experimental time-based work, mobile media, and gaming. Her artwork deals with the politics of perception and the capacity of speech and language to produce political change. Crean has received fellowships and commissions from Art in General, the Bronx Arts Council, Harvestworks, NYFA, NYSCA, Rhizome and Creative Time. She would like to thank her husband Jordan Parnass for his amazingly creative and patient editorial and graphical contributions to the piece.

Notes

1. Elisabeth Bumiller, "We Have Met the Enemy and He is PowerPoint" *The New York Times*, April 26, 2010. http://www.nytimes.com/2010/04/27/world/27powerpoint.html

2. Thomas E. Ricks, *Fiasco* (New York: Penguin Books, 2006).

3. Dr. T. X. Hammes, "Dumb Dumb Bullets," *Armed Forces Journal*, July 2009. http://armedforcesjournal.com/2009/07/4061641

4. Steve Vogel, "Trying Some Disney Attitude to Help Cure Walter Reed," *The Washington Post* February 25, 2008. http://www.washingtonpost.com/wp-dyn/content/article/2008/02/24/AR2008022401993.html

5. Danielle Tumminio, "Lessons from Disney to the US Government" October 11, 2011. http://www.huffingtonpost.com/danielle-tumminio/lessons-from-disney-to-th_b_1005837.html

6. The National Security Archive, "Iraq: The Media War Plan," May 8, 2007. http://www.gwu.edu/~nsarchiv/NSAEBB/NSAEBB219/index.htm

7. The National Security Archive, "Top Secret Polo Step," February 14, 2007. http://www.gwu.edu/~nsarchiv/NSAEBB/NSAEBB214/index.htm

8. The National Security Archive, "Iraq: The Media War Plan," May 8, 2007. http://www.gwu.edu/~nsarchiv/NSAEBB/NSAEBB219/index.htm

9. The National Security Archive, "US Military Hoped for Virtually Unlimited Freedom of Action in Iraq," June 13 2008. http://www.gwu.edu/~nsarchiv/NSAEBB/NSAEBB252/index.htm

10. Lee Cockrrell, *Creating Magic: 10 Common Sense Leadership Strategies from a Life at Disney* (New York: Doubleday, 2008).

PART V. ALERTS AND PROVOCATIONS

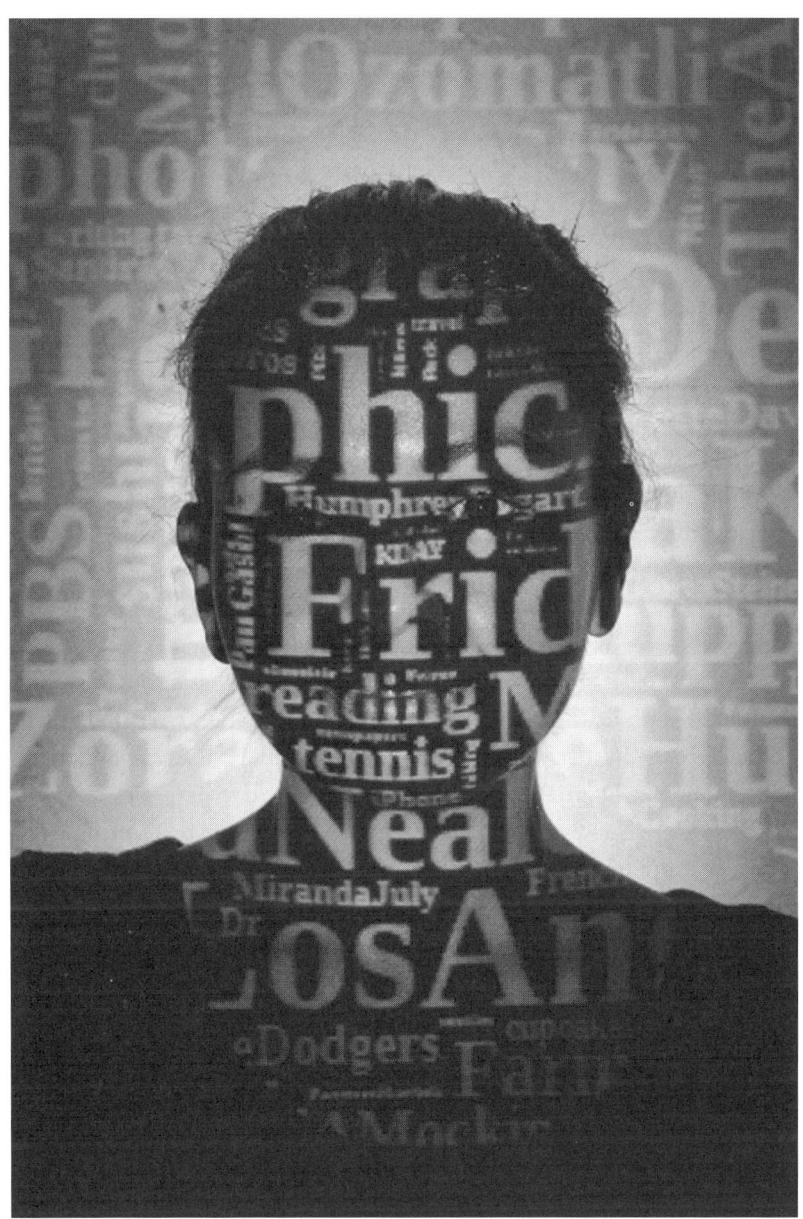

Veronica

Media In Our Image

Johanna Blakley

Most people do not realize that women outnumber men in every age group on social networking sites around the world and they spend significantly more time on these sites than men do. Social media is having a transformative effect on traditional business models in every media industry, including publishing, TV, radio, film, music, and games. I am convinced that the growing influence of social media will help dismantle some of the silly and demeaning stereotypes that characterize media and advertising globally. In particular, I think that social media may help free us from the absurd assumptions we, as a society, have about gender.

Traditional media—which makes its living giving audiences what they seem to desire—has provided us with a surprisingly distorted mirror of our lives, and especially our gender. Most media businesses today use rigid segmentation methods in order to understand their audience. These methods are driven by classic demographics, which sum up human beings with a handful of restrictive labels based on how much money we make, the color of our skin, and our age and gender.

When marketers use demographics, they assume that certain demographics predict certain interests, which can predict a certain kind of purchasing behavior. Demographic-based marketing rose to dominance because it was too expensive to figure out people's *actual* interests, which is the marketer's holy grail because interests are much more closely aligned with purchasing behavior than any demographic model ever could be. But, because marketers, advertisers, and media companies could not reliably track the specific interests of individual members of very large audiences, these companies made a lot of assumptions about what people in certain demographic categories enjoy and want to buy.

 WSQ: Women's Studies Quarterly 40: 1 & 2 (Spring/Summer 2012)

The consequences of this business model are quite profound. Most of our popular culture is based upon assumptions about the interests of certain high-value demographic categories. The content that we hear on the radio, read in magazines, and see on screens large and small has been carefully crafted to deliver certain demographics to advertisers. The presumptions made about demographic preferences—what women want, what Hispanics like, what poor people prefer—comprise the underlying DNA of global popular culture.

I have studied the impact of demographics on advertising and media for several years. After focusing my attention on social media, I discovered the outsized role that women play in what many industry analysts acknowledge to be the most revolutionary technological development since the invention of the printing press. Digital media, and especially social media, allows audience members to talk among themselves, to critique, remix, and redistribute content on an unprecedented scale. Of course participants in social networks belong to the same old demographic categories that media companies and advertisers have used to understand them, but now those categories mean even less than they did before. Geography and national boundaries are easily surmounted obstacles in our quest to network and converse with people who share our interests. And demographic categories often play no part in those conversations. In short, digital networks allow us to *opt out* of our demographic categories, which are often virtually invisible online . . . and easily fudged as we go about constructing our own unique online identities.

Traditional media companies are desperate to understand these online communities because they realize that the future mass audience will be online and networked. That is the future. But one reason that the music, TV, and film industries are having a hard time understanding and monetizing these audiences is because they are still looking at them (that is, us) through the lens of demographics. Why? Because that is how ad rates are still determined.

But this will soon change. If you look at how people aggregate online, you do not find people clustering around age, gender, and income categories. What you find instead are "taste communities," heterogeneous groups of people who coalesce around the things they care about, which can range from serious political causes to pet toys. These audiences are ad hoc; they shift among sites, across link trails, they enter various walled gardens and then report back on their adventures on sites like Tumblr. Their meandering journeys across platforms and channels are driven by their effort to find compelling content that resonates with their taste, their beliefs, and their curiosity. I call them "transnational taste communities" (Blakley and Kaplan 2009, 37).

As media scholar Henry Jenkins observes, place and culture still matter, but fans who participate in these online communities are released from the constraints of geography to interact in real-time with fans around the world—many of whom have widely divergent understandings of the content that has brought them together, whether it's a Bollywood film, *Twilight*, *Harry Potter* books, or memes like Feminist Ryan Gosling (Jenkins 2006).

Shared values and interests are a far more powerful aggregator of people than age, gender, or income ever were. Those demographic categories are best understood as proxies, clues about what it is a potential customer *might* be interested in reading, watching, and buying. But any rational media company or advertiser would prefer to know what their potential customers have already indicated that they like, enjoy, and desire, which is one reason that online surveillance technologies such as cookies and web bugs are being used to capture the click streams and data trails of online audiences. While online citizens have every right to be alarmed by this new surveillance culture, they should also realize that there is something to be gained from being watched—from having their taste *respected* rather than *presumed*.

The fact that these transnational taste communities are being shaped primarily by women is nothing short of a game changer for global media industries. Although there are more adult men in the global Internet population, women not only outnumber men on social networking sites, they also spend significantly more time on these sites than men do. This is true in every region in the world, (Abraham, Mörn, and Vollman 2010) despite the digital divide between men and women in many traditional countries (Gill, Brooks, McDougall, Patel, and Kes 2010, 3).

Academic studies from a wide variety of disciplines have demonstrated that women do seem to have a much stronger drive to socialize than men. The fact that women, once online, gravitate toward social networks should not surprise us. But this dominance is not just in first world countries, but even in places where women have far less access to Internet-connected computers and smart phones. We do not tend to think about women as early adopters of new technology (Gill, Brooks, McDougall, Patel, and Kes

2010, 7), but all reports indicate that once women are online, they seek out social media sites far more passionately than men.

So what are the ramifications of women's demographic dominance of social media networks? We know that social media is transforming old media business models as companies try to figure out how to make money from online audiences. What might this mean for women, both inside the media industries and out? And what impact will it have on our media-saturated culture?

I believe that the content that makes up our current media environment is going to experience a profound shift. And one reason for this is that women are redefining what audiences are and what they actually want. But I do not believe we will simply trade demographic submission for demographic dominance. I think women will play a key role in planting a stake in the heart of the chick flick and all media content that is based on shallow demographic stereotypes about what men or Asians or young people really want. Instead, media and advertising will be a lot more data-driven and far less determined by demographic stereotypes and hunches about the appetites of eighteen to twenty-four year old men. They will be tailored to the taste of networked online communities where women happen to be the driving force.

But while women have taken over the online social media conversation, women are currently not in a position to dictate the development of those platforms nor the way they will be used by the media companies whose content is increasingly consumed there (Nielsen 2012). In Fortune 500 "technical" companies, women hold 10 percent of corporate officer positions and 11 percent of board of director positions (NCWIT 2010, 7). In the TV industry, only 16 percent of high-powered positions such as writing, directing and editing are held by women—down from a peak in 1998 (Lauzen 2011). Only four women have ever run a major film studio and on screen, the numbers are grim: the Screen Actors Guild reports that 62 percent of roles go to men (Masters, 2011) and a study found that less than 30 percent of all speaking characters in mainstream films were female (Smith 2010, 5).

Women have a tremendous opportunity, right here and now, to permanently adjust this picture. Social media has precipitated the emergence of audiences that were, as Xiaochang Li puts it, "unimaginable" in previous media distribution systems (2009, 77). Women's dominance of social media is a crucial development for feminist activists and scholars, who

Jasmine

Kate

have doggedly documented the appalling way in which women have been represented in media, and the bizarre and destructive tactics that media industries have used to court (and exploit) female consumers. Global media companies and advertisers must learn to live without the primitive methods of audience segmentation that have produced debilitating stereotypes about women and every other demographic group that has been targeted with ad-supported content. Women now occupy the ground floor of the new media revolution: we need to make sure that we build the new media system in our own image, to our own specifications, customized for us.

The Portraits: Media In Our Image

These portraits meld together Renaissance conventions of portrait painting with contemporary visual-data mining. The goal was to create augmented portraits of ourselves that tell people more about our taste, values, and beliefs than about our demographic coordinates. We used word clouds, which reflect the relative frequency of words within a data set, to summarize social media preferences and profile data from each of the portrait subjects. Inspired by the concept of lace veils that both reveal and obscure the subjects, we projected each sitter's own metadata on their physical bodies, creating a veil of revealing data.

The *Media In Our Image* portrait project was conceived by Johanna Blakley, Veronica Jauriqui, Sarah Ledesma, and photographer Jasmine Lord. Thanks to Kate Garner and Krystal Garber for revealing themselves to us. You can find more of these portraits, and more information about what inspired them, here:

http://mediainourimage.tumblr.com/

http://pinterest.com/sarahledesma/media-in-our-image/

JOHANNA BLAKLEY is the managing director and director of research at the Norman Lear Center at the University of Southern California's Annenberg School for Communication and Journalism. Blakley performs research on a wide variety of topics, including global entertainment, cultural diplomacy, entertainment education, celebrity culture, fashion, digital media, and intellectual property law. She has two *TEDTalks*: "Social Media & the End of Gender" and "Lessons from Fashion's Free Culture." Her work has been widely cited, and she has appeared on *Good Morning America*, MSNBC, and Current TV.

Works Cited

Abraham, Linda Boland, Marie Pauline Mörn, and Andrea Vollman. 2010. *Women on the Web: How Women are Shaping the Internet.* comScore, Inc. June 30. http://www.comscore.com/Press_Events/Presentations_ Whitepapers/2010/Women_on_the_Web_How_Women_are_Shaping_ the_Internet

Blakley, Johanna and Martin Kaplan. 2009. *The Business and Culture of Social Media: In search of the People Formerly Known as The Audience.* The Norman Lear Center. Presentation given at The Business and Culture of Social Media conference in Barcelona on June 26. http://www.learcenter.org/pdf/ businessandcultureofsocialmedia.pdf

Gill, Kirrin, Kim Brooks, Janna McDougall, Payal Patel and Aslihan Kes. 2010. *Bridging the Gender Divide: How Technology Can Advance Women Economically.* International Center for Research on Women. http://www. icrw.org/files/publications/Bridging-the-Gender-Divide-How-Technology-can-Advance-Women-Economically.pdf

Jenkins, Henry. 2006. *Fans, Bloggers and Gamers: Essays on Participatory Culture.* New York: New York University Press.

Lauzen, Martha M. 2011. *Boxed In: Employment of Behind-the-Scenes and On-Screen Women in the 2010-11 Prime-time Television Season.* Center for the Study of Women in Television. http://womenintvfilm.sdsu.edu/files/2010-2011_Boxed_In_Exec_Summ.pdf

Li, Xiaochang. *Dis/Locating Audience: Transnational Media Flows and the Online Circulation of East Asian Television Drama.* Master's thesis, Massachusetts Institute of Technology, 2009. http://cms.mit.edu/research/theses/ XiaochangLi2009.pdf

Masters, Kim. 2011. "State of the Industry: Are Things Better? You Might Not Like the Answer." *Hollywood Reporter.* December 13-16.

National Center for Women & Information Technology. 2010. *NCWIT Scorecard: A Report on the Status of Women in Information Technology.* http://ncwit.org/resources.scorecard.html

Nielsen. 2012. *State of the Media: The Cross-Platform Report: Quarter 3, 2011– US.* http://www.nielsen.com/content/dam/corporate/us/en/reports-downloads/2012%20Reports/Nielsen-Cross-Platform-Report-Q3-2011.pdf

Smith, Stacy L. and Marc Choueiti. 2010. *Gender Disparity On Screen and Behind the Camera in Family Films; The Executive Report.* Geena Davis Institute on Gender in Media. http://www.seejane.org/downloads/FullStudy_ GenderDisparityFamilyFilms.pdf

Krystal